Murder in the Stacks

Penn State, Betsy Aardsma, and the Killer Who Got Away

David DeKok

Guilford, Connecticut

Project Editor: Lauren Brancato
Layout Artist: Adam Caporiccio
Map: Alena Joy Pearce © Morris Book Publishing, LLC

Library of Congress Cataloging-in-Publication Data

DeKok, David.
Murder in the stacks : Penn State, Betsy Aardsma, and the killer who got away / David DeKok.
pages cm
Summary: "The book weaves together the events, culture, and attitudes of the late 1960s, memorializing the stabbing death of Betsy Aardsma in the stacks of Pattee Library at Penn State University's main campus in State College and her time and place in history"-- Provided by publisher.
ISBN 978-0-7627-8087-7 (paperback)
1. Aardsma, Betsy Ruth, 1947-1969. 2. Haefner, Richard Charles, 1943-2002. 3. Murder--Pennsylvania--State College--History. 4. Murder--Investigation--Pennsylvania--State College. 5. Pennsylvania State University. Libraries. 6. Campus violence--Pennsylvania--State College. I. Title.
HV6534.S68D45 2014
364.152'3092--dc23
[B]

2014015185

Printed in the United States of America

Every unpunished murder takes away something from the security of every man's life.

—DANIEL WEBSTER, 1830[1]

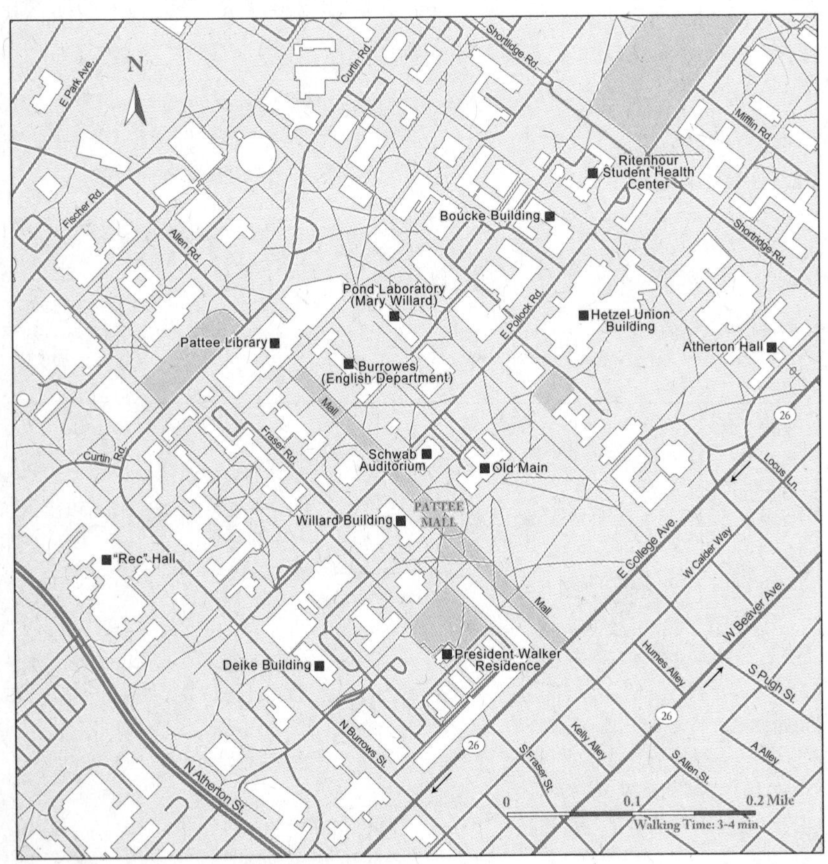

Penn State University campus in 1969.

Contents

Introduction

This is not a tidy true crime narrative of the sort in which a murder occurs, the police labor to solve it, and the murderer is tried and punished. The stabbing death of twenty-two-year-old Betsy Ruth Aardsma of Holland, Michigan, in Pattee Library of Penn State University on November 28, 1969, went unsolved for more than forty years, and remains officially so as of this writing. But the identity of who killed her is no mystery. Indeed, I have written a dual biography of the victim and her killer, revealing who they were, how they came together, and why the murder went unsolved for so long. Their fateful encounter in the library had long seemed like a collision at a dark intersection between an innocent and a drunk driver. But in truth, it was far less random than that.

There was nothing in Betsy Aardsma's life that marked her for murder. She graduated near the top of her high school class and was full of the spirit of the 1960s—an early feminist, a woman with a yearning to help the less fortunate. She was among the best of her generation. Her killer, on the other hand, while extremely intelligent and book-smart, was a dangerous pedophile with a violent temper that could be triggered by a woman doing something that threatened or annoyed him. Both were graduate students at Penn State and from striving middle-class families.

This story begins in State College, Pennsylvania, the home of Penn State, and makes stops in Holland; at the University of Michigan in Ann Arbor; in Chicago; in Lancaster, Pennsylvania; and in the Death Valley region of southern California and Nevada. All of the names in the book are real, although a couple are shortened to just the first name. I came to this story because Betsy Aardsma was from my hometown of Holland, Michigan, and went to my high school, graduating six years before me. I didn't know her, but I remember well when her murder was front-page news in the *Holland Evening Sentinel.* The hauntingly beautiful portrait of her that ran with those stories and for years thereafter accented the horror. It was a murder that seemed to make no sense whatsoever, standing out even in a year, 1969, when brutal and bizarre murders, such as those committed by the Manson Family, seized the headlines.

Nearly all Penn State graduates since 1969 have heard about the girl who was killed in the library—it quickly became a campus legend—but few know more than a couple of details of what happened, which are often wrong. The failure to apprehend Betsy Aardsma's killer would have consequences for many innocent people. One thinks of the phone call to the state police that could have been made by more than one person at Penn State University and weeps for the victims.

No murder should go unsolved. No murderer should go unpunished. The Pennsylvania State Police tried mightily to solve this terrible crime, but in the end, it was citizens who cracked the case.

Part I: The Murder

That place was a jungle up there. The way it was situated, just everything.

—Sergeant George H. Keibler, Pennsylvania State Police[2]

CHAPTER 1

The Library in Happy Valley

It was a university library but also a dark alley, a place of dread.

Pattee Library on Penn State University's main campus in the community of State College was mammoth, overwhelming, and confusing to newcomers, as important libraries often are. But it was also scary, which most are not. Scary because of the crime inside that nobody—neither the university administration nor the undermanned and ill-trained Campus Patrol—seemed able or willing to do much about. The year 1969 had included bomb threats, arson, and sexual assaults, and W. Carl Jackson, the director of libraries, worried that something terrible was about to happen.[1]

It was nothing anyone on the outside might have expected in a small town and university nearly universally described, without conscious irony, as Happy Valley. Penn State had almost 26,000 students on its main campus in 1969, just about all of them white. Once known for little more than the study of agriculture, mining, and engineering, the university had made great strides in the liberal arts since World War II. English professor Harrison T. Meserole, for example, was the principal bibliographer of the Modern Language Association, which put him in the upper ranks of worldwide literary scholarship. You could do far worse than to complete your undergraduate or graduate studies in State College, whether in English or most anything else. Under President Eric A. Walker, Penn State had completed a massive building program between 1959 and 1969, had met all the enrollment targets set by the board of trustees, and would soon do away with its historical quotas for women students.

The town of State College seemed to jump straight from an *Archie* comic book; rarely was a town more aptly named. It never had much *raison d'être* apart from the university. Less a real community than a collection of classroom buildings surrounded by postwar housing developments, if you went looking for "historic" State College, you wouldn't find much.[2]

A longtime joke was that Penn State, which had become the state's largest and most prominent public university, was equally inaccessible from all parts of the state. Indeed, students in Philadelphia, Pittsburgh, Erie, or Scranton, the four urban corners of the state, could look forward in 1969 to hours of travel, much of it over two-lane highways, before arriving in Centre County, in roughly the geographic center of Pennsylvania. The region north of Penn State was so forested, mountainous, and thinly populated that in 1967, Columbia Gas Co. advanced a serious proposal to use an underground nuclear explosion to carve out a storage cavern for natural gas. It would have been near where Route 144 crosses the Clinton County line, about twenty-seven miles due north of State College.[3]

Most who did their four years at Penn State, in what was once described as "a village lost in the mountains," ever after called it Happy Valley.[4] They reveled in the glory of the football team, the Nittany Lions, who were coming off an unbeaten season in 1968 under Coach Joe Paterno, and were already 9-0 in the fall of '69. And they loved student life. They could go a little wild in the bars on College Avenue and depend on the grace of the university and the State College borough authorities not to get in too much trouble.

Yet Happy Valley was an outlier in Centre County, a modern, scholarly island in a very white, traditionally conservative and rural sea. The rest of the county viewed the university with suspicion, if not thinly disguised hostility. Penn State was not multiracial in the modern sense, but did have a few minorities, very few, which most of Centre County in 1969 did not. They were different worlds with different ways. Happy Valley often felt besieged, both by politically and socially conservative members of the Legislature in Harrisburg, and by the very different world that began at the boundary of State College.

But, from the outside, everything in Happy Valley looked rosy. Pattee Library crowned a gentle hill at the upper end of the Mall, a picturesque walkway lined by stately elm trees that the university went to great trouble and expense to protect from the blight that killed most American elms elsewhere. The Mall began at College Avenue downtown and continued gently uphill, past old and stately academic buildings bearing the names of long-forgotten professors or, in one instance, of steel magnate and über-philanthropist Andrew Carnegie. Even on November 28, 1969, with the leaves gone and winter fast approaching, it was a beautiful walk.

Pattee Library[5] had been built in stages beginning in 1937. The main floor of the library held its large and busy card catalog—endless drawers of index cards bearing the names and locations of books—along with study rooms and attentive librarians. Unlike many large libraries, however, Pattee's stacks, which occupied two floors beneath the main floor and five above it, were open, and had been so since the summer of 1964.[6] This meant students were not required to ask a librarian to retrieve a particular book for them. Instead, they looked up the call number in the card catalog, then went to a small door near the circulation desk and descended narrow stairs more suited to a lighthouse than a library. At the bottom was the gloomy underworld of the stacks, a claustrophobic, dimly lit maze of seven-foot-tall, floor-to-ceiling bookshelves separated by aisles too narrow for two people to pass without one turning sideways. It was easy to get lost. The crazy layout was a result of pasting the 1953 addition onto the original 1937 building, without ever truly rationalizing the combination. The 1937 stacks, which had no windows, became known as the Core.[7] No librarians were stationed here, nor were there any security cameras, which were available even in 1969. There was no regular sweep of the stacks, even at closing time. Carole L. Stoltz, a senior from Flint, Michigan, spent a lot of time studying down in the stacks, and dozed off one night during the fall of 1969. When she awoke, the building was dark. The librarians had turned off the lights and gone home at midnight.[8]

Because people tended to be quiet in libraries, it was not unusual in the stacks to be startled by a fellow student materializing with the scary abruptness of a spectral figure in a carnival funhouse. It was also quite possible to be unaware of someone on the opposite side of a row of books, just inches away. Here and there, one might stumble upon a student in one of the carrels on the periphery of the Core. *Carrel*, like *stacks*, was another odd word from the library lexicon. It referred to an individual desk, a mini cubicle, really, with back and side walls rising up from the table and a half-shelf about eighteen inches above the writing surface.[9] They were highly coveted and assigned to individual graduate students, who all but lived in them at certain times of the year.

Students complained about Pattee's inadequacies, and library director W. Carl Jackson did not disagree. The library had a small staff, much smaller than similar university libraries across the country, and its holdings were not all located in the main building. Some were in specialty branch libraries scattered across the campus; for example, in the Earth and Mineral Sciences Library in the Deike Building.[10] It was fine if you knew you needed something at one of these distant biblio-outposts, but annoying if you discovered that fact while in Pattee and now faced a hike across campus or a long wait for it to be retrieved. Pattee held about 1.3 million books in 1969, which might sound like a lot but made it only the fourth-largest library in Pennsylvania. Nationwide that year, it was far down a list topped by the Library of Congress, with 14.8 million books, and Harvard University, with 8 million. Among state university libraries, the University of Michigan had nearly twice as many books as Penn State, 3.4 million.[11] Jackson would sometimes boast that in 1956, Pattee Library had ranked only 50th in the nation in terms of holdings, but was now "in the mid-30s."[12]

Yet, despite Happy Valley's remote location, the outside world was closing in fast. Neither the university nor Pattee Library had escaped the political and social upheavals of the late 1960s. The Vietnam War had, by the beginning of 1969, killed nearly thirty thousand American soldiers and nearly half a million Vietnamese troops on both sides, plus an uncounted number of Vietnamese civilians in a conflict that seemed pointless and endless. Male college students could still get military draft deferments, but these were about to end. Republican president Richard M. Nixon, who took office at the beginning of 1969, had persuaded

Congress to replace the old method, in which local draft boards had the last word on who would serve, with a national lottery and no college deferments. Nearly every American campus had a dedicated corps of antiwar student activists who were outraged at the carnage committed in their name in Indochina, and who feared they would soon be asked to take part. Penn State's aggressive chapter of Students for a Democratic Society, or SDS, and its faculty advisor, Wells Keddie, marched and conducted sit-ins against the war, against Dow Chemical (maker of napalm) or military recruiting, or in support of black students at Penn State.

Race relations at Penn State in 1969 were a major problem. The university was nearly all white. There were just under three hundred black students, some of them foreign, amid nearly twenty-six thousand whites. The 1970 federal census would show Pennsylvania to be 8.6 percent black, which, one could argue, should have resulted in at least 2,236 black students at the state's largest public university. Penn State's excuse was that it could find few qualified black high school graduates in the state. After Reverend Ralph David Abernathy, who became president of the Southern Christian Leadership Conference after the Reverend Dr. Martin Luther King Jr.'s murder, delivered a civil rights speech in Schwab Auditorium at Penn State on March 8, 1969, black students implored him to help, asking what he thought of a state university in the liberal North with so few black students. Could not the SCLC help here? University students had demonstrated against casual, everyday racism in State College since at least 1960, when a barbershop that refused to serve blacks (there was no black barbershop) was picketed. Later, there were protests against university tolerance of State College landlords who specified racial preferences in ads for student tenants. It had become clear to black activists on campus, as well as their white supporters inside and outside SDS, that at a northern university, bringing about change would be up to them.[13]

Pattee Library soon became caught up in the struggle. In the summer of 1969, Penn State began work on a $4.75 million (more than $29 million in modern dollars) addition, called a "research library," to the east end of Pattee Library. A ground-breaking ceremony on July 5 drew noisy and mainly white protesters from SDS, led by their president, Jeffrey Berger, a bus driver's son from New York City. They held placards proclaiming MORE BLACKS, NOT BOOKS, and decrying $4.75 MILLION FOR BOOKS, NONE FOR BLACKS. One protester yelled, "How about some black students to read those books?" Carl Jackson spoke to the demonstrators afterward and thanked them for their generally orderly behavior—they hadn't become violent, after all. President Eric A. Walker and most members of the Penn State board of trustees, on the other hand, were not amused. Work continued on the research library as if nothing had happened.[14]

But civil rights and antiwar protests were not what gave Jackson sleepless nights. The most fragile of Happy Valley illusions in 1969 was that Pattee Library was safe, a temple of learning where students could go to find scholarly books without fear that the scary outside world would follow them inside. This was the murder year in America, a time of grotesque crimes against young Americans, and especially college women. What set 1969 apart was the shocking instances of serial and cult murders springing not from politics, but from some demonic miasma that had been stirred to life. The Zodiac Killer murdered at least five, and possibly as many as nine, young people in the San Francisco area between December 1968 and October 1969. The Manson Family committed the Tate–LaBianca murders, butchering eight people in Los Angeles on August 9–10, 1969, and John Norman Collins murdered as many as six young women, most of them students, around the University of Michigan and Eastern Michigan University in Ann Arbor and Ypsilanti between July 1967 and July 1969, with most dying during the spring and summer of 1969. It was unprecedented and terrifying.

Jackson's fears might not have extended as far as a murder taking place inside Pattee Library, but he was facing growing security concerns. One of the first memos about security problems in Pattee Library was dated July 12, 1968, and addressed what to do about complaints from students concerning incidents in the stacks and reading rooms, "which, for lack of a better word, could be called 'nuisances' [emphasis in original]." The writer defined this as "problems of boisterous conduct or language and similar unusual situations" but did not elaborate on what the "unusual situations" might be. The library staff was reminded that the

Campus Patrol was on twenty-four-hour call, would respond to these incidents, and that calling them would allow for quicker action and "help reduce the number of phone calls to department heads and supervisors during the evening and weekend hours."[15] But it was not so easy as that.

The Campus Patrol and the auxiliary Student Patrol in 1969 were unarmed security guards, not "sworn" police officers, which meant they could detain suspects but not jail or prosecute them. "They were not a bona fide police department," said Howard "Buzz" Triebold, who at the time worked with Colonel William B. Pelton, director of the Department of Security at Penn State. If a crime occurred on campus, they eventually had to call in the real police. But not the State College Borough Police, even though much of the campus was within the borough, and the local police could be on campus from their downtown station in two minutes. Instead, the Campus Patrol referred criminal matters to the state police at Rockview, who were headquartered a little over six miles from campus in the former warden's house outside the state penitentiary, also called Rockview. It took them ten to fifteen minutes to get to campus, and they did not patrol there in any regular sense. No one today seems to have a solid explanation of how and why this bifurcated jurisdiction developed, though it might have been because, in terms of training and resources, the state police of that era were far better prepared than local police to investigate crime on the Penn State campus, not to mention the rest of rural Centre County.[16]

That the Campus Patrol was unarmed was a consequence of state law and university policy. Officers had little formal training in police methods and procedures, unless they had gotten it somewhere else before joining the force. Campus Patrol officers tended to be middle-aged or older men, while the Student Patrol, which mainly provided traffic and crowd control at football games, were, as their name implied, students. Both patrols were under the jurisdiction of Colonel Pelton, a retired army officer who had once headed Penn State's Reserve Officer Training Corps (ROTC) program. He was generally respected by the state police, if not by the SDS, who called him "Pig Pelton." The problem was that Pelton was a rigid bureaucrat who resisted giving the library any special status when it came to security, despite the unique and mounting threats it faced.[17]

Compounding the situation was the latitude Penn State gave to students—anyone on campus, really—who engaged in socially or sexually erratic behavior (political dissent was another matter). At the beginning of 1969, a library memo discussed staff concerns about a mentally ill student who spent a large amount of time in Pattee Library, even during term breaks, behaving in a "weird," unpredictable manner that disturbed and worried some people. One staffer who interviewed him for a part-time job remembered the "far-out" look in his eyes, and that he appeared to be "high." Others were concerned about his apparently rapid physical and mental deterioration. The memo writer commented that some guidance might help the young man, who appeared from all accounts to be intelligent. No one suggested barring him from Pattee Library.[18]

Charles L. Hosler, dean of Penn State's College of Earth and Mineral Sciences from 1965 to 1985, saw many examples of misbehavior at the university that went unpunished. "I think the spectrum of people in academia is a little broader than in society at large," he said. "You have a lot of people who feel sheltered here. Their behavior would not be approved in the average country town. And there is a reluctance to punish anybody, or to turn anybody in. I saw it in many respects."[19]

Politics and protest compounded Jackson's security problems in the library. The late winter and early spring of 1969 was a time of intense political conflict at Penn State, with black students and SDS members demanding greater black enrollment and greater student freedom, including the freedom to publish an SDS underground newspaper called the *Garfield Thomas Water Tunnel.* It was named after a testing facility of the navy's Ordnance Research Laboratory at Penn State that had helped to develop the submarine-launched Polaris nuclear missile.[20] Penn State president Walker, an admirer of FBI director J. Edgar Hoover, tried to suppress the underground newspaper.[21] Meanwhile, radical student activist Jerry Rubin gave a speech in support of the Penn State students on February 13, 1969, wrapping himself in a Vietcong battle flag. Five weeks later, Rubin and seven other left-wing activists, including Abbie Hoffman, Rennie Davis, and Tom Hayden, were indicted by a federal grand jury for allegedly crossing state lines to incite riots at the Democratic National Convention in Chicago the previous summer.

Yet other Penn State students, led by white fraternity members, were vocal in their support for Walker and President Nixon. During a seven-hour sit-in by 400 black and white students at Old Main, the university administration building, on February 24, 1969, an estimated 1,500 counterdemonstrators stood outside, heckling, some shouting, "Bring out the coons!" Several hundred students assembled at a field near Beaver Stadium to welcome President Nixon on March 6, 1969, when he arrived by helicopter with First Lady Pat Nixon to attend the funeral of his uncle, Ernest L. Nixon, a retired Penn State agriculture professor. Walker, who despised student protesters, supported a bill being considered in the Legislature in Harrisburg that would have sharply increased penalties for students who engaged in campus protests, whether violent and disruptive or peaceful.[22]

Whether directly connected to the troubles on campus or not, Pattee Library became the target of repeated, anonymous bomb threats and at least two arson fires in March 1969. None of the bomb threats proved real, but they were troubling and disruptive to staff and students alike. The fires could have been catastrophic. On March 9, a blaze was set in a section of the stacks housing government documents; Penn State was a federal depository library and received copies of many government documents. Only a quick report of the fire by students, and the concrete floor slabs of the stacks, prevented the blaze from spreading to other floors. The arsonist struck again on March 13, first calling in three bomb threats and then setting another fire in the stacks that was found and extinguished by library employees. Additional small fires were set in April, but again were found and put out by the staff. The arsonist had sprayed lighter fluid onto books and set them ablaze.[23]

As scary as they were, the bomb threats and fires were overshadowed by a more pervasive and disturbing problem in Pattee Library. The stacks were a haven for a variety of sexual activities that the state police termed "vice." They were a popular place for gay cruising, especially among gay teenagers who couldn't get served at the My-Oh-My Bar downtown.[24]

And it wasn't just teenagers; adult male gays, some of whom were teachers and professional men, traveled here from conservative small towns around the region, seeking sex in the safer confines of the library, where they were less likely to be recognized, beaten up, or arrested if caught. Gay sex was still against the law in 1969. Pattee's stacks were intended for scholars, but anyone could go there for any reason. There was no gatekeeper to bar the door to those who came to satisfy their sexual urges.

Not all of the sexual activity was consensual. Male flashers, masturbators, and gropers in the stacks were a continuing problem. Librarians might admonish anyone they caught but tried to avoid confrontations or being the sex police. Penn State administrators sent mixed signals on how far they were willing to go to clear out vice. That fall, Colonel Pelton had ordered the doors removed from the stalls in a men's restroom near the Level 3 Core, hoping to deter their use for gay sex. But after a few days, higher officials in the Penn State administration ordered him to put them back in the name of privacy.[25]

Director of Libraries Carl Jackson considered 1969 to have been an awful year, marred by an excessive number of incidents. There had been occasions of men exposing themselves to female students, engaging in voyeurism, and "otherwise molesting female students. . . . We have had excrement on stairways, have been concerned at gatherings of men students (and some who may not be students) who are suspected of engaging in acts of perversion in our basement areas and in the various men's rooms in the library," he wrote in a memo to Paul M. Althouse, vice president for resident instruction.[26]

Jackson had seen the impact of the sex crimes on women students and was deeply frustrated and angry that he could not get a permanent Campus Patrol presence in the library. He had sat with shaking, weeping young women in his office, waiting for the Patrol to arrive. "When they finally get here," he told Taft Wireback, a writer for *Focus,* a student-run magazine serving the Penn State campus, "the girl would be so upset that she couldn't even remember what her assailant looked like. And, needless to say, there was no chance of apprehending the criminal."[27]

Pelton rejected Jackson's request for a permanent Campus Patrol officer in the library. He argued that with a force of forty-five to fifty officers and 300 campus buildings to patrol, it was impossible to detail an officer only to Pattee. "Just as it is impossible to keep a full-time physician in every residence hall in the event of an emergency," he told the *Daily Collegian*, "so it is also impossible to have a patrolman everywhere." Robert Barnes, a retired state police trooper who worked under Pelton as director of investigations, told Wireback much the same, but without the attitude. "We were aware of the deviation in the library but had a manpower problem. [There were] times when the perpetrators were able to escape before we were able to to respond."

Jackson and Pelton had angry confrontations about increased library security, but the director of security would not back down. Finally, after the fires in March, Jackson used library funds to hire two part-time security guards, one of whom patrolled the library, and especially the stacks, every night from 8:00 p.m. until midnight, when the building closed. That left twelve hours, from 8:00 a.m. to 8:00 p.m., without any security presence, but it was the best he could do with the money he could wring from his budget in an especially tight year. The increased surveillance resulted in several men being caught in sexual acts. "To our surprise, many were not students, but family men," Jackson told Wireback.[28]

Pelton presided over the Safety Council, a monthly meeting of departmental representatives at which safety problems of any sort could be addressed. At the beginning of the 1969–70 school year, the Safety Council arranged for fifteen thousand copies of a pamphlet, "Women Alone: Target for Trouble," to be printed and distributed to female students. But more-typical problems addressed by the Council, including at the November 19, 1969, meeting, ranged from traffic hazards to the fire danger posed by unattended hot plates, immersion coils, and coffeemakers. Much time was spent on the hot-plate issue, with talk of an ad hoc committee being appointed to make recommendations for reform.[29]

During the last week of November in 1969, the Pattee sexual deviants were unusually busy. On Monday, November 24, a man exposed himself to a young woman in the Level 3 stacks. Another coed was accosted by an exhibitionist on the following evening. He ran when she screamed for help and was not caught. Later that evening, a third young woman looking for a book in the Level 5 stacks rounded a corner and was shocked to see a man masturbating in the dimly lit aisle, between two rows of bookshelves. He was "playing with himself," she told librarians.[30]

Sergeant George H. Keibler, the chief criminal investigator for the state police barracks at Rockview, who would dwell on the events of November 28, 1969, for the rest of his life, minced no words about the Pattee Library stacks. "It was a den of iniquity down there," he said.[31]

CHAPTER 2

Somebody Had Better Help That Girl

At five minutes before five o'clock on November 28, 1969, Marilee Erdely, a pretty, blonde graduate student with blue eyes and a porcelain complexion, leaned against a wall just outside the Level 2 Core in the basement stacks of Pattee Library. She was flipping through a book she had just pulled off a shelf.[1]

Erdely, who was twenty-three years old, had come to Penn State from the steel and football town of Aliquippa, Pennsylvania, where her father was one of thousands of workers at the massive Jones & Laughlin Steel Corporation mill along the Ohio River.[2] She had majored in secondary education as an undergraduate and was now pursuing a graduate degree in English. She had gone to the stacks to find a book to complete a term paper for English 501, Research Materials and Methods, a class taught by Professor Harrison T. Meserole and Nicholas Joukovsky, a new and young assistant professor recently arrived from Oxford University. In the class, which was a boot camp for first-year English graduate students, they learned how to conduct proper research and write like scholars. Meserole had assigned them a critical study of a manuscript of their choice, either from the Pattee Library's own Rare Books Room, or one of the photocopies he had made of manuscripts from the collections of the American Antiquarian Society in Worcester, Massachusetts, which collected literary and other works from colonial times up through 1876.

A decidedly portly man—everyone remembered him that way—Meserole was an authority on early American literature and the editor of an important anthology in the field. But in the rarefied world of literary scholarship, he was best known as the principal bibliographer for the Modern Language Association, founded in 1883 to promote the study and teaching of language and literature all over the world. There were few better teachers to introduce a graduate student of English to literary scholarship, and if he seemed like a terror, well, what were drill sergeants at boot camp for if not terror?[3]

Erdely had run into several of her classmates in the stacks that Friday afternoon, all working on their own papers. Just a few minutes earlier, she had spotted Betsy Aardsma, a pretty brunette from Michigan, moving among the bookshelves, and had chatted with her briefly. They had two classes together, English 501 and English 434, Movements in American Literature. The latter class was a recently instituted African-American literature course taught by Professor Charles T. Davis, a pioneer in the field.[4] Where Erdely stood flipping through her book, the lighting wasn't so bad, but that wasn't so in other parts of the stacks, especially in the Core. The lights in each row were controlled by individual switches and not from a central panel and were often turned off for one reason or another.

Pattee Library was by no means deserted on the day after Thanksgiving, even if visitors were down by about a third because of the holiday weekend. Those who remained on campus, especially the graduate and foreign students, found the library a logical place to go on a slow day.[5] One of them was Joao Uafinda, twenty-nine years old, and one of the rare black students at Penn State. He was far from home, a refugee from the war of independence against Portugal then raging in his home country of Mozambique in southern Africa. Uafinda was short, just five-foot-five, and had close-cropped hair and a handsome, friendly face. He was walking toward Erdely but had not quite reached her.[6] Perhaps thirty feet away, fifty-two-year-old writer Richard Sanders Allen had just finished making copies at a coin-operated Xerox machine. He was visiting his son Robert that weekend, and was killing time until his son got out of class. (Penn State expected professors to hold classes on Black Friday, even though it was an unofficial holiday for much of the nation, and some actually did.) Allen, who lived near Saratoga Springs, New York, was an engineering historian who wrote for *American Heritage* magazine and was an authority on covered bridges. His latest book, *Covered Bridges of the Middle West,* was due out in about a month.[7] He put the copies in his briefcase and began walking toward Erdely, intending to go up a nearby staircase that led to the main floor. Allen did not know Erdely or Uafinda, but the lives of all three were about to intersect and change forever.[8]

Allen thought he heard something from the stacks but wasn't sure what. Uafinda heard a thump, like a fist hitting a chest, quickly followed by a gasp.[9] But no one heard any angry imprecations, no pleas, no screams of mortal terror, no struggle to the death. A physician familiar with the process of death found the victim's silence hard to explain, even after a wound that proved so quickly fatal. "It's just unbelievable that there was no scream," he said.[10] It was as if the murderer and his victim both observed the ancient rule that no noise is to be made in a library. But not for long. Moments later came a crash and the sound of books hitting the floor. A stranger emerged from the Core, coming at Erdely and Uafinda like a speeding train. He looked to be about twenty-five years old, about six feet tall, and big, but not husky. He had one of those professional faces one tends to associate with foreign correspondents on television. He was better dressed than the typical student, wearing a sport jacket over khaki work pants. Allen, who of course had never seen the young man before, thought he was wearing a white shirt and tie.[11] Neither Erdely nor Uafinda recognized him either.

When the running man saw the two students, he slowed but did not stop. "Somebody had better help that girl!" he said, gesturing back toward the noise. But *he* was not going to help her. The stranger continued moving toward the stairs, but then saw Allen, who was still standing well apart from Uafinda and Erdely. The running man whirled and headed back in the opposite direction, but on a route that took him around, not through, the Core.[12]

Uafinda's native language was Portuguese, and he knew some French, too, but his facility with English was so-so, acquired after arriving in the United States in 1965. He thought he heard the stranger say, "We've got to help the girl!" and followed him. Uafinda followed the running man at a trot back around the Core, back to where Marilee Erdely was deciding what to do, then back into the Core, where he lost him. After one more circuit looking for the stranger, Uafinda left and presumably walked home in the cold darkness to his downtown apartment at 232 West College Avenue. Allen also left, and did not realize for some months that he had been a witness to the aftermath of a murder.[13]

Meanwhile, Erdely, scared and alone, walked hesitantly into the Core, looking for the source of the noise. Passing the aisle between rows 50 and 51, no more than twenty feet from where she had been standing, she was shocked to see a slender, beautiful young woman in a red sleeveless dress and white turtleneck sweater lying on the floor, half on her side, her reddish-brown hair askew. It was Betsy Aardsma, her classmate from English 501, with whom she had spoken so recently. One leg was propped up on a bookshelf, as if she had been trying to climb to safety before falling to the floor.[14] Books lay around and on top of her, and one of the lower shelves hung crazily downward. Her eyes were closed, she was still, and there was a puddle on the floor, later identified as urine. But there was no blood—none that Erdely could see anyway. Erdely told Keibler and his investigators in the coming days that she assumed Betsy had fainted.

Kneeling down, she began smoothing Betsy's hair, adjusting her red dress, and putting some of the books back on an unbroken shelf. Her actions would infuriate the state police and, however briefly, give her the unwelcome status of someone the police thought might know more than she was telling them.[15] Erdely was in shock, rapidly falling to pieces, a breakdown that would mystify investigators. Why did she become hysterical if she thought Betsy had only fainted?[16]

Erdely would later insist that she cried for help for fifteen minutes or more while a number of Penn State students, like the priest and the Levite in the biblical parable of the Good Samaritan, passed by and averted their eyes. But it only seemed that long, and her mistaken perception would become part of the mistaken lore of what happened that day. In fact, help arrived almost immediately. When the books crashed to the floor at 4:55 p.m., the sound traveled up through a floor grating and was heard by librarians in the Circulation Department directly above. One of them went down to investigate, saw a young woman lying on the floor being attended to by Erdely, and went back upstairs to inform Elsa Lisle, the chief librarian at the circulation desk, that a girl had fainted in the Level 2 Core. Lisle placed a call to the campus ambulance at Ritenhour Health Center, the student clinic, at 5:01 p.m. The small hospital was a short distance from Pattee Library, not even a minute away by ambulance, or five minutes at a leisurely walk. Even as Erdely, in her mind, was crying for help, two librarians were already at her side, trying to revive the fallen girl.

One of the two librarians who came to Erdely's assistance was Murray Martin, associate director of Pattee Library, who was in charge that day because Jackson, the director of libraries, was out of town for the holiday. Martin was not surprised when Lisle phoned him; coeds fainted with some regularity in the basement stacks, which were overheated and poorly ventilated. He and another librarian, possibly the original woman who had checked on the noise, had gone down immediately. They turned Betsy on her back, and Martin began mouth-to-mouth resuscitation. He thought he detected a faint pulse.[17]

The two ambulance drivers, both students themselves, struggled to maneuver a stretcher down the narrow stairs to Level 2. A librarian led them to where Betsy Aardsma lay. As they drew near, passing as many as nineteen onlookers, they heard Erdely's hysterical sobbing. Seeing her slumped against the bookshelf, they wondered for a moment if it was *her* they were supposed to pick up. But they quickly deduced it was the girl in the red dress on the floor who needed their help. One of the drivers observed that Betsy's face was flushed and wondered aloud if she had suffered an epileptic seizure. The other saw a spot of blood on her blouse—and it was just a spot—and concluded that perhaps she had bitten her tongue during a seizure. The idea of a murder in the Penn State library was far from his mind. Indeed, when he felt her wrist, the driver, too, thought he detected a faint pulse.[18] Regardless, they would take her to Ritenhour and let the physician on duty decide what to do. They lifted Betsy onto the stretcher and strapped her down. They also brought her purse, which had fallen to the floor when she did. Squeezing between the bookshelves, they moved her toward the stairs. It was 5:08 p.m.

Erdely pulled herself together and caught up with them at the base of the stairs, which they had begun to climb before realizing the impossibility of maneuvering a loaded stretcher around tight turns. They asked a librarian hovering nearby if there was any other way out, and were led to the freight elevator at the eastern end of the stacks. Before the doors closed, Erdely rushed in behind them. They emerged from the warmth of Pattee Library into the cold darkness outside. At that time of year, the last hints of daylight were gone by 5:15 p.m. They loaded the stretcher into the ambulance and Erdely climbed inside. She seemed very fragile, and there was no time to argue.

The ambulance turned into the Ritenhour courtyard around 5:15 p.m. and pulled up to the door. The student attendants wheeled Betsy into the waiting area, where they were met by Dr. Elmer Reed, an ear, nose, and throat specialist who had joined the clinic staff the previous summer. He had just come on duty for an all-night shift and was the only physician on duty. Two registered nurses working the 4:00 p.m.-to-midnight shift were also there. Given what Elsa Lisle had reported when she called, Reed was expecting a student who had fainted and could be quickly revived, but this looked far more serious.[19] The attendants told him she had been found unconscious on the floor of the library, lying in a puddle of urine. Maybe there was a pulse, but they weren't sure. Reed, suddenly filled with dread, motioned to them to follow him to the emergency room through a door to the left. Erdely, holding Betsy's purse, moved to follow, but was told by Dr. Reed to wait on one of the wooden benches. The doors closed and Erdely was left by herself.

Ritenhour had sixty-five beds and sixty-six full-time employees, including fifteen physicians and about twenty-two nurses, and a twenty-four-hour emergency room. But it was in no sense a major hospital or trauma center, even in the way that term was understood in 1969. If one of Penn State's twenty-six thousand students that year had pneumonia or the flu, an ankle sprain, needed birth control pills, or had problems with asthma or any number of other common ailments among students, including alcohol poisoning, Ritenhour was fine. They could get medicine and hospitalization for as long as necessary, which typically was no more than two to three days. The problems came in the rare instances—rare in a large population of mostly healthy young people—of serious illness or injury. There were simply no good options at Ritenhour, or nearby, for advanced care.

Penn State had been trying to improve student and regional health care since 1966, when it donated thirty acres of land near Beaver Stadium for construction of a new Centre County Hospital to replace the old and poorly regarded hospital in Bellefonte, the county seat. That hospital was eleven miles from campus over two-lane roads. The State College area suffered from a severe physician shortage in 1969, and dependents of married graduate students, not eligible for treatment at Ritenhour, often had trouble getting even the most basic care. The new hospital project was fraught with politics, and not much had happened yet in terms of bricks and mortar. The closest real hospital, with a fairly good (for 1969) ER, was in Altoona, forty-one miles away over a mountain highway. In the other direction was Geisinger Medical Center in Danville, seventy miles from campus. The new Milton S. Hershey Medical Center, location of Penn State's fledgling medical school, was nearly a hundred miles from the main campus in Hershey, the famous chocolate town. There were no helicopter ambulance services then in Pennsylvania, or in most parts of the country, for that matter. Those would be one of the few positive legacies of the Vietnam War.[20]

For Betsy Aardsma, it no longer mattered. Dr. Reed checked her vital signs and pronounced her dead, although of what he remained uncertain. He did not have the attendants move her from the gurney onto the examining table. At 5:20 p.m. Reed drew a sheet over her corpse and went to find out who she was. Walking out, he was surprised to see Erdely going through Betsy's purse. He barked at her, demanding to know what she was doing. Still in shock, she stared at him as if in a trance, and said, "I don't know." She handed over the purse. Inside, Reed found a Michigan driver's license identifying the victim as Betsy Ruth Aardsma, age twenty-two, of East 37th Street, Holland, Michigan. There was also a Penn State student identification card. He didn't doubt that she was a student, but it was good to have confirmation.[21]

Reed placed a telephone call to Dr. John A. Hargleroad II, director of the University Health Services, and told him what had happened. Hargleroad, in turn, called Raymond O. Murphy, dean of student affairs, and Charles L. Lewis, vice president of student services, to let them know a student had died under mysterious circumstances. It was up to Murphy to notify Betsy's parents, who lived nearly 550 miles from State College. After pulling Betsy's student information card, he contacted the Aardsma family pastor, Reverend Gordon Van Oostenburg of Trinity Reformed Church in Holland. He agreed to go to the Aardsma home, about a five-minute drive from his parsonage, and inform her parents. At the time, he knew only that Betsy had collapsed in the library shortly before 5:00 p.m. and had been pronounced dead a half-hour later. He was not told how she had died, because at that point, Murphy didn't know.[22]

The pastor drove his car through the snowy, darkened streets of Holland, dreading the task he faced. He had several children of his own. Tall, balding, and gregarious, with a big smile, Van Oostenburg had led Trinity Reformed Church for seven years and was known for his compassion. He turned off Lincoln Avenue at the Salad Bowl restaurant and proceeded onto East 37th Street. The street was lined with silver maples that loomed ominously in the winter night. The Aardsmas lived toward the end of the street on the right, a few houses before it dead-ended at a playground and ball field. They lived in a modest, very typical, two-story middle-class house on a street of similar houses. Their house had two bedrooms down and one up, a broad front yard, and a vacant lot on the south side. The garage was attached to the house by a breezeway.[23]

Holland was a small city of twenty-five thousand on the western side of the state, near Lake Michigan. The inhabitants, including the Aardsma family and Reverend Van Oostenburg, were mainly of Dutch descent, and routinely religious. Although there were wide variations in devoutness within the community, the surprise would have been if the Aardsmas had *not* been church members. He turned into the Aardsma driveway, crunching the gravel before reaching the pavement and parking his car. Outside it was in the mid-20s, warmer by nearly 10 degrees than the previous night, but he still missed the car's warmth as he walked toward the front door. It was just before 8:00 p.m., and Betsy had been dead for three hours.[24]

Inside, where it was warm and bright, the Aardsma family had finished a dinner of Thanksgiving leftovers. Carole Wegner, Betsy's older sister, and her husband, Dennis, were visiting from Madison, Wisconsin, and were preparing to go out to a movie. Their young son, Lorin, would stay home with his grandparents. Kathy Aardsma, at age thirteen the youngest child of Dick and Esther, had gone to visit a friend. Dennis Wegner heard the door open, looked up, and was surprised to see Reverend Van Oostenburg enter the house with a somber expression. In a flash, the Aardsma world collapsed into that special agony and confusion known only by parents who are told, without any warning, that they must prepare to bury a child.[25]

Reverend Van Oostenberg gave them Raymond Murphy's phone number. Dick Aardsma called immediately, recalling later that the Penn State official was "very cold and short," telling him he would need to wait for the state police to tell him how Betsy had died. Murphy remembered the call as a simple, businesslike conversation to verify the bad news and let the family know their daughter's body would be taken to the Koch Funeral Home, the only funeral home in State College. Van Oostenburg stayed to pray with the parents, and Dennis and Carole drove to pick up Kathy. "We all went to bed an hour later, but none of us slept very well," Dennis later recalled. "We all kept waking up and thinking it was not real, and it all was just a bad dream." As they drifted off into fitful sleep, they had no idea that Betsy was not just dead, but had been murdered.[26]

CHAPTER 3

The Long Night

Around 6:00 p.m., after having notified university officials, Dr. Elmer Reed placed a call to the Pennsylvania State Police barracks at Rockview. He told the desk man that a female student had been found dead of unknown causes in Pattee Library. Startled, the officer took notes and passed the information to the shift supervisor, who went to look for Trooper Mike Simmers, the youngest criminal investigator at the Rockview barracks, and the only one on duty that night. Simmers was twenty-three years old, just a year older than Betsy. He worked undercover on campus, monitoring the political activities of left-wing students, as well as the illegal drug trade, and he knew the campus well. In fact, he was a student himself. [1]

The Pennsylvania State Police had been created by the Legislature in 1905, at a time when the state was little more than a resource colony of Wall Street, providing vast amounts of lumber, oil, coal, and iron to the American industrial machine. The state police replaced the so-called Coal and Iron Police, a motley collection of corporate security forces authorized by the Legislature in 1900 to protect business property, mainly mines, from strikes and other union activities. After the United Mine Workers of America was victorious in the big anthracite coal strike of 1902, a cry went up to replace the hated Coal and Iron Police with an official state police force, the first in the nation, that would serve and protect all citizens, not just Wall Street. Unions, doubting the state police would really be evenhanded, fought the proposal and managed for a time to limit the number of state troopers to just 228 for the entire state. Over the years, the numbers grew, although in 1969 they still had fewer than three thousand troopers, all white men. They worked out of barracks in the rural areas of Pennsylvania, wearing crisp gray uniforms, black boots, and distinctive Smokey Bear hats with chin straps. They enforced traffic laws on the highways and the criminal code in small municipalities without a police force of their own.[2]

The state police had a command structure similar to the army, with nearly as many rules and regulations. Recruits often came directly from the military, almost never from college, and indeed, for many years, prior military service was a requirement. Troopers were already accustomed to the regimental life when they put on the uniform. They received three months of training at the state police academy at Hershey. Those who passed their final exams were put straight to work. Whether a trooper did traffic enforcement or investigated a murder depended mainly on chance and circumstance. "We did everything," said Corporal Eugene Kowalewski, stationed at Rockview in 1969, and long retired. "If you came on it, you handled it." If more work on a case was needed, the commander might send out one of the specialized criminal investigators, such as Corporal Dan Brode or Simmers, from the "Crime Room" at Rockview.[3]

The Rockview barracks was located off Benner Pike near the gates of the State Correctional Institution at Rockview, a minimum-security prison with a "big house" look. The barracks had once been the home of the prison warden. Despite their proximity to the prison, the troopers had nearly nothing to do with security inside, although if there had been a bad riot, they would have helped to restore order. The penitentiary had about six hundred inmates and also housed the state's electric chair, an odd side dish on its minimum-security menu. Death Row was elsewhere; condemned prisoners were transported to Rockview shortly before their execution. Witnesses signed a large ledger book before the electrocution, and a second time, often in a much shakier hand, after they saw the condemned man die. The last inmate to die in the chair had been Elmo Smith, a sex killer from the Philadelphia suburbs, in 1962.[4]

Simmers was in the kitchen, talking to some of the other troopers, when the shift supervisor appeared. He told him a coed had been found dead in Pattee Library. Simmers took courses at Penn State under the federal Law Enforcement Assistance Program (LEAP) and knew the library well. He never thought of it as a dangerous place. Grabbing the keys to an unmarked cruiser, he sped off toward the university. There was little traffic on Benner Pike, and in barely ten minutes he was in State College. He parked outside Pattee Library, where a member of the Campus Patrol was waiting for him. It was around 6:30 p.m.[5]

Simmers was young, and looked young, which is why he had been recruited for undercover work in the spring of 1968, right around the time the campus had been rocked by civil rights and antiwar protests. His superiors wanted him to be the eyes and ears of the state police, quietly monitoring and investigating the protests and protesters and keeping track of the drug dealers. Simmers had the freedom to choose how he looked and dressed on the job and chose a "Joe College" look rather than going hippie, as some of his successors did. He didn't consider himself truly undercover, and, indeed, his identity eventually became known. This didn't sit well with some of his professors, causing him to be barred from a psychology class by one and denounced at a press conference in Old Main by another. Nor did some of his fellow students care much for his role.[6]

Later that year, on November 5, 1968, Simmers tangled with SDS protesters when General William C. Westmoreland, the army chief of staff and a hated symbol of the Vietnam War, came to State College for the Army–Penn State football game.[7] Westmoreland had commanded US troops in South Vietnam from 1964 to 1968. After the disastrous Tet Offensive by the North Vietnamese and Vietcong, he had been relieved of command by President Lyndon B. Johnson. No official announcement of his visit was made until the game began, but word leaked out, and the SDS posted flyers urging students to WELCOME A MASS MURDERER. A car carrying the general and President Walker of Penn State was blocked by about seventy-five protesters from leaving the driveway of the president's official mansion on campus, not far from the lower end of the Mall.[8] Some of them rocked the car. Simmers, in plain clothes, waded into the crowd and began throwing punches to distract the protesters from Westmoreland. He got his ass kicked, but the general got to Beaver Stadium for the game.[9]

Once in Pattee Library, Simmers descended to the Level 2 stacks and was shown where Betsy's body had been discovered. Two other members of the Campus Patrol and several students were there. Colonel Pelton, who headed the Department of Security, was nowhere in sight, and no one appeared to be making sure the scene was not disturbed. The Campus Patrol told Simmers what he already knew: that the unconscious girl had been taken to Ritenhour and pronounced dead. Simmers took their names and asked if they would mind staying and securing the scene—meaning keep people out—until he could figure out what had happened. There wasn't much else he could do, given that he was the only state trooper in the library.[10]

So he walked over to Ritenhour, met Dr. Reed, and was stunned to hear that he now believed that Betsy had been murdered. He told the young trooper that after he had made the telephone calls, he returned to Betsy's body, pulled back her clothing, and found what appeared to be a small knife wound in her left breast. Simmers asked to see the body. Reed took him to the gurney, by that time moved to a hallway, pulled back the sheet, and once again removed her red sleeveless dress and white turtleneck sweater, which had a small bloodstain on the inside. Reed removed her bra and pointed out the inch-wide slit where the knife had entered her breast. There was no doubt that the beautiful and young Betsy Aardsma had been murdered. "Mike, this is a homicide," he said. But where was all the blood?

The young trooper knew he was out of his depth. Simmers had never originated a murder investigation on his own. He phoned back to the barracks and asked the desk man to send Corporal Dan Brode, a more senior investigator, as soon as possible. Brode had been designated by Sergeant George H. Keibler, the chief of criminal investigation, as the on-call "reserve man" for Black Friday night, in case a major crime occurred. Keibler had left Wednesday for his father's hunting camp north of Smethport, in the mountains of McKean County, intending to do some turkey hunting on the last day of that season and go bear hunting when that season opened Monday. The desk man reached Brode and told him to go to Ritenhour. After conferring with the shift supervisor and Lieutenant William Kimmel, the commander of the Rockview barracks, he began calling in other troopers as well.[11]

Another officer, Corporal Eugene Kowalewski, was reached up in Snow Shoe, in the northern part of Centre County, and Corporal Mike Mutch at a party in Pleasant Gap. Mutch, in turn, called an old friend at home, Centre County District Attorney Charles C. Brown Jr., only to learn he was at a high school basketball game. The desk man also summoned Trooper Jan Hoffmaster, who was about to leave for his own hunting camp, and told him to meet up with Brode and Simmers at Ritenhour. When he arrived, Brode ordered him to stay with Betsy's body while he and Simmers went back to Pattee Library. Corporal Kowalewski soon joined them.[12]

Brode, who was considered a loner by his colleagues, was certain he knew who had killed Betsy—the so-called Nittany Mall Rapist.[13] The Nittany Mall, which opened in the late fall of 1967, was located along Benner Pike, midway between the Rockview barracks and the university. There had been two rapes, both of teenage girls—one in the fall of 1968, and another a year later. Each girl had been abducted at knifepoint in the Mall parking lot, driven in her own car a few miles up onto Mount Nittany, above Pleasant Gap, then raped and abandoned. The second girl had the presence of mind to observe that her rapist had had dirt under his fingernails and that his hands were rough, leading police to conclude that he was a country laborer of some sort.

Both of the rape cases were assigned to Brode, who had no suspect. He had the man's fingerprints from the rearview mirror of the girl's car in the second crime but was unable to match them to anyone. In the late 1960s, matching fingerprints to a suspect who wasn't already in custody involved far more luck than science. Even if the police had latent prints gathered at a crime scene *and* a suspect, they could not force him to give new prints without first arresting him. And if they arrested him, they had better have a case. Fingerprints were not the magical identifier of popular belief. Movies and popular fiction distorted the reality. All Brode could do with the prints on the mirror was check them against on-file prints of men released from Pennsylvania prisons or send them to the other state police barracks across Pennsylvania, in hopes that they could find a match in their own files. Not until

Japanese scientists developed the Automated Fingerprint Identification System (AFIS) in the late 1980s was there widespread computerization of American fingerprint files.[14]

As he walked to the library, Brode contemplated what today seems a rather implausible scenario: that a farm laborer from the country had come onto the Penn State campus looking for a victim, went to a library he had probably never visited or even seen in his life, and made his way from the main entrance down into the maze of stacks. There, he happened to encounter Betsy Aardsma, tried to abduct her, stabbed her in the heart when she resisted, and then escaped, all the while making no noise or being seen by anyone. It made little sense, but Brode was undeterred.

Brode was shocked when he arrived in Pattee Library and found the crime scene in disarray. No one was really in charge. Forty-five minutes had elapsed between Marilee Erdely's discovery of Betsy on the floor and the arrival of the Campus Patrol, when Colonel Pelton, who made all major decisions for the security force, had issued vague orders to "close it off." He hadn't told them it was a crime scene. In the interim, and for some time after the Campus Patrol had arrived, high-ranking university administrators—or, as Sergeant George Keibler put it, "people of influence at the university"—had been allowed to tramp through the area where Betsy had been found. Keibler said President Walker was among the visitors that night. Even in those more-casual days of crime scene investigation, this was a bizarre situation.[15]

Corporal Kowalewski remembers encountering curious Penn State students around the periphery of the crime scene. "They were just milling around in there," he said. "We asked several kids if they were in that section of Pattee Library at the time [of the murder]. They said no." He and Brode and Simmers walked among the rows of books, looking for anything that might be tied to the murder. They found nothing, other than confirmation that they were not examining a virgin crime scene.[16]

That was far from the only blunder of the evening. One of the librarians, probably Murray Martin, had ordered a janitor to clean up the crime scene, including the puddle of urine on the floor. It no doubt made perfect sense at the time. The young coed had just been carried off to Ritenhour, unconscious but presumably alive. Why not clean up the mess? However well-intentioned, the effect on the subsequent investigation was disastrous. Books that had tumbled to the floor around her body were moved, some by Erdely, some by the librarians, some by the janitor. A few remained on the floor when Brode and Simmers and Kowalewski arrived. The nearby shelves had been touched, and some had been wiped down. People had walked over the spot where she had fallen. The immediate crime scene and any evidence that might identify the killer had been thoroughly contaminated.[17]

There had also been no move to bar the doors of Pattee Library to prevent potential witnesses from leaving. The doors had stayed open, and the counter showed that 157 people had left via Exit 1, the main door, and 52 via Exit 2, in the hour after the murder. Almost certainly, potentially valuable witnesses, not to mention the killer, had left during that time. Access to the Level 2 stacks was blocked early in the evening, but the rest of the library remained open for business. Students continued to come and go until the library closed at midnight.[18]

Brode ordered Simmers to accompany Betsy's body to Centre County Hospital, where an autopsy would be performed. District Attorney Brown, who had been summoned from the stands at the basketball game, and Lieutenant Kimmel also went to the hospital. But who would do the postmortem? The choices were Dr. Thomas G. Magnani, the only pathologist in Centre County, or an older, better-known pathologist who practiced in Altoona and would have to drive more than forty miles to the hospital.[19]

Fireworks erupted. Brown didn't know Dr. Magnani, who had moved to Centre County fairly recently. He worried about the autopsy results standing up in court in what he assumed would be the inevitable trial of Betsy's killer. In fact, Magnani, who was thirty-six years old and a graduate of Hahnemann Medical College in Philadelphia, had performed many forensic autopsies in Maryland and some in Centre County. By his own account, Magnani went to the basement morgue at the hospital to view Betsy's body, but Lieutenant Kimmel, who agreed with Brown's concerns, told him he was too young and inexperienced to do the postmortem. Magnani stormed out, "mad as a hornet," and drove home, walking in the door to a call from Corporal Mutch, who managed to soothe his anger and persuade him to come back. Mutch remembers saying to Brown and Kimmel, "He's a good man. Let him have it," meaning, do the autopsy. In an alternate version of this story, Kimmel asked Centre County coroner W. Robert Neff about Magnani's qualifications, but loudly and publicly enough that it soon got back to the pathologist, who reacted predictably. In any case, Magnani returned to perform the postmortem. He received no apology from Kimmel, who, the pathologist claimed, had "too big of an ego."[20]

Word of the murder had leaked out to the local press. The state police put out a brief news release late Friday evening, identifying the body found in the library as Betsy Ruth Aardsma, twenty-two, of Holland, Michigan, but listing the cause of death as unknown. Nor would the desk man tell reporters whether foul play was suspected. But a reporter for the *Pennsylvania Mirror*—the State College edition of the *Altoona Mirror*—reached Neff at 11:15 p.m. Neff, free to say what he wanted, told the reporter that the photographing of Aardsma's body had just been completed and that an autopsy would begin in about half an hour.[21]

From the official autopsy report by Dr. Thomas J. Magnani:
Aardsma, Betsy Ruth, 22, Female
Date of Autopsy: 11/28/69
Started: 11 p.m.
Finished: 4 a.m.
Clinical Diagnosis: Stab Wound of Chest

Final Autopsy Diagnosis:
Penetrating wound of left chest involving skin and subcutaneous tissues, sternum, thymus, pleura, pericardium, pulmonary artery heart, left hemothorax 3,000 milliliters, cutaneous contusion, left anterior chest, hemopericardium, abrasion of right ear, abrasion of right mastoid area, tracheobronchial aspiration of gastric content, compression atelectasis of left lung, pulmonary congestion and edema, accessory spleen. The knife went through her left breast. Left pleural space almost

completely filled by 3,000 milliliters of fresh liquid and clotted blood. Wound three inches deep.

The body is that of a well-nourished 22-year-old female that measures 68 inches from crown to heel and weighs approximately 125 pounds. She is fully clothed. The outer garment consists of a red dress without sleeves. This dress has wide lapels and each lapel has fresh bloodstains on it. The right lapel [from Magnani's perspective] . . . contains a transverse linear cut measuring 3/16 of an inch in length. This is surrounded by bloodstains. Beneath this garment there is a white turtleneck cotton sweater. This contains fresh blood stains across its anterior portion just beneath the turtleneck collar. Within these bloodstains there is a linear cut measuring one inch. . . . Beneath the sweater there is a white full slip that contains bloodstains. . . . Beneath the slip is a brassiere which is bloodstained. These stains are larger on the right side of this garment. There is no evidence of a cut within the brassiere. The remainder of the body is clothed with blue underpants and panty hose. All of these articles are intact. Both the underpants and panty hose are soaked with urine. She is also wearing a pair of light tan shoes which show no significant abnormalities. The hair is reddish brown, the eyes are hazel. . . . There are contact lenses in place over both corneas.

The configuration of the skin wound and wound tract suggest that the weapon is a pointed, bladed instrument. The blade of this measures 7/8 of an inch in width and has a minimum length of 3 1/2 inches. . . . The findings also suggest that the wound was inflicted with considerable force at the time of a face-to-face confrontation of the victim and the assailant, and that this weapon was held in the right hand of this assailant. The abnormalities created by the wounds in the heart point to a very rapid, almost immediate collapse following their infliction, and death very likely then followed in less than five minutes.[22]

Translated, the autopsy report said that Betsy Aardsma was stabbed in the chest during a face-to-face confrontation with her killer. The weapon was wielded with considerable force and penetrated her breastbone—no easy feat. The blade sliced through one of her lungs, causing it to collapse, and pierced the pulmonary artery of her heart. Her chest cavity filled with just over three liters of blood, about half the volume in her body. The wounds on her head were most likely caused when she fell to the floor, hitting her head on the bookshelves and the floor itself. She was not raped.[23] And she died very quickly, probably without excessive suffering.

The manner of her death would provoke much debate over the next forty years among the original investigating officers. Some of them, agreeing with Dr. Magnani, swore she only could have been stabbed straight on from the front. Others, just as certain, insisted the killer had grabbed her from behind, reached around, and pulled the knife into her chest.[24] What seemed clear is that Betsy had been taken by surprise by someone who could get close enough to her in the narrow aisle between the rows of books without triggering a retreat or a cry for help. Most likely that was someone she knew, someone filled with silent rage and strong enough to plunge the knife through her breastbone. The autopsy found no defensive wounds on her hands or arms, received trying to ward off a knife. Nor was there any skin of the killer under her fingernails.[25] And there was nothing tentative about the knife wound. The killer had no doubts about what he had wanted to do and drove the blade in with a vengeance, right through her breastbone and into her heart.[26]

Death by exsanguination, the medical term for how Betsy Aardsma died, doesn't take long when a major artery is severed—a few minutes at most, wrote Dr. Sherman B. Nuland in his book, *How We Die: Reflections on Life's Final Chapter.*[27] The loss of three liters of blood in a 125-pound woman was more than enough to stop her heart. Betsy quickly would have gone into a coma and died. Dr. Magnani believes she could have been saved only if she had been immediately hooked up to a new blood supply in a modern trauma center and attended by a skilled thoracic surgeon, none of which (except, in theory, the blood) existed in Centre County in 1969.[28]

And why did so little of Betsy Aardsma's blood escape her body, which deceived the librarians and ambulance attendants into thinking she was still alive, critically delaying the search for her killer? Dr. Magnani said it was because the knife wound was "just a slit" and offered only a tiny, narrow path for the blood to exit her body. Instead, it filled up the pleural cavity, or, in layman's terms, her chest.[29] The severe internal bleeding also caused her face to become flushed, which they mistook for a sign that she had merely passed out from a seizure and was still alive. Dr. John Hargleroad II, director of University Health Services in 1969, said they well could have *imagined* they felt her pulse, because they expected they should feel one. "Maybe you stretch things a little bit to convince yourself that you do," he told reporter Taft Wireback in 1972.[30]

The final issue from the autopsy would, like the manner of the stabbing, be debated among investigators for the next forty years. Magnani made note of a circular black-and-blue mark found on Betsy's left breast just below the knife wound. Simmers thought it might have been caused by the killer's knuckle, or by the part of the knife where the blade met the handle. Mutch thought it might have been made by a wristwatch worn with the face on the killer's inner wrist, as some men do.

Or perhaps it was none of the above. Andrea Yunker, who shared a room with Betsy Aardsma during their junior and senior years at the University of Michigan, said in an interview in 2011 that it wasn't a bruise at all, but rather a birthmark. "It was always there," she said, describing the mark as resembling a large strawberry. "I saw Olga [Lozowchuk, who lived in the same apartment as Aardsma and Yunker] at the funeral, and she said, 'I wonder if they stabbed her in the birthmark?'"

At the conclusion of the autopsy, Dr. Magnani closed her up and sent her to the morgue, from where she would be taken to the Koch Funeral Home in State College. His part of the investigation was over. That of the Pennsylvania State Police had barely begun.

CHAPTER 4

Trying for a Do-Over

Even while the autopsy was in progress, Lieutenant William Kimmel tried for a do-over, a restarting of an investigation that had sputtered and failed before it had gotten very far down the road. He was the commanding officer of the Rockview barracks and was the boss of both Simmers and Brode. Bad luck and serious mistakes by the Campus Patrol and the library had allowed the crime scene to be contaminated and any number of potential witnesses to walk out the door. The murderer had fled into the gathering darkness, running from Pattee Library. What Kimmel did not yet understand was how different, and difficult, it would be to search for a murderer on a college campus. Penn State University was a world unto itself, with its own rules and culture, and he was barely even a tourist. His chief of criminal investigation at Rockview, Sergeant George H. Keibler, had been at the barracks since 1965 and had been commanding officer until the beginning of 1969, when Kimmel arrived from the country to take over. Keibler had had three years to study Penn State and knew it was a different animal. But he was away on vacation, and so Kimmel took personal charge of the Aardsma investigation.

The last murder of a Penn State student had taken place in 1940. Seventeen-year-old Rachel Taylor, a home economics major, was abducted and murdered after she arrived back in State College on a bus from Wildwood Crest, New Jersey, her hometown. She lived in Atherton Hall, the same dorm where Betsy lived, but never made it back to her room from the bus stop. She was seen getting into somebody's car at 1:30 a.m., ten minutes after the bus had arrived. Her nearly naked body was found five hours later in Lemont, three miles outside of town. Taylor's murder was never solved. Too many people came and went at a big university, making it difficult for the police to track suspects. And now Kimmel faced the same dilemma.

When a woman is murdered, police look for a man. The lieutenant told his men to find out if Betsy had a boyfriend. Among the first people questioned was Sharon Brandt, Betsy's roommate, who was a zoology student from Oyster Bay, Long Island. She was in their dorm room when the police located her, and she identified Betsy's boyfriend as David L. Wright, a first-year medical student at the new Penn State College of Medicine in Hershey.

Kimmel arranged for two detectives from the state police barracks in Harrisburg, the state capital, to drive to Hershey and wake up Wright for questioning. Detective Cornelius Shovlin and his partner—no one today can remember his name—drove down Route 322 into Hershey, fifteen miles east of Harrisburg and even smaller than State College, veering off before they passed the Reese and Hershey plants that made the town famous among candy lovers. Their destination was the Milton Hershey School, a private academy for disadvantaged youth started in 1909 by chocolate magnate Milton Hershey and his wife. Surplus housing at the school was being used as temporary quarters for the medical students, and Wright and several classmates shared one of the redbrick cottages. He was about to find out that the boyfriend, if there is one, is always the number-one suspect when a young woman is slain and the killer gets away.[1]

The two detectives pounded on Wright's door around 2:00 a.m. They told him to get dressed and come downstairs, where they sat him down at the kitchen table. According to Wright's memory of the incident forty years later, they spent twenty minutes questioning him about his whereabouts that afternoon before telling him why they were there.[2] He told them several times in several ways that he had been in the gross anatomy laboratory, dissecting a cadaver, around 5:00 p.m. Other medical students in the house could vouch for him. Finally they told him the awful news—that Betsy Aardsma, his girlfriend, had been murdered in Pattee Library. In his mental agony, Wright "wanted to scream," he told Kevin Cirilli, a writer for the Penn State *Daily Collegian,* and later, for *Politico,* but seemed unable to move his vocal cords. To Wright, it seemed increasingly obvious from the questions that he was their chief suspect.[3]

But the interrogation was not over. Detective Shovlin and his partner roused the other occupants of the house, including Wright's roommate, John Misiti, and Steven W. Margles. The detectives separated the young men and questioned each individually about David's alibi. Each confirmed that their friend had been with them, dissecting cadavers, around the time Betsy was murdered. Later on, they had gotten together to study microbiology. There was no way David could have been at Penn State's main campus. Indeed, it would have taken him two hours to drive to State College and two hours to drive back. But perhaps he had hired someone to kill her? His friends knew of no serious quarrels between David and Betsy. In fact, the couple had just spent Thanksgiving Day in the cottage and, with the other students who stayed on campus, enjoyed a homemade turkey dinner cooked by some of the women students. From everything his friends could see, David and Betsy had a good relationship.[4]

Margles came to believe that the state police were slow to drop David as a suspect because of the seeming medical precision of Betsy's fatal wound, a wound that had bled almost entirely inside her body. But he was skeptical of their reasoning. "I mean, I couldn't hit that if I tried, knowing the anatomy pretty well," Margles said. "And if you're going to kill somebody, are you going to do it in the middle of Pattee Library?"[5]

After the detectives left, Wright, shaken, went to the hall telephone and called his father, Dr. Donovan Wright, a psychiatrist in Elmhurst, Illinois, a Chicago suburb. He poured out what had happened, telling him that his girlfriend had been stabbed to death. After his son hung up, Dr. Wright placed a call around three in the morning to the Aardsma family to offer his condolences. Dick Aardsma answered the phone and heard for the first time that his daughter had been stabbed to death. In his grief and confusion, he thought it was the state police calling.[6]

Not wanting to repeat the mistakes that had allowed the crime scene to be contaminated, Kimmel ordered Trooper Ken Schleiden to look for evidence in Betsy's room in Atherton Hall and remain there until he was relieved in the morning. Schleiden was almost as young as Simmers but had been on the force slightly longer. Atherton Hall had become Penn State's first coed dormitory that fall and was only for graduate students. The ground-floor room shared by Betsy and Sharon Brandt, Room 5A, was in a corner near a stairway that led down to an exit door. A Campus Patrol officer unlocked the room for Schleiden, who went inside and flipped on the light. Brandt was long gone, ordered by the Campus Patrol to stay away until the state police had finished their investigation. She would stay with friends in Atherton until Christmas break began, then move to a different room with two other girls in January. Room 5A was on the small side for two people, Schleiden observed, but nice enough and kept scrupulously tidy by the two young women. Nothing seemed out of place. Schleiden opened Betsy's desk and dresser, looked in her closet, and found notes she had written—but no formal diary—and many, many doodles. There was nothing among her effects that would have embarrassed Betsy's mother. And nothing that provided any clue as to why someone might have wanted to plunge a knife into her chest.[7]

Meanwhile, Corporal Brode had persuaded Lieutenant Kimmel to let him pursue his cockamamie theory that the country rapist who abducted the two teenage girls from the Nittany Mall in 1968 and 1969 might have killed Betsy, which meant Brode's time and energy would be diverted from more promising avenues of inquiry. It would not be the last wild goose chase by the state police, but in fairness, few major criminal investigations are without them. Lieutenant Kimmel brought many strengths to the Aardsma investigation, including experience in managing a big, high-profile case. But he brought significant weaknesses, too, including a certain tendency to want to "fight the last war" and a certain indifference to the sensibilities of the community where a crime occurred. Kimmel had been closely involved, as the sergeant in command of the Huntingdon barracks, in running the massive and successful manhunt in the spring of 1966 for the so-called "Mountain Man" rapist and killer, William Diller Hollenbaugh, a forty-four-year-old recluse who had terrorized people, especially women and girls, in and around the village of Shade Gap, about sixty-eight miles south of State College.

The problem was that Kimmel's tough tactics in the Mountain Man investigation had offended the community. After Hollenbaugh fired guns into the home of a young woman whose husband was at work, then broke in and raped her while muttering Bible verses, Kimmel ordered his investigators to begin checking the alibis of all the men in the area, inquiring with employers whether certain men had really shown up for work. Robert V. Cox, a reporter for the Chambersburg *Public Opinion* who won a Pulitzer Prize for his coverage, wrote in a subsequent book on the case that "dozens of men" were taken to Huntingdon for polygraph examinations. Many in the community considered their treatment by the state police, and especially by the polygraph examiner from Harrisburg, to be shabby and offensive. "And that caused an awful lot of trouble," Sergeant George H. Keibler said. "When you go into a mountain area, there are different types people than there are in the city of Harrisburg. And you'd better treat them a little different. They didn't do this." The state police did not gain the trust of the local people, and the Mountain Man remained at large longer than he might have, with tragic results.[8]

Matters came to a head on May 11, 1966, when Hollenbaugh forcibly abducted Peggy Ann Bradnick, age seventeen, at gunpoint while she and five younger brothers and sisters walked home from their school bus stop. He fled with her, dragging her by a chain around the neck, into the wilds of Black Log Mountain, part of the Tuscarora Mountains, where he had stocked three caves with cans of beans and corn and a supply of water. He told Bradnick that he had been spying on her for months. He wanted her to live in the forest with him and be his sex partner—a compliant, willing sex partner. "All I want is the sensation of touching a woman," Hollenbaugh told her. "I never did that."[9]

Kimmel launched what is often described as the largest manhunt in Pennsylvania history, involving nearly 500 state troopers—nearly a third of the entire force in 1966—plus some 140 FBI agents, dozens of local police, and about 360 members of the Pennsylvania National Guard. Hollenbaugh, sometimes literally dragging the girl along, managed to elude them for nearly a week. Eventually, he lured his pursuers into a trap. Law enforcement was closing in on May 17, helped by two tracking dogs brought in from Arkansas, when Hollenbaugh shot and killed both dogs and then FBI agent Terry R. Anderson, who became the fifteenth agent in FBI history to die in the line of duty. The Mountain Man and his hostage escaped once again. But he died the next day in a shootout with state police and a fifteen-year-old boy, Larry Rubeck, who fired a .12 gauge shotgun loaded with a "pumpkin ball" shell out a window of his home at near point-blank range. Bradnick was rescued, and Kimmel wore the victor's laurels.[10]

The critical question was whether the case might have been resolved more quickly, and without bloodshed, if Kimmel had not employed harsh tactics in an attempt to gain information. The state police had become expert over the years at solving small-town crime that grew out of sexual depravity or dysfunctional relationships between the sexes. The troopers were small-town white boys (still all-male and all-white in the 1960s) and knew how to swim in that rural sea. They understood their neighbors, who often acted in predictable ways that helped them solve terrible crimes. But take them out of that milieu, or violate community hospitality by treating people harshly in an attempt to shake out information, and they were at a decided disadvantage.

One has to believe that Corporal Brode's pursuit of the idea that a country rapist had killed Betsy Aardsma was an attempt by him, at least subconsciously, to re-create the Mountain Man case. He probably believed that Lieutenant Kimmel would be receptive to the idea, since it echoed his greatest triumph. But that was the last war, not the current one. Kimmel, while allowing Brode to pursue his rapist theory, did not want him running the Aardsma investigation. As he gathered his thoughts on Friday night outside the autopsy room, he decided he needed Sergeant George H. Keibler, his most experienced investigator, in charge of the ground game, carrying out the role he himself had played in the Mountain Man case.

When it came to criminal investigations, Sergeant Keibler was second to none. He was whip-smart, a master organizer who could keep track of the myriad pieces of information and evidence that accumulated during an investigation, while at the same time—without benefit of computers—analyzing that evidence and drawing insights and conclusions. He was one of fourteen criminal investigation specialist-3s in the state police, the best of the best. Keibler spoke in a police dialect all his own, a patois, where to mount an intensive investigation was to "run everything," to name a suspect was "to get him into it," and to clear a suspect was "to get him out of it," all punctuated with frequent *hells* and *damns*. He had a wicked sense of humor and loved to kid his subordinates about their job performance, as Trooper Mike Simmers would soon learn. In many ways, Keibler was the right investigator for the Aardsma case, and if the case had not been such a mess when he arrived on the scene, he might well have solved it. The problem that evening was that Keibler was at his father's hunting cabin, which had no telephone, and no one knew how to reach him. His wife and son were with him at the cabin, not at their home in Bellefonte.

His biography was not that different from many other state troopers of the era. Nearly all of them were from small towns and farms, not big cities or suburbs. Keibler grew up in New Kensington, a small town on the Allegheny River northeast of Pittsburgh, where his father was an elected justice of the peace. He joined the US Air Force at age eighteen, spending three years in West Germany. Returning home in 1953, he contemplated his career options and eventually joined the Pennsylvania State Police. He had met a number of state troopers as a teenager when they came to his father's office to file papers or appear at hearings. They seemed like good men.[11]

After working his way through various barracks in western Pennsylvania, notably in Uniontown, which served a high-crime area, Keibler was promoted to sergeant and made commanding officer of the Rockview barracks on October 10, 1965. Here he would face new challenges. Not long after taking command, he was invited by Colonel Pelton, Penn State's director of security, to observe a speech on campus at Rec Hall by Henry Cabot Lodge, who had been President Kennedy's ambassador to South Vietnam, and was another symbol of the hated Vietnam War. Pelton was expecting trouble, and it came. A group of SDS students clashed with right-wing students from the campus chapter of Young Americans for Freedom, who prevented them from going inside to protest Lodge's speech. Keibler was stunned by the violence. Why was this happening? What should he do in response?[12]

Under Keibler's direction, the state police at Rockview began to monitor civil rights and antiwar activities on the Penn State campus. For example, when the university chapter of SDS held a supposedly secret meeting on January 31, 1967, to plan a demonstration the next day in front of Old Main, the state police had an undercover officer present. SDS had no idea they were being infiltrated. The demonstration was to protest President Walker's refusal to respond to a letter demanding to know whether he planned to turn over their names to the House Un-American Activities Committee in Washington, which was investigating groups opposed to the Vietnam War. When the demonstration began at 11:00 a.m. the next morning, an undercover agent was with the thirty-five students when they occupied a dean's office and refused to leave. A detailed description of the day's events was contained in teletype bulletins sent by the state police to Governor Raymond P. Shafer in Harrisburg.[13]

But many of the protests had to do with civil rights, not the Vietnam War. Number one on the list of SDS and black student demands was a doubling of the black student enrollment at the main campus, from two hundred to four hundred—out of twenty-six thousand students—by the fall of 1968. They demanded one thousand black students by the fall of 1969, and 10 percent of the undergraduate population thereafter. Four days earlier, the university had put out a press release saying it was going to admit "a number [ten] of *marginally qualified* [emphasis added] black students from the Harrisburg area." The implications of that statement were insulting and infuriating to black Penn State students. Their other demands included naming a building after Dr. King, bringing in more black athletes, and offering black literature courses in the university's English curriculum.[14]

If Keibler was sympathetic to the grievances of the Penn State black students, he did not let on. He was a by-the-books, law-and-order, *Dragnet*-style police officer, and much later, when he was in his eighties, listened regularly to conservative talk radio. He joked about the foibles of the black student organizations and was fond of telling a story about how he tracked their use of university cars (provided for recruiting new black students) through gasoline credit card receipts, discovering that they had attended an Angela Davis rally in Detroit; however, there was no evidence he harbored any personal animosity toward blacks. They lived in a different world he didn't fully understand. As a law enforcement officer, he had to respond if they broke the law during their protests. It was as simple as that.[15]

And then abruptly, at the beginning of 1969, Keibler was no longer commander of the Rockview barracks, although he remained in charge of criminal investigations. It all had to do with state police regulations and the department's byzantine seniority rules. The state police used a complex formula based on the number of troopers at a station, the number of calls handled by that station, and the number of calls anticipated based on the area's population to determine when a station headed by a sergeant should instead be headed by a lieutenant. Rockview had reached that critical mass. There had been eighteen troopers assigned to the barracks when Keibler became commander in 1965, and two of those were driving examiners. By 1968, there were thirty-three, mainly because of the Penn State political troubles and a rise in drug trafficking.[16]

So, who would be the new lieutenant? It could never be so simple as moving up the sergeant who was already there—Keibler, who was thirty-eight years old and one of the state's best criminal investigators. Kimmel, who was forty-four, had recently been promoted from sergeant at Huntingdon to one of three lieutenants at Troop G headquarters in Hollidaysburg. In the end, the state police commanders chose Kimmel. Keibler, who wanted to stay in criminal investigation work and didn't want to move his family, accepted the change. Kimmel would be fine. He just didn't know the territory.[17]

Frustrated in his attempts to figure out how to contact Keibler, Lieutenant Kimmel phoned Keibler's mother in the wee hours of the morning, waking her up. He pleaded with her to tell him how George could be reached. He desperately needed him to lead the investigation of the murder of a Penn State coed. She finally relented, giving him the phone number of a neighbor. Around 3:00 or 4:00 a.m. on Saturday, November 29, the neighbor knocked on the cabin door and brought Keibler back to his house. Kimmel explained over the phone what was happening and asked him to return and take over the investigation. The sergeant agreed to be there by mid-afternoon on Saturday.[18]

CHAPTER 5

Miss Marple Arrives at the Library

In the early morning hours of Saturday, November 29, long before Keibler returned, a very short, plump, and elderly lady strolled purposefully into the Level 2 stacks of Pattee Library. She greeted the troopers who had been there all night, took off her coat, and began to look around as if she owned the place.[1] The indomitable seventy-one-year-old chemistry professor, Mary Louisa Willard, the Miss Marple of State College, had arrived to help her boys find whatever material evidence might remain after the unfortunate contamination of the crime scene early Friday night. She was certain that something was still there to find.[2]

Lieutenant Kimmel, appalled by what had happened, had phoned Willard on Friday night and asked for her help. He probably wondered whether he should send a car to her home at 363 Ridge Avenue to fetch her, because every police officer knew she was the worst driver in town, barely able to see over the wheel as she drove down the middle of the road. But when it came to gathering evidence at a crime scene and analyzing it in her lab, she was second to none. Willard was the daughter of Joseph Willard, the late chairman of the mathematics department at Penn State and namesake of the Willard Building. She had been born on the Penn State campus in 1898, in what was later called Moffat Cottage, torn down in 1965 to build the library's new research wing. And she had been a member of the Penn State faculty, active or emeritus, for fifty years.[3]

Mary Willard had obtained bachelor's and master's degrees in chemistry from Penn State and her PhD from Cornell University. At Cornell, she studied under Professor Emile Chamot, a master of chemical microscopy, and probably from him picked up the bug for using science in the public interest, especially crime solving. In 1899, Chamot proved that most wallpaper sold in America contained dangerous amounts of arsenic, bad if your toddler liked to lick the wall or if you were a fireman battling a house fire. In 1902, he helped the police in Syracuse, New York, convict a seventeen-year-old girl of murdering her late husband's brother with strychnine after he spurned her advances. A court had the body exhumed, and the Cornell professor found enough poison in him to kill a horse.[4]

Lieutenant Kimmel's request for Willard's assistance was not unusual, even though under departmental regulations all crime scene analysis was supposed to be done by the state police crime lab in Harrisburg. She had been doing this work for the Rockview barracks since 1946, when her brother had become district attorney. The troopers got around the rules by having District Attorney Willard request that Professor Willard do the work, a subterfuge that subsequent DAs continued. Troopers often sent their DUI blood tests to Willard for processing so they didn't have to drive them down to Harrisburg. Willard was "highly regarded" by the Rockview troopers, according to a 1954 FBI memo.[5]

But they didn't simply use her because it was convenient. An internal FBI memo of February 20, 1961, sent to FBI director J. Edgar Hoover, accused the state police commissioner, Colonel Frank McCartney, of pushing use of the Harrisburg lab by local police departments, "despite the fact he knows he does not have qualified experts." State troopers in the field were under no illusions about the lab's competency, the memo continued, "and whenever possible endeavor to have local police work on the same case and send the evidence to the FBI Laboratory." Or, in Rockview's case, by Mary Willard. In 1967, the District Attorneys' Association of Pennsylvania complained to Governor Raymond Shafer that the facilities of the Pennsylvania State Police Crime Laboratory were "simply inadequate," though the complaint centered on understaffing rather than technical incompetence. Shafer replied that his administration was working on an ambitious plan to raise state police pay, build a new crime laboratory, and establish a statewide laboratory system that would ensure that crime lab services were not so far away.[6]

Kimmel knew it could be hours before a technician made it up to State College from the capital, and there had been too many mistakes and delays already. Plus, Mary Willard was a better crime scene investigator—she called her work "criminalistics"—than anyone in the troop, or anyone sent up by Harrisburg. Each troop had a couple of officers who were called lab people, but in practice they could do little more than take pictures and process fingerprints. They had no training in the sorts of things Mary Willard could do blindfolded. We can only imagine how different the investigation of the Betsy Aardsma murder might have turned out if Willard had arrived in Pattee Library before the Campus Patrol.[7]

After all, she had been doing criminalistics since 1932, when law enforcement agents brought her bootleg liquor for analysis in the waning days of Prohibition. She had even been called as an expert witness for the defense in the original murder trial of Dr. Sam Sheppard in 1954 in Cleveland, Ohio. This was the notorious case that spawned *The Fugitive,* first as a television series from 1963 to 1967 and then as a feature film starring Harrison Ford in 1993, about a physician wrongly convicted of his wife's brutal murder. In 1961, Willard declared emphatically to the *Washington Post* that Sheppard was innocent. "Those marks on her body could only have been made by a left-handed man," she said. Sheppard was right-handed. Helping to solve murders was Willard's life's work. "There are so many kinds of murder," she told a reporter for the Lake Charles (Louisiana) *American Press* in early 1965, when a retrial of Sheppard was looking more likely. "But I'm not talking about someone taking a gun and shooting someone. I'm talking about the cases such as the Sheppard case, that I was called as a technical consultant on. Here you had a case where fibers, hairs, blood, soil, and many other things had to be analyzed." A jury in the second trial found Sheppard not guilty, and he was freed in 1966, after ten years in prison.[8]

After Betsy's autopsy was completed early Saturday morning, Trooper Simmers took some of the tissue samples back to the Rockview barracks and put them in the refrigerator. He then picked up Trooper Ken

Schleiden at Betsy's room in Atherton Hall and drove with him to Pond Lab to pick up Willard and take her back to Pattee Library. This time she brought along a black light, because black lights cause bloodstains to glow. Since Betsy had been stabbed, it made sense to her to look for blood, even though very little of Betsy's blood had left her body.[9]

Willard was not squeamish about her work. Joe Willard, her nephew, recalled driving his aunt to burned houses, wrecked cars, and other places where her services were needed. One of his earliest memories was driving her to the Scranton area so she could pick up a badly charred set of human remains. He loaded them in the trunk of the car and drove her back to State College and her laboratory on the first floor of Pond. She was unflappable. Given what she was about to find in the Level 2 stacks of Pattee Library, that was a good thing.[10]

The first state troopers to arrive on the scene Friday night had conducted an intensive search of the bookshelves near the crime scene, looking for the murder weapon. They didn't find it. The troopers also looked for fingerprints, one of the few technical areas of crime scene investigation in which they had training. A soda can with a partial print was found near the murder site, but it turned out to have been left by one of the Campus Patrol officers. Nearly a hundred library books, including the ones that fell to the floor when Betsy was stabbed to death, were boxed up as potential evidence. Some of Betsy's belongings, including books and her coat, were retrieved from her study carrel by Charles H. Ness, associate director of public services for the library.[11]

What happened next should have been no surprise, given the vice problems in Pattee Library. Three rows over from where Betsy was slain, toward the back of the room, was a carrel on which two glossy, illustrated books featuring hard-core heterosexual pornography lay open. "Hard-core" at that time had a specific meaning for American law enforcement. It was a designation reserved for photographic portrayals of sexual intercourse involving vaginal, anal, or oral penetration. This particular book had been published in the Netherlands, where pornography had been legalized earlier that year, and carried an eye-popping price tag for 1969 of $10. This was well above the typical price for porn, which ranged from

$1.50 to $2.25 (a non-porn paperback at the drugstore might cost 50 to 75 cents). They were simply too expensive to casually abandon. Whoever owned them had left in a hurry, so agitated that he had forgotten about them. Or didn't dare take the time to circle back.[12]

Trooper Simmers said a subsequent search of the the area turned up twenty to thirty other cheap paperback porn books, known in the trade as "sex pulps." They were stuffed in the shelves among the scholarly titles. Sex pulps were once soft-core pornography, more like today's R-rated movies, but in the late 1960s had begun to include more blunt language about sexual acts, descriptions once limited to hard-core books.[13] They, too, were boxed up for transportation to Rockview. There was no telling how long the sex pulps had been there. The US Supreme Court, in the *Stanley v. Georgia* decision of April 7, 1969, had legalized possession of pornography in the privacy of one's own home, but possession in a public library still fell well outside of what the court said was legal.

During her search, Mary Willard turned on her black light and began crawling along the floor of the library near where Betsy was murdered, shining the light over every square inch, and providing a running commentary to the troopers. Something glowed, and she recognized it not as the dark black color of dried blood, but the unmistakable yellow-green fluorescence of human semen. She continued her search and found many other semen spots on the floor throughout the Level 2 Core. Then she lifted the light to the shelves, to the books themselves, and was stunned to find semen stains on the books, too. The troopers were in a state of shock. "It looked like [they] had orgies on the floor," Trooper Ronald Tyger recalled. Schleiden remembered that the area "was covered." Simmers said, "You cannot imagine the amount of semen." Betsy Aardsma had wandered into a dark place where men with broken souls masturbated onto library books.[14]

Finally, Willard stood up and announced that she needed to gather up anything that was on the floor at the murder site. And because she had none of the specialty vacuum suction devices or other collection tools used by police today, she was going to wipe the floor with her skirt and take it back to her laboratory for analysis. She looked inquisitively at the young troopers. "Do you boys have girlfriends?" she asked. Informed that they did, she wasted no time doffing her skirt, then got back down on her hands and knees and used it to wipe the floor as the troopers turned away in embarrassed disbelief. She carefully gathered it up, put on her long coat, and walked out of the library and back to her laboratory, as if an old woman walking across campus without a skirt was the most natural thing in the world. She was secure in her belief that her methods were sound and would be accepted in the Centre County court and, indeed, in most courts of the land.[15]

"She was the expert on anything and everything," said former district attorney Charles C. Brown Jr., later a county judge. "Handwriting? She was the expert. Blood analysis? She was the expert. You name it, she was the expert. Of course, you look back now and say, wait a minute! Somewhere along the line, she couldn't have been the expert. But she qualified in court all the time when I had her . . . and virtually no defense attorney ever really challenged her. Now in this day and age, she'd be challenged on everything, and probably rightfully so, on some of her areas of expertise. But she was a delightful person, and she just charmed the hell out of everybody."[16]

In the days that followed the Aardsma murder, Mary Willard made several more trips to the library. One of the specimens she analyzed was a spot of blood found on the wall by the stairs that ascended to the main floor from the Level 2 Core. It turned out to be Betsy's blood. Keibler believed it had somehow been smeared on the wall when the ambulance attendants tried and failed to get the stretcher up those stairs. But even he considered this a "very strange" explanation. Had the killer gotten a little of her blood on his hand and then touched it to the wall ever so slightly as he fled up the stairs?[17]

CHAPTER 6

Bringing Her Home

Whereas ye know not what shall be on the morrow. For what is your life? It is even a vapor, that appeareth for a little time and then vanisheth away.

—James 4:14, King James Bible

Dick and Esther Aardsma barely slept. There had been the call from David Wright's father around 3:00 a.m., and at dawn on Saturday, November 29, the telephone rang again. This time it was the Pennsylvania State Police officially informing them that a small knife wound had been found in their daughter's breast and that she had been murdered.

After Reverend Van Oostenburg left on Friday night, Esther phoned her sister, Anna Ruth Cotts, who lived in Michigan City, Indiana, to pour out her grief. Mrs. Cotts and her husband, Louis, were as devastated as the Aardsmas. Betsy was their favorite niece. She was always somebody's favorite something, so why would anyone want to kill her? Ruth told Esther that of course they would accompany her and Dick to State College to bring her body home. By chance, their son Ron, a Delta Airlines pilot, was visiting. He offered to fly back to Michigan City early the next morning in his own small plane. Then he would fly them up the Lake Michigan coast about a hundred miles to Holland to pick up the Aardsmas. Then he would fly them all back to O'Hare Airport in Chicago, where they could catch an Allegheny Airlines flight to Pittsburgh and on to State College. His work schedule precluded him from taking them all the way.[1]

Cotts touched down at Tulip City Airport, which was less than three miles from the Aardsma home on East 37th Street. Carole and Dennis Wegner, Betsy's sister and brother-in-law, stayed in Holland to look after Kathy, who that morning phoned her friend, Arlene Pelon, who lived a couple of doors down, to tell her she couldn't play because her sister had died. Esther and Dick were ashen and "absolutely silent" during the flight back to Chicago, Ron Cotts recalled. "Almost didn't say a word." Later that day, after transferring in Chicago, the four adults arrived at Black Moshannon Airport on a mountain plateau near Philipsburg, about twenty miles from Penn State. They checked in to the Holiday Inn in downtown State College and were visited by some of Betsy's friends, including Sharon Brandt, who told them about her life at Penn State. One of them mentioned the perverts in Pattee Library. The Aardsmas also arranged with Koch Funeral Home for the return of Betsy's body to Holland on Monday.[2]

Most of the Penn State community, especially students who went home for the Thanksgiving weekend, was focused on the last Nittany Lions football game of the regular season, which they could watch on national television that afternoon. Coach Joe Paterno and his team were in Raleigh to play North Carolina State, a team with a 3-5-1 record. Penn State, already picked to play Missouri in the Orange Bowl on New Year's Day, won its twenty-first straight game, 33–8. It was another triumph for the Charlie Pittman–Franco Harris ground attack that all fans believed would surely lead the team to the national title. Football was everything at Penn State. Paterno was already a legend.[3]

Betsy's murder jumped out from the front page of the *Holland Evening Sentinel* on Saturday afternoon. Randy Vande Water, city editor of the *Sentinel,* was a member of Trinity Reformed Church and knew the Aardsmas, though not well. It was rare at that time for anyone from this small city of twenty-five thousand to be murdered, especially a girl like Betsy from a good, Dutch, middle-class, churchgoing family. Saying you were Dutch in Holland was like saying you were Irish in Dublin. Not everyone was of Dutch descent or had a Dutch name like Aardsma—just 85 percent of them. Vande Water included Betsy's University of Michigan senior portrait with the story. This haunting photograph became her death mask, reprinted by many newspapers and magazines over the next four days and, indeed, for the next four decades. It was a particularly striking image of her, making her look beautiful and even a little glamorous. That description would have surprised and amused her friends, who were used to her casual, artsy ways, but it was cemented in place for all time by that photo.

Because the murder received national press coverage, Betsy's friends heard about it whether they still had family in Holland or not. Peggy Wich, a close friend from Holland High School, had moved to Washington, DC, after graduating from Marquette University in Milwaukee and was working as a waitress in a hotel restaurant near Dupont Circle. She had last spoken to Betsy in August, right before she left for Penn State, but they had stayed in touch through letters. Peggy, in fact, had just sent her a letter, dropping it in a public mailbox near the restaurant. Her father heard about the murder in Holland and phoned her long distance with the devastating news. On Sunday, she worked the breakfast shift. When she went to take the order from her first customer, she saw he was reading that day's *New York Daily News.* It was open to the same photograph of Betsy that Vande Water had used, under the headline COED IS MURDERED IN COLLEGE LIBRARY. Peggy managed to hold it together even as she inwardly reeled.[4]

George Arwady, a journalist who had briefly dated Betsy at Hope College, where she spent her freshman and sophomore years, was shaken by the same story in the *Daily News.* Andrea Yunker, Betsy's roommate during their junior and senior years at the University of Michigan, was at her parents' house in Sturgis, Michigan. She came downstairs and walked into the kitchen, where her father's transistor radio was playing. She was half listening when the news came on about a girl named Betsy Aardsma being murdered at Penn State. Andrea's head spun. She called the radio station to confirm the news, then drove to a restaurant, ordered breakfast, and broke down when the waiter came. "My best friend's been killed!" she sobbed.[5]

Adults who knew Betsy were similarly shaken. Verne C. Kupelian, a former teacher at Holland High School and former owner/manager of the Edgar Allan Poe teen club, now lived in his hometown of Columbus, Ohio. He heard about her death on the popular and ubiquitous *Paul Harvey News and Comment,* which ran on his local radio station at noon on Saturdays. Shaken, Kupelian made a long-distance call to another former student up in Holland, who confirmed the news. He could never understand why someone like Betsy would be the target of a murderer, chalking it up to somebody's momentary violent outburst. "You should never be alone," he said. "I kept telling kids that."

Among Penn State students still on campus, word spread slowly. There was no effort by the university administration to alert them to the murder, as there almost certainly would be on any college campus today. One of the main sources of information, the student-run *Daily Collegian* newspaper, had suspended publication until after New Year's, as it always did at that time of year. The paper's editors were huddling and about to decide, given the gravity of events, to publish on Tuesday, December 2. Local radio broadcasts in the State College area carried the news on Saturday, as did the *Centre Daily Times* newspaper in State College, but not all students listened to the radio or read the town newspaper. So the grapevine, with all its limitations, remained the most likely source of the news among students stuck on campus that weekend.

Thomas D. Witt, a freshman journalism major, lived in Thompson Hall, a hundred yards west of Pattee Library. One of his classes actually met Friday afternoon, and in the early evening, he had an intramural basketball game at Rec Hall up the street. Still, Witt didn't hear about Betsy's murder until Sunday, when his roommate returned from break and said, "Hey, did you hear about that girl in Pattee Library?" Students who went home for Thanksgiving had a better chance of seeing a story about the murder than those who had stayed on campus. Marge Wissler, who lived near Lancaster, Pennsylvania, read about the crime Saturday night in the Lancaster *New Era* newspaper. The story was on page two: PENN STATE COED DIES OF STAB WOUND. The morning paper, the *Intelligencer Journal,* ran nothing until Monday.

Back in State College, getting more investigators was Lieutenant Kimmel's number-one priority. He had initially requested that ten criminal investigators be assigned to the case, more than the Rockview barracks could provide. That number rose to twenty by Monday, and then to forty a few days after that. The Pennsylvania State Police had about 1,600 troopers in 1969, compared to more than 5,000 today. Lieutenant Calvin Richwine arranged to bring in troopers from other barracks in Troop G, including Hollidaysburg, Bedford, McConnellsburg, Huntingdon, and Philipsburg. Some from Carlisle and Harrisburg in Troop H also were dispatched to help. As the out-of-town troopers arrived, they reported to a command post Kimmel had set up in Room 109 of the Boucke Building, which was across the street from the Ritenhour Health Center and a quick walk from Pattee Library. Some of the new arrivals were housed in the Holiday Inn, the same place Betsy Aardsma's family was staying, and others at a different motel.[6] Kimmel's rationale was to throw a lot of men at the crime and hope that one of them came up with something; albeit on a smaller scale, this was the same approach he had used in the Mountain Man case in 1966.

From the start, the Aardsma investigation was dogged by morale problems. Some of the troopers assigned to the case were upset at missing the start of deer and bear season, a much-anticipated event in rural Pennsylvania, which opened a half-hour before sunrise on Monday, December 1. They stayed four to a motel room and, not yet having their first union contract, received no overtime pay for their very long days and endless weeks.[7] Trooper Tom Shelar was sent from Carlisle up to State College on Tuesday, December 2, the second day of hunting season, and recalled that he was peeved. But he, like the others, did his duty.[8]

When the first troopers arrived on Saturday, Kimmel ordered them to search again for the knife, in case the killer had dropped or hid it as he fled. They searched in trash cans, on rooftops, and along logical escape paths through the campus, looking for anything of interest that might have been discarded. But despite several sweeps, nothing was found. Kimmel also arranged for video cameras borrowed from Channel 3, the Penn State television station, to be placed in the Level 2 stacks, in the hope of catching someone acting suspiciously. Given the size of video cameras in 1969, hiding them was no easy task. One was placed at the end of the aisle where Betsy was murdered but wasn't very well hidden. Albert Dunning, news director of WDFM Radio, the student-run station, went to the stacks that weekend out of curiosity, hoping to better understand what had happened. Right away he spotted the cardboard box with a lens-size hole sitting on a top shelf and chuckled to himself.[9]

As he drove home from his hunting camp on Saturday afternoon with his wife and son, Sergeant George Keibler thought about the murder case that, unbeknownst to him, was about to take over his life. During the year prior to ceding command of Rockview to Kimmel, he had attended a major-case school and conference at the state police academy in Hershey. The instructors were from the FBI as well as the state police, and they reinforced the dos and don'ts of handling a major case. Thus, he had a good idea of what he needed to do to keep the investigation running on track. But that didn't solve the crime. His three years as commander of Rockview had given him as good an understanding as anyone in the state police of the social changes that were engulfing Penn State at the end of the Peace and Love Decade, which those days seemed anything but. The question now was whether Betsy Aardsma's brutal murder had grown out of political radicalism or had welled up from the same foul miasma that had spawned the Michigan, Zodiac, and Manson Family murder sprees. Or maybe it was something else entirely.[10]

After dropping off his wife and son at home, Keibler drove on to Pattee Library, arriving around 4:00 p.m. Trooper Ken Schleiden heard Kimmel tell Keibler that he had to run the Aardsma investigation from the inside, as the data collector and analyst, and not from out in the field with the detectives. This wasn't quite what Keibler expected, and he wasn't happy about it for a time, say those who know him. But Kimmel soon made it clear that Keibler was really running the show, even if he, Kimmel, was the public face of it. He ultimately allowed Keibler to go out on witness interviews whenever he saw a need to do so. "There was no one else who could have done what he did," Simmers recalled. "And Kimmel knew that." After visiting the crime scene, Keibler drove to the Rockview barracks, where he got a look at the pile of library books collected as evidence. They included eleven volumes of *The History of the Rebellion and Civil Wars in England* by Edward, Earl of Clarendon, *Alice's Adventures in Wonderland* by Lewis Carroll, and *Controlled Fertility* by Regine K. Stix. All had been scooped up from the floor at the murder site, or from adjoining shelves, and would not be returned to Pattee Library for nearly two years.[11]

On Sunday, November 30, Keibler and Corporal Mutch went back to Atherton Hall to conduct a more thorough search of Room 5A. Sharon Brandt was still being kept out, and the room had been sealed and guarded since Friday night. Keibler wanted to assure himself that nothing had been missed in the first going-over but also wanted to determine whether any of Betsy's personal effects could be given to her parents before they returned to Holland. The two investigators searched the room thoroughly, a process that took a couple of hours, but found nothing important.[12]

They then drove to the Holiday Inn to meet Esther and Dick Aardsma and Ruth and Louis Cotts. Mutch recalled that the family was "down and desperate" but very much in control of their emotions. Keibler expressed his condolences, gave Mrs. Aardsma two personal items from Betsy's room, and explained that they would have to keep her purse and the clothing she was wearing when she died. Then he settled down to the business at hand. He had a number of questions, standard, but intrusive nonetheless, about Betsy's life. These were aimed at ferreting out any dangerous personal habits, such as drug or excessive alcohol use or promiscuous sex, and any possible enemies who might have wanted to harm her. They were standard because so often the answers led to the killer. This time, they didn't.

"I told the police that Betsy had no enemies," Mrs. Aardsma told *Daily Collegian* reporter Ted Anthony many years later. She was upset, believing that Sergeant Keibler expected her and Dick to solve the case for him. And Esther was bitter about one thing. "My God," she told Keibler. "Betsy came here to avoid Michigan."[13]

During her senior year at the University of Michigan in Ann Arbor, Betsy had faced a difficult decision. Her family urged her to get out of Ann Arbor and follow her boyfriend, David L. Wright, to Penn State, where he would start medical school in the fall. This was not so much for love but because they were worried sick about the serial killer then stalking and killing coeds in Ann Arbor and around nearby Eastern Michigan University in Ypsilanti. The so-called Coed Murders, sometimes called the Michigan Murders, took place between July 1967 and July 1969 but mostly in the spring and summer of 1969. Pretty brunettes like Betsy were his favorite target. Reluctantly, she agreed to go.[14]

Already on Friday night, Lieutenant Kimmel had decided that Sergeant Robert Milliron, a veteran criminal investigator from the Hollidaysburg barracks, and Trooper Ronald C. Tyger, from Philipsburg, would go to Michigan to see if there were any possible links between Betsy's murder and the Coed Murders in Ann Arbor. By that time, John Norman Collins had been arrested and charged with the murder of the final victim, eighteen-year-old Karen Sue Beineman of Grand Rapids. The Michigan police at one time had been looking for a second man who supposedly helped Collins. Had this supposed accomplice somehow known Betsy and followed her to Penn State? The questions seemed endless, the answers less so. They would also conduct an in-depth investigation of her personal life aimed at laying bare who Betsy Aardsma really was. They would talk to everyone they could find in Holland and Ann Arbor who knew her. There had to be some reason she was murdered, some moral flaw that would lead them to the killer. This was another time-tested scenario from Murder 101 and something they always looked for, just as it made perfect sense to Kimmel to tell Shovlin to haul David Wright out of bed and question him that first night. Many murders boil down to sex or money. Money didn't seem to be an issue here, so that left sex. But with whom?[15]

The Aardsmas and Cotts flew back to Michigan on Monday afternoon, December 1. Betsy's coffin went on an earlier flight and was taken upon arrival to the Notier-VerLee-Langeland Chapel, a funeral home on 16th Street in Holland, not far from the first home where she had lived as a young child. The family was still coming to terms with what they had seen and heard at Penn State. Ruth Cotts, who wrote thank-you notes for her sister, sent one to the Pattee Library staff at Penn State expressing bewilderment at what had happened to Betsy and displaying more than a hint of anger toward the university for allowing the murder to happen.[16]

> *We know you share in some small part our sorrow in this tragic event. We hope and pray whoever committed this heinous crime may be found, to protect other innocent young girls. . . . Could there not be some way of keeping non-students from entering the library? Some of Betsy's friends said there were "hangers-on" who used the library as a refuge.*[17]

Grief was more private in Holland than in some places. Cards and casseroles might arrive, but a stream of visitors to a house in mourning was rare. Families tended to retreat behind closed doors and drawn shades until the funeral and burial were over. The idea of a Jewish shiva or an Irish wake, with toasts by friends to the recently deceased, would have been deeply foreign, even offensive, to many in Holland. That was their culture. They were not an effusive people, at funerals or in any other way.

The Aardsmas struggled with preparations for the viewing on Tuesday night and funeral on Wednesday. They were in turmoil. Dennis Wegner tried to pretend Betsy's murder was a bad dream. But when he saw her body at the viewing at the Notier chapel, the bubble burst and he fell to pieces.[18] Kathy Aardsma, Betsy's younger sister, was hurt by the reaction of her teachers and counselors and fellow students at E. E. Fell Junior High School, who acted as if nothing had happened. No one from the school reached out to her. Esther Aardsma began a slide into deep depression, and Dick Aardsma reached for liquid comfort, a problem that was bad before Betsy died and would grow worse over the years.[19]

Reverend Gordon Van Oostenburg recognized that this was no ordinary funeral; no funeral of a young person ever is. But Betsy had been murdered, and the shock and horror had left the many who knew her in Holland reeling. On Sunday, November 30, he departed from his prepared sermon and instead preached on James 4:14, a verse that is widely interpreted as a warning to Christians not to be arrogant, that they are living on borrowed time and subject to God's will as to whether they live or die. He had preached similar sermons after the King and Kennedy assassinations the previous year. Later, he began thinking about what he would say at the funeral. Even though he had been the pastor of Trinity for seven years, he did not know Betsy well and would have to reach out to others to define her.[20]

David L. Wright, her boyfriend, was torn over whether to attend Betsy's funeral, which was just days before his first semester final exams at medical school. His parents convinced him he needed to go, and he conceded afterward that he would have felt bad if he hadn't. He also sent a dozen roses. His psychiatrist father, Dr. Donovan Wright, accompanied him to the service. He told David he counted only eleven roses in the bouquet, but he then realized that the twelfth had been placed in Betsy's hands in the coffin, which was open prior to the service. Several of David's fraternity brothers from the University of Michigan came to the funeral, as did several of Betsy's friends from Hope College and U of M. One of her high school boyfriends, Tom Bolhuis, served as one of the pallbearers. He hadn't seen her in several years and was surprised when he received a call from Betsy's parents.[21]

Just before the service began, David and the Aardsma family entered the church from a door on the left near the front of the sanctuary and sat in a front pew. Trinity was a big old church, built in 1911 in the traditional cathedral style of many churches of the era. Today it was nearly full. All eyes were drawn to the pulpit, which was in the middle of the chancel in front of three high-backed chairs and a large wall cross. Many Christian churches place the pulpit off to one side so as not to block the altar, but Reformed Churches do not have traditional altars. When Reverend Van Oostenburg mounted the pulpit, he towered over the congregation like a figurehead on a sailing ship, surveying the stormy seas ahead. Now he would try to explain the death of a young woman who had grown up in his church but who he did not really know very well. She had been influenced in her moral beliefs by what she heard there but had gone further into the world than many of her elders found comfortable. Betsy had embraced what was good about the 1960s, especially the fight for civil rights for blacks, an end to the war in Vietnam, and the beginning of new rights for women. In the end, uncertain about what to say, Van Oostenburg fell back on doctrine and Scripture and preached about her death no differently than he would any other. It did not go over well.[22]

One of Betsy's friends from the University of Michigan, he informed the mourners, told him that Betsy had been worried enough about the Coed Killer the previous spring that she had thought about her own funeral if she was murdered. And she wanted an Easter resurrection message to be preached. So Reverend Van Oostenburg told them they should celebrate her entrance into Heaven. Esther Aardsma had provided him with a copy of a poem, "Why Do I Live?," which Betsy had written during her senior year in high school. The poem compared her God-centered moral values with those of a more self-centered, worldly ex-boyfriend. "I am living in preparation for death / What I live for will last," the pastor read from the poem. Expanding on his Sunday message, he declared that the poem meant Betsy had accepted both the reality of her death and the fact that her death would be God's will. Of course, whether that remained her attitude four years later, when she was in love with David L. Wright, was unknown, but Van Oostenburg proceeded as if it was. He did not reach out to those who considered her violent death at a young age, and her loss to the world, to be an unspeakable tragedy.

This did not sit well with a number of Betsy's grieving college friends and some in her family, who were unwilling to take only the eternal view and saw nothing to celebrate about her murder. Her college friends, in particular, knew Betsy as a modern, educated, outward-looking young woman who had embraced the cultural and political changes of the 1960s and longed for a life in the outside world. Now, Reverend Van Oostenburg seemed to be dragging her back into the insular, Calvinist, small-town church culture in Holland from which she had longed to escape. The pastor had no ill intent, but some were angry about the sermon even forty years later.

"I still recall her funeral with a great deal of anger toward Reverend Van Oostenburg," said Dennis Wegner, her brother-in-law. "Rather than dealing with why someone who was young and making a difference in the world was murdered, he merely dusted off his fill-in-the-blanks, 'old lady dies of cancer,' stock funeral sermon. He seemed to say it was not Christian for us to grieve, because Betsy was in heaven, and we should celebrate her life. That is, not only did I feel bad, but the preacher said I should feel bad about feeling bad. It took me a long time to find a healing perspective on that." Olga Lozowchuk, one of Betsy's apartment mates during her senior year at the University of Michigan, found the sermon "not very personal" and "not very comforting at all."[23]

Linda DenBesten, who had been Betsy's freshman-year roommate at Hope College, was dumbfounded and then furious as she listened to the pastor. "It made me so angry. And I remember leaning over to her mother after the funeral. I said, this is not God's will. And she said, I know it, I know it." DenBesten poured out her tears and anger in the car as her husband drove them home to Illinois after the funeral. The one good thing about the funeral, she said, was that she finally had a chance to meet David L. Wright, "who seemed just as decent as I would have expected him to be."[24]

Perhaps nothing Van Oostenburg could have said that day would have eased the grief that Betsy's friends and family were feeling. The death of a young person upsets the natural order of things, and her friends wanted an affirmation of her worthy life and lost potential rather than Calvinist theology that probably was perfectly appropriate when, as Wegner put it, an old lady died of cancer. Barbara Timmer, a friend of Betsy's from Hope College, who is Van Oostenburg's niece, defended her uncle as a loving and compassionate man who was never harsh or judgmental. She did not attend the funeral but found the reaction of Betsy's friends who did to be upsetting and hard to comprehend. But she knew Gordon Van Oostenburg in a different way than they did.[25]

Tom Bolhuis remembered the physical shock of placing his hand on one of the six handles of her coffin and helping to carry it to the hearse. Her body was taken from the church to Pilgrim Home Cemetery, final resting place for generations of prominent and ordinary Dutch Americans in Holland.

Esther Aardsma continued to send David birthday presents for many years. Thirteen-year-old Kathy Aardsma took it upon herself to keep up

Betsy's habit of sending him a letter nearly every day, not realizing that it kept the pain of her sister's death alive for him. David Wright called them "a very, very nice family. It's just a tragic thing. . . . You sort of want to forget something like that," Wright said. "But boy, she kept that up for about two years." He would soon meet another woman and move on but could never truly escape the shadow of Betsy's murder, which he did not talk about to his own children until 2008, after a series by the author on the murder ran in the Harrisburg (PA) *Patriot-News.*[26]

Part II: Searching for the Killer

It was a damn shame, but we worked hard. We worked months on that. We had a hypnotist and everybody else in there. There were six hundred people we interviewed who were in the library at the time, but absolutely nothing.

—Lieutenant Calvin Richwine[1]

CHAPTER 7

The Running Man in the Core

As a light snow fell on State College, Lieutenant Kimmel arrived at the Boucke Building on Monday, December 1, 1969, to hold his first news conference about the Aardsma murder. The snow, which had been falling since the night before, made the roads slippery but pleased thousands of deer and bear hunters who had trooped into the woods of Centre County an hour before dawn for the start of both seasons. Now it would be easier to track their prey, whether by footprints or blood. Kimmel had neither footprints nor blood to lead him to Betsy Aardsma's killer, save for the one tiny drop of her blood on the library wall. He was depending on Sergeant Keibler to study the evidence and determine the path to follow.

About forty people were waiting for the news conference, although the journalists were far outnumbered by state troopers, Campus Patrol officers, and university officials. Kimmel told the press that he was particularly eager to identify and question the *two* men—yes, two—whom Marilee Erdely claimed had come running out of the Level 2 stacks shortly before she had discovered Betsy's body.[1]

Nearly all of Penn State's twenty-six thousand students had returned the previous day from Thanksgiving break, had learned that one of their own had been brutally murdered, and were clamoring for information. Kimmel had decided to tell the public what he knew, or at least what was safe to release. The problem was that some of the things he believed that morning were later proven to be wrong or misleading.

The only witness to the immediate aftermath of the slaying the state police had found thus far was Marilee Erdely. She had been in shock after finding Betsy's body and may well have thought she saw two men running at her. At the news conference, Kimmel did not call the two mystery men suspects in Betsy's murder, saying only that "we consider them very important for questioning." What the press was never told was that Keibler eventually concluded that one of the men almost certainly *was* the killer and that the other was Joao Uafinda, the student from Mozambique who had followed the killer around the Core. Erdely did not know Uafinda, and he had not yet come forward. Nor had Richard Sanders Allen, the man at the copier, who would not find out that Keibler wanted to talk to him for many months. Because no obvious clarification was ever issued, the "two men" narrative became embedded in the public mind. So did the time of the murder. Kimmel told reporters it had occurred between 4:30 and 4:45 p.m. Keibler, after analyzing the available evidence, changed that to 4:55 p.m., but Kimmel's time was the one people remembered.

The lieutenant's frustration at the lack of solid leads was evident at the news conference, as was his growing realization that the state police, after four years of crackdowns on political dissent and illegal drug use, had an image problem on campus. Perhaps he remembered what had happened when his men got too tough with the locals during the search for the Mountain Man. At the press conference, Kimmel urged any student or professor with information about the murder to contact his investigators as soon as possible. "We want it understood that we are *not* coming around talking to people as suspects at this time," Kimmel said at the news conference. "We don't want anyone to think that this is a stigma on them if somebody comes to talk to them. We have a serious problem as far as we can tell at this point." The "serious problem" Kimmel referenced was the lack of material evidence. He called it a "crime without clues."[2] All they had were the books, including the pornography, a soda pop can collected at the scene, the splash of Betsy's blood on the wall by the staircase, and the body tissue samples taken at her autopsy. Kimmel had no physical evidence that could be used to identify the killer.

Trooper Simmers took the books and the soda pop can to the state police crime lab in Harrisburg later in the day. Normally, the evidence would have gone to Troop G headquarters in Hollidaysburg for iodine fuming, the classic method of raising fingerprints. But the state police had recently begun using the new ninhydrin method, which could only be done in Harrisburg. The technicians did find fingerprints on the soda can, but they matched the fingerprints of one of the Campus Patrol members at the scene that night. Nothing was found on the books. Betsy had not been raped, so the semen samples collected on the floor by Mary Willard were a curiosity at best, proof, however shocking, only of the sort of perverted behavior that went on in Pattee Library. Even if the murderer was one of the perverts, the semen didn't prove much since there had been no rape. All they had to go on was what Erdely had told them.[3]

Marilee, who shared an apartment with another girl at 133 North Patterson Street, exactly a mile west of Pattee Library, was not identified by name at the news conference. Instead, Kimmel referred to her as "the student" or "the girl student." He was concerned about her safety, since the killer was at large, and she was the only witness they had. For several weeks, according to the man she later married, Erdely was provided with security, including troopers who accompanied her to classes and waited outside the door.[4]

Kimmel dismissed any significance to reports by Penn State coeds that they had been "bothered" by men, as he put it, in Pattee Library in recent weeks. This unwanted attention was a serious matter, including groping, flashing, and public masturbation, which were all forms of sexual assault. But Kimmel downplayed the incidents as routine. "You have reports of peeping toms, men following girls, bumping into them, talking to them, all the time in colleges and communities everywhere," he said. His skepticism was common to many policemen, physicians, and other male authority figures of the time.[5]

Of course, sometimes events seemed to lend support to those attitudes. On the morning after Kimmel's first news conference, there was concern that the killer had tried to strike again, this time at Clarion State College in the picturesque small town of Clarion, ninety-five miles west of State College. The victim of the attack, an eighteen-year-old freshman psychology major, claimed to have been in bed in her dorm room around

2:30 a.m. on December 2 when the assault occurred. She said a strange man pressed a pillow over her face and slashed her on the neck and abdomen with a double-edged razor blade, then fled into the night. The victim, bleeding and seemingly terrified, went to another room for help. Her fellow students took her to the college dispensary for treatment of what turned out to be superficial cuts. She was released after treatment.[6]

The state police were called only at 9:00 a.m., the victim claiming she delayed because a college official in the dorm told her not to call police. Trooper William E. Lees, the investigating officer, could find no other student in the dorm who had seen or heard anything that night. Increasingly skeptical, the state police announced that they were going to ask the victim, who was recovering from her wounds at her parents' house outside Pittsburgh, to take a polygraph examination. She apparently flunked and ultimately confessed that she had inflicted the cuts herself and made up the account of the attack. She dropped out of Clarion after her confession.[7]

During the three weeks he was in charge of the Aardsma investigation, Lieutenant Kimmel was at the Boucke Building nearly every day, accompanied by Lieutenant Richwine. On that first Monday, he asked Sergeant Keibler to compile and write the official investigative report on the murder. Keibler was provided with a clerk-typist, a woman from Troop G headquarters, to help organize a comprehensive filing system for the never-ending river of information that was flowing in from the forty investigators, converting it to three-by-five index cards and assembling those in ways that made sense and could easily be retrieved later. It was also Keibler's job to pick the brains of the investigators, to analyze the information they uncovered and suggest where to look next. In an era when personal computers did not exist and mainframe computers were something for NASA, not the Pennsylvania State Police, George Keibler was the human computer of the Aardsma investigation. When he found that two plus two didn't equal four, he would make a note and advise Kimmel to send someone to check further.

Whenever new information replaced the old, some of the main investigative report, which eventually ran to more than 1,700 pages, had to be rewritten to keep the overall narrative accurate. Kimmel's job was easy in comparison.[8]

Some of Keibler's investigators, including Mike Mutch and Ronald Tyger, were veteran detectives. Others, like Mike Simmers and Ken Schleiden, were young and had long careers ahead of them. Tyger welcomed the presence of the younger men, even while boasting that seasoned investigators could "look beyond the horizon." The problem was that some of the troopers on the Aardsma case had no practical investigative experience at all. They were traffic cops who had been drafted into the case because Kimmel wanted more feet on the ground.[9]

That posed a problem. Keibler, who had a better understanding of the university culture than Kimmel, worried about sending troopers into the different world of the Penn State campus who had never dealt with faculty and their prickly sensibilities. "You were reaching out and getting a trooper who may not have been to college, didn't know a damn thing about it, and we sent him to interview a professor," Keibler said. "[Some troopers] are not used to college-type people and the bullshit you get. You know in interviewing the average faculty member, he wants to be in charge of the interview. You see, the troopers aren't used to him being in charge, and here comes Assistant Professor So-and-So and smoke comes out of his butt. He's going to tell the trooper what to do. . . . And the professor's looking down at him, and the professor is in charge. And here's a trooper trying to interview a professor, and he doesn't know how to go about it, really. My academic opinion on the thing is that people in universities look down on someone who doesn't have their level of education. Now there's a way to handle that and a way not to handle it. But it causes problems when you bring people in who aren't aware of that."[10]

Keibler recalled the time he investigated the death of a Penn State graduate student in chemistry who committed suicide by swallowing cyanide. "His dad was a military officer, the Vietnam War was going on, and the kid felt his dad was disgracing him. Wrote about four or five suicide notes and never destroyed one, that was the strange thing," he said. One of the dead student's teachers, a full professor, came to see Keibler. "You probably think suicide is wrong," the professor said. Keibler admitted that yes, he did. "'Well, that's the difference between you and me,' he said. And I said, 'What do you mean?' And he said, 'Well, Johnny went out and sat under a tree and took cyanide. He weighed all the things he had that were good, and all the things that were bad. This outnumbers this.'" Keibler considered the professor's argument to be nonsensical and held it up as an example of the sort of things the state police ran into on the Penn State campus that they didn't typically encounter elsewhere. "Lord knows what you're going to find," he said.[11]

Many years after his role in the Aardsma investigation was over, Keibler conceded that he had about thirty more investigators than he could effectively use. It was Kimmel who wanted more boots on the ground, not him. "See, the more people you get, the more problems you get. It's a shotgun approach. If you get ten people—and I could handle that very easily—you can get your briefings. Briefings are the most important thing that a policeman can do with a group. If you arrive at eight o'clock in the morning and you're working for me, and the other guy comes in and he goes out that door and we don't get together, we've lost him. And again, I can understand the bringing in of forty. There's a helluva lot [of investigative work] to do. You had a trip to Michigan to start with. You're in a situation where you've got an awful lot of people that you're to interview." He worked from dawn till dusk and beyond, as did Lieutenant Kimmel, whose wife recalled that he didn't come home to Huntingdon for many days.[12]

A murder investigation on the other side of the country was about to bump the Aardsma case out of the headlines. Later on December 1, Los Angeles police chief Ed Davis announced arrests in the Tate-LaBianca murders, in which seven people, including actress Sharon Tate, the wife of director Roman Polanski, had been stabbed, slashed, or shot to death on the evenings of August 9 and 10, 1969. Davis said a "roving band of hippies" was believed responsible. Two of the suspects, Charles "Tex" Watson, twenty-four, and Patricia Krenwinkle, twenty-one, were already in custody. A third suspect, Linda Kasabian, nineteen, was still being sought.[13] All three were members of the so-called Manson Family. The cult leader, Charles Manson, thirty-five years old, was a short and wiry ex-con turned hippie guru. Davis said four or five other suspects, including Manson (although he wasn't mentioned that day), were already in custody in Independence, California, the county seat of Inyo County.[14]

The arrests followed months of intensive police work that ran the gamut from brilliant to incompetent. Although the crimes took place in upscale neighborhoods of Los Angeles, the Manson Family members had been arrested at their hideout near Death Valley National Monument, more than two hundred miles northeast of the city. Manson had led his followers to this barren land in the fall of 1968, telling them it was a place where "things aren't so crazy." He mesmerized them with talk of finding the "Hole in the Desert," a supposedly bottomless pit beneath Death Valley that led to a beautiful underground world complete with light, fruit trees, and a flowing river. Manson and Paul Watkins, his nominal second in command, spent their days searching for the Hole, driving stolen dune buggies through Death Valley at breakneck speeds. Susan Atkins and two other girls from the Family occasionally panhandled in Shoshone, a tiny desert oasis and crossroads about fifty miles from the Barker Ranch, where the Manson Family was hiding out. It had a store, restaurant, motel, gas station, and a high school that served the disparate and scattered children of the desert, plus an easygoing, live-and-let-live lifestyle. There were always tourists passing through during the cooler months.[15]

Surprisingly, there was often a Penn State University presence as well. Lauren A. Wright, a professor of geology at Penn State and chairman of the Department of Geology and Geophysics, taught geology of North America and did his research in Death Valley during the fall term nearly every year. Shoshone was his base of operations, and he would often bring along a graduate student. During the fall terms of 1967 and

1968, he was accompanied by Richard C. Haefner, who went by Rick, a strange, distant young man from Lancaster, Pennsylvania, who wore khaki pants every day and, as Wright observed out of curiosity, often carried a homemade knife.

CHAPTER 8
Hypnosis

Soon after Betsy's murder was discovered, the state police had begun contacting and questioning every student they could find who had been in Pattee Library on Friday afternoon. These included forty-six who had checked out books in the hour before she was found on the floor and as many students as could be identified among the six hundred who passed by the checker's desks during that hour but did not actually leave with books. The latter task was difficult, since these patrons were identifiable only if the librarian happened to know and remember them or if they came forward on their own. Reports had been received of a male student leaving one of Pattee Library's two exits in a hurry sometime between 4:00 and 6:00 p.m. on Friday. Another young man had been seen running away from the library around that time. Was either one of them the killer? Maybe. But ultimately, the tips led nowhere. Betty Arnold, one of the Pattee librarians, remembers a state trooper telling her, "We'll be lucky to ever find out who did this."[1]

The not-so-secret video cameras in the stacks also yielded nothing, or at least no footage of the murderer returning to the scene of the crime. Albert Dunning, news director of WDFM Radio at Penn State, took Kimmel aside after one of the news conferences early that week and asked him if they had gotten any leads off the videotape. The lieutenant froze, and Dunning said, "Well, it's really not very well concealed."

Around that time, W. Carl Jackson, director of libraries, and Charles H. Ness, assistant director of public services, went down to the Level 2 Core and were picked up on the very same video camera. When a Campus Patrol officer viewed the tape, he was certain they were the two men being sought for questioning by the state police. "They came back!" he exclaimed. "The sons of bitches have come back!" Lieutenant Kimmel himself became briefly excited when he viewed another tape and saw that a young man whom he had spotted in an earlier tape had returned to the Level 2 Core. His height and general description seemed close to that of the running man. The student lived out in Boalsburg and was brought in for questioning. But he had an airtight alibi. "It wasn't him," Keibler said.[2]

They also questioned students assigned to study carrels around the Level 2 Core. This raised alarm among foreign graduate students, who had a number of the carrels there. According to Dante Scalzi, then director of the Office of International Student Affairs, the international students believed they were being singled out for suspicion. Many of them spent hours in the library daily. The attention from the police left them shaken, especially those who came from countries where the police did not have a good reputation and were widely mistrusted by the citizenry. Many foreign students were there on scholarships or assistantships from Penn State or had some sort of financial support from their home government, all of which made them feel vulnerable.[3]

Whether it was overly tough questioning or not, it led to the first break in the case. Joao Uafinda, the student from Mozambique who had followed the running man around the Core before losing him and going home, either had a carrel himself or was told about the questioning by someone who did. He came forward nine days after the murder and identified himself to the state police. Uafinda spoke freely about what he had seen and done in the Core that day, but he was vague on key points and nervous when Keibler questioned him. A look at his background explains why.[4]

In 1969, his home country of Mozambique was in its 471st year of benighted colonial rule by Portugal and wracked by revolution. Some two hundred thousand white Portuguese had long exercised dominion over seven million blacks without any noticeable concern for their welfare beyond their utility as near slaves, creating wealth for Lisbon.

Uafinda was the youngest of five children of a poor farmer and did not begin school until about age twelve, when the missionary friars of the Italy-based Capuchin order saw potential and plucked him from his family to raise and educate. They hoped he would become a priest. Even so, his prospects were bleak.

Blacks had no political rights and could be arrested by the feared Portuguese secret police, the International Police for the Defense of the State (PIDE), as traitors if they criticized their racist treatment. They were subject to arrest and torture if they tried to leave the country, for higher education or anything else. To Uafinda, police officers meant danger, even death.

When the revolution against Portuguese rule began in the fall of 1964, he was in seminary. A supporter of independence, he fled his homeland after a political crackdown. Over the Christmas holiday in 1964, Uafinda took a bus as close to the border with Malawi as he dared. Then he crossed over, probably through the bush on foot, and made his way to the US consulate in Blantyre. He told American officials that he wanted to go to the United States for a university education and become a physician.

Uafinda arrived at the University of Rochester on a full scholarship from the US government in May 1965. An intake form said he arrived with an interpreter. "He [Uafinda] was well dressed—seemed somewhat timid, but fairly at ease. He will need to be put in [an] English language course immediately." Uafinda stayed at Rochester for two years, studying geography and English—medicine had fallen by the wayside—before transferring to Penn State in the summer of 1967.[5]

And now he was living in downtown State College, taking geography classes at Penn State and facing the stern detectives of the Pennsylvania State Police. He must have wondered if they were anything like the PIDE and would torture him. Uafinda gave them the benefit of the doubt, as his American friends encouraged him to do, but the language barrier remained an obstacle. He was not perfectly conversant in English, and his police interrogators were never quite sure if he fully understood what they were asking him.

Sergeant Keibler interviewed Uafinda several times and took him back to the Level 2 Core, but he remained maddeningly vague about what he had seen. Keibler finally went to Scalzi and requested his help, asking him to take Uafinda to the Core and ask the questions he wanted asked.

Scalzi said he would. When he returned, he told Keibler that Uafinda was nervous around police because in Mozambique, a police officer meant danger. He did not trust the state police, even though he had been told that in America it was different and the policeman was his friend. Scalzi decided that Uafinda was not holding anything back; he simply didn't have the answers Keibler was seeking.[6]

His other witness, Marilee Erdely, was a problem in her own way. On the surface, she was a perfectly pleasant, pretty, blonde twenty-three-year-old from Aliquippa, Pennsylvania. She had a classic western Pennsylvania childhood, the kind seen in the films *The Deer Hunter* or *All the Right Moves.* Her father, Edward, was a steelworker, a machinist at the giant Aliquippa Works of the Jones & Laughlin Steel Corporation along the Ohio River. Her mother, Mary, was a homemaker. The family had strong Slavic roots, even if her parents had changed the family name from Erdelyi, which was always being mispronounced as *Erdley-eye,* to Erdely, which people tended to guess right.[7]

Marilee, an honor student at Hopewell High School, wanted to be a high school English teacher. She spent her freshman year at Edinboro State College, then transferred to Geneva College, a conservative Christian school in Beaver Falls, for her sophomore and junior years. She didn't get to State College until the summer of 1967 but received her degree in secondary education from Penn State in the spring of 1968. After taking a year off, she began working on her master's degree in English, with an emphasis in English literature, which she probably hoped would make it easier for her to land a good teaching job.[8]

But she had behaved oddly on the day of Betsy's murder, and Keibler didn't know what to make of her. He couldn't understand why she had "flaked out," as he put it, upon discovering Betsy Aardsma's body in Pattee Library. "The strange thing about Erdely is, she's up there, she's a grad student. She's in Betsy's class. She knows her," Keibler said. "When she goes into the Core area, the noise has occurred, and lying on the ground is Betsy. [Erdely] goes completely ape. As a matter of fact, when they [ambulance attendants] came downstairs, they thought *she* was the victim. It's a puzzle in my mind why she reacted that way." He mentioned how Dr. Reed found her almost in a trance, aimlessly rooting through Betsy's purse in the waiting area at the Ritenhour Health Center. Keibler shook his head. James L. Severs, who married Erdely years after the murder, said his wife believed that for a time, the state police suspected her of having something to do with Betsy's death. So there matters stood. Erdely was questioned as extensively as Uafinda, but her answers were incomplete or lacked clarity.[9]

Lieutenant Kimmel hoped to obtain enough information to create a verbal description and composite sketch of the running man. What he got from Uafinda, Erdely, and a third man, another student in the English 501 class who Keibler, the protector of secrets, would not identify to the public, was barely enough for the verbal description. A week after the initial press conference, Kimmel told reporters that the running man was in his early twenties, approximately six feet tall, weighed 185 to 200 pounds, had short, light brown hair, and might have been wearing glasses. As far as clothing, he was wearing khaki work pants, a lightweight sport jacket, and light-colored sneakers.[10]

Because the three witnesses were frustratingly vague on some details, creating a composite sketch was a problem. These sketches were rarely, if ever, done freehand by a trained artist. Rather, the state police relied on a kit that resembled a Mr. Potato Head game, albeit with human features. "They were very basic," Trooper Mike Simmers said. "You plug a nose in, and plug a hairpiece, and then take a picture of it or get someone to do a drawing of it."

His description perhaps oversimplifies the process. The person providing the description first looked at a series of transparencies with different hairdos, different sideburns, different noses, and so forth. Then the matching features were added to the plastic head. The kit was intended to make it possible for any police department to draw a composite sketch, even if they had no sketch artist. The problem was that the kit sent up from Troop G headquarters dated from the 1930s, with hats and hairstyles from that era. Given that it was 1969 and men's hairstyles had changed dramatically, Kimmel realized he had a problem. He arranged to borrow a newer version from the State College Borough Police that apparently had never been used.[11]

The two composite sketches ultimately released to the public blended information received during the initial interrogations of Uafinda, Erdely, and the third English 501 student. Descriptions received from people who had seen a young man running outside of Pattee Library shortly after the murder occurred were also thrown into the mix. The reason for two composites was that the witnesses couldn't agree on whether the suspect was wearing eyeglasses, but they were also slightly different in other ways. In the eyeglasses sketch, the figure has slightly more hair, and it's combed in a different style. But they were intended to be the same person, the running man in the Core.

Keibler considered the composite sketches to be "general, neutral composite" sketches that would fit a lot of suspects. Indeed, it was not hard to imagine that David L. Wright, Betsy's boyfriend, resembled the sketch without eyeglasses, even though he had been in Hershey, dissecting a cadaver, at the time she was murdered. Keibler never placed much stock in the composites and said they did not play a significant role in the investigation. Their release to the media was an accident, he said, because they were not yet ready to go. But they were never publicly recalled by the state police, either.[12]

It was Lieutenant Kimmel's idea to bring in a hypnotist, hoping that in so doing he could extract more details about the running man from the minds of the two principal witnesses at that time, Uafinda and Erdely. Hypnosis could reach into the unconscious brain where seven-eighths of memories are stored, including disturbing or "unsafe" memories a person had suppressed. "This is why witnesses to very traumatic crime situations, such as homicides, are often unable to recall what they have seen," wrote Vernon J. Geberth, a New York City detective sergeant, in his 1983 book, *Practical Homicide Investigation.* "Hypnosis has been used to enable people to recall names, places, or details including the actual verbalizations which took place during the crime."[13]

There are downsides to hypnosis, Geberth wrote. People can lie under hypnosis. Recollections may be colored by past experiences, or the mind of the person under hypnosis may fill in memory gaps with imagined or distorted information. He recommended that any information obtained through hypnosis be independently corroborated.[14] What it all boiled down to was that although hypnosis could occasionally pry information out of the minds of witnesses, it wasn't a magical mental truth serum. There were also legal risks. Hypnosis was an accepted investigative tool in 1969, but only barely, and there were still judges who believed it could implant false memories. Hypnosis proponents had cheered the ruling in *Harding v. Maryland,* issued in 1968 by the Maryland Court of Appeals, which ruled for the first time that the testimony of a witness to a crime obtained through hypnosis could not be excluded from trial *per se.* The defense could challenge the credibility of the hypnosis-aided testimony but not its general admissibility. This ruling was soon adopted by other federal and state courts. Keibler worried about tainting the prosecution of whomever they arrested for Betsy's murder, but went along with Kimmel's plan. Neither Erdely nor Uafinda had witnessed the actual murder, he reasoned, only the immediate aftermath, so the risk was less.[15]

Kimmel asked Colonel Pelton if he knew of any qualified hypnotists. Pelton knew of a dentist in Hazleton, Pennsylvania, Dr. Phillip T. Domin, whom the university had used once in a noncriminal matter. Domin had graduated from the University of Pennsylvania dentistry school in Philadelphia. He was a strong champion of hypnosis to relieve pain and stress in the dental chair, but also during chemotherapy, menstrual cramps, and any number of other uncomfortable situations. He once hypnotized an injured man in the field for painless transport to a hospital. And now Domin would try to help the witnesses relax themselves into a state where they might be able to identify Betsy Aardsma's killer. Pelton obtained permission from Penn State administrators to pay Domin's fee and fly him from Hazleton to State College in the university airplane.[16]

Plans were made to have Domin hypnotize Uafinda, Erdely, and the second rape victim abducted from the Nittany Mall just a few months earlier, who agreed to be hypnotized so long as it was done by a professional. Brode's theory of the country rapist coming to Pattee was still alive more than a week into the investigation. Keibler said the first Mall rape victim was off-limits for hypnosis because she was studying to become a psychiatrist, and her own analyst had forbidden her to undergo hypnosis.

The hypnosis was conducted in a room in the Boucke Building that was wired for sound so state troopers and Campus Patrol officers could listen in on the session. Inside, it was just Domin and Uafinda, and after he put the Mozambique student into a trance, he began asking the questions Keibler wanted answered. Under hypnosis, Uafinda told Domin far more than he had told Keibler or Scalzi in his previous interviews. He was able to confidently remember the height of the man running out of the Core, estimate his age, and describe how he was dressed, which gave them more confidence in the information they had obtained from Erdely and the other English 501 student.[17]

Erdely's first hypnosis session was a failure, although it did yield some squad-room humor. Trooper Mike Simmers, the young criminal investigator who had been the first state trooper to respond to the murder, had been sent out by Sergeant Keibler to locate a student they wanted to interview. As he was leaving the Boucke Building, he passed an attractive blonde in the hallway. Their eyes met briefly as they checked each other out. Simmers didn't think anything of it and didn't know she was Marilee Erdely.

He returned later to the Boucke Building and went to the war room. Keibler was smoking his pipe. Simmers asked how the hypnosis session went with Erdely. "Great," Keibler answered. "We got a real good composite sketch of the guy." Simmers, excited, asked if that meant the running man would be identified, and Keibler responded, "No doubt in our mind. In fact, you know him." He handed Simmers the sketch and watched the young trooper's face as he realized the sketch looked exactly like him. "Can you explain yourself, Simmers?" he said, trying not to laugh. Mortified, the young trooper explained what had happened. Dr. Domin, still in the room, theorized that since Erdely had gone into the hypnosis session right after eyeing up Simmers, her memory of him overrode her memories of the Core. The other troopers erupted in laughter.[18]

Erdely was brought back for a second hypnosis session and did better. She was able to recall in greater detail some of the things she saw that day, including the running man and the chase by Uafinda. But Keibler still considered her a puzzle. It was nothing he could put his finger on, but there was something about her that troubled him. The second rape victim added detail to what she had told Brode after she was assaulted in the fall but was not able to identify her assailant or contribute in any way to the Aardsma investigation. Brode's theory continued to be a wild goose chase. Kimmel released the final composite sketches to the press, even though Keibler was not really satisfied with any of them.[19]

CHAPTER 9

Frustration on the Road

That Betsy Aardsma was a good girl, a smart young woman dedicated to literature, art, and progressive causes, was briefly mentioned in news stories in the days following her murder. An Associated Press story published that first Monday suggested that had she lived, Betsy might have become "a dedicated doctor's wife, an artist, a professor of English literature, or a teacher on an Indian reservation." An unidentified friend told the reporter that Betsy was very interested in minority groups and loved black literature, especially the work of James Baldwin, the gay black American author who had moved to France in 1948 to escape his home country's racism, then largely absent in France. After her freshman year at Hope College in her hometown of Holland, Michigan, she had spent a couple of weeks working on an Indian reservation in New Mexico. Someone else remembered her love of sketching. One of her professors, not identified in the story, said she "had the deep sensitivity of an artist for others' feelings—and a keen sense of observation in addition to her natural abilities." She had been at Penn State only eight weeks but had still managed to make a number of close friends and impress teachers in that short final act before she was murdered.[1]

Yet after this brief burst of humanizing news coverage, Betsy receded back into victimhood and, eventually, rumor. She had no family in Pennsylvania, no one who could be her advocate, her voice from beyond the grave. College friends can only fulfill that role for so long. The state police were as befuddled as everyone else over the apparent lack of a motive for her murder. Kimmel hoped the troopers he sent to Michigan would be able to uncover something, anything, that would tell him why the killer had plunged a knife into her chest. They would find little but frustration as they drove from town to town in the Wolverine State.

Esther Aardsma, during her brief sojourn in State College after the murder, had voiced suspicions about a student named Darryl whom Betsy had dated at Hope College and who, subsequently, like her daughter, had transferred to the University of Michigan. Betsy had dated a number of Hope men, mostly without incident, but her brief relationship with Darryl, her mother remembered, had ended badly. Esther told police that he had "attacked" Betsy one evening in the lobby of Voorhees Hall, where she lived on campus. Betsy indeed saw the incident as sinister and scary, although her freshman-year roommate, Linda DenBesten, thought it was just overly dramatic behavior on Darryl's part. There doesn't seem to have been any physical violence. In any case, Betsy had taken up with him again at the University of Michigan at the beginning of her junior year. In a letter to a friend, Betsy said that the young man had changed and was now "a beautiful person. The fact that my parents don't approve adds a certain intrigue to it all," she wrote. It didn't last long, but there was no more drama.[2]

Upon hearing about the ex-boyfriend, Corporal Mutch and Lieutenant Richwine phoned the Michigan State Police around 11:00 a.m. on December 1, even as Kimmel was concluding his first news conference in the Boucke Building. They spoke to Detective Sergeant George Smith and asked for his help. Could he gather as much information as possible on the ex-boyfriend's whereabouts around the time of Betsy's murder? And could the Michigan State Police assist in other ways in a background investigation of Betsy? "They have talked with the victim's parents, who allege she is a good girl. However, they would like to know more about her," Smith wrote in his memo about the call. He agreed to help and conducted several interviews of Betsy's friends and ex-boyfriends during the coming weeks. Darryl soon was eliminated as a suspect.[3]

The two Pennsylvania state troopers dispatched to Michigan shortly after the murder, Sergeant Robert Milliron and Trooper Ronald Tyger, were sent mainly to look for possible links between John Norman Collins and the Coed Murders and the murder of Betsy. For that reason, they went first to Ypsilanti, where Detective Sergeant Smith worked out of the Washtenaw County Crime Center of the Michigan State Police. Washtenaw County, which surrounded the two university towns, was where the Coed Murders had taken place. Their second goal was to search for anything in Betsy's past that might lead them to the killer. Smith arranged for Detective Ken Kraus of his department and Deputy Gene Alli, a Washtenaw County sheriff's deputy, to accompany the pair while they were in the Ann Arbor–Ypsilanti area. Collins, who had been arrested the previous August for the murder of Karen Sue Beineman, was in jail awaiting a trial that would begin the following summer. He had not been formally charged with any of the other seven murders that police believed he had committed, but the string of murders had stopped with his arrest.

Still, for all police knew, there could have been a copycat killer at work. Indeed, one of the murders long attributed to Collins—that of Jane Mixer—is now officially attributed to a male nurse, Gary Leiterman, who was convicted of the crime in 2005 and sentenced to prison for life.[4]

Because the records released by the Michigan State Police were redacted, it is not possible to name all of the people to whom Milliron and Tyger spoke during their stay in Michigan, which lasted from about December 1 through 5. They certainly spent time in Ypsilanti that first day, speaking to Smith, and on December 2, according to a memo by Smith, "made contact" with someone of interest at her job in Ann Arbor. At some point, they also interviewed David L. Wright's friends in the Alpha Delta Phi fraternity who were still in Ann Arbor. In the afternoon, they were driven by their handlers to the state police station in Ionia, not far from the state's reformatory, which had the same forbidding "Big House" look as Rockview penitentiary back home in Pennsylvania. There they were passed off to Detective Herb Brown from the Grand Haven station, who was their escort when they did interviews in the Holland area.[5]

The Michigan State Police, under intense political pressure to solve and close the Coed Murders, kept close tabs on Milliron and Tyger during the trip. The two Pennsylvanians came to believe their hosts were fearful they would inadvertently do something to screw up the prosecution of John Norman Collins. "They assigned a criminal investigator with us. And boy, he got us up in the morning and put us to bed at night," Tyger recalled.[6]

They visited the Aardsmas at home, probably on December 4, the day after the funeral, finding them still in shock and bewildered. They could offer nothing that might help. The detectives went to the Hope College campus and interviewed professors who had known her during freshman and sophomore years. They all said much the same thing: that she was a good girl, nice, fun-loving but not a troublemaker, and smart as a whip. No one thought Betsy smoked pot or used any other drugs. "She was clean as a whistle," Tyger said. He found it deeply frustrating.[7] Strangely, one thing they did not do was attend Betsy's funeral, even though they were in Holland. Tyger said they were too busy doing interviews during the day and consolidating their notes at night to spend several hours at her funeral and burial, watching for anyone who might seem out of the ordinary.

On Friday, December 5, they were back in Ann Arbor interviewing one of Betsy's apartment mates from her senior year at the University of Michigan, probably Terrie Andrews. Detective Sergeant Smith, who wrote up a report for his own department, said the only valuable information gleaned from the conversation was that one of their other former apartment mates, Andrea Yunker, knew Betsy better than she did. Yunker, Andrews, and Olga Lozowchuk, all University of Michigan students, had shared a two-bedroom apartment with Betsy at 441 South First Street in Ann Arbor, a fifteen-minute walk from Angell Hall and the Diag in the heart of campus. Angell Hall was where the English Department was located, and the Diag, a large plaza, was ground zero for antiwar and other protests by leftist students. Betsy and Andie had shared one of the bedrooms, Terrie and Olga the other. It was late in the day, and the detectives didn't have time to talk to Yunker but obtained a promise from Smith that he would look her up as soon as he could. They flew back to Pennsylvania the next morning, frustrated that they had not been able to find anything useful.[8]

"Now as far as Betsy, we brought her up from the day she was smacked on the bottom to the day people thought [incorrectly] she was having an epileptic fit," Tyger said, meaning the day she died. "We didn't leave any stone unturned when we did the background on her. That's one of the first things you do, is get a background on the young lady or the victim. To find out what there was, and possibly put a motive to their killing. We couldn't find one."[9]

David L. Wright had checked his mail at school the day after the murder and found a last letter from Betsy. She had mailed it from State College on Friday, the day she died, and here it was, in his mailbox in Hershey on Saturday. Letters from her had arrived almost daily during the fall. She sent him letters and sent her friends letters in the way a young woman in the twenty-first century sends e-mails or texts. It made sense. Stamps were cheap, but long-distance telephone calls in 1969 were not. Betsy carried on an epistolary romance with David and epistolary girl talk with her friends Peggy Wich, Olga Lozowchuk, and Jan Sasamoto. Peggy and Jan had graduated with her from Holland High School, and Jan had gone on to the University of Michigan, where Betsy joined her two years later. For a young man, opening a handwritten letter from his girlfriend could be sweet (or bitter, depending on the content). He might catch a hint of her perfume and wonder what she was doing at that moment. But for David, Betsy's last letter was only a reminder of her violent death and what he had lost.

Detective Shovlin was not through with him—not by a long shot. After David returned to Hershey from the funeral, Shovlin and his partner began visiting him at the medical school almost daily, asking the same questions in a dozen different ways. It reached the point where Dr. George T. Harrell, dean of the medical school, told David to mind his studies and told the officers not to come on campus again. He did not want him subjected to further questioning. Wright didn't obey. "I just sort of went against his rule, just because I was so devastated by the whole thing and wanted to find out as much as I could," he said. Shovlin and the other officer still came two or three times a week, but they met him at a diner on Route 322 across from the medical school. They bought him lunch and pumped him with questions. Finally Wright asked, "Am I a suspect?" and they laughed and said "Not at all." But he did not fully believe them. At the medical school, the rumor circulated that Betsy may have been a "hippie" involved in drugs at Penn State, and that her murder was somehow related to that. Like the police, the public demands a logical explanation for murder and reaches for the tried and true, whether true or not.[10]

David's father flew to Harrisburg a few days before Christmas, and together they drove home to Illinois in David's car. Leaving Hershey on Route 322, they stopped first at the Rockview barracks. David asked to see Sergeant Keibler, whom he had last seen when he went to State College to see the Aardsmas after they came to bring Betsy's body home. Keibler was at his home in Bellefonte but hurried over to the barracks when he heard the student wanted to talk to him. "I think maybe he thought I had some new information, but I just wanted to get an update because it had been a month since I talked to him," Wright said.[11]

The state police came to believe that David L. Wright had no role in, nor foreknowledge of any plans for, Betsy's murder. Keibler says that the repeated, intensive questioning was "to get him out of it," meaning they had to clear him or arrest him, not leave him in boyfriend limbo. About two months into the investigation, in a little-noticed interview with a student newspaper far from State College, Lieutenant Kimmel proclaimed that Wright was innocent. "As to the report that the victim's boyfriend may be involved, we can say that he has been interviewed many times and that he is not connected with the slaying," he told Charly Lee, a reporter for *The Nittany Cub,* the student newspaper at Penn State University Behrend Campus in Erie in early 1970.[12]

But Wright still felt the eyes of the public upon him. On the Penn State campus, the rumor was that the murder weapon was either an ice pick or a surgical instrument, and wouldn't a medical student have access to surgical tools? Andrea Yunker, when interviewed by Detective Sergeant Smith on December 12, blurted out "David did it!" then could not explain why she felt that way beyond the fact that a woman's killer is often her boyfriend or husband.

Smith interviewed Yunker in Room 135 of the Undergraduate Library at the University of Michigan, where she worked as a librarian. She talked freely about about Betsy's funeral, which she had attended with Olga Lozowchuk, about David and Betsy's relationship, and how David first met Betsy. They had become "informally engaged," the report said, quoting Yunker. But David was not her first boyfriend. Betsy had dated at least three other boys, including Darryl, the drama king. There was also a naval ROTC student at Michigan who was now aboard the USS *Chicago,* a missile carrier then in home port at San Diego. The third boy she described as short, five-seven or five-eight, and slim, no more than 130 to 140 pounds. He had blond hair and blue eyes and acne scars on his face. Yunker said this boy had tried to get serious with Betsy but was rebuffed.[13]

Possibly on the same day, Smith also interviewed Lozowchuk, who was then a graduate student at Wayne State University in Detroit. She had told police earlier that she had corresponded with Betsy about twelve times between May of 1969, when they had graduated from Michigan, and the end of October. Although Lozowchuk thought she had kept the letters, when she arrived at the interview, accompanied by her parents, she confessed that she could not find them and believed she had thrown them away. Lozowchuk did confirm the names of the three young men Yunker said Betsy had dated at U of M in addition to David L. Wright.

On December 12, Lieutenant Kimmel announced that he was sending two detectives back to Michigan to conduct further interviews with Betsy's friends and family. "We still have a lot of work to do on her background," he said. "We have a lot to learn about her former associates, her schools, her attitudes, and the like." His use of the term *former associates* struck an odd note, like something one would say about a criminal suspect. That wasn't his intention, of course, but he seemed in some ways then to be flying on autopilot. By now, two weeks had passed since the murder, well beyond the forty-eight-hour window in which most murders are solved, *if* they are solved. This time it would be Corporal Mike Mutch going to Michigan with Tyger. They drove out to Holland and did not have handlers from the Michigan State Police.

It is unclear exactly when Keibler heard about a former assistant professor of English at Penn State, Robert G. Durgy, who was rumored to have had some kind of a relationship with Betsy or, at the very least, an obsession with her. Durgy was a promising young literary scholar of Fyodor Dostoevsky, the Russian author, and had just edited a critical translation of *Notes from Underground*, which was Dostoevsky's 1864 novel about an ugly, sick, and nasty man living on the fringes of society, a man who does horrible things yet revels in his vanity. "I got to the point of feeling a sort of secret, abnormal, despicable enjoyment in returning home to my corner on some disgusting Petersburg night," the Underground Man said in the novel, "actually conscious that today I had committed a loathsome action again, that what was done could never be undone, and secretly, inwardly gnawing, gnawing at myself for it, tearing and consuming myself till at last the bitterness turned into a sort of shameful, cursed sweetness, and at last—into positive, real enjoyment. Yes, into enjoyment, into enjoyment! I insist upon that." Durgy's book had been published earlier in 1969.

Durgy was from Grosse Pointe, an affluent suburb of Detroit. He was five years older than Betsy and had spent most of the 1960s at the University of Michigan after enrolling as a freshman in the fall of 1960. He graduated in 1964 and was admitted to the well-regarded graduate English program at Michigan to continue studying English language and literature.[14]

He completed his master's degree in eighteen months, and in early 1966 married Martha Travis, a librarian. They had two sons fairly quickly. His wife remembers they had "a good marriage. Bob was a lot of fun, very clever, very witty, loved his children. We were both very young, so you don't have a lot of patient wisdom. But apart from that, we had a good social life, good friends." He began work on his PhD right away and was recognized by the English department as a rising star. Everything seemed to be going his way. By the time he was hired as an assistant professor in the English Department at Penn State in the fall of 1969, he still needed to finish his dissertation and have it accepted to receive his doctoral degree in comparative literature.[15]

There was a demon stalking Durgy, though, and it was clinical depression. He had struggled with it for years and attempted suicide around age twenty-one, possibly during a summer break, as there is no obvious gap in his academic transcript. Hospitalized for a time, he recovered "beautifully," his wife said. When he moved to Penn State with his wife and children in the summer of 1969, even buying a new car for the new job, the demon returned with a vengeance. Martha Durgy blamed the stress of the new job and the pressure to finish his dissertation, which has taken down more than one graduate student. The family lived in Bellefonte, where the real estate was more affordable than State College. Durgy began teaching undergraduate English classes—not the sort of classes that a graduate student like Betsy Aardsma would have taken—but soon found himself unable to get up and face his students. "This anxiety set in, and he kept trying to teach. He said to me, 'I just get up there and make no sense; I just can't do it,'" his wife recalled.[16]

Martha Durgy doesn't believe her husband had an affair with Betsy Aardsma at the University of Michigan or Penn State, and he may not have even known her, despite the rumors that swirled. Betsy arrived at the University of Michigan as a junior in the fall of 1967 and majored in English. It is possible that they knew each other from their time in the Angell Building. "I certainly never heard her name," said Martha Durgy. "She wasn't an important person, or even a familiar person in our lives."[17]

Martha sat up with him nights and helped him go over the lecture material and talk about it. But Durgy was on a downward spiral and reached the point where he simply could not teach. He went to see Dr. Henry Sams, the chairman of the English Department, whom Martha Durgy called "a wonderful man." Sams granted him sick-leave status. Once that was out of the way, Durgy packed up the car and returned to Ann Arbor with his family, leaving many of their belongings behind in the Bellefonte house. It was right around Thanksgiving. Martha Durgy is said to remember that it was November 27, recalling that they missed their Thanksgiving dinner because they were on the road.[18]

If that had been where Durgy's part in this story ended, it is doubtful he would have become a person of interest to the police. He saw a psychiatrist in Ann Arbor upon his return, but on December 19, Durgy got in his car and began driving north. It was three weeks to the day, almost to the hour, since Betsy Aardsma had been murdered. Assuming he started in Ann Arbor, he drove north on US Highway 23 for about nineteen miles, turning west onto Interstate 96, a freeway, at Brighton. He continued toward Lansing, the state capital, for another twenty-seven miles. It was 7:00 p.m. and dark, and he was traveling through farmland, but he might have seen the lights of a house about three hundred yards to the south just before he veered off the highway and crashed into the middle abutment of the Dietz Road overpass. Durgy died of his injuries the next morning at a Lansing hospital. Martha Durgy believes her husband committed suicide.[19]

That was not the only out-of-state trip made by Pennsylvania state troopers during the Aardsma investigation. Toward the end of the active phase of the probe, Keibler told Ken Silverman, a reporter for the *Daily Collegian* at Penn State, that he had sent investigators to Michigan, Washington, DC, New York, Indiana, West Virginia, Ohio, and even New Mexico. (Some of these may actually have been phone calls. Jan Sasamoto, who lived with her husband in Charleston, West Virginia, at the time Betsy was murdered, said she talked to a trooper over the phone, but that he never came to their house.[20])

The trip to Washington, which is about two hundred miles south of State College, had to do with a mysterious postcard and Peggy Wich, one of Betsy's closest friends. Wich lived in Washington for a time after graduating from Marquette University and worked as a waitress at a hotel near Dupont Circle. It was there, the day after her friend's murder, that she chanced to wait on a customer who had the *New York Daily News* open to a picture of Betsy and a story about her death. Wich had mailed a letter to Betsy just before she died, dropping it in a public mailbox on Dupont Circle near the restaurant. Her letter, with the postmark identifying the station where it was processed, was now in police custody. So was a postcard to the state police from an anonymous writer that had been processed around the same time, at the same station. This postcard urged the detectives searching for Betsy's killer to "Look for the guy in the work pants in the library."[21]

Two Pennsylvania state troopers, accompanied by a DC Metro detective, came to Wich's apartment. Had she mailed that second postcard? No. She knew nothing about it. How had Betsy met David? The usual answer. If one of Betsy's friends had been involved in the drug business, would she have reported her? "I said no," Wich recalled. "She would not have gotten involved. It would not have interested Betsy at all. Because we talked about that kind of stuff."

Her roommates listened in fascination from the top of the stairs as the police questioned Wich. She convinced the troopers she had nothing to do with the anonymous postcard, despite it being posted from the same station, and they did not come back a second time. The question raised by the mysterious postcard remained: Who was the student in the library wearing work pants? *Work pants,* of course, is an indistinct term. The writer might have meant jeans or he might have meant khakis, but the anonymous author did not elaborate.[22]

CHAPTER 10

Dragnet

Nearly every morning that first month, the forty Pennsylvania state troopers involved in the Aardsma investigation assembled in Room 109 of the Boucke Building to receive their daily list of students or faculty members to interview. On the assignment sheet was the person's name, where they allegedly were at the time of the murder, what they were allegedly doing, and where to find them, plus "just a little bit of background on the individual," Trooper Carl Cseko said. Astonishingly, the state police interviewed at least two thousand students and an unknown number of faculty during those early weeks. Students were questioned because they were in the English 501 class or lived on Betsy's floor in Atherton Hall, had been in Pattee Library that day, were friends of Betsy's, or simply because someone thought there was an off chance they might know something.[1] Often it was the Campus Patrol who tracked down the students wanted for questioning. Other times it was Trooper Simmers, a student himself, who would bring them back. From his undercover work on campus, he knew the lay of the land. Most of the troopers brought in from outside did not.[2]

As Lieutenant Kimmel already knew, the problem was that many students, though not all, viewed the state police on campus not from the perspective of besieged settlers welcoming the arrival of the US Cavalry, but more from the perspective of the Indians. Not all Penn State students saw the state police and Campus Patrol as the good guys. Leftist students in Happy Valley had numerous grievances stemming from crackdowns on civil rights and antiwar protests since 1965, and over freedom-of-expression issues. There was a vast gulf between these students and the police, which they found difficult to cross to report mere suspicions.

Trooper Simmers knew the tensions all too well. "They did not like the state police; they did not like authority," he said. Much of his work on the Penn State campus up until now had been spent monitoring the SDS and a group he called the Coalition for Peace. His superiors did not always try to preserve his undercover status—for example, ordering him to be the one to make arrests. Then everyone knew who he was. "There was no love at all by the professors or the students for the state police. No respect at all," Simmers said. Keibler agreed. "Some of us were probably looked at as pigs," he said. But attitudes varied. The reluctance of students to talk to investigators seemed to depend on which academic department they were in, with art students being the hardest to interview. "I think art students in the university are a different breed of cats," Keibler said.[3]

The Michigan State Police had faced similar problems during their investigation of the Coed Murders and had found no real solution. "The net result was that there were many college students who viewed the police as puppets for the government," wrote Earl James, the Michigan state trooper who prepared the murder case against John Norman Collins. He blamed the problem on police having to do their jobs and facing the inevitable fallout of doing what was necessary to keep the peace and protect property. In the eyes of many students, that made them the mailed fist of the establishment, the same establishment that, if they were boys, wanted to cut their hair—no joke at the time—and send them off to fight in the hated Vietnam War. The late 1960s saw the first battles in the culture wars that would convulse America well into the twenty-first century. Students watched TV in the summer of 1968 and saw other students being beaten by helmeted police on the streets of Chicago during the Democratic National Convention. It should have come as no surprise that suddenly all police everywhere were potential *pigs* in their eyes.[4]

Things were not all bad for the state police investigating Betsy Aardsma's murder. For all the detractors of the police, probably as many Penn State students retained an instinctive respect for law enforcement that was a legacy of their small-town upbringing. This was the campus, after all, that had turned out counter demonstrators to the Penn State SDS chapter in 1965 and 1969 and a non-ironic welcoming committee for President Nixon when he arrived on campus for his uncle's funeral. Trooper Lee Fisher, part of the team of forty investigators, believed that most students gave information if they had it, even if they were upset by state police crackdowns on dissent.

But murders aren't solved by limiting interviews to conventional, clean-cut students who respect the police. Keibler and his detectives needed to reach out to the angry half and hope that students who knew something would come forward, whether they were summond or not, whether they liked the state police or not.[5]

If there was any low-hanging fruit, it was likely to be found among students in the graduate English boot camp class, English 501, Materials and Methods of Research. Betsy Aardsma and Marilee Erdely had been in Pattee Library on November 28, working on term papers for the class. Linda Marsa, Betsy's best friend at Penn State, was also in the class. So were fifty-seven other new graduate students in English, including a quiet young man from a farm north of Harrisburg, Larry Paul Maurer, who would soon attract police attention. Many of them, including Maurer, had been in the library that day. The state police made plans to question every one of them.

When English 501 next assembled in a lecture hall in the basement of the Willard Building, where it met, the mood was somber. Professor Harrison Meserole opened the class with consoling words and then explained why there were state police detectives in the room. They were here to ask questions about what each of them remembered about Betsy, he said, and whether they had any thoughts on who might have wanted to kill her. If they had seen anything suspicious in Pattee Library that day, they should mention that, too. The students were then divided into groups of six and taken away in turn to different rooms for individual questioning by the detectives. David R. Johnson, one of the students questioned, recalled being asked point blank if he was having an affair with Betsy.[6]

In the days to come, students speculated about who among their number could have been the killer. Their suspicion fell on one particular young man who was widely disliked for his loud, arrogant behavior in class, even while not being particularly smart. "I think there were some people who wanted him to be guilty just because they didn't like him," said Nicholas Joukovsky, who co-taught the class. He said this was not Maurer, whom he remembered as a very quiet young man.[7]

The state police would occasionally stop by Joukovsky's office in the Burrowes Building to show him images gathered by the not-so-hidden video camera at the crime site. He never recognized any of the faces. Joukovsky sensed that the investigators had no solid leads. In addition, they seemed "incurious," as he put it. He was surprised that they did not interview him in greater depth, given that he knew the members of his class better than anyone, except perhaps Professor Meserole. There was no follow-up interview—at least, not the sort of interview where an investigator or team of investigators bores into a subject to extract anything he might know. He reasoned that perhaps they were directing their most probing questions to Meserole, who was a full professor, after all, and eighteen years older than he was. Still, Joukovsky thought, wouldn't it still make sense to talk to me anyway?[8]

The state police pressed their student informants on campus for anything they might know. Keibler and his men were especially interested in knowing what the drug dealers were saying. Given the times, it was inevitable that suspicions arose regarding a possible connection between Betsy's death and drugs, with scenarios ranging from the possibility that she had come upon a sale in progress in the stacks to speculation the she had somehow run afoul of a drug dealer in some other way. Today, her friends find the idea that she was involved in the drug trade, either as a buyer or seller, to be laughable. But it was one of the ideas pursued by the police in that cold month after she was murdered. And, as with nearly every aspect of the case, there were tantalizing hints that perhaps, just maybe, this was the right trail.[9]

On the night of the murder, a young man from New Jersey, remembered only by his last name of Landis, had been found passed out in a dark corner on the first floor of Pattee Library. Keibler said he was a small-time drug dealer, peddling LSD on the Penn State campus. Whoever discovered him had removed his wallet and turned it over to a librarian, who either did not go to check or did not wake him up and tell him to leave. Nor did any of the police officers in the library investigating the murder that night notice him. Landis slept there until the next morning. The librarian turned over the wallet to the Campus Patrol. Around the middle of the following week, Robert Barnes, a former state trooper who was second in command to Colonel Pelton, contacted Keibler and told him what had happened. Barnes said the student had been "screwed up" that night, based on what the librarian told him.

Keibler went through the wallet, which among other things contained a list of safe houses for draft resisters and army deserters heading to the Canadian border. He passed the list along to army intelligence. Then he had Barnes summon Landis on the pretext of returning his wallet. "I got on him and interviewed him with Barnes present," Keibler said. "He admits he was in the library upstairs, high on LSD. He didn't even know there was a murder, and nobody ever [questioned] him. He was lying on the floor in a corner! Unbelievable." After he extracted whatever information he could, Keibler ordered Landis (who was not a student) to leave the campus and never come back. Landis protested angrily, saying, "You can't do that!" Keibler disagreed. "I'm just going to let the word out that you're working for me. He said, 'Well, they'll kill me.' And I said, 'That's your problem.' And he left campus." Keibler said the situation after the Aardsma murder was "just crazy as hell."[10]

Then there was the case of the mysterious drug dealer from Philadelphia, one of a number of young men suspected by the state police of transporting drugs from the City of Brotherly Love for sale in Happy Valley. He was believed for a time to have been the running man followed by Uafinda shortly after the murder, and also the person seen running from the library and across the quad in front of Old Main minutes later. It later turned out he was in Philadelphia at the time. The incident passed into the lore of the Aardsma case, fated to be brought up by people who remembered bits and pieces of the story but not how the entire narrative played out.[11]

One of the weirder rumors on the Penn State campus was that Betsy and her mother and father had been drug agents for the Federal Bureau of Narcotics, a predecessor of the Drug Enforcement Agency, and that her murder had been carried out by a professional hit man. The idea seems as preposterous today as it did in 1969. Her mother, for the record, was a college-educated homemaker, and her father, a college-educated tax auditor for the state of Michigan. Unless they led a *True Lies* sort of existence, with secret lives as crime fighters unknown to the people closest to them, this one can be dismissed. Keibler, who heard the rumors, certainly did. Tyger, who had gone to Michigan looking for dirt on Betsy, proclaimed her "clean as a whistle." He and Milliron and Mutch were unable to find any links to drugs in her life. David L. Wright, her boyfriend, told one of his Hershey housemates that as far as he knew, she "wasn't into drugs or anything like that." Did she ever take a toke? Who can say.[12]

The state police did get tips from student informants, from the Campus Patrol, and from people walking in the door, calling on the telephone, or writing letters. These could be good, intriguing, silly, wrongheaded, or useless. But they all had to be checked out. Keibler believed you just never knew. "You had to get them out, because you can't tell who's crazy and who isn't when you're getting a tip like this," he said. "If I would sit down and try to figure out how many diversions we had, it's in the dozens." He said that in any major case, "you'll get stuff like this. It's coming at you. You can expect it."[13]

Consider, for example, the investigation of the so-called "vicious lesbian" who had supposedly attacked two or three people affiliated with the university. The Campus Patrol had been "working with" her, Keibler said, because she had a history of being sexually aggressive and very physical. Some of his detectives were tied up for a week investigating her. "Not that it was wrong to look, but then they realized that she wasn't connected to this," he said. "There's a person who is physically afflicting her views onto female students. Well, you have to get her out of it."[14]

As far as homosexuality as an explanation for the murder, some of the state police investigators considered it possible that Betsy had been slain because she chanced upon some form of gay sex in the stacks at a time when it was still illegal under state law. "One of the biggest theories was [that] she walked in on a gay professor and a student going down on each other, [and that] one stabbed her and the other ran. A possibility," said Trooper Simmers. Trooper Tyger, who considered the stacks to be "a hell-hole," also leaned toward this theory. So did Corporal Mutch, who found support for the interrupted-sex theory in the odd positioning of five chairs near the murder site. The back story to their theories, of course, was the discovery by Mary Willard of deposits of dried semen on the library floor, shelves, and on the books themselves. If gay sex was going on, might she not have surprised a man masturbating or performing oral sex on another man, or stroking himself while viewing pornography? They had found all that pornography stuffed in the shelves, after all, as well as the expensive Dutch pornography left in one of the carrels.[15]

A critical question is whether anyone she interrupted would have been scared of exposure to the point of committing murder. Trooper Kent Bernier, one of the later investigators (2005–09) assigned to the Aardsma case, disbelieved the interrupted-sex theory for that reason. He wondered why there were no other reports of gay violence in the library if that was what happened. "It's covered in the report," Bernier said, referring to the 1,800-page main report on the Aardsma murder that the state police keep locked away. He doesn't believe that an interrupted tryst, especially at a relatively tolerant place like Penn State, would lead "to an unbelievably vicious murder." Trooper Roger Smith, who studied the Aardsma case file in the 1990s, thought it was simply the wrong time of day (4:55 p.m.) for a sexual tryst to be taking place. Masturbation, though, might have occurred at any time.[16]

In considering any of these scenarios, it is important to remember the near silence in which the crime occurred. Nothing was heard except a sound like a fist hitting a chest, which suggests that Betsy Aardsma was struck down completely by surprise by someone who could approach her without raising alarms. That seems unlikely in the interrupted-tryst scenario, but perhaps not if she had happened upon someone she knew reading pornography and masturbating at one of the carrels. Her friends think she was more likely to have pretended not to see it and moved on, searching for a book—but perhaps not before registering a look of disgust that was observed by the man at the carrel, who then knew that she knew. Given the lack of physical evidence linking anyone to the porn books, however, it was only a theory, albeit one of the more interesting ones.

There seemed to be no end to the craziness. A woman turned over several letters allegedly written to members of a Church of Satan cult in the region. Keibler did not identify the woman beyond saying she was the mother of one of the cult members. They were followers of Anton LaVey, who organized the original Church of Satan in San Francisco in 1966. The letters were written by the local chapter's archpriest, who lived in Dubois, about sixty miles from Penn State. In the letters, he talked about wanting to commit a human sacrifice. The mother heard of Betsy Aardsma's murder and wondered if she had been the victim sacrificed to Satan. Keibler and his detectives looked at that story for a while but concluded that the archpriest's proclaimed intention to sacrifice a human was more braggadocio than anything else. Nevertheless, "we couldn't ignore it," Keibler said.[17]

Keibler also believed in the possibility that some people would concoct elaborate stories because they were trying to send the police a coded message about who the killer was. That was why he ordered an investigation of a report that three students with a Ouija board had come up with the name of the killer. The state police eventually figured out who the students were and concluded it was just a story. "You didn't know if these people were trying to give you a legitimate name and they didn't want to come forward, so they said they got it off a Ouija board. So that's why we spent a lot of time on that," Keibler said.

There were blackly humorous moments. A State College woman who was a church organist was practicing on Thanksgiving evening, the night before Betsy was murdered. She reported seeing a shadowy figure, a man she didn't recognize, moving through the church. A few days later, she concluded that he must have been there to murder her, but for some reason didn't do so and then killed Betsy the following night. Her husband decided to pass along details of the incident to the police by writing an anonymous letter and driving ninety-six miles to Indiana, Pennsylvania, to mail it. It was addressed to State College police chief John Juba, who turned it over to Keibler. The state police had a good laugh when they read it, because the man had left his name off but included his return address. Keibler sent Trooper Thomas L. Jones, one of the troopers sent up from Harrisburg to assist with the investigation, to interview the man. "I said, 'Jones, when you go down to this guy to interview him, he's going to want to know how the hell you found him. Don't you dare tell him. Just say, we've got our ways!'"[18]

One of the more sensitive areas of the Aardsma investigation was how to approach the clergy and psychiatrists serving the twenty-six thousand students on the Penn State campus. Sensitive, because under a Pennsylvania law adopted in 1959, most clergy (except for self-ordained ministers and denominations where all members were considered clergy) could neither be compelled to give testimony nor provide it voluntarily without the permission of whomever had gone to the pastor to "get it off his chest." It was much the same for psychiatrists. In practice, Keibler said, the courts did not take an absolutist approach to the privilege, interpreting the law as granting a privilege *unless* a patient or penitent revealed plans to commit a specific crime, such as a troubled husband saying that he was going to kill his cheating wife on the following Tuesday when the kids were at Grandma's house. Keibler had to walk a fine line and try to persuade the counselor that he or she would not be linked to the information. He told them, "I'm not going to go down and knock on the guy's door and say, 'Doc So-and-So sent me.' That's not going to happen." Perhaps not surprisingly, given the wording of the 1959 law, most clergy believed they had a complete privilege, Keibler said. Psychiatrists, on the other hand, tended to accept that they had to report impending crimes, although they varied in their degree of cooperation.[19]

Because of this qualified privilege, police normally shied away from approaching members of either profession for help. But as the Aardsma investigation hit roadblock after roadblock, the temptation became greater. Keibler said he did talk to some pastors during the Aardsma investigation. His method was to gently persuade them to pass along names of any Penn State students who had shown a sudden interest in religion and seemed to be in a troubled frame of mind.[20]

There were a number of psychiatrists in the State College area in 1969, some on the staff of the Ritenhour Health Center, and others in private practice. Keibler worked closely with both of the Ritenhour psychiatrists (the normal complement was three, but there was a vacancy). One of them insisted to Keibler that all his patients were "real good," but as he said it, Keibler noticed the baseball bat beneath his desk. In the end, he believed the psychiatrists helped him within the limits of their professional code. He had his men check all the Penn State students who had dropped out of school at the end of 1969 for no apparent reason, including those who left for psychiatric reasons. "Hell, yeah, you do that," he said. "You have to do that." At least two students who had been barred from campus for serious psychiatric problems had been seen on campus the day Betsy was murdered.[21]

One thing Keibler never did was make a direct, public appeal to the Penn State faculty to come forward and report suspicious behavior by any of their students. He avoided this because the faculty was, in some instances, even more anti-police than their students. "They don't want it *known* [*emphasis in original*] that they are in any way, shape, or form cooperating with police," he said. When they did want to talk, it might be to discuss something that was of interest to them but of little relevance to the investigation. Trooper Lee Fisher recalled being sent to talk to a professor who, in the sort of situation Keibler had predicted, sought to take control of the interview. The professor, it turned out, had invited Fisher to find out whether the state police were looking for people with the supposed "criminal chromosome" in their genetic makeup. "I thought, geez, we can't go test everybody for this criminal factor, this criminal chromosome factor," Fisher said. The gap between the faculty and police was nearly as wide as the chasm separating the cops and many of the students.[22]

One of the more salacious rumors was that Betsy Aardsma had been a nude model for the art department at Penn State, and that her murder somehow grew out of that. To those who knew her, it made no more sense than her being a narc, although few denied her beauty. Keibler said the rumor arose early in the investigation and took "a helluva long time" to chase down. The experience seemed to have permanently soured him on art students. "They're nuts. I can't understand a guy sitting here, and he has a nude model up there, you'd think he was sketching a nude model, but he's really sketching an apple, or if he's sketching a model he has a knife through her," he said, adding: "There's more psychological problems with art students than anything in the world." He said they questioned four or five art students until finally concluding that there was nothing to the nude modeling rumor.[23]

That trail led them, however, to another of the odd characters who occupied the fringes of the Aardsma investigation. Bill Spencer, who was forty-one, was a sculptor who lived with his young wife in the former Waddle School outside State College. His claim to fame was that he and his first wife, Lena Spencer, had cofounded the Caffe Lena in Saratoga Springs, New York, in 1960, where in June 1961 they had hosted the young and unknown Bob Dylan in his first concert outside New York City since moving east from Minnesota five months earlier. The two-night stand was a spectacular failure. Bill Spencer, furious, went onstage to reprove the crowd. "You may not know what this kid is singing about and you may not care, but if you don't stop and listen, you will be stupid all the rest of your lives. Listen to him, dammit," he implored. By the time of the murder, Spencer, a notorious tomcat, had split from Lena for a Skidmore College coed and decamped to Boston. He later got a job teaching art at a high school in upstate New York but was fired for his eccentricity. He had persuaded the school to let him bring some junk cars onto the school grounds in the name of art, then let his students attack them with sledgehammers. Later he moved to the State College area, where his latest wife was a graduate student in English at Penn State.[24]

Spencer got Keibler's attention when he phoned one day and announced that he had solved the Aardsma murder. A trooper was dispatched to interview him at home. When he walked in, the trooper couldn't help but notice a painting above the sofa showing a naked couple having sex. Spencer saw him looking and commented, "That is the ultimate release. You know what that is? That's my mother, and I'm having sex with her." The trooper held his tongue, nodded, and took notes. Spencer's claim to have solved the crime stemmed from allegedly being in State College on November 28 around the time of the murder and supposedly seeing the murderer walking fast or jogging away from the university in a westerly direction. How he knew it was the murderer was not really explained, beyond his perception that the young man was acting in a suspicious manner. Spencer offered to sculpt a bust of the murderer and give it to Keibler, which he presented at the Boucke Building about eight days later.[25]

Keibler concluded that Spencer was "wacky as a coon." His young wife, he recalled, was beautiful and knowledgable. "And she said, in no way is he seeing anybody or has anything [to do] with this. She basically said, 'Just disregard him.'" Eventually, they did, and State College became a way station for Bill Spencer on his downward slide from minor footnote in the history of Bob Dylan to oblivion. The state police, unable to avoid spending time investigating Spencer, were no closer to solving the mystery of Betsy Aardsma's murder.[26]

Perhaps every unsolved murder, too, causes people to notice strange coincidences, sometimes long afterward. Take the matter of the Rolling Stones song "Midnight Rambler" and its seeming, though unproven, relation to Betsy Aardsma's murder. The band had released its album, *Let it Bleed,* in the US on the morning of November 28, 1969. "Midnight Rambler," which was loosely based on the crimes of the Boston Strangler in the early 1960s, was on the album and had been performed in concert since the summer of 1969. Their US concert tour had begun on November 7 and they had performed the song at least fourteen times, including in Philadelphia on November 25 and in Baltimore the following night.

On the night of Betsy's murder, Mick Jagger and the Rolling Stones again took the stage, this time at Madison Square Garden in New York, and again sang "Midnight Rambler." You can hear that particular performance on their live album, *Get Yer Ya-Ya's Out!*, which was released in September 1970. It is a creepy, nine-minute, rock-and-roll *tour de force.* The song is sung by Jagger from the perspective of a serial killer who lurks in the shadows and concludes with the chilling words, "I'll stick my knife right down your throat, baby, and it hurts!" That was close to how Betsy had died. Had a deranged fan on the Penn State campus decided to kill someone in tribute to the song? It is, as they say, an interesting possibility, but there is no evidence that her killer was a Stones fan of any variety.

Keibler's men began to show the strain. Hours were long, morale was low, and those troopers who were brought in from long distances, and were now living four to a room, wanted to go home. There was no overtime pay to make the endless hours seem worthwhile, especially with no break in the case. "No one was sharing information," Trooper Simmers said. "No one was completing the report." What he meant was that some investigators withheld things, hoping to use the information to advance their own careers if they could personally break the case. A detective with a hot lead might write that he had interviewed someone but omit the interesting details the witness provided. Not everyone did this, Simmers cautioned. But some did. "There was no sharing, particularly with the guys that came in from Harrisburg, from Philadelphia, and those CIS guys, they were called. Criminal investigation specialists."[27]

But it happened among the Rockview troopers, too, he said. Corporal Brode was notorious. "If Dan Brode had a lead, it never went into the report. He kept it for himself," he said. "Dan Brode had an ego, and he wanted to solve that case. He would actually mislead the other investigators onto a wild goose chase. Oh, yeah." Keibler agreed that Brode would do that, but said it is a common trait among police officers. He didn't believe Brode withheld anything important in the Aardsma case. "He didn't have anything to hide," Keibler said. Brode continued to believe that the country rapist was a likely suspect in the murder of Betsy Aardsma. He was an eternal optimist, telling Buzz Triebold of the Department of

Security every time he saw him that "We're going to clear this thing up in such and such a time. And I would ask, based on what? Well, [Brode would say], I think we got a pretty good suspect lined up, and once we can talk to so-and-so and this person and that person, I think we'll be able to get this narrowed down. Well, time went on and on and on, and that never materialized, of course." Keibler agreed that this sounded like Brode. "If you'd say, 'How you doing on the case?,' he'd say, 'Oh, it's just a matter of time; we'll have that sucker.'"[28]

CHAPTER 11
Trouble in Old Main

Penn State coeds and their parents were consumed by fears of a killer on the loose. Duty officers in the women's dorms fielded scores of telephone calls from parents during the weekend after Betsy's death, wondering if it was safe for their daughters to return to campus. Many students gave considerable thought to whether it was safe to continue using Pattee Library, and more than a few concluded it wasn't. Some women drafted their boyfriends as bodyguards if they couldn't avoid going into the stacks.[1]

Barbi Stine, a reporter for the *Daily Collegian,* remembered the murder of Betsy Aardsma and the aftermath as "horrifying but surreal. How could that happen? Everybody stayed out of the stacks, for sure." A freshman in the fall of 1969, Stine didn't go back into the stacks until her senior year, when she had an unavoidable need for a book shelved not far from where Betsy was murdered. As soon as she found it, she ran out of the stacks and smack into a graduate student, who subsequently became her boyfriend for about a year. "But I was just so freaked out by being up there, because they had never caught the guy. So everybody was pretty nervous that way, I guess," Stine said.[2]

Rebecca Craven, a senior at Penn State in 1969, said most students felt safe before the murder, believing nothing bad could happen in Happy Valley. She worked as a volunteer leader in a high school youth ministry, had gone home for a Thanksgiving weekend of activities, and didn't hear about the murder until she returned. She had often studied by herself in the stacks, but never did so again. Neither did many of her friends, especially after Betsy's death began to appear to be random, not the revenge of some deranged old boyfriend. "We had feelings of dread, that none of us were safe," Craven said.[3]

Albert Dunning, news director of student-run WDFM Radio, was struck by how Betsy seemed like such a "wholesome, studious, red-blooded all-American girl, with no enemies." How does someone like that get murdered? Tom Gentzel, a 1969 graduate of State College Area High School and a freshman at Penn State that fall, said the murder was so shocking because murder was so rare in State College. The violence of her death and the fact that the police had no solid leads set everyone on edge. "No one knew if this was an isolated incident," Gentzel said. "Or whether this was the start of other violence."

To no one's surprise, female students in English 501, the research methods class that was the proximate cause of Betsy being in Pattee Library that day, showed "great reluctance" to return to the library, according to Joukovsky. They talked about it in class and in private meetings with him. This was a problem, because the final assignment for the semester required a lot of research in the library. "We had to cut some of the students some breaks in terms of their not being willing or able to go in," he said. "We encouraged them to go in together in groups, which they mostly did."[4]

A rumor took hold among students at Penn State that Betsy Aardsma had been the victim of an "Alphabet Killer." There were a couple of variations of this rumor. One was that the killer would target the student who was first in the campus directory for each letter of the alphabet. Betsy, with a family name that began with two As, was indeed the first student in the Penn State directory that fall. The other variation was that the killer would target all women whose last name began with A. Neither prediction came true, but they reflected the student state of mind that December.[5]

Students who knew Betsy, such as her English 501 friend Linda Marsa, struggled with grief, a phenomenon that in 1969 was not as well understood as it is today. "In those days, we didn't know about grief," Marsa told writer Kevin Cirilli decades later. "It took me several months to come out of this funk. It was a pretty bad experience, and I blocked it all out." The librarians were forced to relive their own emotions about the murder with every news story in the *Daily Collegian*.[6]

The feelings of Carl Jackson, director of libraries, regarding Betsy Aardsma's death can only be imagined. On Monday, December 1, their first day back at work after the Thanksgiving holiday, he huddled with Charles H. Ness, his assistant director for public services, and Francis E. Hooley, his manager of business operations, to discuss Betsy's murder and what should be done. He asked them to calculate the cost of expanding the hours of the security guards for the rest of 1969 and all of 1970. Ness costed out a number of options, ranging from full- to part-time coverage in Pattee, and also the specialty branch libraries on campus. Jackson also asked Hooley to pull together all documents that "present a fair picture of our concern for both patron and employee in the area of safety-security." Hooley reported back on December 3 that he had located a fair number of memos and letters.[7]

Paul M. Althouse, vice president for resident instruction, had just been designated Penn State's contact point "relating to all matters dealing with the coed's murder," as an official memo put it, rather coldly. On December 3, Jackson appealed to Althouse for approval of the library's proposal to hire more uniformed security for the indefinite future, insisting, "I have a legitimate concern for the safety and well-being of all members of the academic community, and particularly those working in or utilizing library facilities." Jackson described the horrible year in Pattee Library, the arson fires, men committing sexual offenses against women, and "acts of perversion" (gay sex) in the stacks and restrooms, all backed up by the letters and memos Hooley had collected.[8]

Jackson's appeal was successful, and Penn State approved funds for a uniformed security guard to be stationed in Pattee Library at all times the building was open to the public, meaning 7:45 a.m. to midnight. Because the guard was not under the jurisdiction of the Campus Patrol, he was not subject to being called away from the library for traffic control or other assignments from Pelton or Barnes. Some students and faculty actually objected to the presence of the uniformed guard, but the number of incidents in Pattee Library dropped dramatically. As a further safety measure, reflective of an era when paternalism toward women was still tolerated, if not expected, female staffers were barred from working alone at night in the branch libraries and in sections of Pattee away from main corridors and lobbies. Jackson and Ness were not completely satisfied but acknowledged that the situation was better than before Betsy Aardsma was murdered. Of course, if Pelton and the Penn State administration had listened to Jackson earlier in the year, the tragic events of November 28, 1969, might well have been averted.[9]

Four days after Betsy's murder, Representative David S. Hayes (R-Erie) and nine cosponsors introduced a resolution, HR 161, calling for the appointment of three members of the Pennsylvania House of Representatives to investigate security at all of Pennsylvania's state-owned or state-related (Penn State was in the latter category) colleges and universities. "The tragic death of Betsy Aardsma in the Pennsylvania State University Library raises a serious question as to the effectiveness of the security system of our colleges and universities. We must ensure that our children are as secure in their schools as they are at home," Hayes wrote in the resolution. At twenty-nine, Hayes was one of the younger members of the Legislature. He wanted the investigators to have subpoena and contempt power. But his commonsense proposal went nowhere. HR 161 never made it out of the Rules Committee. Committee chairmen and the majority party leadership have great power over which bills see the light of day in Harrisburg, and lobbyists know it. Whether Penn State's lobbyists had anything to do with that is impossible to determine at this juncture. The resolution received no known news coverage and only came to light because a copy turned up in the University Library Administration Documents in the Penn State Archives, meaning that some at the university knew of the resolution. Indeed, it is inconceivable that Penn State's lobbyists did not immediately forward the measure to university president Eric Walker. What his position on Hayes's proposed investigation might have been remains one of the mysteries of the Aardsma murder.

The question of how much Penn State cooperated with the investigation has been much debated over the years, especially by the state police detectives who worked the first weeks of the Aardsma case. They remain deeply divided over whether the university fully cooperated with the Aardsma investigation. Interviewed at the end of his life, when he was dying of cancer, Lieutenant Kimmel said the university was "very, very" cooperative. "Well, of course, they should have been, but they were," he said. "There was no question about cooperation." Then Kimmel added, as if sensing the intent of the question, that the university was not the reason the case was never solved.[10]

Sergeant Keibler said there was no official pressure from the university not to pursue certain angles that might bring scandal to Penn State. He did sense reluctance from faculty members to answer questions about other faculty members, which he believed was due in part to the sexual overtones of the murder. "Normal thing. Would happen today," Keibler said. "But no, you can't say we were blocked in any way with it. Did we get all the information that we would have liked to have had? Hell, no. But we got an awful lot that I can't even talk about." Keibler had a close working relationship with Colonel Pelton, the director of security who oversaw the Campus Patrol. Although he was critical of how Pelton handled the first ninety minutes of the investigation, when both the killer and any usable clues were lost, Keibler praised Pelton's help and cooperation from that point forward. "There is nothing that happened in the Aardsma case that they knew or were working on that I didn't know," he said. He did not believe there could have been a credible suspect in Betsy's murder that Pelton knew about but he, Keibler, did not. Pelton had a good working relationship with President Walker and so, eventually, did the sergeant.[11]

Penn State also helped to fund the Aardsma investigation, Keibler said. He calculated that the most intensive months of the investigation had cost the state police $250,000, or just over $1.5 million in today's money. But other costs were borne by Penn State. "Anything we needed from the university, in regard to money or things like that, it was there," he said. The university provided access to copiers and paper, paid for some of the hotel rooms used by the state troopers who came to assist the Aardsma investigation from other cities, flew the hypnotist to State College to help in the questioning of Uafinda and Erdely, and provided meals to the investigators, plus their pens, pencils, and notepads. Former troopers Ken Schleiden and Tom Shelar recall getting access to everything they needed, in addition to a "huge, nice-sized office." But both troopers said they didn't know what was happening farther up the food chain.[12]

Among the original investigators, Mike Simmers, who rose to the rank of captain, was the most skeptical of Penn State's response to Betsy Aardsma's murder. He believes that Penn State exercised control over the investigation in terms of what information was released to the public and what wasn't. "[It's] not that we didn't have some good people, like George Keibler, heading it up. George had his hands tied with the lieutenant and also with the university. The university had a lot of control over this. They truly did." Simmers said the university took its concerns to "Harrisburg," meaning Governor Shafer, who called himself "Penn State football's No. 1 fan" and attended many games, sometimes flying to away games with the team, and to Colonel Frank J. McKetta, the state police commissioner appointed by Shafer. "We were told we were basically under a thumb," he said.[13]

Simmers believes that Penn State wanted the Aardsma murder to go away to avoid having the crime damage the image of the university among prospective students and their parents. The university especially did not want the state police to publicly speculate that another student might have been the killer. "Unless you arrest him, don't you dare say it was a student," Simmers said. "Say it was Ted Bundy, say it was somebody like that, say it was some deranged guy from out of town, a drug dealer from Philadelphia." Simmers says the state police were actually told not to raise public suspicions that the killer might have been a student "until you have enough to make an arrest and the DA agrees." And they never did. In none of the available public statements did the state police speculate that a student might have been the killer, even though they privately [apart from Corporal Dan Brode and his rapist theory] believed that to be the case. Simmers readily acknowledged that on the surface, at the lower levels, Penn State's cooperation was fine. But that did not mean President Eric Walker was willing to let the chips fall where they may.[14]

Trooper Ronald Tyger tended to agree with Simmers. He called the situation "political," meaning that most colleges and universities, not just Penn State, were reluctant to release damaging information. "They don't want anything that's going to interfere with them getting students back, or getting more students on board," Tyger said. Penn State didn't want anything to come out that would "rock the boat. As a result, it was very tough obtaining records and information that you were looking for." Trooper Kent Bernier, who was the investigator of the Aardsma murder from 2005 to 2009, pointed to Penn State's mishandling of the first ninety minutes of the investigation. "I don't think they wanted anything to do with this, once they determined what it was," he said of the university.[15]

One would normally turn to the university archives, both to President Walker's official papers and to the papers of relevant university offices, for documents telling the story of a murdered student and how the university responded to help the police in their massive, on-campus investigation to find her killer. Unfortunately, that is an exercise in frustration. The Penn State archives appear to have been largely scrubbed of documents relating to the Aardsma case—either that or they never arrived. How else to explain the nearly complete lack of memos, reports, expenditure approvals, and the like regarding a major campus trauma? There is but a single folder of press clippings and press releases related to the early days of the investigation.[16]

Any researcher who has delved into the archival records of government or university bureaucracies would expect to find scores of relevant documents. Did Eric Walker never receive any reports on the crime itself and the progress of the investigation or write one of his frequent memos-to-the-file? Did the presence on campus of forty state troopers investigating the first murder of a student in nearly thirty years, questioning two thousand or more students and faculty members as well, generate not a single scrap of paper from campus officials? Were there no letters from concerned parents to Walker? Or between Walker and the board of trustees? The minutes of the January 10, 1970, meeting of the board of trustees—found in the Pennsylvania State Archives in Harrisburg, not at Penn State—contain a brief statement that Lieutenant Kimmel "reported on the investigation into the recent homicide involving Miss Betsy Aardsma." One can easily imagine that a flurry of memos and letters preceded that appearance, but one searches for them in vain. No bureaucracy preserves all documents, but most preserve records related to major events, if only to be able to give an accounting of what was done. It is entirely possible that a file cabinet full of Penn State documents related to the murder of Betsy Aardsma is stored on campus apart from the archives to keep them from public scrutiny. If the Jerry Sandusky investigation at Penn State has shown anything, it is that Happy Valley's darkest secrets sometimes yield only to subpoena power or extreme public outrage.

Another curious aspect of this case is the cold, clinical treatment of the Aardsma family by Walker and his staff. One searches Walker's papers in the Penn State archives in vain for any letter of condolence written by him to the Aardsmas, even though the record shows he wrote such letters to at least six other grieving families in the three months following the murder. Dick Aardsma, Betsy's father, told reporter Taft Wireback in 1972 that the phone call he made to Raymond O. Murphy, dean of student affairs, on the night his daughter was slain was the only time the family spoke to a university official. And that call did not go well. Wireback wrote in his *Focus* article that Aardsma was upset by Murphy's tone. "Whoever he was, he was very cold and short and told me that I would have to wait for the police to call" to get any additional information, Betsy's father said. When Wireback sought out Walker in 1972 to find out why the Aardsmas had received no condolences from him, the former Penn State president claimed not to remember that a murder of a student had occurred during his tenure.

There was a rumor, one of many circulating at Penn State, that Walker believed Betsy Aardsma was one of the radical students disrupting his campus. But his assessment, if he indeed believed that, does not ring true. She probably would have called herself a liberal and was a supporter of Senator Eugene McCarthy (D-Minn.), the Democratic peace candidate in 1968, and other liberal causes. Many other students held similar views. It didn't make her a dangerous radical or a member of the SDS, although university administrators of the day had a habit of lumping all leftist students together. Trooper Simmers, who was an undercover officer on the Penn State campus and has heard the rumor, said it simply wasn't true. "She was never on the [radical] list I had back then, a big card file," he said. "Oh, the SDS was big. I used to go to those meetings. She was never involved in anything like that." Indeed, the most violent confrontations between student radicals and the university occurred before her arrival at Penn State and after her death, in the spring of 1970.[17]

Nearly twenty years after the murder, Esther Aardsma remembered how university officials failed to console the family. "We were completely ignored," she told *Harrisburg Patriot-News* reporter Phil Galewitz in 1988. Twenty months later, in a conversation with reporter Ted Anthony of the *Daily Collegian,* she softened her opinion in one way but sharpened it in another. "The school was quite nice, but we really never met with the administration," Aardsma said. "I think they were very worried the university would get a bad name. So the victim is sort of pushed aside, I guess."[18]

Penn State administrators from 1969 say little to dispel that notion. Charles L. Lewis, the unpopular vice president for student services in 1969, insisted nearly forty years after the murder that Penn State officials were "all shook up" by Betsy Aardsma's murder. He sought to put their cold response into perspective: "She was a graduate student," Lewis said. "We would have no or little contact. She would not be a residence hall person [*sic*]. Her family would come in and claim the body. They would go in and take care of the apartment wherever she was living, and move on. There was just no reason for us to be involved. Why I'm telling you all this crap, a murder is a serious thing; it's always serious. But there's nothing you can do except try to calm the students down and be courteous to the family. You've got twenty campuses and you've got something bouncing all the time." Raymond O. Murphy, the dean of student affairs who was at the other end of Betsy's father's telephone call on the night of the murder, wondered what all the fuss was about. "There was a limited amount of local interest or information once it happened," he said in 2008. "She was taken home to Holland and that seemed to be pretty much it. I would have to say, she was a grad student. So nobody would know her particularly. In the administration."[19]

Esther Aardsma probably had it right in 1989 when she lamented that her daughter had been pushed aside, forgotten in the name of the glory of old State.

CHAPTER 12

Here Sits Death

As 1969 drew to a close, Lieutenant Kimmel and Sergeant Keibler believed that the solution to the murder of Betsy Aardsma still lay somewhere in Happy Valley. But they had no "A-1 suspect," as Kimmel put it. They needed the Penn State faculty and students to get past their negative feelings toward the state police and help to solve the crime. He even said publicly that the state police were on campus "to work on the murder case and only the murder case." Not, in other words, as an occupying army aimed at crushing student civil rights and antiwar dissent or busting them for pot smoking in the guise of investigating Betsy Aardsma's death. But nothing seemed to work. Kimmel was frustrated that very few students were walking in on their own to report information or suspicions. Those who were contacted by troopers were generally cooperative, but they needed people to volunteer tips. A letter sent to all twenty-six thousand students on December 19, a week after they went home for Christmas break, pleaded for information about any known or rumored threats to women students. It yielded almost no responses, and those few tips that did trickle in contained nothing useful.[1]

Just before Christmas, Kimmel told Keibler that he was now in full charge of the investigation, saying, "Aardsma's yours." Kimmel was moving back to Rockview to resume day-to-day administration of the barracks. The investigation seemed to be fading away; the university announced on December 23 that daily news releases by the Department of Public Information would be discontinued "until such time as there are new developments to justify releases." No doubt the state police commanders in Harrisburg hoped that Keibler could turn things around. Kimmel still hoped for a dramatic arrest but was clearly frustrated. "We're stalemated right now," he said a day after classes resumed at Penn State for the winter term on January 5, 1970.[2]

A promising lead had recently come to naught. A couple of weeks earlier, the state police had first talked to Larry Paul Maurer, the English 501 student who would occupy their thoughts and suspicions for the next four decades, even though he was never arrested and charged, and even though the most that detectives could muster against him was a gut feeling that he had something to do with the Aardsma murder. It was a strange situation.[3]

Maurer had grown up on a farm in the Mahantongo Valley of Northumberland County, north of Harrisburg. He was tall and blond, according to his description in the 1964 edition of *The Bruin,* the yearbook of Mahanoy Joint High School (today Line Mountain High School), and wore eyeglasses. The caption beneath his photo read that he "likes firearms," not uncommon in the country. Maurer was an avid hunter and fisherman and came off as a bit woodsy. He routinely carried a small hunting knife. Maurer was remembered by Nicholas Joukovsky, one of the two professors who taught the English 501 class, as a very quiet young man. His problem was that when he spoke to the police, he couldn't stop talking.[4]

Maurer lives today in Maryland and is retired from the super-secret National Security Administration [NSA]. He will not talk about the Betsy Aardsma case or the suspicion that fell upon him. "I'm not interested in talking to anybody about this anymore, because I feel like it was a tar baby that I got involved in, and the less I have to do with it, the better," Maurer told the author. "Sorry, but I'm not talking to anybody."[5]

When troopers Tom Shelar and Lee Fisher went to Maurer's room in Atherton Hall to talk to him shortly before Christmas break, they had no reason to believe it would be anything other than a routine question-and-answer session, similar to those they were conducting with other members of the English 501 class. They did not have or need a search warrant, Keibler said, because they were not looking for anything. Shelar, the senior investigator, began chatting with Maurer, who admitted he had been in the Level 2 stacks of Pattee Library, in the English literature section, around the time Betsy had been murdered but had not seen her. They continued to talk. Meanwhile, Fisher, who had been on the force only a year, glanced around the room. His eyes were drawn to words carved into the arm of a wooden chair. Moving closer to get a better look, he saw that it read HERE SITS DEATH IN THE GUISE OF MAN. The carving looked fresh. Fisher took Shelar aside and told him about the chair. Maurer casually admitted that it was his handiwork—that he had carved it because it was "a neat saying," Shelar said. The troopers took notes and left.

Shelar went to find Trooper Tom Jones, another senior investigator, and went back to interview Maurer at greater length. This time Maurer admitted he had asked Betsy out on a date and been turned down. Jones asked him what he had used to carve the inscription in the chair, and Maurer told him he had a knife. "Why do you own a knife?" Jones asked. "To cut cheese," Maurer said. He didn't seem at all nervous, even though he had to have known how the knife, his interest in Betsy, and his presence in the Pattee stacks near the murder site not long before Betsy died might be construed by the detectives.[6]

Keibler remembers Jones returning to the Boucke Building, "so damn excited I thought he was going to fall over on the floor. I said, 'What the hell?' He said, 'I got him!' And I said, 'What do you mean, you got him?'" Jones told him about the crude inscription on the chair and of the knife used by Maurer to make the carving. According to Keibler, Jones acknowledged that he and Shelar didn't have solid evidence, "but that has to be him," meaning the killer of Betsy Aardsma.

Lieutenant Kimmel was just as excited, and he ordered that Maurer be polygraphed and put through the wringer. The examination was scheduled for after New Year's Day but before classes resumed at Penn State for the winter term. Jones and Shelar drove to the Maurer farm in Northumberland County and picked him up. They drove him up Route 147 to Sunbury, where they crossed the bridge over the Susquehanna River and drove to the state police barracks outside Selinsgrove, where the polygraph examiner from Harrisburg had set up his bulky machine. Maurer was not accompanied by anyone—not by his father, not by a lawyer.[7]

Jones and Shelar grilled Maurer hard. "He was respectful, and very cool," Shelar said. "We actually accused him of the murder, and he was very cool in denying it. We always figured that any normal person would be aggravated, excited if they were accused. Not him! He just calmly said he didn't do it, even though he admitted being in the [English] Lit stacks at the time of the murder. But he said he didn't see her."[8]

Only then was Maurer hooked up to the polygraph. The two troopers were stunned when the operator came out and told them he had passed the test. "We always figured he beat the operator, not the machine," Shelar said. Back at Penn State, Kimmel paced the floor nervously, waiting for a call he expected from Jones, telling him that the student had confessed and that they were driving him back to State College for arraignment. He was bitterly disappointed when they arrived back at Rockview and told him Maurer had passed the test. Simmers witnessed the aftermath of the meeting. He was in the kitchen, which was next to Kimmel's office. "If anyone thought they had the cat in the bag it was those three," Simmers said. "And Kimmel come [*sic*] out and his chin was down to the ground. [They] just thought for certain that they had him, and they couldn't get him to talk."[9]

Robert W. Sams, second son of Henry W. Sams, chairman of the Penn State English Department, remembers his father talking about the Aardsma investigation. "I remember sort of toward the tail end . . . it came up again, and what I remember clearly is Dad saying, 'Well, they know who did it. They just don't have enough evidence.' That was his impression at the time. I got the impression that he knew who they suspected, but he didn't say. I got the feeling that he knew enough detail about the possible suspects to either make a judgment or to have been told who they were suspecting."[10]

The police admitted they had no evidence—just a heaping pile of suspicion that even today raises eyebrows, but which, as late as 2007, when it was considered again, was not enough to move authorities to take any further action. "Well, basically, during the time I had it [the investigation], there was never any evidence that [Maurer] should be arrested," Keibler said. "There was no evidence that he was a high suspect. It's that simple."

CHAPTER 13
Sleep Mode

There comes a point in any failed criminal investigation when it goes into sleep mode, which can be defined as a couple of detectives still looking and hoping for a break even if their superiors are skeptical. Sleep mode may occur suddenly or it may be gradual, beginning with a small reduction in the number of detectives assigned to the case. Think of it as the last stop before "cold case" status.

For the Aardsma investigation, the beginning of the end was around the time of another infamous crime in Pennsylvania: the murders of United Mine Workers of America union reformer Joseph "Jock" Yablonski, his wife, Margaret, and their daughter, Charlotte. Their violent deaths closed out the American murder year of 1969. In the wee hours of December 31, three weeks after Yablonski decisively lost his electoral challenge to the corrupt UMWA president, W. A. "Tony" Boyle, a trio of paid assassins crept toward the family's fieldstone farmhouse near Clarksville in the southwest corner of the state, about 165 miles from Penn State University. They first cut the telephone lines to the house and disabled the family car parked in the driveway. Once inside, Paul Gilly, thirty-seven, a housepainter and gun collector, Claude Edward Vealey, twenty-seven, a professional burglar, and Aubran "Buddy" Martin, twenty-three, described as "a pretty, blond sociopath," went upstairs and carried out their orders to murder Yablonski and anyone else who was in the house. Martin executed the sleeping Charlotte, twenty-five, with two shots to the head, then killed Jock, fifty-nine, and Margaret, fifty-seven, after Vealey's M1 rifle misfired.[1]

The bodies were discovered five days later by Kenneth Yablonski, one of their sons. Both the Pennsylvania State Police and the FBI worked on the case, helped by physical evidence at the scene—a plethora of fingerprints—that the state police Aardsma investigators did not have because of the mishandling of the crime scene by the Penn State Campus Patrol and library administrators. Arrests in the Yablonski case came just three weeks later. Convictions and death sentences followed.

Tom Shelar, one of the Aardsma investigators, believed the Yablonski case diverted the attention of state police higher-ups. "Because a couple of guys said, 'Well, there goes the pressure off of us.' It all went onto the Yablonski thing because of the union connection and all that," he remembered.[2]

For a couple of days, state police investigators thought the Yablonski and Aardsma cases might somehow be linked. Around January 9, 1970, a few days after the gruesome scene at the Yablonski house was discovered, Shelar learned of a twenty-eight-year-old Penn State student who was hospitalized in Ritenhour Health Center, the apparent victim of a mental breakdown. The student had been babbling, "They killed Aardsma, they killed Yablonski, I'm sorry, I'm sorry." The student's parents lived about thirty miles from the Yablonski home. Shelar asked the Yablonski investigators to do a background check on the student. After interviewing his parents, they concluded that he was mentally ill and unlikely to have real knowledge of either murder. It was one more frustration.[3]

The top commanders of the state police in Harrisburg were still concerned about solving the Aardsma case, enough so that one of them, a major whom Keibler would not identify, called a few months into 1970 with an extraordinary request. The major, who clearly had never been to Pattee Library, told Keibler, "We don't want to be embarrassed. Take all those books out of the library to make sure the knife isn't there." Relating the story, Keibler chuckled. "Well, they had no idea what the Pattee Library was. He thought it was a room like this," Keibler said, gesturing to the finished basement of his house. "And I explained to him that it would take five hundred men six months to do this. . . . He did not realize the magnitude."[4]

That may have been the strangest call, but it was hardly the only one Keibler received from farther up the chain of command. "You had people from all over the state police, high command, picking the phone up and contacting me, saying, 'Do this and do that,'" Keibler said. "Make sure we do this, follow that. And most of them did not have the knowledge of what was going on at Penn State, nor did they have the experience of a criminal investigator to know what the hell they were talking about." Officers who had access to the main report would call him and announce that based on what they were reading, he needed to look closely at a certain person right away. "And I would say to this person, if you're on page 27, if you'll look at page 65, you'll see that he's been cleared."[5]

Keibler was not particularly upset about the reduction in the staff assigned to the Aardsma investigation, from forty down to about twenty to twenty-five at the beginning of 1970. He believed he could have done a better job from the start with just ten veteran investigators. "When you have forty bodies here, you have a large number of them that are just bodies sent to you to help. They're unfamiliar with how to deal with the campus. They've never been on campus, they don't know a damn thing about it; you have that problem, okay? You have people coming in who have never been on the campus. So they have a hell of a time just getting around and knowing what to do. Fortunately, you're able to take care of that by giving them assignments they can handle," Keibler said.

The decision to downsize the Aardsma investigative staff was done, he said, "to get it down into a workable thing. Besides, I think the people at the top felt they'd covered their tail. They'd put a lot of people in there, there's nothing that we need a lot of people for, we'll get it down now to an investigative thing. And the people that I had, I could handle it with." If one week he needed five more people, Keibler said, all he had to do was pick up the phone and he could get five more people.

But there was less and less work to do. They had rounded the bases several times without scoring a run. Albert Dunning, news director of WDFM Radio, said the daily briefings on the case trailed off to no briefings at all. Why hold a press conference if there was nothing new to report? District Attorney Charles Brown made the same observation. "I was getting fewer and fewer updates," he said. "There was not much to report other than to say things are the way they were the last time we talked." Keibler sent detectives out to Michigan again in the spring to take one more look at whether there was any connection between the Coed Murders and the Aardsma case. There wasn't, or if there was, they couldn't find it.[6]

By the time spring drew near, the Aardsma investigation was no further along than it had been in January. It was Lieutenant Kimmel's idea, not Penn State's, to offer a sizable reward for information leading to the arrest and conviction of Betsy's killer. He approached Penn State president Eric Walker, asking where they could obtain funding for a reward. Walker, as Kimmel probably hoped, agreed to have the university put up the money. On March 9, 1970, a reward of $25,000 was offered, enough at that time to buy a house or start a small business—or to disappear. It was the equivalent of more than $150,000 today, enough to draw even the most reluctant tipster out of the shadows. A committee of five prominent Centre County residents led by attorney Wayland F. Dunaway of State College would decide who got the reward. State troopers and their families were not eligible. Other members of the committee were Mahlon K. Robb, president of the Bellefonte Trust Co., Jerome Weinstein, editor of the *Centre Daily Times,* J. Alvin Hawbaker, developer of Park Forest Village, the first large postwar housing development in the State College area, and Dr. J. Reed Babcock, a Bellefonte surgeon.

The reward and the involvement of important members of the community showed how seriously State College viewed the murder of Betsy Aardsma, a young woman who had been among them for barely three months, and the urgency they felt about finding her killer. It was basic human decency at work. But no one ever claimed the reward, and no one ever mentioned it when they did talk to investigators, according to Keibler. It finally expired on January 1, 1972, without stirring the conscience of the one man in the community who could have helped—or at least, not enough to make him pick up the telephone.[7]

In one of the last news releases by the state police during the active part of the Aardsma investigation, on March 9, 1970, Lieutenant Kimmel said they were looking for "a man and a woman known to be having a conversation in the area where Miss Aardsma's body was found." Was it Betsy and her killer? Or the killer asking one of her fellow English students where to find her? Or two people who just happened to be passing by? The tendency is to reach for straws, to assign importance to the smallest detail. Events would soon put a stop, at least temporarily, to even these last ditch efforts to solve the murder.

The descent of Penn State into chaos began on April 14, 1970, when about fifty student demonstrators occupied the Shields Building in support of demands made by black students at Penn State Ogontz, a branch campus outside of Philadelphia, for black student rights and black studies courses. The next day, about five hundred students rallied in front of Old Main at the main campus in support of their own latest list of demands to the administration. These included open admissions to Penn State, meaning no academic admission requirements that blocked black students struggling with the legacy of inferior inner city high schools; an end to Penn State ties to military research; an end to the ROTC program on campus; and support by Penn State for the freeing of Black Panther leader Bobby Seale, who was then serving a four-year sentence for contempt of court handed down during the Chicago Seven conspiracy trial. (Seale was the eighth defendant, but his case was severed from that of the others after the contempt sentence.) He had no known ties to Penn State, but ending his incarceration was a *cause célèbre* among student protesters at the time. Between one hundred and three hundred of the students entered Old Main and began a sit-in while attempts were made to deliver their demands to President Walker. After windows were broken and other damage done, including vandalism of wall murals, university officials went to Centre County judge R. Paul Campbell and obtained a cease-and-desist order, which was read to the students at 4:00 p.m.[8]

Meanwhile, Keibler was ordered to put the Aardsma investigation on hold and bring his men in riot gear—helmets and wooden batons—from the Boucke Building to the front of Old Main. Keibler said Wells Keddie, the SDS faculty advisor who was with the student protesters in Old

Main, persuaded state police commanders to order their men to remove their helmets and put away their batons. Why? They were a "provocation," Keddie insisted. Who actually gave the order to disarm is in dispute. Keibler said it was Captain Earl O. Bergstrom, commander of Troop G. Trooper Mike Simmers, who was there undercover in plainclothes, trying to blend in among the students, says it was Major Robert A. Rice, a former marine, who until his promotion to major was the commander of Troop H, Harrisburg. Whoever gave the order, the results were disastrous. "They got the hell beat out of them," Keibler said.[9]

The forty students inside Old Main surrendered, but other students outside attacked the disarmed and unhelmeted state police, hurling rocks, dirt balls, and pieces of wood. Some of the projectiles hit home, causing head injuries to at least ten troopers. An unidentified physician at Centre Community Hospital, where five of the injured troopers were taken, commented to the *Centre Daily Times* that if the troopers had been wearing their helmets, virtually none of them would have been injured. Five other troopers were admitted to Ritenhour Health Center and kept overnight.

Some of the students who came out of Old Main managed to escape, but twenty-nine others were herded onto buses and taken to Beaver Stadium, which was used as a holding pen. From there, they were transported to their arraignments and then to either Centre County Prison or, after the county lockup ran out of cells, to the Rockview state prison. The male students had their long hair—and beards, if they had them—shorn off at the prison. Keibler, wearing civilian clothes, drove a wrecker back to Old Main and managed to tow away a bus destroyed by the students. They didn't realize who he really was.[10]

But the worst was yet to come. On April 18, some six thousand students jammed Rec Hall to hear an incendiary speech by radical lawyer William Kunstler, the lead attorney for the Chicago Seven defendants, and Rennie Davis, an antiwar activist who was one of the defendants. Kunstler and Davis had dinner before the speech at the Tavern in downtown State College with Jeffrey Berger, president of the Penn State SDS chapter. They told Berger they had to be careful during the speech to avoid inciting major demonstrations that could get them arrested once again for inciting to riot.[11]

Nevertheless, the speech turned into a leftist pep rally that left Penn State students even more radicalized and eager to take on the university administration and the state police. Kunstler gave an interesting and moving account of the Chicago Seven trial and of his verbal jousting with Judge Julius Hoffman. "I don't want to see us bathed in blood," Kunstler thundered. "Only a madman would say that. But change has to come by any means necessary, or we are a doomed and lost people in a doomed and lost world." Davis, shouting to be heard over the students, who were chanting "All power to the people," told them that their demands of the Penn State administration "make all the sense in the world if you have the power to see them through." They were appealing to the best instincts of a generation, to youthful idealism and disgust over the Vietnam War and racial discrimination. And in those tense days it was like throwing gasoline on a fire, provoking a descent from idealism into *Lord of the Flies* nihilism.[12]

On the morning of April 20, President Walker announced that there would be no amnesty for the twenty-nine students arrested at the Old Main sit-in five days earlier. That angered many leftist students, but Walker was unyielding when he met with them. That evening, they took over the HUB and made it their "strike" headquarters. Some decided to vent their frustrations against the Penn State president, who at that time lived in a mansion in the heart of the campus. SDS president Jeffrey Berger remembers hearing one of the more militant students say, "We're going over to the president's house." A mob of students appeared outside the mansion at 10:50 p.m. and began smashing windows. Finally, they used an uprooted stop sign as a battering ram to break open the front door, but then lost their nerve and took off running.[13]

"He had different thoughts and a different approach to the SDS after that happened," Keibler said of Walker. "Because he saw that he could have been hurt. He could have been killed."[14]

Many windows were smashed, but the scariest thing was the setting of fires. Through the wee hours of the morning, small fires were touched off at five girls' dormitories among the East Halls, forcing their evacuation, but were brought under control. False alarms forced the evacuation of two boys' dormitories. Dumpsters outside McAllister, the Human Development Building, and Oak Cottage were set afire but quickly extinguished. A Molotov cocktail was thrown through a window at Tyson Building, starting a fire that destroyed a high-protein corn research project that a graduate student had worked on for three years as part of his doctoral dissertation. He was shattered by the loss, Keibler said. The last fire was reported at 6:15 a.m., nearly an hour after sunrise, in Stone Hall, a girls' dorm. In all, fires were set in ten to twelve buildings before the long night was over.[15]

The next day, April 21, a contingent of 280 more state police arrived in State College and established a headquarters at the Holiday Inn. The campus settled down, as if spent. President Nixon's announcement on April 30 that he was mounting an invasion of Cambodia touched off an estimated twenty student strikes per day around the nation, but not at Penn State. Even student anguish over the killings of four students by the Ohio National Guard at Kent State University on May 4 did not bring a resumption of the violence, although there were peaceful marches and the suspension of classes for one day. The students who were arrested for mischief during the April riots by and large won their cases when they appeared before the justice of the peace. Wells Keddie, the labor studies professor who joined the students on the barricades, and who accused the police of brutality in their response to the protests, was denied tenure by Penn State a year later. He sued on First Amendment grounds, claiming he was the victim of retaliation for his political activities. But a federal judge in Harrisburg in 1976 ruled that the tenure committee had sufficient grounds apart from politics to deny him a permanent place on the faculty.[16]

Even through the turmoil around them, Betsy Aardsma's friends in the English Department did not forget her. The graduate students created the Betsy Aardsma Fund, from which any graduate English student could borrow money without interest. It was funded through book sales, and one of Betsy's friends, Betty Bechtel, worked to publicize the annual event. Linda Marsa bought a first-edition copy of *The Sun Also Rises*, Ernest Hemingway's first novel, at the first auction. She inscribed the book and sent it to Dick and Esther Aardsma.[17]

Buzz Triebold, one of Pelton's top aides in the Department of Security, believed nothing was really accomplished during the investigation. Not ever. "So there was really nothing that was fruitful that we found in the weeks or months after this happened," he said. "We kept working on and trying to find out what happened from people—who was seen, and who might have been in there—and the direction in which she was stabbed, where the person was, whether he was behind her or in front of her, whether she startled him." Lieutenant Richwine, with his gift for pithy quotes, said simply, "It was a damn shame, but we worked hard."[18]

The Aardsma investigation petered out to almost nothing during the year that followed the riots. By the summer of 1971, no more leads were coming in. The investigation became mostly Keibler, a single detective trying to unravel what had led someone to murder Betsy Aardsma. He had three theories about Betsy's murder. The first was that the slayer was not concerned about being identified by Betsy, because he fled without waiting to see if the single stab wound was fatal. The second was that she might have been murdered to silence her after she had stumbled upon someone doing something illegal or improper in the library. And the third was that her killer had determined that for some reason, Betsy had to die, and he was only waiting for the right time to do it. He actually had a fourth theory, too—that the owner of the expensive Dutch porn books found near the crime scene was the killer, the one who had abandoned them in haste when he fled. "The reader of those books either saw the killing, or he was the killer," Keibler said. "And in all probability, he *was* the killer."[19]

Betsy Aardsma remained a puzzle, unlike nearly every other murder victim Keibler had encountered or would ever encounter in his long career. He and his investigators had turned her past upside down more than once, looking for evidence of character flaws that would lead them to a motive, and then to the man who killed her. But this time it didn't work. As Keibler told one reporter, "We've examined in detail all the letters we've been able to obtain that Miss Aardsma wrote, both to her parents and to friends, and from everything we've learned, she led a singularly blameless and uncomplicated life."[20]

The first was true, but the second depended on how you looked at it. In some ways, Betsy Aardsma had made her life very complicated with her dreams and ambitions, her desire to leave home and fly toward the sun, to become smart and educated and to save a little bit of the world. Who could criticize that? At the same time, while not a Pollyanna, she was friendly and trusted people. Had she been less ambitious, or more cynical, she might not have ended up dead on the floor of Pattee Library. Those were the complications, but they were also what made her life and death so compelling and utterly tragic.

Part III: The Good Girl and the World Outside

Two Hollanders a church, three Hollanders a heresy.

—Traditional saying [1]

CHAPTER 14

Betsy Who Dreamed

One of the earliest mentions of Betsy Aardsma in the pages of the *Holland Evening Sentinel* is on March 14, 1956, when she was just eight years old. In a roundup of news from the various Camp Fire Girl and Blue Bird groups in Holland, Michigan, the *Sentinel* reported that when the Happy Blue Birds of Longfellow Elementary School held a meeting on March 5, Betsy Aardsma led the group in singing "The Blue Bird Wish," verses of nearly unbearable sweetness, optimism, and innocence.[1] Betsy and her friends sang of their intention to have fun, to learn to make beautiful things, to finish what they began, to keep their temper in check "most of the time," to go to interesting places, to know about trees, flowers, and birds, and to make friends. It is unbearable because we know how it all ends for the girl leading the song.[2]

Betsy's birth came on July 11, 1947, nine months after her father, Dick Aardsma, was discharged from the army. She was of the Baby Boom, one of 3.8 million American babies to begin life that year in the golden glow of postwar optimism. Among her fellow 1947s in the Midwest were Mitt Romney, born in March, and Hillary Clinton, born in October. In his 2009 book, *Boomers: The Cold-War Generation Grows Up*, Victor D. Brooks wrote that the postwar optimism was short-lived but real. Children existed, he wrote, "in a world of stable and seemingly happy marriages where divorce seemed to be a feature primarily of the Hollywood acting community, and where fatalities from work accidents, disease, and childbirth were substantially reduced." Murder rates, too, were low and getting lower, not that murder had ever been a big problem in Holland. It was almost nonexistent, really, and the few that occurred, often many years apart, most often involved outsiders killing outsiders.

Around 1946, Betsy's parents, Dick and Esther, had moved the family to a house at 144 East 16th Street. It wasn't far from the home of John and Bessie Van Alsburg, Esther's parents, at 455 College Avenue on the corner of East 19th Street. John Van Alsburg was a well-known coal dealer in Holland, in business since 1925. Betsy's first home was not as nicely situated as that of her grandparents, who lived on a leafy block of pleasant older homes across from a city park and ball field, but it would do. What more does a baby need than four good walls and a roof and a loving family?[3]

Dick Aardsma, who majored in history at Hope College in Holland, worked as a bookkeeper for the H. J. Heinz Co., which made most of its pickles at a large factory on the shoreline of Lake Macatawa, a small lake that opened onto the giant Lake Michigan. A couple of years later, he switched to a similar job for Venhuizen Auto Co., which sold Studebakers (FIRST BY FAR WITH A POSTWAR CAR, went one ad in the *Holland Evening Sentinel*) in Holland. Around 1951, he was hired by the State of Michigan as a sales tax auditor, a steady job he would keep for the rest of his working life. He exercised his mind and a yen for history by reading biographies of historical figures. The family moved that year to 180 East 24th Street, across the street from Baker Furniture Co. and kitty-corner from tree-covered Prospect Park. A couple of years later they moved again, this time to 165 East 26th Street, a solidly middle-class block with no factory in sight. Esther Aardsma, even though she had a Hope College degree in English, followed the custom of most women of her era and did not work outside the home after children began arriving. By 1956, the Aardsmas had four: Carole, Betsy, Richard II, and Kathy.

The Aardsmas were relatively unusual for a Holland family at the time, in that both parents had college degrees. Both Dick and Esther were of Dutch descent, as were so many other people in Holland. Esther had grown up there, and Dick had come from Chicago's Roseland neighborhood, then a tidy Dutch enclave but much different today. They had met at Hope College, graduating together in 1940. Hope was affiliated with the Reformed Church in America, one of two major Calvinist denominations in Holland, and a Van Alsburg family tradition. Esther's siblings Donald and Ruth Van Alsburg had graduated from Hope before her. The Van Alsburgs were bound up in the unusual history of Holland, a pioneer family that had prospered in the New World. That Betsy Aardsma had the option to follow her Icarus dreams into the world outside was due in no small part to the choices her ancestors had made.[4]

It is difficult to understand the currents of Betsy's short life without understanding the history of Holland. The city, located on the western side of the state's hand-shaped Lower Peninsula, is 150 miles up the Lake Michigan coast from Chicago, or 90 miles as the crow flies. In 1969, Holland had almost twenty-five thousand people and had not yet undergone the late-century television and chainstore-driven homogenization that ironed out the unique wrinkles of so many American small towns, ethnic or not. The Holland phone directory could be mistaken for that of a smaller Dutch city, and outsiders often commented on the number of blond-haired people they saw on the street. Hollanders were split nearly evenly along religious lines between the Reformed Church in America, whose members in 1969 could fairly be said to be moderates on Calvinist and other theological and social issues, and the Christian Reformed Church, which took a very strict, ultraorthodox view of those same matters. What was left was an oddly schizophrenic community. It was divided by an invisible wall of separation that dated to 1857, and it affected many aspects of life in Holland.

The founder of the town was Reverend Albertus C. Van Raalte, a well-educated and fairly well-to-do *dominie,* or minister, from Arnhem in the Netherlands. He was an important leader of the conservative opposition to the state church. The state church, headed by the Dutch monarch, was Protestant and Calvinist. So were Van Raalte and his peasant followers, known as Seceders. The difference was that Seceders, who comprised about 2 percent of the Dutch population, followed John

Calvin's teachings with a vengeance. Their rules barred any desecration of the Sabbath, including children playing outside. They banned attendance at community fairs, drinking, gambling, going to the theater, and dancing. They condemned the Dutch king for his tolerance of Catholics, Jews, and Anabaptists, or Mennonites. Even in the 1800s they were out of step with much of the Netherlands; today, when Van Raalte's Arnhem has sex clubs advertising on the Internet, they seem like the Dutch from another planet.

Harassment by state church supporters and ultimately by the Dutch government caused Van Raalte in 1846 to lead a group of his followers to America. They traveled to Michigan, where in the dead of winter at the beginning of 1847 Van Raalte set them to building a Calvinist utopia shielded by the wilderness where they could practice their religion without interference. Other Dutch settlers followed that year, including two great-great-uncles of Betsy Aardsma's on her mother's side, John and Henry Van Alsburg, sons of a potato farmer who had probably heard Van Raalte preach. Their brother, Dirk Van Alsburg, Betsy Aardsma's great-grandfather, followed them to America in 1854.[5]

But isolation did not stop the Dutch settlers from quarreling among themselves, ostensibly over religious doctrine. Clerical critics of Van Raalte condemned the "awful, poisonous heresies" they saw among his followers, including tolerance of Masonic membership, use of church organs, adding lightning rods to church steeples (displaying lack of faith in God), placing flowers on caskets, and even church picnics. These are hard to understand today. But underlying it all, at least for the conservatives, was fear of assimilation into the American culture, which loomed ever larger as the wilderness was cut down, and loss of their Dutch language and identity. In 1857, the Reformed Church in Holland broke apart, with about a third of the congregations forming the ultraorthodox Christian Reformed Church.

There was no physical barrier between the two communities, just that invisible line. They coexisted but did not engage each other, even when they played their roles in the annual Tulip Festival, a celebration of Holland's Dutch heritage that included nearly all the children in the elementary schools dressing up in Dutch costumes and parading down

8th Street. It was entirely possible to go through life knowing no one from the other side of the line, or at least not well.

The Reformed Church, which included Betsy Aardsma's family, moved toward embracing the American culture, the English language, and public schools while holding on to a more moderate interpretation of Calvinism. The Christian Reformed Church, which eventually ministered to just under half of the Holland community, sought to protect its faithful from contamination by the outside world, including members of other faiths. It did this by creating its own schools and institutions, even its own version of the Boy Scouts and, for a time, its own Pinkie/Candy Striper program at Holland Hospital. They struggled to preserve the Dutch language, but by the very early twentieth century, it was increasingly a lost cause.

Their conservative piety and adherence to the old ways survived. When television arrived in Holland in the 1950s, the Christian Reformed elders considered it little different than moviegoing and added TV watching to their list of banned activities. But not all of the faithful agreed, and the story was that console televisions—the kind where the television was inside a nice cabinet with doors, intended to make the TV set look like another piece of furniture—were especially popular in Christian Reformed households. When the pastor came to call, the doors on the TV were quickly closed. How he could miss seeing the aerial on the roof was unexplained, but it was a good story, one that illustrated the cultural divide in Holland and the strictures under which one side lived.

The rest of Holland, while never liberal, became increasingly moderate after World War II, helped by an influx of executives from national corporations who were not Dutch, and sometimes not even Protestant. In 1951 Parke, Davis & Co., the pharmaceutical manufacturer, opened a plant in Holland to make chloromycetin, one of the early wonder drugs, employing some 350 people. Even more significant was the arrival of a General Electric plant in 1954, to build hermetic motors for refrigeration and air-conditioning units. That factory employed nearly eight hundred people, including some seventy-five executives who comprised the headquarters unit for the motor division. They moved into the community, bringing with them different outlooks, different experiences, and, in many cases, different religions, including Catholicism. Their children enrolled in the Holland public schools.

Also changing Holland after the war was the arrival of Mexicans and Mexican Americans who came as migrant labor to work in the fruit and vegetable farms around the town, staying for the factory jobs. They were curiosities among their fellow students in the public schools, so brown and non-Dutch. The new arrivals, whatever their background, did not change the overall tenor of Holland, but they stirred the mix and intrigued young people like Betsy Aardsma, who yearned to know the world outside of a hometown that was so often blond and bland and hyper-pious. Because her ancestors had cast their lot with the Reformed Church, she had a better chance to do so, but the path was still not easy.[6]

From the start, Betsy Aardsma was a top student, always one of the smart girls, seemingly destined for great things. She attended Longfellow Elementary School from kindergarten through fourth grade, from 1952 to 1957, and left her friends with lifelong memories of her artistic drive and love of drawing. Sandy Vande Water, a classmate, remembered her bursting into tears one day when she didn't have time to finish an art project. "Typical artistic, emotional little girl at that time of her life," she remembered more than fifty years later. "Kind of a delicate—what we would think of as an artistic—personality. That's what I remember about her. And she followed that love of drawing and writing and anything in the creative arts." Margo Hakken, who was a fellow Blue Bird, remembered Betsy as "very brilliant, real artistic, a lot of fun, and really creative." Even at the end of her life, Sergeant George Keibler of the Pennsylvania State Police marveled at the "doodles" she left behind in her room in Atherton Hall.[7]

With four children, Dick and Esther Aardsma needed more space, and they moved in the late summer of 1957 to the 100 block of East 37th Street. This was a neighborhood that had not yet been annexed to

Holland. Betsy spent three years at Maplewood Elementary, which went to seventh grade, before moving on to E. E. Fell Junior High School in Holland for eighth and ninth grades. Fell, located along River Avenue between 16th and 15th Streets, was a three-story brick edifice of the kind one would have found then in a thousand American small towns. It had up-staircases and down-staircases, and only the bravest students dared to use the wrong one and risk a detention.[8]

On that first day of eighth grade in 1960, Betsy met and befriended another new student, Jan Sasamoto, a Japanese-American girl and only child whose background was as different from her own as she was likely to find in Holland. Ted and Toshi Sasamoto, Jan's parents, had arrived in Holland around 1944. Originally from Los Angeles, Mr. Sasamoto had traveled around the country working for poultry growers as a chicken sexer. He could tell at a glance whether a hatchling was male or female (most male chicks were euthanized because they couldn't produce eggs). When World War II broke out, his father was interned at a camp in Colorado because he served on the board of a Japanese school, which offered after-school instruction in Japanese language and culture. So was Toshi Sasamoto's sister, who had married a man in an internment camp. Internment, which was driven by fear of a Japanese fifth column in the American homeland, but also by racism and economic envy, was not uniformly imposed on all Japanese Americans. Indeed, the experience of the Sasamoto family made it seem almost arbitrary. With travel to distant jobs becoming increasingly difficult, Ted and Toshi decided to move to Holland, where they had friends and there were plenty of chicken farms. They married and bought a house on Harvard Drive in Holland Heights, near the Holland Country Club.[9]

Eighth-grade homeroom for Betsy and Jan turned out to be the school library, and they met because they happened to sit at the same table. The homeroom teacher asked them to elect officers. Betsy leaned over to Jan and whispered, "What do you want to be? I'll nominate you if you nominate me."

"That's how it started," Jan said. Their friendship deepened over time, she said, explaining how in French there is one word, *camarade,* for "classmate," and another, *ami,* for "close friend." She and Betsy started as the first and gradually moved to the second. They didn't have that many classes together in junior high and didn't often eat lunch together that first year, Jan recalled. But little things pulled them together, like sneaking down the hallway without a pass. "Betsy would say to me, 'Just look like you know you have a hall pass, because we've got a good reputation.' And they never did question us!" she said.[10]

If likes attract, it was not surprising that Jan became Betsy's best friend. They were among the top students at E. E. Fell. In the spring of ninth grade, both were honored, along with seven other students in her class, for having maintained perfect 4.0 grade point averages during junior high. The two girls couldn't wait to get to high school, crashing the senior high dances "well before we were eligible," Jan recalled.[11]

The rarity of murder in Holland could understandably lull anyone there into thinking the world was a safe place, especially if you associated with the right kind of people and didn't stray far from home. Even Holland's most terrible murder, which occurred on April 29, 1961, wasn't enough to shake that complacency. On that date, James Scott Stephens, a seventeen-year-old boy who was mentally ill and liked guns, shot to death two innocent young girls, Margaret S. Chambers, eleven, and Carol Gee, twelve, while they were picking flowers in the dunes along Lake Michigan near Macatawa Park. Stephens, a student at Saugatuck High School who lived in the same neighborhood as the girls, claimed it was accidental, the result of having tripped, but could never explain how he shot them eleven times by accident. He fled on his thumb, hitchhiking to the Upper Peninsula of Michigan and then west across the UP, across Wisconsin and Minnesota to South Dakota. He was finally spotted by a local police chief and arrested in a cafe in Kadoka, a lonely prairie town near the Badlands. Stephens was convicted and sentenced to a long prison term—Michigan never had the death penalty—and committed suicide in his cell a few years later. The murders shocked the Holland community, which reached out to the girls' families. The Gees, who were Catholic, were established in Holland, while the Chambers family, Baptists, had roots in the South. Margaret and Carol were buried in Pilgrim Home Cemetery.

And the city moved on. It was still possible, if you lived in Holland, to pass off this tragedy as an aberration, something that involved outsiders, and believe your world was still a pretty safe place. At least if you stayed close to home.[12]

In the fall of 1962, Betsy Aardsma and Jan Sasamoto moved to the new Holland High School. Built along Van Raalte Avenue, it was laid out more like a college campus, with two main classroom buildings, a domed fieldhouse, a separate performing arts center, a library and administration building, a visual arts building, and a building for wood and metal shop and mechanical drawing. Holland High was a far cry from most American high schools of that day, or any day. The differences extended to attendance policy. If you didn't have a class during a particular period, you could leave campus and do what you pleased, so long as you didn't get into trouble and showed up for your next class. There was no sign-out or sign-in required. In practice, most students went to one of the four Commons areas in the two classroom units and spent their free periods working on homework or talking to friends and solving the problems of the world. No teacher directly monitored the room, although students were expected to hold down the volume of their conversations. There was no cafeteria, just coin-operated hot- and cold-food machines. Such a progressive attendance policy might only have worked in a conservative, relatively homogeneous, churchgoing community like Holland, but it did work for many years. Holland Christian High School, run by the Christian Reformed Church, maintained strict, traditional discipline and rules.

Betsy hung out in the Commons with a group of other girls bound for college, including Jan Sasamoto; Judi Jahns, whose father was a GE transplant; Peggy Wich, whose family had moved to Holland from Detroit so her banker father could start a new finance company; Leslie Nienhuis; Sandy Vande Water; Margo Hakken; and a few others. "It was one of those clique things," Sasamoto said. "We had friends outside it, but we were pretty tight." She said they weren't the popular girls, as that term is understood in most high schools, but were officers in every club, notably the Publicity Club, or "Pub Club." "I don't think we were the cutest," Wich added, then reconsidered her opinion. "Well, we were pretty cute. But [we were] the [girls] who wanted good grades and were going to college." Another common thread among about half of Betsy's friends was that they were not Holland natives.[13]

They were all Dutch Dancers, part of a unique Holland tradition. At Tulip Time, dozens of girls from the three Holland-area high schools would put on traditional Dutch peasant costumes and wooden shoes, somewhat like clogs, and perform folk dances. Also known as *Klompen* dancers, after the Dutch word for "wooden shoes," they had been a highlight of Tulip Time since 1935. Girls paired off, one dancing the female role and the other the male; recruiting boys was deemed a lost cause. Betsy and Jan were a Dutch Dance pair, with the male role danced by Betsy, who was several inches taller than her friend. The costumes either were sewn by a girl or her mother from approved patterns or acquired at an annual community Dutch costume exchange. Wooden shoes were manufactured by the Wooden Shoe Factory in Holland, one of the city's thematic tourist attractions for many decades. They were not uncomfortable if you wore enough layers of socks. Sometimes a dancer would lose a wooden shoe on a high kick and watch in horror as it sailed into the mob of parade spectators along 8th Street. The Tulip Festival celebrated a Netherlands that no longer was. The traditional costumes had vanished from Old Holland, save perhaps in the most remote island villages, and wooden shoes, while still practical for Dutch farmers working in damp ground, had pretty much become historical relics as well.[14]

Even though the Netherlands of Tulip Time no longer existed, Holland was recognized by the Dutch government and royal family as a special place. Crown Princess Juliana visited Holland in 1941, while she and her children were in exile in Canada because of the Nazi occupation of the Netherlands. She became queen in 1948 after the abdication of her mother, Queen Wilhelmina, and returned to Holland for another visit as queen in 1952. Other members of the royal family visited in later years.

Kids who grew up in Holland got used to this, as different as it might seem to outsiders. But blond/bland, that overwhelming sense of tidiness, and the sense of being part of a theme-park attraction could become old. Some Holland kids yearned for any splash of color they could find, longing to escape the confining walls of the citadel that was Holland.[15]

None of Betsy's friends remember her as boy-crazy. They say she dated from time to time but was more interested in her studies. According to Jan Sasamoto, she was "no prude," but not promiscuous either when it came to physical relationships. "Lots of girls in high school are after the guys, and she wasn't that type of person," said Vicki Sparks, "although she [did have] many male friends." Jan thought that Luke Kliphuis, who had a mild "bad boy" reputation among the girls at Holland High, was the closest Betsy came to a serious boyfriend. "We used to have lunch together and stuff like that," Kliphuis said. "And there was a little slap and tickle going on, but it wasn't anything, really. We were good friends for a long time." Much of that was communal activity, the usual group of girls plus a few guy friends like Kliphuis who would join the table during their free periods. "To me, [Betsy] was good-looking, but she wasn't one of those people who augmented herself," Kliphuis said. "She didn't wear a lot of makeup, or any. She was just kind of a normal kid." He didn't find her intelligence intimidating. They had a biology class together. "She wasn't somebody who stood out in a class. She was one of those quiet people who took good notes and got all the stuff right," he said.[16]

That was perhaps the greatest difference between them. Kliphuis worked the evening shift at the Hitching Post restaurant kitchen, or at the Warm Friend Hotel as a bellhop, or at a service station pumping gas, back at a time when most stations hired men or boys to do that. His studies suffered. Working jobs during the school year and not doing well in school set him apart from Betsy and the other members of her group. "Those kids got allowances and had a lot of support," Kliphuis said. "All those girls had parents who guarded them pretty closely. . . . They were really focused on getting ahead in life." When she was fifteen, toward the end of 1962, Luke took Betsy to the Horizon formal dance at the Holland Civic Center, picking her up (he was sixteen and had his license) in his father's white Lincoln. He remembers meeting Dick Aardsma, who he recalled as nice, but "pretty intense," and really into "success through focus and stuff." Afterward, Kliphuis remembered, they went back to the Sasamoto house with Jan and her date, Allen Holleman. Whatever they had didn't last. Kliphuis may have been the unnamed subject of the poem read at Betsy's funeral about the boyfriend whose values were too worldly.[17]

By the time the next Horizon formal rolled around in June, her date was Tom Bolhuis, who says they met at a high school dance and became acquaintances, then friends. Anything more than that was precluded by the disconcerting discovery that they were second or third cousins by her maternal grandmother, Bessie Bolhuis Van Alsburg. Betsy hosted a prom pre-party at her house for twenty-one of her friends and their dates. Her mother was always putting little news snippets about family doings into the *Holland Evening Sentinel,* so it is easy to determine who was there.[18]

The friendship between Betsy and Jan deepened in high school. They mostly hung out at Betsy's house, but when they went in a group, going to a home or away basketball or football game, it was Jan's father who drove. Betsy didn't particularly like sports, Jan said, but went along for the socializing. Gradually, she and Jan became fast friends, despite their different personalities. "She was the artist," Sasamoto said. "She put the color in my world, and I think I put a little structure in hers." They were comfortable enough with each other that neither got jealous if the other spent time with different friends.

Several of Betsy's friends, including Jan, described her as artistic and "quirky," which they meant in a nice way, but in a way that set her apart from the Holland norm. "A little bit of a different stride," Jan said of Betsy. "In a lovely way. Not weird, not strange, a very light spirit." On St. Patrick's Day during their senior year, in 1965, Betsy came to school with her hair dyed green, she recalled. One of her male friends, Brad Spahr, who went to the Naval Academy after graduation, took one look at her hair and uttered an exaggerated, "Why?" Not everybody "got" her humor, Jan conceded, and this could hurt her in popularity contests, such as getting elected to the Athletic Sisters—a group of girls who wore red blazers and sold candy and Cracker Jack at the boys games—and Student Council, although she eventually was elected to the latter. "They didn't dislike her," Sasamoto said. "She just was a little different."[19]

Indeed, Jan believed that many Holland High boys found Betsy too different to be prime girlfriend material. "Betsy was different in a time when different wasn't celebrated. So a lot of guys thought she was funny and cute and smart and all that, but that wasn't the kind of girl they were looking for at that time. I don't think they valued that," she said. "The kind of guys she attracted were a little intimidated by her in some respects, because she was kooky and smart and artistic. And so she never had a problem finding someone to dance with at dances or go out with to the big dances."[20]

Peggy Wich defined *different* in Betsy's case as being artistic and saying what was on her mind. "She was authentic and had her own ideas about stuff. Interesting observations that other people didn't make," Wich said. In their senior year, she and Betsy went to visit her brother, Hank Wich, at St. Joseph's College, a Catholic liberal arts school in Rensselaer, Indiana. The Chicago Bears held their summer training camp at St. Joseph's, and the tearjerker 1971 film about the team, *Brian's Song,* was filmed on campus. Peggy was an observant Catholic and made a point, when out with Betsy, to not eat meat on Fridays, then a strict rule in the Catholic Church. "And I forgot [once] and ate a hot dog, and she said it was the high point of her life, to watch me eat a hot dog on [a] Friday," Wich said. Betsy was a notoriously bad driver, getting her license late and never having any great desire to operate a motor vehicle. "Let's put it this way," Sasamoto said. "I would always volunteer to drive. She would go, 'Why is that person honking?' And I would say, 'Maybe because you pulled out in front of him?'"[21]

But people also remembered Betsy for the best of human qualities. Jo Ann Pelon, who lived a couple doors down from Betsy on East 37th Street and was six years younger, remembered her neighbor as "smart, kind, and beautiful." Wich said her friend "was just so easy. She was a really easy person and just liked everybody. She was just easy for people to be with, and not very judgmental at all." Margo Hakken recalled that Betsy "never had any enemies, because she never said a cross word about anybody." And Sasamoto couldn't remember ever bickering or fighting with Betsy. "It was just that kind of friendship; it was give and take," she said. "We were just easy with each other." Another girl remembered her "sunny personality." For her old friends, the memories flowed like water.[22]

During her junior and senior years, she began dating Jeff Lubbers, whose father, Dr. Julius Lubbers, was a dentist who had successfully pushed for the fluoridation of Holland's drinking water. Dr. Lubbers had also graduated from Hope College, and in the same class, 1940, as Dick and Esther Aardsma. Betsy and Jeff would walk on the Lake Michigan beach near his parents' cottage just south of Camp Geneva, near the end of Riley Street. Late at night, the two of them, plus Jan and other friends, would hang out at the Howard Johnson's on South Washington Avenue, downing coffees and Cokes. Betsy was the kind of girl you wanted to marry, Lubbers said, the cute girl next door. He remembered her baggy sweaters, French beret, and "artistic" aura. "She was friendly, easygoing—just a great person," Lubbers said. Nevertheless, he did not consider her his girlfriend.[23]

There was never any doubt in Betsy's mind or anyone else's that she would go to college. But for what? She was torn between her love of English and art and her desire to work in medicine. Peggy Wich remembers her as a voracious reader, more interested in books than the Beatles or the other rock-and-roll music on the radio. Her tenth-grade English teacher was John Noe, a Marine Corps veteran of World War II who bore literal scars of battle on his face. From Noe's personal records, we know that Betsy received a C on a punctuation test and a B+ on a book report but finished the course with a straight A. She moved on to honors English in eleventh grade and achieved As there, too.[24]

But the world she saw in the news and heard about from missionaries who visited Trinity Reformed Church nagged at her and made her wonder if she should do something more relevant, something that would enable her to make her mark and ease human suffering. Dennis Wegner, her brother-in-law, recalled in 1972 that Betsy "loved America and loved its people. The fact that many people were in desperate need of food, medical attention, warmth, and understanding were sources of great pain to her." The problems were real, and she was not alone in her beliefs among her 1960s generation. It was an idealistic time.[25]

By the time she reached her junior year, Betsy had decided she wanted to become a physician. Not a nurse, mind you, the traditional route to the medical world for a female, but an MD. That was still a bold, even radical, ambition for a young woman when only about 7 percent of US medical school graduates were women. Any woman who overcame the barriers and was admitted to medical school could expect a difficult and possibly lonely four years. At one time, Sasamoto remembers, Betsy toyed with the idea of becoming a medical illustrator instead, combining two of her passions. But there seems little doubt that her overarching goal at that time was to be a physician.[26]

The pre-med sequence at Holland High, although it was not formally designated as such, consisted of biology, chemistry, and physiology, the last a difficult and challenging full-year course taught by Dirk Bloemendaal Sr., who remembered Betsy well. "That was a class that was slanted toward the top kids in school," he said. "And she was a very hard worker. Excellent student. I think I ended up giving her a straight A in the class, and it was not an easy class." Not only that, in 1965 Bloemendaal named the fourth of his five children after her, according to what Betsy told her first college roommate, Linda DenBesten. Bloemendaal trusted both Betsy and Jan to the extent of giving them the key to his classroom over winter break so they could attend to plants that were part of an experiment they were doing, to measure the effect of growth hormones on plants. "Just water my plants, too," he told them.[27] Betsy could charm and impress, not through her physical appearance—although that didn't hurt—but through her intelligence and personality.

An important part of Bloemendaal's physiology class, remembered by all his former students, was the dissection of a cat. Each pair of lab partners—for Betsy, this, of course, was Jan—received a preserved cat from a laboratory supply house and was required to do much of the dissection at home. "We worked on learning the muscles and origins and insertions," Bloemendaal said. "And then we did the circulatory system. The cats came all injected with red and blue. And the kids loved working on it." The kids might have, but their mothers often didn't appreciate what came in the door. Toshi Sasamoto made a big fuss, her daughter recalled, and so all the dissection homework was done at Betsy's home in the breezeway between the house and the garage. "Betsy and I would spend a lot of time poking around. She was always so much more meticulous than I was. . . . So I was always happy when she took it home, because I always knew she was going to be dissecting when she had time and cleaning it up. She was very careful that way," Sasamoto said. "Betsy was very, very bright, and she worked very hard. And she was very dependable. If she said she'd do something, she did it. We were perfect lab partners, because she did all the illustrations and I wrote out the technical procedures."[28]

Betsy also participated during her senior year in what was called the Cooperative Training (or Co-op) Program at Holland High, which offered what today would be called internships. She was a nursing trainee, or Pinkie (for their uniforms) at Holland Hospital, which was a few blocks up the hill from Trinity Reformed Church, where her family worshipped. Thirty-five students from Holland High, West Ottawa High School, and, for the first time, Holland Christian High School entered the program in the fall of 1964. Holland Christian, in line with the church's separatist beliefs, had previously operated its own Pinkie program apart from the two public schools. Thirty-three of the students were girls, and nursing trainees. Two were boys, and X-ray trainees. Just as the notion of female doctors puzzled many Americans in 1964, so did the idea of male nurses.[29]

It was her last English teacher at Holland High School, Olin Van Lare, who made Betsy wonder if she had made the right choice of career. She took Van Lare's English literature course the second semester of her senior year and was captivated. He became her favorite teacher, at least after Bloemendaal. Judi Jahns, in the class with Betsy, remembers Van Lare's intense love of poetry and him taking the class to Chicago to see a production of the Oliver Goldsmith play, *She Stoops to Conquer*.[30]

Everyone remembered Van Lare as a character. He had grown up in the small town of Wolcott, New York, along Lake Ontario. After graduating from Hope College in 1937 with a degree in English, and from the

University of Michigan with a master's degree in music in 1942, he had taught elsewhere for fifteen years, including in postwar Japan as the music director of the American School in Yokohama. The Holland school board hired him to teach high school English in 1957. An excellent teacher, he spoke in an epicene voice that some boys found off-putting and was prone to classroom histrionics. Van Lare referred to his students as "kiddles" in class. His will—he died an early death in 1975, at age sixty—contained a bequest for an Olin C. Van Lare Scholarship at Hope College for a deserving student, preferably from Holland High School, who wanted to pursue the study of literature. It was too late for Betsy.[31]

Betsy had a near-perfect grade point average in high school, scoring As in most of her classes and Bs only in advanced algebra, physics, gym, and in her nursing co-op program. She ranked fifth in her class and was inducted into the National Honor Society as a junior, which required a minimum 3.5 grade point average and the good opinion of one's teachers. Her SAT scores were 625 verbal and 598 math under the old scoring system. In the spring of 1965, she was one of several Holland High students, including Jan Sasamoto, to win Michigan Competitive Scholarships, a generous state grant that could be used at either public or private colleges in the state.[32]

She was going to Hope College and Jan was going to the University of Michigan. Betsy also had applied to Michigan, had been accepted, and wanted badly to go. The girls had already talked about rooming together on campus. But in Hope College families, the pressure to go to Hope can be intense. In Betsy's case, her mother, father, older sister, and several aunts, uncles, and cousins had gone to Hope. They argued, they negotiated, and she finally agreed to go if she could live on campus. She could have done worse. Hope was strong in pre-med. Her career goals would not suffer, and at least two of her friends would be there, Leslie Nienhuis and Margo Hakken. Betsy told Linda DenBesten that in the end she agreed to go to Hope to please her parents. They, in turn, took out loans to pay the extra cost of the private school.[33]

The culture of the 1960s had barely touched Holland in 1965, but that was about to change. Radio from Chicago brought that world to the transistor radios of Holland teenagers. In the spring of 1966, the director of the seventh-grade band at E. E. Fell Junior High felt the change in the air and arranged a Top 40 radio hit from the previous fall, "Hang On, Sloopy" by the McCoys, for the marching band to play during that May's Tulip Time parades, instead of a traditional Sousa march.

Something indeed was in the air. A group of antiwar protesters from Hope College joined one of those same Tulip Time parades that spring, demanding an end to the Vietnam War. Anyone who thought Hope College would stand as a bulwark against a fast-changing society would be sorely disappointed. Anyone who expected it to be as liberal as the University of Michigan would likewise be frustrated.

Betsy Aardsma, 1969
COURTESY OF MICHIGANENSIAN YEARBOOK

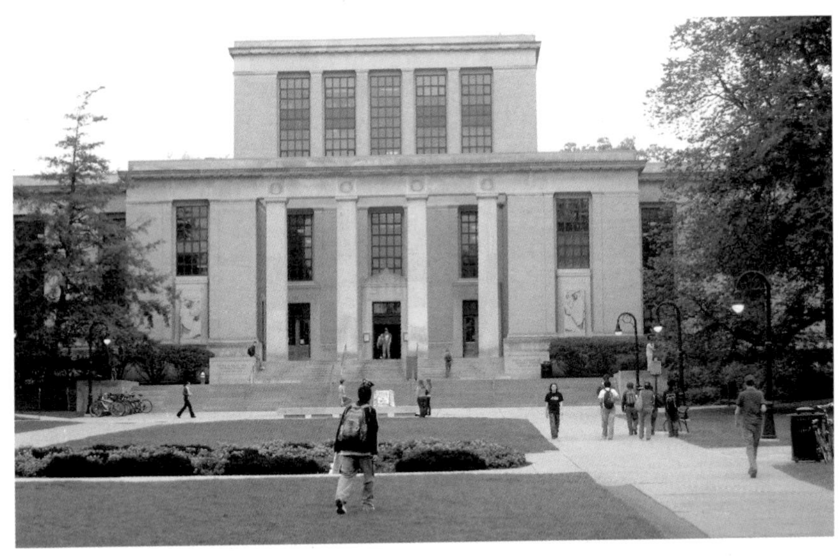

Pattee Library from a distance
DAVID DEKOK

Entrance to the murder site, Pattee Library
DAVID DEKOK

Joao Uafinda, witness to the events immediately after the murder of Betsy
COURTESY OF RARE BOOKS AND SPECIAL COLLECTIONS, UNIVERSITY OF ROCHESTER ARCHIVES

Richard Sanders Allen, witness to the events immediately after the murder of Betsy, with his grandson, circa 1969
COURTESY OF DICK ALLEN

Marilee Erdely, witness to the events immediately after the murder of Betsy
COURTESY OF HOPEWELL HIGH SCHOOL, ALIQUIPPA, PENNSYLVANIA

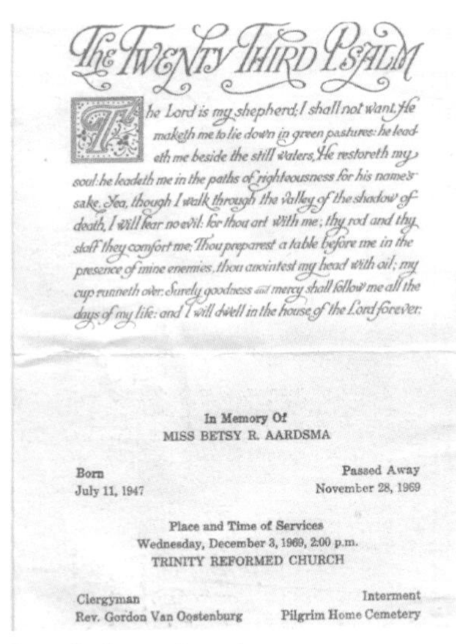

The Twenty Third Psalm

The Lord is my shepherd; I shall not want. He maketh me to lie down in green pastures: he leadeth me beside the still waters. He restoreth my soul: he leadeth me in the paths of righteousness for his name's sake. Yea, though I walk through the valley of the shadow of death, I will fear no evil: for thou art with me; thy rod and thy staff they comfort me. Thou preparest a table before me in the presence of mine enemies: thou anointest my head with oil; my cup runneth over. Surely goodness and mercy shall follow me all the days of my life: and I will dwell in the house of the Lord forever.

In Memory Of
MISS BETSY R. AARDSMA

Born	Passed Away
July 11, 1947	November 28, 1969

Place and Time of Services
Wednesday, December 3, 1969, 2:00 p.m.
TRINITY REFORMED CHURCH

Clergyman	Interment
Rev. Gordon Van Oostenburg	Pilgrim Home Cemetery

Betsy's funeral card
COURTESY OF ANDREA MARCHAND

nent to Labor's 40. It
fourth-straight victor

Friends of Co…ed Question In Stabbing at Penn Sta

…IVERSITY PARK, Pa.— … — State Police were …tioning "a long list of …" Sunday in the mys… …s death of a Pennsylva… …tate University graduate …t whose body was found … floor of Pattee Library.

…ce said they had al… questioned a number of …s, most of them Penn students, but had filed …arges in the death of Aardsma, 22, of Hol… …ich.

…body was found on the … floor of the campus li… Friday evening by an …ified student. State Po… …id the girl's body was … with blood.

…e County Coroner Rob… …ff said an autopsy … the girl died of a stab … of the chest. No weap… found near her body.

Betsy Aardsma

A State Police spokesman said 15 officers had been assigned to the case.

"There is a long list of people we are talking to and that will take several days," he said.

THE DEAD GIR… Mrs. Carol Wagne… land, said she and … bers of the Aards… had talked to Bets… phone on Thanksg… that "everything w…

Mrs. Wagner sai… ter did not go home … gan for Thanksgivin… the Christmas recess … Penn State on Dec.

A graduate of th… sity of Michigan, Mi… ma was doing grad… in art and English … State.

State Police said … have been working … search paper in the l…

Mrs. Wagner said h… lived in a dormitory … campus and was en… David Wright, a … Penn State's Mil… School of Medic…

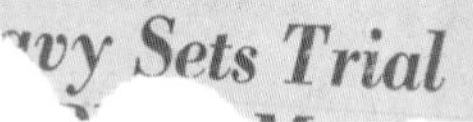

…vy Sets Trial

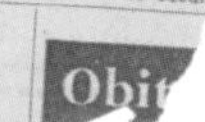

Obi…

Photo of a story about Betsy torn from the newspaper
FROM THE AUTHOR'S COLLECTION

Close-up of Betsy's grave, Pilgrim Home Cemetery
DAVID DEKOK

Aardsma Family, 1967 (not pictured: Carole Aardsma)

TRINITY REFORMED CHURCH

Betsy at age 16

COURTESY OF BOBBI FREY

Betsy and friends, Holland High School graduation photo, 1965: from left, Peggy Wich, Margo Hakken, Vicky Lewis, Nancy Gebben, Jan Sasamoto, Judi Jahns, Betsy Aardsma, Barb Stoner, and RuthAnn VanDyke

COURTESY OF PHYLLIS VANDENBERG

David L. Wright, York Community High School Y's Tales yearbook picture, 1965
COURTESY OF YORK COMMUNITY HIGH SCHOOL LIBRARY, ELMHURST, ILLINOIS

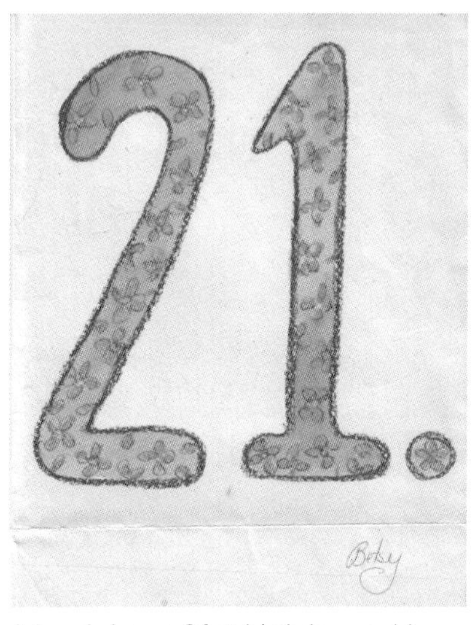

A hand-drawn 21st birthday card by Betsy for Andie
COURTESY OF ANDREA MARCHAND

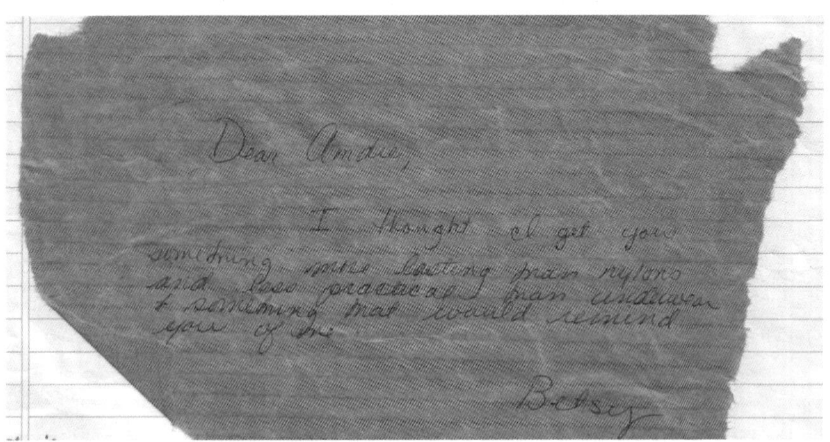

Dear Andie,

I thought I'd get you something more lasting than nylons and less practical than underwear & something that would remind you of me.

Betsy

A note from Betsy to Andie Yunker on her birthday
COURTESY OF ANDREA MARCHAND

Lt. William Kimmel, Pennsylvania State Police

PSP YEARBOOK PHOTO

Mary L. Willard, crime scene analyst

COURTESY OF JOSEPH WILLARD

Sgt. George H. Keibler at his retirement dinner, 1983

COURTESY OF GEORGE H. KEIBLER

Mike Simmers (second from left) subdues a demonstrator on the PSU campus, April 21,1970
DICK BROWN

Pennsylvania State Police "War Room," Boucke Building, PSU campus
PENNSYLVANIA STATE POLICE

CHAPTER 15

Way Station to the World

We are people of this generation, bred in at least modest comfort, housed now in universities, looking uncomfortably to the world we inherit.

—Tom Hayden, opening lines of the Port Huron Statement, Students for a Democratic Society, 1962

At Hope College, Betsy moved into Room 69 on the third floor of Voorhees Hall, an aging, creaking, three-story dormitory for women students built of red-orange bricks in 1907 in the style of traditional Dutch architecture in the Netherlands. Her freshman-year roommate was Linda DenBesten from South Holland, Illinois, a Chicago suburb that was another center of Dutch settlement and only six miles from the Roseland neighborhood of Chicago, where Betsy's father grew up.

Linda remembers Betsy as an easy roommate, willing to give her first choice of bunks and seemingly unconcerned about her untidy ways. "I would come in from class and I would always take a nap in the middle of the afternoon. I would flop down on her bed," she said, referring to the bottom bunk. More than once, Betsy came back to find Linda sleeping on her bed. "I'd hear her kind of groan," DenBesten said. "But then she'd just go up on my bunk. If I had garbage all over the place, which I frequently did, she ignored it." Musing about Betsy's fate, she wondered, "Who could she have annoyed? She just never annoyed anyone." Linda found her bright and artistic, as did most everyone else, and an interesting conversationalist about nearly anything, but especially literature and theater. The only thing that bored Betsy was dorm gossip. "That was just not her thing," her former roommate said.[1]

She was not a complete grind, however, and her first year included typical college activities and hijinks. Margo Hakken, Betsy's classmate at Holland High School, lived at home and commuted to classes at Hope. But she often hung out with Betsy and other friends in Voorhees, and she recalled the pranks, such as the time juniors and seniors in the dorm put wet leaves in the beds of first-years. Betsy and some of her classmates retaliated later in the semester. They broke off icicles that hung from the third-floor roof, put them in the beds of their tormentors, and then taped the doors shut so the icicles would have plenty of time to melt.[2]

Betsy dated a number of men that year, including George Arwady, a budding journalist and editor of the Hope College student newspaper, the *Anchor*, who remembered her as "smart and pretty." He recalled being in an honors English class with Betsy that employed dance movements as part of the learning process. She also dated a boy named Darryl and had an angry breakup with him that her mother remembered after her death, even though Betsy by that time had long since reconciled with him. Tom Bolhuis, her date for the Horizon summer formal in 1964, was also a freshman at Hope and ran into her once or twice, although they never went out again. DenBesten said Betsy dated a lot of guys and wasn't exclusive with any of them. That was the pattern of her young life.[3]

Young women at Hope College in the fall of 1965 were still bound by rules from a different era, which were enforced by the housemother in their dorm. Women students—this didn't apply to men—had to be back in their dorms by 9:00 p.m. on weeknights, with lights out at 10:00 or 10:30 p.m., DenBesten remembered. On weekends, women students could stay out until 11:30 p.m. "The idea was that if the women were in, the guys couldn't get into too much mischief," she said. All first-years, female or male, had to attend 8:00 a.m. chapel services at least two days of the week. That was an improvement, depending on how you looked at it, from earlier decades, when daily attendance was required. Men were barred from ever going past the lobby in Voorhees, except on homecoming weekend, when male family members and friends could visit the girls in their rooms. It wasn't unusual to see couples making out in the darkness outside the main entrance of the dorm. DenBesten remembers visiting Columbia University in New York in the summer of 1967 and wondering at the lack of amorous couples outside the dorms. "I later learned that men were allowed in women's rooms and everything became immediately clear!" she said. Women students at Hope were even barred from traveling alone to other cities unless they could provide the name of a relative they were visiting. The paperwork alone was daunting.[4]

Betsy Aardsma certainly had doubts about staying in Holland and enrolling at Hope College. But she was fortunate to arrive at a unique time, when Hope was slowly moving toward a more culturally and religiously diverse faculty, a new moderation on student life issues, and a student body that was both larger and included students, especially from the East Coast, who were political liberals and willing to apply their Christian principles to trying to solve America's social problems. Betsy Aardsma, so eager to embrace the world outside of Holland, found herself shaped by these new liberal currents at Hope College. She gravitated toward the civil rights struggle and opposition to the Vietnam War.

The man behind Hope's transformation was Calvin A. Vander Werf, who became president of the college in 1963. He had been an organic chemistry professor and chairman of the chemistry department at the University of Kansas in Lawrence for more than twenty years. Even though he was a Hope graduate, the valedictorian and commencement orator of the Class of 1937, and the son of a Reformed Church minister from Wisconsin, Vander Werf and his wife, Rachel, had belonged to a liberal Congregationalist church in Lawrence. She had been raised as a Quaker. They were deeply committed to the cause of civil rights and improving the lives of black people and had been frustrated for years by the stubborn persistence of segregation in Lawrence in hotels, restaurants, and movie theaters. Vander Werf and others in the Kansas chemistry department recruited blacks from the South as graduate students in the 1950s, and several received master's or doctoral degrees. Perhaps his most famous black undergraduate recruit was the Philadelphia high school basketball star Wilt Chamberlain. Together, Calvin and Rachel

Vander Werf founded the Lawrence League for the Practice of Democracy to promote civil rights. With the League's help—this was Rachel's project—the local YWCA opened the first interracial residence for students at Kansas.[5]

Vander Werf carried out a number of reforms at Hope College before, during, and after Betsy's time there. His mantra was that "piety is no substitute for excellence." As one geology professor, J. Cotter Tharin, put it, "He took Hope College from a college that was somewhat sleepy and backward and tried to make it into a first-rate liberal arts college." Vander Werf believed that religious-based liberal arts education was an antidote to many of the world's ills, whether racial discrimination or nuclear proliferation. But during his tenure, he took the control of the college board of trustees away from the Reformed Church clergy and gave it over to businesspeople and other non-clerics who could provide more of the financial support Hope College needed in order to change and grow. He also hired the first non-Protestant faculty, including Catholics and nonbelievers (the first Jew was not hired until 1971, after he left), and strengthened Hope's already strong reputation in the natural sciences.[6]

But the changes students remembered most applied directly to their own lives. Vander Werf ended the ban on dancing on campus (1963); opened the college library on Sundays (1967); invited black comedian and social activist Dick Gregory to speak in Dimnent Chapel, where he delivered a mildly profane, eye-opening look at the black condition in America (1968); eliminated mandatory chapel attendance for students (1970); and started the ball rolling on the end of parietal hours for women students (it finally happened in 1972, after he left). Parietal hours were rules governing when women students could be visited by men students.[7]

Vander Werf also hired Reverend William "Bill" Hillegonds as college chaplain and alter ego. Hillegonds opened a draft counseling office in the basement of Dimnent Chapel, where any young man, whether a Hope student or not, could go to learn his options if facing military induction for the Vietnam War. In the spring of 1966, when some four hundred thousand US troops had already been sent to South Vietnam and heavy bombing of North Vietnam had commenced, he brokered negotiations between thirty students and the Holland city attorney that allowed the students to carry signs protesting the war in one of the Tulip Time parades.

Hillegonds found himself at the center of Hope's social, racial, and political tensions, striving to keep the lid on the cauldron while still letting it simmer and endeavoring to stay in the middle of the debate. It wasn't always easy. Many more black students were recruited to Hope during Vander Werf's tenure, which Hillegonds considered a good thing, but they were not the "scared . . . Uncle Tom types" of the late 1940s when he was a Hope student. "We had blacks that were very aggressive, very hostile, very suspicious," he said, adding that many of them especially distrusted white clergy. "We had strikes on campus, we had mass meetings in the chapel, we had late-night sessions trying to keep the peace." He understood. And there were First World problems on his plate, too—students who would rather be marching with Dr. Martin Luther King Jr. but couldn't find the nerve. White, middle-class young men came to Hillegonds in anguish over the conventional futures their parents demanded of them, saying they wanted a chance to change the world, not work in their father's insurance agency. He heard it all, and listened with a kind ear—unless he thought a student was bullshitting him.[8]

Conservatives on the board of trustees and in the Reformed Church were agitated by many of the changes, and faculty, especially in the social sciences, sometimes felt left out of Vander Werf's promotion of the natural sciences or steamrollered by his personal style. One political science professor, Al Vanderbush, who was a liberal Democrat, criticized Vander Werf for allegedly wanting to turn Hope College into "the Colgate . . . or Reed College" of the Midwest, which he felt would hurt average students. But his harshest criticisms were reserved for what he saw as Vander Werf's tendency to be a self-centered autocrat. "He didn't work with people; people had to work with him," he said. Vander Werf ultimately was deposed—not exactly fired, but not exactly urged to stay on, either. But from 1963 to 1970, he changed Hope for the better, and most of his reforms were not rescinded by his less-contentious successors. It was Calvin Vander Werf's Hope College that greeted Betsy Aardsma in the fall of 1965, doing much to turn her focus to the problems of the outside world.[9]

For all of Betsy's high school dreams of going to medical school, she seems to have changed her mind by the end of her freshman year at Hope. Her transcript shows her taking classic pre-med courses only in her freshman year, when she had two semesters of chemistry and one of zoology. There were no biology, physics, or math courses on her transcript. She took far more English, art, and German than anything remotely related to getting accepted to medical school. Linda DenBesten says Betsy did well in the pre-med courses she took but decided partway into her first year that she liked her English courses a whole lot more. The idea of being a physician never completely left her conversations with friends, but she took no further concrete steps toward medicine.[10]

DenBesten wondered if social pressures and conventional expectations had worked against Betsy's dream. In retrospect, she considered her friend a feminist, even though the word wasn't yet part of the common vocabulary in 1966. "She wanted to be a doctor. I think that's pretty feminist [for] the time. And then she talked about being a lawyer. That never would have worked out," DenBesten said. "I thought it was kind of gutsy to say you were going to be a doctor. I didn't know anybody else who was going to be a doctor. In the [pre-med] classes she was in, she was one of the few women." Most women she knew at Hope planned to be teachers. Betsy wanted to be different, but literature—a safe, conventional choice for a woman in 1966—won out.[11]

It was probably Al Vanderbush who got her thinking about politics. Vanderbush was a crusty former football coach with short-cropped hair and a trademark bow tie. He had morphed into one of the best and most influential political science professors the school had ever known, despite not having a doctoral degree. His gift was for teaching, not scholarship. A liberal Democrat and devotee of the New Deal, he turned his National Government classes into spirited dissections of the workings of governments and politicians, and made it all absorbingly interesting. With his piercing eyes and near permanent scowl, Vanderbush radiated intensity. Like Professor Kingsfield in *The Paper Chase,* a movie that came out a few years later, he used the Socratic Method in his classes, asking probing questions of his students. Woe unto he or (rarely) she who arrived unprepared to join in the discussion. That could trigger a volcanic tirade about "wasting your parents' money."[12]

Betsy Aardsma and her high school friend Leslie Nienhuis sat together in the front row of Vanderbush's classroom in Van Raalte Hall, and they were always prepared. "We just had a ball in that class," Nienhuis said. "We both did well and we enjoyed him." It is quite likely that Betsy's mental dance with the idea of becoming a lawyer grew out of Vanderbush and his National Government class. Betsy was politically liberal, at least by Hope College standards, according to DenBesten. "She wasn't a political nut, but she could talk on any topic; politics was just one of them."[13]

Betsy spent the summer of 1966 exploring her new interest in public service and mission work. She participated in a program to teach art to low-income black children in Grand Rapids, a city about seven times the size of Holland and twenty-five miles away. Few details of her participation in this program are known, but it was mentioned to reporters after her death by people who knew her and later confirmed by Dennis Wegner, her brother-in-law.

Also that summer, she traveled on a World Deputation Mission from her church to the Mescalero Apache Reservation in New Mexico, about two hundred miles south of Albuquerque. Trinity Reformed Church provided mission support to Mescalero Reformed Church, one of five Reformed churches serving Native American communities in the American West. The church had three pastors, Reverend Frank Love, Reverend Herman Van Galen, and Reverend Robert Zapp. Love, who was an Indian himself and a graduate of Western Theological Seminary in Holland, said the poverty on the reservation was profound. The federal government had built "some pretty nice homes" for the Mescaleros in the 1960s, he said, but that barely made a dent in the problem. When church youth groups came to help, they would typically work in the church's Vacation Bible School or summer camp or help repair or paint buildings, Van Galen said.

That fall, Betsy made a presentation to her church about the trip, as did three other young people from the congregation who had visited other mission churches. She thought about joining the Peace Corps when she graduated from college.[14]

When they were all back in Holland for the summer, Betsy and her friends did what most young women their age did: They went out dancing. She and Jan Sasamoto were still inseparable, and they were often joined by Peggy Wich, Judi Jahns, and Leslie Nienhuis. One of their favorite destinations was the Edgar Allan Poe Club, a dry teen hangout that occupied the former Nibbelink-Notier Funeral Home at the corner of 9th Street and River Avenue, next to the National Guard Armory. The proprietor was Verne C. Kupelian, a former history teacher at Holland High School who opened the club in 1965. He kept it open until 1968, when he moved back to his hometown of Columbus, Ohio. Kupelian was another favorite teacher of Betsy and her friends, and he would remember them fondly four decades later. The Poe Club was open to young people between the ages of seventeen and twenty-four. On a typical night, he drew two hundred young people, but on a good night, when a popular band was playing, he could draw as many as six or seven hundred customers from as far away as Muskegon and Grand Rapids. Sometimes Kupelian hired bands from Chicago with Top 40 hits, such as the Buckinghams ("Kind of a Drag") or New Colony Six.[15]

Betsy and her friends roamed far and wide to dance. Jan Sasamoto recalled driving as long as an hour, or even ninety minutes on occasion. But often, if they were headed out of Holland, it was to Saugatuck, a rollicking, gay-friendly resort town just ten miles away by highway but light-years distant from Holland in social attitudes. Downtown Saugatuck, which was built along the Kalamazoo River about a mile before it entered Lake Michigan, was full of bars like Coral Gables that offered dancing and were open seven days a week. In summer, the village was choked with visitors, both straight and gay, from Chicago and elsewhere in the Midwest. Some drove there and others arrived by boat, docking at their favorite riverside watering hole.

Betsy and her friends were still underage, but Kupelian also had a summer teen club, Noah's Ark, in Saugatuck in a shed used to store cabin cruisers and sailboats during the winter. In the summer it was empty. One side of the building was open to the river, and the noise from the bands tended to annoy cottagers in Saugatuck's sister city of Douglas, on the other bank. "It was a corrugated building, and the water magnified the sound," Kupelian said. Betsy and her friends would go there, sometimes after a visit to Laketown Beach, which was between Holland and Saugatuck, or Oval Beach in Douglas.

Kupelian didn't remember Betsy for her beauty so much as the way she was. "Her personality was super, and everybody gravitated around her," he said. He thought for a moment, then added: "And you know, those kind of people probably never saw anything evil in anybody."[16]

In the fall of 1966, Betsy began her sophomore year at Hope College with a new roommate and a new dorm, Durfee Hall, just down the street from Voorhees. She was still on good terms with Linda DenBesten, who moved to Phelps Hall, and would have been willing to room with her again. "But she said, 'I just think it's important to have lots of experiences.' So she roomed with somebody else," DenBesten said. Their friendship endured. Betsy was a bridesmaid in Linda's wedding in June 1968 and gave her one of her paintings as a gift. Linda came to Betsy's funeral eighteen months later.

Abandoning pre-med and changing her major to English, Betsy dove into humanities courses, studio art, and art history. She never took another science course. Even with her dedication to her studies, though, there was still time for fun. She joined the cast of *Winnie the Pooh,* the sophomore class play in the annual Nykerk Cup competition at Hope. Nykerk pitted the sophomore and freshman girls against each other in singing, oration, and drama. Betsy's class lost that year. Hope's boys had the Pull, a brutal and physically demanding tug-of-war across the Black River between carefully selected and trained teams from the freshman and sophomore classes. Each puller had a reinforced pit about two feet deep in which he could brace himself and a Morale Girl at his side to cheer him on, wipe his brow, and give him water during the ordeal. The event could last for hours before one team broke and was dragged across the river. As much as Hope College tried to combat racism during the Vander Werf years, feminism was definitely a novelty. There were still well-defined roles and rules for men and women students.[17]

Student demonstrations on the Hope campus were rare but not unknown. In November 1966, approximately forty women students "slipped out of the back door of Voorhees Hall at midnight," the *Anchor* reported, and walked to the nearby home of President Vander Werf to protest the lack of fire safety in their dorm. They sang Christmas carols and chanted, "We want fire escapes!" They had a point: Voorhees had a single, inadequate fire escape, plus a fire alarm system that could not be heard on all floors. A request from students on the second and third floors for rope ladders for emergency escape had been turned down, according to students interviewed by the *Anchor*, because the college administration feared they would be used to sneak out after closing hours. Vander Werf later claimed to have slept through the commotion. The Voorhees housemother was furious, and the dean of women, Isla Van Eenenaam, condemned the "thoughtless, inconsiderate, and immature way of getting their point across" used by the girls, who, she said, should have gone through "proper channels." She vowed to discipline them for leaving the dorm after closing hours.[18]

DenBesten said that the longer Betsy was at Hope, the more she wanted to leave. She applied to transfer to the University of Michigan in Ann Arbor during her sophomore year and moved home for the second semester to save money. Both her brother-in-law, Dennis Wegner, and her close friend, Peggy Wich, said she transferred for "academic reasons." Leslie Nienhuis believed it was because Hope College did not have what she wanted but was a good place to go for a couple of years. David L. Wright, who would become her boyfriend at Michigan, believes it was for the richer course selection and the much larger campus and student population. "For a better education," he said.

In February 1967, the *Anchor* ran a story examining the reasons that students gave for transferring from Hope to other schools. The number-one reason cited was the Hope academic program, notably the limited course selection and too many required courses. Second was the "all-encompassing regulations," i.e., the nannylike regulation of women students, on and off campus. Third was the quality of the campus social life. Students who were surveyed commented that if one was in a relationship, social life at Hope could be fine. If you weren't, it was a bore, and Holland had little to offer. All of these applied to Betsy Aardsma to some extent. She was eager to leave.

And there were personal reasons as well. Dick Aardsma, her father, who was a serious alcoholic, separated from his family in 1967 and moved to Douglas, the small town across the river from Saugatuck. He was fifty-one years old. The reason may have been his alcoholism, or that may only have pointed to something else. The full story remains a deeply guarded family secret. In the fall of the year, he wrote out and signed a will at the office of a family law attorney in Plainwell, Michigan, in which he stated that he lived in Douglas and was leaving all of his estate to his wife, Esther; if she was dead, his estate was to be divided equally among the four children. He named Betsy the executrix of his estate, passing over Carole, the eldest child. If Betsy was dead (a routine provision in a will), the executrix would be his lawyer, not another family member.[19]

The summer of 1967 was the Summer of Love in San Francisco, a flowering of psychedelic rock music and hippie life, but in Holland it began as just another West Michigan scorcher, hot and humid and, for Betsy, filled with longing for Ann Arbor. She worked at least two jobs to raise money for school. One was at the Wooden Shoe Factory, an old-line Holland tourist attraction that actually did carve wooden shoes to sell to tourists and the Dutch Dancers at local high schools. One of Betsy's jobs was to run out and slap Wooden Shoe Factory bumper stickers on cars in the parking lot. Her other job, later in the summer, was at the H. J. Heinz pickle factory, where her grandfather, John Van Alsburg, had been a foreman on the ketchup line in the early years of the twentieth century, before becoming a coal dealer. Heinz only made pickles and pickle relish at the Holland plant by this time.[20]

It was miserable work, made tolerable only by its short-term nature. Green season, when the regional cucumber harvest was in progress, began in late summer and lasted three to four weeks. Truckload after truckload of "cukes" arrived daily at the plant. They soaked in huge wooden vats of brine before being turned into dill pickles, gherkins, and other condiments. Heinz hired large numbers of temporary workers during green season, often young people eager to earn some summer cash. A typical job was to stand on the line for a ten-hour shift (there were short breaks) and shove pickles in jars as they passed on the conveyor belt. You could never escape the smell, which was overpowering. When the shift ended, every piece of clothing you wore smelled like pickles.[21]

One wonders why Betsy felt the urgent need to earn money, since she was moving to a state school, albeit a great one, that cost considerably less than Hope College. Total tuition, room, and board for an in-state undergraduate at the University of Michigan was $1,400 in the 1967–68 school year, while at Hope it would have been $2,100. Were her parents unhappy about her change of schools? Did they refuse to pay, or pay as much? Or was this tied to the Aardsma family turmoil and worries that her father might lose his job? Perhaps she was simply being a good daughter and helping out with the cost. Whatever the reason, Betsy transferred to the University of Michigan and was accepted into the honors program. She made plans to move to Ann Arbor and began picking out her courses from the plethora of choices.

It was a strange summer in many ways, and Betsy was probably glad when it came to an end. What normally made the hot and humid Holland summer bearable—few people then had home air-conditioning—was the beautiful Lake Michigan beaches. She and her friends could be at Oval Beach, Laketown Beach, Ottawa Beach, or Tunnel Park in a half-hour or less, and often were—but not this year. On June 15, 1967, a scientist from the US Water Pollution Control Administration was flying over the lake looking for pollution sources when he spotted an endless white carpet of dead fish, all belly-up. The carpet was about fifty feet wide and stretched nearly forty miles, between South Haven and Muskegon. Holland was in the middle. The dead fish were alewives, a silvery member of the herring family, and the wind was blowing them toward shore. Within days, beaches up and down the Michigan coast were fouled by billions of dead alewives. Many also drifted through the channel at Ottawa Beach into Lake Macatawa. The stench was unbearable, extending a mile or more inland. Then the wind shifted and the dead alewives began piling up on Chicago beaches. It was like a biblical plague, and all that could be done was to bulldoze them into trenches.[22]

The fish were not the only catastrophe in Michigan that summer. In late July, a raid by Detroit police on a speakeasy where a welcome-home party was under way for two black Vietnam veterans triggered a week of rioting that engulfed the state's largest city, and ultimately led to forty-three deaths and untold looting and property damage. It was one of the worst urban upheavals in American history. Governor George Romney, father of Mitt, sent thousands of troops from the Michigan National Guard, including Company B from Holland, to help the Detroit police. Company B was "assigned to a completely burned-out riot area to protect firemen from sniper fire and to guard against looting," the *Holland Evening Sentinel* reported. The paper's first major headline on the rioting, NEGROES ON RAMPAGE IN DETROIT, was spread across the top of page one on July 24. The gulf between white and black residents of Michigan was wide and unyielding. President Lyndon B. Johnson, at Romney's request, also sent units from the 82nd Airborne Division—federal troops—to back up the National Guard. The show of force ended the riots by July 28. It was little wonder that young Americans like Betsy Aardsma were "looking uneasily" to the world they stood to inherit.[23]

CHAPTER 16

A Desirable Young Woman

Betsy Aardsma was not the only member of her extended family to enroll at the University of Michigan in the fall of 1967. Her second cousin, Chris Van Allsburg, the future author and illustrator of such popular works of childhood fantasy as *Jumanji* (1982) and *The Polar Express* (1985), both Caldecott Medal winners for their illustrations, started there as a freshman, majoring in art. Neither knew the other very well. The son of a Grand Rapids dairy owner, Van Allsburg (his branch of the family spelled it with two Ls) said the two families were not close, even though the ties are mentioned in the 1953 obituary of John D. Van Alsburg, Betsy's maternal grandfather, and in the Van Allsburg Family genealogy on file in the Herrick District Library in Holland. Some families just drift apart, and this apparently was one of them.[1]

Arriving at the University of Michigan in the fall of 1967, Betsy would have realized almost immediately that she wasn't in provincial Michigan anymore. This was a big school, with nearly forty-five thousand students. The Doors played the homecoming dance on October 20, renowned in the band's history as a spectacularly bad performance by a very drunk Jim Morrison. Many of the five thousand students in the Intramural Sports Building left in disgust. One student, though, was enthralled by Morrison's stumbling, incoherent performance. Jim Osterberg, later Iggy Pop of the Stooges, credited the birth of his punk rock persona to that show. He, like Morrison, would end up in the Rock and Roll Hall of Fame. It was all part of the craziness of University of Michigan homecoming, which in those years could feature go-go girls, elephant races with real elephants, and a big, loud parade through the streets of Ann Arbor. There was something for everybody. Those who didn't like the electric rock of The Doors could have heard folksinger Buffy Sainte-Marie perform that weekend in an Ann Arbor coffeehouse.[2]

But Ann Arbor and the Michigan campus were not just rock and roll. They were politics, too, deeply left-wing student radical politics. Here was where Students for a Democratic Society (SDS) was founded in 1960, and where its members organized the first teach-in against the Vietnam War in March 1965. (Teach-ins were originally somewhat similar to debates, with both sides represented, but evolved into something more like a campaign rally.) SDS leaders Tom Hayden, Carl Oglesby, Bill Ayers, and Rennie Davis, among others, were students here at one time or another in the 1960s. Hayden, editor of the *Michigan Daily,* the student newspaper, authored the Port Huron Statement, adopted in 1962 as the SDS manifesto. He and Davis were among the Chicago Seven, radicals put on trial in 1969 for allegedly conspiring to disrupt the Democratic National Convention in Chicago the previous year. Ayers, who was a national leader of the violent SDS Weather Underground faction, went on the lam for a time with his lover and later wife, Bernardine Dohrn, and spent most of his later life as a respected academic in Chicago. His younger brother, Rick, also a Michigan student in the 1960s, was briefly the lover of Gilda Radner, an acting student at Michigan from 1964 to 1969, and later, a member of the original cast of the long-running NBC late-night comedy show, *Saturday Night Live.* It remained for the director Lawrence Kasdan (Michigan '70) to memorialize his fellow radicals at U of M, capturing their Reagan-era angst and guilt in his 1983 film, *The Big Chill.*[3]

We know how Betsy Aardsma felt during her first weeks at Michigan because of a letter she wrote in September to her high school friend Peggy Wich. She missed her friends at Hope College and was surprised to find that Ann Arbor wasn't necessarily the modern-day Athens she seems to have expected. "Intellectually," Betsy wrote, "this place is not as alive as it should be. I run into asses every day. Michigan seems to have a good share of university zombies and fact regurgitators. It also has a good number of acutely aware people. That's the wonderful part of it; it has a good number of almost any classification." She admitted to veering from being happy and excited about her new world to feeling lonesome amid her forty-five thousand fellow students. She also worried about the tougher academic standards at Michigan.

Betsy told Peggy she was planning to go to "some damn fraternity orgy" that night, even though she didn't expect to enjoy herself. "I don't make that kind of scene very well," she admitted. A friend named Bill, apparently an old boyfriend from Hope College, had not contacted her since he, too, had transferred to Michigan. That left her feeling both let down and relieved; relieved, because she dreaded getting involved with him, which she was certain would only lead to "an emotional disaster. And yet I feel like I'm being cheated." Betsy liked the attention from men that she received but was wary of letting anyone, male or female, stand in the way of the life she wanted. She wasn't cruel—no one ever accused her of that—but she wanted a regular infusion of new friends and experiences. Sometimes old friends or old places fell by the wayside.

But old ghosts sometimes returned. Betsy told Peggy that she had resumed going out with Darryl, the young man from Hope College with whom she had had an angry, dramatic breakup during the second semester of her freshman year. "He's at Michigan, too," she wrote, "and he has also changed. He is a beautiful person. The fact that my parents don't approve adds a certain intrigue to it all. Damn—why can't I fall in love with a more sensible type?"[4]

Her roommate at Michigan was Andrea Yunker from Sturgis, Michigan, a small town of about ten thousand located a hundred miles west of Ann Arbor, near the Indiana border. They lived in the Oxford Houses, which opened in 1963 and housed about four hundred women students in seven, modern-style buildings. Betsy and Andie were randomly assigned as roommates but stayed together for the next two years. Both were English majors, although they shared no classes. "Oh, we got along great," Andie said. "I had a little motorcycle and sometimes she would ride on the back. I feel like I got along great with her."[5]

Every young man who met Betsy was crazy about her, Andie recalled. Her friend was pretty, if not drop-dead gorgeous, and was smart, provocative, and interesting. Even though she had mild acne scarring on her face,

Betsy could "cover it up with a great big smile. I don't think I ever saw her use any kind of makeup," Andie said. She and Betsy talked about boys while they smoked cigarettes in their dorm room. "I never considered her a saint," Andie told a reporter many years later. "She didn't carry herself that way." As Jan Sasamoto had said about her high school years, Betsy was no prude, but not promiscuous, either. She was a normal college girl, trying things out, sometimes making mistakes, and unwilling to settle down with any one man. Jeff Lubbers, one of her prom dates at Holland High School, was also a junior at Michigan, where he was majoring in pre-med. He lived off-campus in an apartment but would run into Betsy now and then, walking around campus. They got together two or three times at parties and once at his apartment, but that was all, much to his regret.[6]

In the spring of 1968 she also dated Elbert Magoon, whose mother, Johanna Meijer Magoon, was one of the founders of the Meijer Markets/Thrifty Acres chain in Michigan. By that time, the Magoons had been cut out of the company by Fredric Meijer, Elbert's uncle. Magoon, who became an ophthalmologist, recalled taking Betsy to a dance on their first date and on a couple of movie dates, but the relationship didn't last long. Like so many who knew Betsy, he had warm memories of her.[7]

Betsy's friendship with Jan Sasamoto hit a brief rough patch when she transferred to Michigan. As high school seniors, they had talked about rooming together, but then Betsy acceded to her parents' demands and went to Hope College while Jan went off to Ann Arbor. They saw each other during breaks and summer vacation during their freshman and sophomore years. They both took summer school classes at Hope College after their sophomore year, leaving "Hi!" notes on each other's cars. But by the time they were juniors and living on the same campus, their worlds had changed, and a number of factors conspired to limit their time together and, at least for a time, put a damper on their once-intense friendship.

Jan had joined the Alpha Gamma Delta sorority and lived in the chapter house at 1322 Hill Street, not that far on foot from Oxford Houses. Betsy was not a fan of either sororities or fraternities, considered by many students of the time to be über-establishment and decidedly uncool, and resisted being drawn into that scene. Ironically, Jan did not see herself as a rah-rah sorority girl either, viewing membership mainly as a better housing option than dorms or off-campus apartments. She never tried to recruit Betsy to join Alpha Gamma Delta. But another important factor was that Jan now had a steady boyfriend, her future husband, Jim Brandt. They began dating during the second semester of Jan's sophomore year at Michigan and were spending a lot of their time together. In high school, Friday had been girls' night and Saturday was date night, but things were more complicated in college. Betsy was dating a number of young men, but no one exclusively or for any length of time. With her desire for new people and experiences, Betsy seems to have wanted her friendship with Jan to be different, not quite as close and intense as it was in high school. There were geographic issues, too, on the sprawling Michigan campus. Jan was studying physical therapy and spent much of her day on the Medical Campus, a considerable distance from Angell Hall, where Betsy went for her English classes. In the end, they viewed the situation as the normal ebb and flow of a friendship and expected that, once they were out of college, they would be close again. But there was no doubt that high school was over. When Betsy hung out or went to the movies, it was more likely to be with Andie than Jan, who does not recall ever meeting Andie.[8]

What first got Betsy actively involved in the politics of the day is hard to say. It could have been the death of a high school friend, Scott Freestone, who was in the army in Vietnam. He was mortally wounded in the Tet Offensive on February 12, 1968, while giving first aid under fire to a wounded comrade, and died three days later. The offensive by the North Vietnamese Army and its Vietcong allies in the South had begun on January 30 with a coordinated series of attacks across South Vietnam. Tet ultimately was a tactical defeat for the Vietnamese Communists, but a victory for them in the minds of the American people, who were shocked by the ferocity of the offensive after having been repeatedly assured by General William Westmoreland, the commander of American forces in South Vietnam, that the enemy was no longer capable of mounting major operations. Unlike the Battle of the Bulge during World War II, the last major offensive by the German army, Tet presaged ultimate victory for the enemy rather than defeat. Among other things, it led to the entry of Senator Eugene McCarthy of Minnesota and then Senator Robert F. Kennedy of New York into the Democratic primaries in opposition to President Johnson, and to Johnson's announcement on March 31, 1968, that he would not run for reelection.[9]

Betsy's mother did not call her about Scott Freestone, but Jan heard about it from her mom and called Betsy to break the news. One or both of Jan's parents drove to Ann Arbor to pick them up and bring them back to Holland for the funeral, which was held on February 29, 1968, at Bethel Reformed Church in Holland. Burial was in Pilgrim Home Cemetery. Afterward, they talked about how ironic it was that Scott, a short-timer, had been counting the days remaining until his twelve months in the country were up and he could go home. Jan thought of the silent peace vigils she had observed on the steps of the Graduate Library at Michigan. She and Betsy were becoming close again. That summer, Betsy took the bus to Ann Arbor to celebrate her twenty-first birthday with Jan, which was on July 11, a Thursday. Jan, who was taking summer courses in her physical therapy major, wasn't yet twenty-one, so she declined to join Betsy at the bar. Betsy went out by herself and reported back later that she had her first drink with the bartender. When Jan turned twenty-one later in 1968, Betsy gave her one of her paintings.[10]

Andie remembered visiting Betsy in Holland during the summer of 1968 and going out to one of the Lake Michigan beaches, probably Oval Beach near Saugatuck, where a Eugene McCarthy supporter was handing out MCCARTHY FOR PRESIDENT buttons. They each took one and wore them proudly. She remembered her friend as "fairly political," as do Betsy's other close friends. That apparently didn't extend to membership in SDS or any other group on the Michigan campus, although one of her senior-year apartment mates, Terrie Andrews, remembered her going off to various meetings of a political nature.[11]

During their senior year, beginning in the fall of 1968, Betsy and Andie shared a two-bedroom apartment at 441 South First Street, Ann Arbor, a nondescript, modern apartment building on a street of 1920s bungalows that appeared to have about twenty-four units. Their apartment was on the second floor in the back and had a balcony overlooking the parking lot. Angell Hall was about a fifteen-minute walk from here, or less if they cut across the railroad tracks at the rear of the parking lot. Oxford Houses had been a little farther away in the opposite direction from Angell Hall, but not by much. The advantage here was that the rent was lower, plus they were among many other students of both sexes. Andrews, who had lived on the same floor in Oxford Houses as Betsy and Andie, and Olga Lozowchuk, who had answered an ad in the *Michigan Daily,* shared the second bedroom.

Terrie Andrews was from Union Lake, Michigan, a little town in a picturesque lake district in Oakland County on the far northwestern edge of the Detroit suburbs, almost in farm country. She, too, was an English major but planned on becoming a high school teacher.[12] Like so many others, Terrie thought of Betsy as an artist who marched to her own drummer, someone who was fully aware of the issues of the day. "And would speak her mind from time to time," she added. Then there was Betsy's quirky personal style. "She did what she wanted to do and dressed the way she wanted to dress, and didn't feel affected by peer pressure and didn't feel she had to impress anybody or prove anything to anybody," Terrie said. Expanding on that, she said Betsy was a little bit flashier than most girls, though not in a slutty way and not in a hippie way. "But at the same time . . . she had her own taste. If she wore louder clothes, and clothes that maybe clashed a little bit more, or wore long scarves when nobody else was wearing a long scarf, you'd have said, 'That's Betsy.'" Terrie considered herself a small-town girl with a conventional approach to life, too busy trying to get good grades to get involved in issues like the Vietnam War. When there were demonstrations planned on the Diag, the grand plaza in the middle of campus, she tried to avoid going near. "It was a very turbulent time, and I remember there were a lot of protests going on. It's not that I didn't care, but I just didn't get involved." Betsy did, to a certain extent. Terrie saw her as a good person, with strong ethics and morals, "and she wasn't into drugs or anything wild or weird."[13]

Olga Lozowchuk, who was born and raised in Detroit, had been a pharmacy major during her freshman and sophomore years but had switched to sociology as a junior after being assigned a human cadaver for dissection in anatomy class and deciding a career change was in order. Her opinion of Betsy dovetailed with that of Terrie. Betsy was "quiet, studious, dependable, even-keeled, nonconfrontational, artsy," Olga said. To Andie, Betsy was the girl who, after they all returned to the apartment from a three- or four-day vacation, could whip up dinner from whatever was in the refrigerator. And when Andie got angry about something, or was having a bad day, it was even-keeled Betsy who was the conciliator, Terrie said.[14]

Another reason Terrie Andrews liked the apartment at 441 South First was that her boyfriend, Jerry Newman, lived in the apartment directly above them. They had been dating since high school, making it the most serious sort of relationship. Like her, Jerry had three roommates, Jim Schoolmaster, John Burpee, and David L. Wright. All were members of the Alpha Delta Phi fraternity. Both Jerry and David were pre-med. In due course, Betsy was introduced by Terrie to all four of the young men upstairs. It was David that she hit it off with, and that seems to have surprised nearly everyone.

David was from Elmhurst, Illinois, an upscale western suburb of Chicago, and as noted was the son of a respected psychiatrist, Dr. Donovan Wright. His family had high expectations that he would become a physician, and David was dedicated to getting the good grades he needed to get into medical school. This has never been easy, but the hurdles were higher in the late 1960s, when there were fewer seats in American medical schools. "David was a lot of fun," said his friend and roommate Jim Schoolmaster. "But he was as devoted to getting into medical school as anyone I knew. He may have had a few drinks like everyone else does in college, yet David was one of those individuals who would [still] get up at eleven o'clock in the morning and go study." Schoolmaster recalled how David took one of the early University of Michigan pass/fail courses and still got an A in it. Nothing diverted him from his goal of getting into medical school and becoming a doctor.[15]

But he did not spend all of his time with his nose to the grindstone. Jim and David and the other two apartment mates enjoyed late-night bull sessions while watching television. Even at the University of Michigan in

1968, women students had parietal hours, although they were far more liberal than at Hope College: midnight on weekdays, 2:00 a.m. on weekends. Jim didn't mind that so much. After they "got rid of" their dates, it was back to the apartment for some late-night TV. John Burpee and Jerry Newman worked at Krazy Jim's Blimpy Burger, an Ann Arbor institution not far from the apartment, and would bring burgers home after their shift let out. "I really enjoyed spending time with [David]," Schoolmaster said. "He had a real nice sense of humor."[16]

David and Betsy began dating. In his recollection, two of the young women who lived in the apartment below—Andie and Terrie—were pushing him together with Betsy, not that he minded. Betsy told Peggy Wich that their first date was for ice cream. They went to parties at his fraternity or to dinner in Detroit. Sometimes they studied together at the library. She accompanied him to the Pretzel Bell, aka the P-Bell, a popular Ann Arbor bar, on the eve of his twenty-first birthday and watched him buy and drink his first legal beer just after midnight. Traditionally, at least among some students, the first drink was an entire pitcher of beer consumed while standing on the table. This sort of excess, though, was out of character for David. His roommate, Jim Schoolmaster, considered him "kind of a Nixon type of person," Republican and conservative. They all wondered how well David would mesh with Betsy, who was liberal and Democratic, a Eugene McCarthy supporter who was eager to save the world.[17]

Like so many others, David was smitten by her. "She was just a very brilliant person, extremely smart. . . . Good sense of humor. Just a wonderful person," he said. And he could overlook things that were not consistent with his worldview. "She was Democratic, I'm sure," David said. Politics wasn't something he particularly cared about one way or another at this stage in his life. He was nearly totally career-oriented, and getting into medical school was everything. He admired Terrie Andrews, who had nearly all As, for her dedication to her studies, calling her, "the world's best grade-grubber." Jim Schoolmaster, David's roommate, got to know Betsy a little bit when they walked together toward Angell Hall. He considered her a free spirit, kind of "a hippie person," no different than many young women at the University of Michigan.[18]

Terrie, despite her role in getting David and Betsy together, wasn't sure that they would ever really click. Betsy was not a rah-rah girl and was indifferent to football, school spirit, or fraternities and sororities. "None of that really interested her," Terrie said. "They really seemed to be like oil and water in some respects, [and] I just didn't ever think they would match up." She thinks David may have seemed too conventional to Betsy at first, but that she succeeded in loosening him up. "They seemed to be really, really enjoying each other's company." Olga Lozowchuk, however, didn't think much of David or the relationship. He and Betsy seemed to be polar opposites, and not only in personality. He was from a big-city suburban, well-to-do family, and she was small-town and middle-class. "I didn't know David very well. He did not give me the time of day," Olga said. "I viewed him as a typical, vain frat boy, opportunistic and self-centered. Betsy was down-to-earth, no hidden agenda, wanted to do good things for others." Her gut feeling was that David was "just using Betsy." Andie thought Betsy was "head over heels" in love with David and was "very physical" with him. She acknowledged their very different personalities, "but that doesn't matter, does it?"[19]

What attracted Betsy to David? Perhaps he was finally the conventional man she wrote about longing to fall in love with in her letter to Peggy Wich, when she first came to Michigan in the fall of 1967. In that letter, she longed for someone she could love who also would be acceptable to her conservative parents. David almost certainly met that test. A future doctor was the stereotypical good catch. But would Betsy's goals in life be compatible with his goal of becoming a physician? A wife of a physician in 1968 was expected by social convention to be a traditional helpmeet, taking care of the house and children and doing charity work while her doctor husband treated the sick and earned a good salary. Even as they became closer, Betsy hedged her bets and was never completely exclusive with David. That was her personal style. She wanted to experience everything life had to offer, and occasional friendly encounters with other men fell into that category.

It is very possible that the author Kurt Vonnegut Jr. was one of them. He came to Michigan as the second writer-in-residence of the winter term (following Jerzy Kozinski) in mid-January 1969, when the manuscript of his novel, *Slaughterhouse-Five,* was at his publisher, but not due for publication until March. He was supposed to stay for two weeks, his cult following hanging on his every word. Betsy's cousin, Chris Van Allsburg, remembers passing Vonnegut on the sidewalk outside East Quad [Vonnegut had a room in South Quad] a couple of times. He was a big fan of the author's 1963 novel, *Cat's Cradle,* but was too shy to walk up and talk to him. Betsy was not. Or perhaps Vonnegut approached her. She was well into her English and literature studies at Michigan by the start of the second semester in 1969, although she was taking only one English course in her final term, English 494, [George] Meredith to the Present, taught by Professor Bert Hornback. Two art history courses and a Psychology of Religion course rounded out her complement. Clearly, Betsy was a student who was in good standing with her English professors, because she had an opportunity to meet and talk with Vonnegut the day he arrived on campus, or shortly thereafter. And to charm him with her beauty, wit, and intelligence, as she did so many other men.[20]

Vonnegut, according to his recent biographer, Charles J. Shields, was at that time looking for a way out of his twenty-year marriage to Jane Cox and bedding any number of younger women. During the fall of 1968, he had conducted affairs with Jane "Jimmy" Miller, the widow of a former student of his at the Iowa Writers' Workshop, and then Suzanne McConnell, who had been one of his students at Iowa. Betsy invited Vonnegut and his English Department minder to a small party she and her apartment mates were having one Friday night in early January in their apartment at 441 South First Street. It may even have been a throw-away invitation by her, one she hoped he would accept while expecting that he probably wouldn't.[21]

The party began around 7:00 p.m. and was still going at nine-thirty when there was a knock at the door. Outside was a man with dark, bushy hair and a mustache. Betsy greeted him and ushered him inside. Olga Lozowchuk thought it was a little late to be arriving at a party, but the man explained that he had gone out to dinner with his minder, and that the professor didn't want to come to the party because he had small children at home. He handed over a six-pack of Guinness Stout, which none of the roommates had ever seen, let alone drank. Betsy pointed to a sheet of paper hanging on the back of the door and asked him to sign his name and write something profound, as the other guests had done. He was reluctant at first, but finally wrote his name: Kurt Vonnegut. Of course, they all knew who he was, as nearly every literary-minded college student of the era did. Regrettably, Olga could remember no other details when recounting the story more than four decades later. It was like one of those memories poured from a vial into the pensive in the *Harry Potter* movies: brief, intense, incomplete. Betsy talked about Vonnegut to her friend Linda Marsa after she arrived at Penn State eight months later, but again, no details. We don't know whether Vonnegut talked only to Betsy, how long he stayed, or whether he left alone.[22]

Vonnegut, who was forty-six years old, spent only a week of his contractual two weeks at Michigan, deciding midway that he was sick of interacting with people. "I don't particularly like to talk to people or listen to people," he told an American Studies class one night. When a student inquired why he was there, Vonnegut responded, "We aren't necessarily rational beings, you know." He had also been scheduled to speak at Delta Community College in Bay City, Michigan, about a hundred miles north of Ann Arbor, where one of his lovers, Suzanne McConnell, was teaching that term. He called to cancel, then showed up at the school, scooped her into his car, and drove up the Lake Huron coast. They spent the night together at a motel and he left in the morning, heading back to his home on Cape Cod in Massachusetts. The probability seems high that he had gone to Betsy's party hoping to score with an attractive, interesting coed, but left frustrated. By that time, she was deeply involved with David L. Wright.[23]

CHAPTER 17

In the Shadow of a Killer

He was among the more sadistic of serial killers, a leader in that benighted fraternity of cruelty. The Coed Killer who stalked and murdered young women around Eastern Michigan University and the University of Michigan from 1967 through 1969, but mostly in the latter year, did not merely take the lives of his six victims, as if that was not enough. He also raped them, tortured them, bashed in their faces, and finished them off with knives, ligatures, blunt instruments, or, one time only, gunshots. Even then he was not always finished. In at least one instance, he peeled off large sections of his victim's skin, postmortem. Unlike Buffalo Bill, the fictional serial killer in Thomas Harris's 1988 crime novel, *The Silence of the Lambs,* the Coed Killer is not known to have made clothing from the skin. Nor were his victims chubby, as in the book. On the contrary, they were all petite. Betsy Aardsma was slim but much taller than the girls he murdered, eight inches taller in one instance. But like her, they were all pretty brunettes, which the news stories often mentioned, and which alarmed her family.

The Coed Killer may have ended forever the insouciance about personal safety characteristic of so many young women of that era, whether they were students at one of the two universities or townies. They did not fully understand that there were some men, even in a university town, who would kill them for sport or to satisfy sexual demons. They did not completely end their casual hitchhiking, the accepting of rides home from total strangers, or their trust in the basic goodness of fellow humans. But they came to realize that a monster could be out there waiting to snare them, and things were never the same afterward.

From Betsy's comments to one of her apartment mates, probably Andie, it seems that she, too, worried about the Coed Killer. According to comments Reverend Van Oostenburg made at her funeral, she said that spring that if she was murdered, she wanted a resurrection-themed sermon at her funeral. Her roommates and friends, interviewed more than forty years later, do not seem to have been overly fearful themselves, but fear tends to diminish over time. In Betsy's case, the gut-wrenching fear induced in her family by the Coed Killer would have a profound effect.

The Coed Killer started slowly. His first victim was Mary Fleszar, an Eastern Michigan University student, nineteen years old, who left her stiflingly hot apartment in Ypsilanti on the evening of July 8, 1967, to go for a walk and never returned. Her parents in Willis, a small farm town southeast of Ypsilanti, waited eleven days to report her disappearance to the police, hoping against hope that their daughter would appear at their door. They, too, were in denial about the changing nature of American society. Mary's badly decomposed body was not found for a month. Two fifteen-year-old boys plowing a field north of Ann Arbor on August 7 spotted her naked corpse facedown in front of their tractor. Mary's feet, one hand, and the fingers of the other hand had been chopped off to make identification difficult, but her dental records were enough. The medical examiner ruled that she had died of multiple stab wounds to the chest. The location where Mary's body was found was described by police as adjoining a lovers' lane. That would be true of many of his future victims, as well. The Coed Killer, who knew no love and hated women, possessed a sick sense of irony.[1]

He waited almost a year, until June 30, 1968, to commit his second murder. She was another EMU coed, Joan Schell, who wanted to teach art to young children and had a boyfriend who was an army deserter. She was twenty years old and decidedly petite, at five feet and ninety pounds. That night she wore a blue miniskirt. Her roommate pleaded with her not to hitchhike to Ann Arbor. She followed Joan out of the EMU Student Union to the street, imploring her not to be stupid, but saw her get into a car with three young men. As the car sped off, she saw it turn the wrong way if they were going to Ann Arbor. Five days later, construction workers followed a strange odor to Joan's body in a forest along a road on the northeast side of Ann Arbor. She had been stabbed twenty-five times in a bloodlust frenzy. In addition, she had been raped, and her blue miniskirt was wrapped around her neck. Police immediately saw the similarities between the murder of Mary Fleszar a year earlier and this new murder, but that was as far as things went. Both murders had been written up in the press, but they had occurred in midsummer, when most students were home, and so passed them by. Betsy and her friends barely took notice.[2]

His true reign of terror began in March of 1969, during Betsy's final semester at the University of Michigan. For years afterward, everyone thought the Coed Killer's next victim was Jane Mixer, a twenty-three-year-old student at the University of Michigan Law School, who had twice been the women's debate champion at Michigan. She had posted a note on the ride board at the Law School looking for a lift to Muskegon, where her parents lived. She received a call from a young man who gave his name as "David Johnson" and is believed to have left with him that night. The next morning, her body was found in the Denton Cemetery, located about fifteen miles east of the Law School off of Interstate 94, near Belleville Lake. She had been shot twice in the head with a .22 caliber pistol and strangled with a nylon stocking, but had not been raped. A copy of Joseph Heller's novel, *Catch 22,* very popular at the time, lay at her side. Long attributed to the Coed Killer, the crime was solved in 2004 when a DNA test implicated Gary Leiterman, who lived in Washington State but had worked as a pharmaceutical sales representative in the Ann Arbor area in 1969. He was tried and convicted and sentenced to life imprisonment, although doubt remains about the DNA evidence. At the time, though, Mixer's murder was believed to be the latest work of the Coed Killer.[3]

Perhaps the well-publicized murder of Jane Mixer stirred his competitive instincts. The next day, he went out looking for a victim of his own, and he found her in Maralynn Skelton, a troubled, drug-using, sixteen-year-old hippie chick and recent high school dropout from Romulus, Michigan. Her parents had recently moved to Flint in the hope of getting her away from the drug culture of Ann Arbor and Detroit. On March 22, her brother drove her from Flint to Ann Arbor to meet her fiancé but couldn't take her all the way to his house. Hitchhiking the rest of the way, she was apparently picked up by the Coed Killer and murdered. Her body was found three days later in a forest near Michigan's North Campus, not far from where Joan Schell's body had been found in the summer of 1968.

Maralynn was lying naked on her back, her legs spread and a stick jammed into her vagina. She had been whipped with a belt with a large metal buckle. Her face, particularly her right eye, was a mess, and a garter belt was tied around her neck. Ann Arbor police chief Walter Krasny described her condition as one of the worst things he had seen in thirty years of police work. It didn't take Krasny long to connect the dots between Skelton's murder and the murders of Fleszar and Schell, but even then he was uncertain about Mixer, who had been shot and not raped. Sheriff Doug Harvey of Washtenaw County, which surrounds Ann Arbor and Ypsilanti, summed up what everyone was thinking: "There's somebody mentally deranged around here who has to be caught quickly—I mean, fast." Her parents buried Maralynn in a pale yellow dress in a light green casket covered with red rosebuds.[4]

And then came Dawn Basom, just thirteen years old and an eighth grader at West Junior High School in Ypsilanti. Inevitably, she was short, just over five-foot-two, pretty, and a brunette, but, unlike the others, quite strong. She lifted weights, unusual for a girl at that time, and could bench-press seventy pounds, more than her brother could. For a girl who weighed 120 pounds, that was saying something, then or now. Her mother was a widow, and Dawn seems to have had a great deal of freedom to go where she wanted. On the evening of April 15, 1969, she announced that she was bored and was going out to see friends. In fact, she was going to the Depot Town section of Ypsilanti to see her boyfriend, who was five years older than her. Dawn spent some time with him, then began walking back home, a distance of nearly two miles.[5]

Along the way, she encountered the Coed Killer and went off with him, possibly on his motorcycle. He took her to an abandoned farmhouse north of Ypsilanti, dragged her to the dark, dank basement, and strangled her with a piece of wire he found at the old farm. Police speculated that he must have had an accomplice, given her strength and feistiness.

The question of accomplices was never answered, on this murder or any of the others, despite the clues. Her body was found along a country road not far from her home, yet another "lovers' lane." She was semi-naked, no jeans, no panties, and probably had been raped, although the lab test was inconclusive. Her legs were spread wide and locked in rigor mortis. Dawn's blouse had been ripped to pieces, and part of it was stuffed in her mouth. The wire was still around her neck. There were slash marks on her breasts, but, for whatever reason, he had not mutilated her to the extent he did the others. Nor had he plunged a knife into her chest or beaten her in the face. A small favor? Or perhaps Dawn did fight back and he had to kill her quickly rather than entertain himself with her slow, excruciatingly painful death.[6]

On the other side of Michigan, the headline in the Benton Harbor *News-Palladium* read SLAYINGS TERRORIZE 2 UNIVERSITY TOWNS. Similar headlines were composed in newsrooms around the state, in the Upper and Lower Peninsulas. The story about Dawn Basom in the *Holland Evening Sentinel,* almost certainly read by the Aardsma family, was POLICE COMB AREA OF FIFTH MURDER. The *Sentinel* covered all the Coed Killer's depredations after he resumed his work in March. What would any parent think if they had a pretty, brown-haired daughter at one of those schools?

Betsy's life was complicated that spring. She fretted over a visit to Ann Arbor by David's parents and worried about what to wear when the four of them went to dinner. Although Olga Lozowchuk suspected that David wasn't really interested in Betsy, the relationship seemed to grow deeper. That was a pleasant surprise to Terrie Andrews, one of the other apartment mates. Complications also had arisen from Betsy's home in Holland. No one from Betsy's own family came to visit her that year, possibly an indication of continuing problems regarding her father. "I believe she told me that her father had a drinking problem and that the home environment was not very healthy," said Olga, who had the impression that Betsy couldn't wait to put Holland behind her. She doesn't remember Betsy ever going home for the weekend, either, unless it was a holiday. Nor did her parents come for graduation, and Olga ended up using Betsy's tickets for her own family.

Jan Sasamoto put a different spin on that omission, saying that Betsy didn't want to attend the ceremony, so why should her parents come? "She just sort of blew it off," Jan said. "She just wasn't interested in participating." Graduation at the University of Michigan indeed was an impersonal cattle call, with thousands of graduates and their families jammed into the huge football stadium. When your class was called, you stood up, Sasamoto recalled. She got to stand up twice, once for her regular class, and a second time with her fellow physical therapy graduates. No one marched across the stage and shook hands with the president as their parents beamed and took pictures. There were simply too many graduates for that to be practical.[7]

What Betsy would do after graduation remained undecided. She had long wanted to join the Peace Corps and do a tour in Africa, talking about it as early as her freshman year at Hope College. Terrie Andrews remembered her wanting to give something back to the world and being particularly concerned about underdeveloped countries and people in them who were struggling to survive. The University of Michigan had a special and historic connection with the Peace Corps, ever since October 14, 1960, when Senator John F. Kennedy, fresh off one of his presidential debates with Vice President Richard M. Nixon, had stood outside the Michigan Union at 2:00 a.m. (he had just arrived; a crowd of students had been waiting since 10:00 p.m.) and announced his idea for a program that would send idealistic young Americans to underdeveloped countries to help educate and uplift their people. Today, a plaque on the building near the spot where he stood notes that Kennedy was cheered by a large crowd of students, "for the hope and promise [his remarks] gave the world." After he was elected, JFK created the Peace Corps by Executive Order on March 1, 1961.[8]

Peace Corps recruiters were at the University of Michigan from February 3–7, 1969, setting up shop in Room 3529 of the Student Activities Building. This presumably is when Betsy Aardsma took the tests and filled out her application. She told them she wanted to go to Africa.

However, she did not hear back immediately from the Peace Corps, and in the meantime considered a fallback option: graduate school in English. Betsy had done well at Michigan. She would receive her degree "with distinction," which at Michigan meant she was in the top 25 percent of her class, and "with honors" in English, the lowest of three honors levels, but very good nonetheless. It generally signified a grade point average of at least 3.4 on a 4.0 scale and having demonstrated capacity for independent work. She should not have had much of a problem getting into what was one of America's better graduate programs in English. Joann Manz, whose boyfriend and future husband, Nicholas Lekas, was a close friend of David L. Wright's, had even talked to her about sharing an apartment in Ann Arbor during her first year of graduate school at Michigan.[9]

But her family was adamantly opposed to her staying in Ann Arbor. Her father and mother, Dick and Esther Aardsma, now apparently reconciled, and her uncle and aunt, Louis and Ruth Cotts, were alarmed by the thought of her staying and enrolling in graduate classes at Michigan when there was a serial killer still preying on pretty, brown-haired young women. Her beloved uncle, in particular, urged her to get out of Ann Arbor.[10]

And then two letters arrived, one for her and one for David, and they changed everything. Her own letter was her acceptance into the Peace Corps. Olga Lozowchuk remembered the day Betsy's letter arrived. It contained a penny, proffered as "A penny for your thoughts," and offered her an assignment believed now to have been in the West African country of Sierra Leone, a former British colony where in 1969 there were about 260 Peace Corps volunteers, primarily engaged in teaching. Betsy was excited but realized she was at a crossroads in her life. David's letter was his acceptance to the Penn State College of Medicine in Hershey, Pennsylvania, which had opened in the fall of 1967. They could not pursue their own dreams and stay together—at least, not easily.

Betsy broke the news to David one night after the letter arrived. He had pulled into a parking space behind the apartment building where they both lived, and she told him she had been accepted into the Peace Corps and would be leaving in the summer for three months of stateside training, followed by two years in Africa. She hoped he would wait for her. She wanted him to wait. David, though, was noncommittal, telling her that she might meet a new love in the Peace Corps, and he might meet someone in Pennsylvania. "I sort of selfishly said, 'I don't know what will happen,'" Wright said. "I guess that's probably the truth." It was not the answer she wanted. She loved David and was devastated, uncertain what to do. Going to Africa was her dream, even more so than becoming a physician had once been.[11]

Later in the spring, probably in late May or early June, Betsy called up Jeff Lubbers, her old prom date, and asked if she could come out and see him at his parents' cottage along Lake Michigan, north of Holland. They went for a long walk on the beach. Jeff had also wanted to join the Peace Corps, but his dentist father was strongly opposed and his friends were unsupportive. So he didn't even apply. As the waves rolled over their bare feet, dampening the first few feet of sand, Betsy talked about the pros and cons of going to Africa, the dangers, everything. She felt that her choices, because of her family's opposition to her staying in Ann Arbor, were to go to Africa or follow David to Pennsylvania. If she went to Africa, she would probably lose David. And if she went to Pennsylvania, then what? She knew no one there and knew little about Penn State University. The medical school was a hundred miles from the main campus, so they would still be apart even if she could still get into the graduate English program at this late date. Betsy made no decision that day.

Jan Sasamoto, who was getting married in Holland on August 25, was pressing her for a decision on whether she would be one of her bridesmaids; if she went into the Peace Corps, she would be gone by late August. Around the beginning of June, with Betsy still undecided, Jan picked a sorority sister to take her place in the bridal party.[12]

The body of another pretty brunette, twenty-one-year-old Alice Kalom, was discovered in a field seven miles north of Ann Arbor, near North Territorial Road and US Highway 23. She had been raped, shot twice in the head with a .22 pistol, her throat cut so deeply that her head was nearly off, and stabbed ferociously in the chest—a classic, Coed Killer sex-and-bloodlust frenzy. Alice was from Portage, Michigan, about sixty miles southeast of Holland. She was a senior at Michigan and should have graduated on May 3, when Betsy did, but still needed to complete a photography project to receive her art degree. Alice Kalom and Jim Schoolmaster, David L. Wright's roommate, had both graduated from Portage Northern High School and were acquaintances. Alice was last seen at 2:30 a.m. on Sunday, June 8, leaving a private dance party at the Depot House at 416 South Ashley Street, Ann Arbor, with an unidentified male companion. A former railroad station then used as a band rehearsal space, the Depot House was just beyond the railroad tracks that ran behind the parking lot of Betsy's apartment building at 441 South First Street, an almost-literal stone's throw away. You could see their old apartment from the Depot House. Even though Betsy had moved home by then, it placed the Coed Killer well into the fear zone of her world.[13]

Betsy was hoping that David would ask her to follow him to Pennsylvania, Jan Sasamoto said. She did not want him to be able to say "Well, I never asked you to follow me," if things ended badly. This was a big deal for her. The social conventions of the time prevented Betsy from simply asking David whether he wanted her to come to Penn State with him. He had to pop the question. Jan believes he finally did. Indeed, according to what David told Kevin Cirilli in 2009, he told Betsy that he didn't want her to leave, but that it was her decision. She chose him. Betsy gave up her dream, informing the Peace Corps that she would not be accepting the assignment to Sierra Leone. She applied soon after for the English graduate program at Penn State and was accepted. Michigan was known as a far superior program, so logically, her decision didn't make any sense, but logic had little to do with it. Fear of the Coed Killer was certainly one factor; her family was relieved that she was leaving Ann Arbor for Pennsylvania. And then, of course, there was love.[14]

She and Jan spent a lot of time together during that last summer. And what a summer it was! Holland, or rather, nearby Saugatuck, had its first serious rock festival during the July Fourth weekend, featuring mostly Michigan bands, including the MC-5, Bob Seger, the Amboy Dukes (Ted Nugent in his pre-NRA days), and the Stooges, but also one British headliner, Procol Harum, and three famous blues singers, Muddy Waters, John Lee Hooker, and Big Mama Thornton. It didn't hold a candle to the now-famous Woodstock Music and Art Fair that took place near Bethel, New York, a few weeks later, but what did? Above their heads that summer, well above, was the first Moon landing on July 20, 1969. All of America and much of the world watched the ghostly, black-and-white video images of astronauts Neil Armstrong and Buzz Aldrin loping across the Moon's dusty surface. It was the high-water mark of the American century.

But it was also the long, hot summer of the murder year. The Coed Killer had been briefly quiescent, but in northern California, the Zodiac Killer—so named because he supposedly consulted his horoscope to determine when to attack—was targeting teenage couples parked on lonely "lovers' lanes" around Vallejo, thirty-five miles northeast of downtown San Francisco. Zodiac reveled in the public terror he created. Unlike the Coed Killer, he taunted the public and especially the police, daring them to catch him. Letters received on August 1, 1969, by the Vallejo and San Francisco newspapers contained part of a 408-symbol cryptogram that Zodiac claimed would reveal his identity. He demanded that it be published on the front pages of the papers, and it was. Two readers decrypted it, but it was just another taunting message. Zodiac continued murdering young people through the fall of 1969 and was never apprehended. The author Robert Graysmith believes he knows who Zodiac is, but no arrest was ever made. Authors can draw strong conclusions about guilt from available evidence and logic, but law enforcement needs proof that will stand up in court.[15]

On August 9, 1969, members of the Manson Family, a hippie cult devoted to Charles Manson, a thirty-five-year-old guru and ex-con, went to a house in Los Angeles and slaughtered five people: actress Sharon Tate, who was married to director Roman Polanski; Jay Sebring, a noted celebrity hair stylist and Tate's former lover; Wojciech Frykowski, a friend of Polanski's from Poland who was an aspiring screenwriter; Abigail Folger, Frykowski's lover and heir to the Folger's coffee fortune; and Steven

Parent, an eighteen-year-old boy who was in the wrong place at the wrong time. (Polanski was in London.) On the following night, Manson Family killers traveled to the home of supermarket executive Leno LaBianca and his wife, Rosemary, and killed both of them.

If there were any doubts in the minds of Betsy's family members that she was doing the right thing in leaving Ann Arbor to accompany David to Pennsylvania, they were probably erased by the murder of Karen Sue Beineman on July 23, 1969. Beineman, a tiny, blue-eyed brunette from Grand Rapids, was just five-foot-two and weighed one hundred pounds. She was eighteen years old and had just started the summer term as a first-year student at Eastern. Karen was last seen in her dorm around noon that day and reported missing at eleven that night. She was observed accepting a motorcycle ride from a young man outside the shop where she had just bought a wig. "I've only done two foolish things," she told the wig-store manager as she was leaving. "Buy this wig, and accept a ride from a stranger on a motorcycle."

Her body was discovered three days later about midway between Ann Arbor and Ypsilanti, not far from Concordia University, a Lutheran college. Similar to the other murders by the Coed Killer, she had been raped and strangled, her face beaten beyond recognition. She was naked except for sandals, and appeared to have been rolled down an embankment. Police needed to use fingerprints taken from her dorm room to identify her. A pathologist said large patches of her skin were stripped from her body. Michigan students still in Ann Arbor for the summer marched in protest on July 29 to denounce Washtenaw County sheriff Doug Harvey's failure to find the Coed Killer.[16]

And two days after that, police arrested John Norman Collins, twenty-two, a classically handsome and athletic former Eastern Michigan University English major who had wanted to be an elementary school teacher. He considered himself to be a superman of the Nietzschean variety, exempt from the petty laws that constrained lesser men. When the police searched his Olds Cutlass, they found the Cliff Notes to Fyodor Dostoevsky's *Crime and Punishment* in the glove compartment. They charged him with the murder of Karen Sue Beineman.[17]

Born in Canada, Collins had grown up in Center Line, Michigan, a suburb of Detroit. Most recently, he had stayed in a rooming house three blocks from the EMU campus and across the street from where one of the earlier victims, Joan Schell, had resided. Mary Fleszar had lived two blocks away. He was the nephew of Michigan State Police corporal David Leik, who thought highly of his nephew and had urged him to consider joining the state police. Collins often hung out with cops—including those on the task force searching for the Coed Killer—in the Bomber Restaurant in Ypsilanti. He went motorcycle riding with an officer from the Eastern Michigan University police force.[18]

Collins had murdered Beineman in Leik's basement while his uncle and his family were up north on vacation. He had tried to hide the bloodstains with paint. Leik figured it out and did his duty, alerting his superiors. Collins would be tried and convicted a year later and sentenced to life imprisonment (Michigan, as previously noted, never had the death penalty). But he was not charged with any of the other murders, even though police strongly believed he was connected to all of them except that of Jane Mixer, about which they had doubts. Although District Attorney William Delhay said Collins was the only suspect in the other killings, he said there was insufficient legal evidence to charge him in any of the others, and might never be. Enough ambiguity remained in the case—in particular, regarding the other men seen hanging out with Collins around the times of a couple of the abductions—to make the Pennsylvania State Police wonder if all the killers had been arrested. That was why they could not pass over the Coed Killer case when they investigated the murder of Betsy Aardsma later that year.[19]

It was too late for Jan to put Betsy back into her corps of bridesmaids. Her place had already been taken by one of Jan's sorority sisters, dresses purchased, plans made. Betsy accepted the lesser role of co–punch bowl attendant with Jan's cousin, Jean Yamaoka, with good humor. The rest of the summer leading up to the wedding and Betsy's planned departure for Penn State was as typical as a summer like that could be. Jim Brandt,

Jan's fiancé, was working for DuPont in Charleston, West Virginia, so Jan and Betsy saw a lot of each other. The Sasamoto family was hosting some Japanese exchange students, and Jan and Betsy showed them around Holland. That was one of the things Jan remembered about that last summer with her old friend. She said Betsy seemed very happy with the idea of marrying David and having children rather than going into the Peace Corps.[20]

Betsy also bade farewell to Peggy Wich, who was moving to Washington, DC, on August 11. They went out for drinks at Coral Gables in Saugatuck on the evening of Saturday, August 9, the same weekend as the Tate-LaBianca murders in California. After that, they drove to Oval Beach across the river in Douglas, where they sat on the warm sand, listened to the waves lap on the shore, and talked about David and how he had changed her life. "And that was the last I saw her," Peggy said.[21]

CHAPTER 18

Making the Best of Things

After Jan's wedding on August 25, 1969, Betsy occupied her time working as a volunteer at Holland Hospital, much as she had done during her senior year in high school. David, meanwhile, prepared for the start of medical school, which he assumed would begin at roughly the same time as Betsy's graduate school courses in State College. But he was wrong. A couple of weeks before David thought he was supposed to be there, he received a letter from the medical school informing him that orientation had begun, and where was he? David phoned Betsy in a panic. As always, she was the voice of calm, saying, "Let's get ready and go."[1]

David would be one of 155 students at the medical school, and one of 35 from outside Pennsylvania. He would be a hundred miles away and busy during nearly every waking hour with his studies. That was how it was. That was how *he* was. She had learned this early on in their relationship, when they were still seniors at the University of Michigan. Not that her study habits were lax, but his were ferocious. When they kissed and said good-bye, she promised to write him every day and—having no car—come to see him on weekends via the bus that ran between State College and Harrisburg, the state capital. Betsy watched David's car with the Illinois plates fade in the distance and realized that she knew the name of no one on the Penn State campus except her new roommate, Sharon Brandt, a zoology student from Oyster Bay, Long Island.[2]

If not for David, she would have been in the Peace Corps in Sierra Leone, fulfilling her dream. Or, at the very least, starting graduate work in English at Michigan. But her mother and father and uncle and aunt had been unrelenting about her not going back to Ann Arbor. David had left little doubt he would move on if she went to Africa. So she had come to Penn State, to an English program that was good and getting better but had nowhere near the prestige of the one at Michigan. One of her fellow graduate students, Robert Braman, even asked her about it one day after class—the "Why Penn State?" question. Her answer was not about the program or about David, but about the "creepy murders" at Michigan and the need to escape that danger.[3]

And then she remembered that she loved David and vowed to make the best of it. Betsy walked back to her room in Atherton Hall, a four-story redbrick dormitory at the corner of College Avenue and Shortlidge Road, built in the 1930s. Atherton was a smallish, genteel sort of place as dorms went, a notch above the typical utilitarian accommodations at Penn State. There were just under three hundred rooms. In the lobby, a massive grandfather clock showed students how much time they had left when they were hurrying to wherever they were going. Betsy unlocked the door to Room 5A, which was in a corner on the ground floor near an exit door. Sharon was not there. Like most roommates, they were alike in some ways and different in others. Betsy smoked and Sharon didn't, for example, but Sharon remembered that Betsy was "a polite smoker" who was considerate of her feelings. The room was tidy and there was no unpacking left to do. Betsy was a neat freak and had already hung up her dresses in her closet and put the rest of her clothes in her dresser. Plopping down at her desk, she sketched a couple of aimless doodles, which she was always doing, then decided she wanted to be outside on such a beautiful day in late September.[4]

The differences between Penn State and Michigan were many. Happy Valley was a little over half the size of the University of Michigan and offered about as many cultural events in a semester as Michigan offered on a typical weekend. Detroit and its suburbs added even more, and Chicago was a three-and-a-half-hour train ride away. Penn State was in the middle of nowhere, and if you didn't have a car, you were stuck. An advertisement in the Penn State *Daily Collegian* on September 21, 1969, the start of new student orientation, joked: "Woodstock? Not quite, but we're trying with Blood, Sweat, and Tears." The jazz-rock band, then at the peak of its popularity, had performed at Woodstock that August (it was left out of the movie, a fate shared by several bands) but was still a B-list attraction, and everyone knew it. Now they were scheduled to play the HUB—Hetzel Union Building—on October 5.

Politically, Penn State was not nearly as radical as Michigan, at least not overall. It just seemed that way from time to time, as the smaller campus and student body magnified the serious turmoil that did take place. The Happy Valley chapter of the mostly white Students for a Democratic Society, and the Black Student Union and the Frederick Douglass Association, comprised of activist black students, had relentlessly targeted the Vietnam War and civil rights issues, especially the shamefully low enrollment of black students. Unlike Michigan, Penn State also had a contingent of conservative students willing to publicly confront the leftist white and radical black students. But the activist students on the left had the upper hand in the fall of 1969, and they made that clear on September 21 at the opening convocation.

The event was held in Rec Hall and attracted an estimated five thousand students. SDS members distributed leaflets outside opposing the Vietnam War and sold copies of the *Garfield Thomas Water Tunnel*, the SDS underground newspaper that the administration had tried to suppress via obscenity arrests. Inside, the Black Student Union held up a large banner attacking the administration's failure to increase black enrollment, which stood at somewhere between two hundred and three hundred, about 1 percent of the nearly twenty-six thousand students on campus. President Walker delivered an unintentionally comical speech that could have come straight from *Animal House*: "In the years ahead, you are going to have to pick up more knowledge than any other generation before you—simply because there is now and will be much more knowledge than ever before," Walker told the students.

Then he got around to the campus unrest. Addressing the protests and sit-ins of the previous year, Walker didn't talk about any of the student grievances, didn't defend the university, but instead called attention to "good" black students who had organized a Black Arts Festival and "a weeklong series of programs and forums known as Colloquy." Walker noted that while 250 black and white students were carrying out a sit-in at Old Main in 1968, some 25,000 other students were attending classes. And he equated the earnest student protests over low numbers of blacks on campus to students upset about the beginning-of-year housing shortage. It was all the same to him, and not worthy of a serious response. Walker was almost asking for trouble.[5]

Ted Thompson, the black president of the Undergraduate Student Government, followed Walker to the podium and delivered a blistering rejoinder. "They tell us not to question; they tell us to be patient, not to challenge the established order of things. They tell us that institutional racism no longer exists, but they tell us that higher education must continue to be a privilege and not a right," Thompson said. "Just who keeps telling us this bullshit? I'll tell you who. It's those damn downtown merchants who drain you of every penny you have. It's those hypocritical members of the faculty who hide behind their cloak of academic freedom so that our education remains stagnant. It's the money interests tied into this university. It's our holier-than-thou state legislators who play political football with our education. And it's those rich bastards of society who give one or two scholarships with instructions in contentment and complacency. This is what we are up against."[6]

Thompson's incendiary words were remembered more than four decades later by Thomas Witt, then an incoming freshman from New Jersey. Witt also recalled that when a student group attempted to present an award to Walker, students in the back of the room shouted, "You're a goddamn racist."

Things got no better as the year went on. Black students staged an on-field protest during halftime of the Penn State–Boston College football game on November 1. They had permission from the university to do so, but that didn't mean anyone in authority was happy about it. The Pennsylvania State Police, in a two-page, single-spaced confidential memo sent out by Lieutenant William Kimmel on October 28, said 130 demonstrators were expected, and that the university was trying to prepare the football public in advance, "to acquaint them with the shock." The demonstration went off without incident, according to police, but the black students didn't see it that way. Spectators in the stands at Beaver Stadium, believed to be white students, attempted to drown out the black students' eight-minute speech on racist American society. The protesters raised their fists in the black power salute before exiting the field. Some students cheered when the Penn State Blue Band came onto the field for the remainder of halftime.

Four days later, the Black Student Union issued a news release accusing the Penn State athletic director, whom they called "Rodent" McCoy (his real name was Ernest), and the state police of allowing them to be harassed in various ways, including stopping a contingent of like-minded white students from joining them on the field. Two letters to the *Daily Collegian,* apparently from white spectators, decried the attempt to shout down the black speakers.[7]

Also in the fall, an *ex officio* member of the Penn State board of trustees, state secretary of Mines and Mineral Industries, H. Beecher Charmbury, a former geology professor at Penn State, delivered a speech to the Bellefonte Kiwanis Club saying that the nation's "greatest pollution problem is the pollution of Americanism by Communism." Charmbury, who was the state official most responsible in the early 1960s for allowing an underground mine fire to burn out of control in Centralia, Pennsylvania, eventually destroying the town and scattering its residents, made it clear he thought the Democratic Party and the Communist Party were one and the same, out to subvert the youth of America. "But for the future of our country, we must not respect or even tolerate their disorderly conduct, their disrespect for law and order, their defiance of the draft, their contempt for our flag or their use of drugs, which undermines their morals," he said of students in general, and Penn State students in particular. His remarks caused an uproar on campus—the *Daily Collegian* in particular was not amused—but Charmbury refused to apologize, saying he had many supporters.[8]

The new graduate students in the English Department were thrown together early and often. Betsy, who never had trouble making friends, met and befriended Linda Marsa, a first-year graduate student from Bayside, Queens. Her father was a civil engineer. For ten years before she got married, her mother had been a model in the Garment District in Manhattan. Marsa had done her undergraduate work in English at SUNY Buffalo in Buffalo, New York, where many of the students were fellow New Yorkers. Buffalo was a fairly radical campus, and she had transitioned from Goldwater Girl to left-wing radical in the course of four years. Penn State seemed tame by comparison. She came to Penn State in part because of the reputation of Henry W. Sams, the chairman of the English Department. "It was kind of an up-and-coming department," she said.[9]

Marsa, who became a science and medical reporter for the *Los Angeles Times* and later worked for *Discover* magazine, took to Betsy almost immediately, despite the difference in their backgrounds. Betsy seemed a small-town girl in the best sense: neat and tidy, smart, funny in a wry way, and generous, but with a level of broad-minded sophistication that belied her roots. "She always seemed like a young Katharine Hepburn," Marsa said. "You know, with these kind of angular features and this curly reddish hair that she pinned up. Lean and lanky with that same kind of sarcastic, funny, witty attitude. Slightly askew attitude. And that was something I liked. I was pretty radical at the time, and we were all antiwar and really upset with what was going on in the country. She and I united on that."

They became close and spent a lot of time together, or at least as much as busy graduate students could. Given that they had a heavy load of studying and writing, and could flunk out if their grade point average fell below 3.0, this consisted mostly of a few minutes hanging out after class, grabbing dinner, or going to Pattee Library. On occasion, if Betsy wasn't going to see David on a weekend, they might go downtown. Linda lived off-campus, in a garden apartment on Wapalani Drive. She wasn't a drinker, so she didn't often hit the bars. Her memory of being downtown with Betsy in State College in 1969 was the Old College Diner and their famous grilled sticky buns.[10]

They had two classes together: English 501, Research Materials and Methods, and English 434, Movements in American Literature. The latter was an African-American literature course taught by Charles T. Davis, a pioneer in that field. There was also a third course on Betsy's plate,

English 582, Hawthorne and Melville, but Linda wasn't in that one. There were sixty students in English 501, which met in the basement of the Willard Building. The class, as previously noted, was aimed at whipping new graduate students into shape as budding scholars. John Swinton, who was a graduate student in the department when Betsy was there, said the course "was really tough and required an awful lot of library work. And sometimes a lot of digging in the library. A lot of work in the Rare Books Room, a lot of photocopy perusal." The course introduced students to the ways and means of solving literary mysteries, how to do good research.[11]

The first paper of the term was a bibliographic essay of fifteen to twenty pages. Students were to take a minor English author and identify all the important scholarship about him. "It was very challenging," said Nicholas Joukovsky, the professor who assigned it. They were instructed to identify the best editions and most scholarly texts available, as well as the best critical writing on the author. Betsy wrote her essay on Dr. John Arbuthnot, an eighteenth-century physician, satirist, and contemporary of Jonathan Swift.

It was the black literature course that may have been Betsy's favorite. This may seem odd for a young woman raised in Holland, Michigan, then almost entirely white, with a smattering of Mexicans and almost no blacks. There was only one black student in her high school class. Yet it reflected her growing interest in the African-American community and civil rights issues, and perhaps, too, her thwarted dream of going to Africa with the Peace Corps. Davis's course offered a broad menu of the best in Afro-American (the term he used) literature, which he and fellow Penn State professor Daniel Walden, white and Jewish, were about to edit into an anthology, *On Being Black: Writings by Afro-Americans from Frederick Douglass to the Present.* It would be published in 1970. Davis was a liberal but seemed moderate compared to the activist black students on campus, and he occasionally was approached by state legislators who thought he might be a useful Uncle Tom. He wasn't. Davis appears to have liked Betsy and Linda Marsa. A scrap of paper bearing her parents' address in Holland, and Marsa's in State College, was in his papers at Yale University, the final destination of his academic journey. There seems little reason for it to be there unless he sent condolences after Betsy was murdered.[12]

Betsy's favorite black writer was James Baldwin, who would be represented by "John's Conversion" from *Go Tell It on the Mountain* in the Davis and Walden anthology. Baldwin was small, thin, gay, and defiantly black, unwilling to tone down his opinions or his art, either for whites or middle-class blacks made uncomfortable by his rhetoric. As Fern Marja Eckman wrote in her admiring 1966 book, *The Furious Passage of James Baldwin,* "This slight, dark man is salt rubbed in the wounds of the nation's conscience. He is the shriek of the lynched. He is an accusing finger thrust in the face of white America. He is a fierce, brilliant light illuminating the unspeakable and the shameful." You get the idea. Baldwin was as far from the white, conservative sensibilities of Holland, Michigan, as a writer could be, and Betsy Aardsma embraced him.[13]

Betsy and David settled into a long-distance relationship, if a hundred miles can be considered long distance. She wrote a letter to him nearly every day. Long-distance telephone calls were a luxury then, reserved for special occasions. On many, but not all, of the nine remaining weekends in her life, Betsy went to see him at the medical college in Hershey. David remembered visiting her in State College maybe once, but no more than that, and could not remember the names of her friends. "I knew she had a group of friends; they're people I didn't know. I never met them," Wright said. Marsa, though, remembered that he was "a very nice man."

Restless as ever, Betsy considered whether she was doing the right thing in jumping on the marriage express with David, Marsa recalled. What may have shaken her confidence was a dinner she attended at David's house in Hershey on one of the first weekends after they arrived in Pennsylvania. It was her, David, and several other medical students. "The memory I have is of an attractive gal with a nice figure, pretty but not a knockout, who was very casually dressed," said Ian C. Osborn, David's medical school friend. "I don't think she said very much. The talk was pretty much between the medical students." For a young woman whose Hope College roommate recalled how she liked to hold forth on many subjects, it had to be irritating. In addition, Betsy still wondered if she was cut out to be a doctor's wife. There was actually a formal Hershey Medical Student Wives Club in 1969. One of the club's stated goals was to prepare young women like Betsy, married to or dating male medical students (there were females in the class, but not many), "for their role as physicians' wives." Meetings of the club were mentioned in the *Vital Signs* newsletter at the school. Betsy must have taken note.[14]

Sexism was also pervasive at Penn State's main campus, not just at the medical school. Some women believed that female applicants to Penn State were required to have higher academic qualifications than male applicants, and that there was a quota for women. As it happened, this was true. Penn State officials acknowledged publicly in January 1970 that two and a half men were admitted for every woman at the main campus. Things had been worse in 1958, when four men were admitted for every woman. The imbalance had gradually lessened but was still a factor. By 1971, Penn State would be facing the threat of litigation over the imbalance and dropped preferential admission for men at the main campus the following year.[15]

There were movements for many things at Penn State in 1969, and feminism was no exception, although it was in its very nascent stages. A student-faculty group called the Women's Liberation Front had been organized the previous winter with the goal of making the university community aware of discrimination suffered by women. They didn't have to wait long for firsthand examples. Penn State officials, disapproving of the group's nature and purpose, refused to grant them meeting space in the HUB. So for the first six months, which included the time Betsy Aardsma was on campus, they met in a women's restroom, according to Pam Farley, a member of the group. "It was quite a varied group, and we were all activists," she said. "Of one sort or another." They would sit on the restroom floor and share experiences. After about six months, Women's Liberation Front was granted permission to use actual meeting rooms. Gradually, they began taking their message to a dumbstruck and often-antagonistic outside world.[16]

None of Betsy's friends recall her labeling herself as a feminist, but most remember her saying and doing things that supported the idea that she was. Since high school, she had aimed toward a career outside the home—first as a physician, which was bold for a woman of her day, and then as a scholar of English and literature. There was no sense that she wanted to go the traditional route for women, which would have been nursing or K-12 teaching. From all indications, her ambitions went beyond that.

"One of the things she said to me was that she was a little ambivalent about it," Marsa said of Betsy's feelings about marriage to David. "This is just as the women's movement was gathering momentum. And she said, 'Is this what I want? Do I want the kids and the keys to the Country Squire?' You know, she loved David, she'd go visit him, but she had a certain ambivalence that I think was very natural."[17]

That ambivalence may have led to her decision to go out on casual, "friendly" dates with other men. Pushed out of Michigan by her family, who feared she would become the next victim of the Coed Killer, pulled to Pennsylvania by her medical student boyfriend, who didn't want her to join the Peace Corps, Betsy was lonely in State College. She had no family here, none closer than five hundred miles away. Even David was a hundred miles from her at the medical school in Hershey. All she had was her graduate work in English and one good friend, Linda Marsa. It should come as little surprise that some young men at Penn State saw her as vulnerable and available.

CHAPTER 19

Dangerous Attraction

One of the two students who pursued a relationship with Betsy Aardsma that fall was Larry Paul Maurer, whom we already know from the aftermath of the murder. He had drawn the attention of the state police for carving HERE SITS DEATH IN THE GUISE OF MAN on his Atherton Hall dorm-room desk chair, and later was hooked up to a polygraph and questioned about her murder. He passed the test, never losing his cool, and was not arrested, then or ever. Maurer was twenty-two years old and, like Betsy, a graduate student in English, also in English 501. He came off as a quiet, outdoorsy young man who enjoyed hunting and fishing, albeit one who kept a small hunting knife on campus. He would tell state police investigators that he used it to cut cheese, not stab young women. But as became obvious during the investigation of the Aardsma murder, Maurer had another side. He seemed to enjoy taunting and toying with the detectives who questioned him.

How Maurer ended up as a graduate student in English at Penn State is anyone's guess. In high school, he was on the industrial track and his stated goal was to become a draftsman. Why he became interested in Betsy is hard to pinpoint beyond the factors that attracted many men to her. There were other pretty girls in the class, but he was drawn to her. Interestingly, his high school nickname was "Aardvark." Perhaps he fancied Aardvark and Aardsma as a couple. And both were dedicated doodlers. He might well have observed her doodling during class, which was held in the basement of the Willard Building.

Another woman in English 501, an attractive blonde from Aliquippa, Marilee Erdely, had taken note of how Maurer gazed at Betsy. Erdely, who was friendly with Maurer, had acted as an intermediary between him and Betsy, who is said to have let him buy her coffee once. But when he asked her out to a movie, she turned him down, telling Erdely later with a laugh that he was too much the "forest ranger." Maurer probably reacted as any boy did in this situation, with a mixture of hurt and embarrassment. Yet he could not avoid her, because he saw her in class each week and in Pattee Library when they had to find research materials.[1]

The other man interested in Betsy was Richard Charles Haefner, a geology graduate student from Lancaster, Pennsylvania. Haefner, who went by Rick, lived in Atherton Hall and had been admitted to the doctoral program the previous June. He was due to get his master's degree in December. Rick was twenty-five years old, just over six feet tall, and handsome. Although he came off as highly intelligent to some people (indeed, his IQ was in the top 5 percent), to others he seemed condescending. Nerdy, clean-cut, and neatly dressed at a time when that was fast going out of style among male college students, it was easy to imagine him as a foreign correspondent in a Burberry trench coat or a college professor in a Harris tweed jacket. The black horn-rimmed glasses he wore could make him appear to be looking down his nose at lesser mortals. Only the khaki work pants he often wore, whether in the hard-baked desert of Death Valley, where he did the field research for his advanced degrees, or the hallways of Happy Valley, betrayed him as a geologist. Haefner considered himself to be on the road to becoming an important member of that profession.[2]

Rick's home on campus since the fall of 1966 had been Room 303 of Atherton Hall. Maurer was assigned as Rick's roommate at the beginning of the fall term in 1969. For whatever reason—either they didn't get along or Rick wanted to live by himself—Rick moved to Room 48 early in the fall semester and, two days after that, to a single, Room 64, when it became available. He was a loner, selective in whom he chose as his friends. Geology professor Roger Cuffey, for whom he worked as a teaching assistant in Cuffey's historical geology course for three terms, saw nothing abnormal about Rick. He found him to be conscientious, decent, and helpful.[3]

But Haefner had a dark side that only a few knew about. He had regularly carried a narrow-bladed homemade knife, a shiv, since his years at J. P. McCaskey High School in Lancaster, when the other boys would taunt and harass him over his perceived homosexuality. According to his cousin, Christopher Haefner, Rick had wanted a weapon that fit comfortably in his oversized hand, and he liked the feel of the cylindrical wooden handle of an awl. There was no one way to hold it. So he removed the steel point of the awl, widened the opening where the shaft had entered the handle, and wedged in a knife blade that was slightly narrower than a penny and three to four inches long. In later years, Chris watched him sharpen the blade on a grinding wheel in his rock shop. He kept a ball of tape on the tip of the blade to avoid nicking himself.[4]

Had the boys at McCaskey known the truth about Rick Haefner's sexual orientation, it might have been even worse. He was a pedophile attracted to prepubescent boys. There had been several incidents in his hometown of Lancaster, where Rick was the scion of a once-great brewery family gone to seed. Although he had been confronted by adults about his pedophilia, he had so far escaped the attention of the police. Haefner had a great fear of being exposed as a child molester, fearing it would wreck his career.

Why did Betsy not sense danger until it was too late? Luke Kliphuis, her high school beau, believes that her sheltered upbringing in Holland left her with no good ability to sniff out peril or deal effectively with people who seemed odd but didn't wear danger on their sleeve. At Holland High School, Betsy had been surrounded by a tight-knit circle of friends and had never even had to deal with a problematic boyfriend, let alone an obsessive stalker. She had tangled with Darryl at Hope College, but that was minor and they later resumed their friendship. At the University of Michigan, she dated a future physician, David L. Wright. His friends were her friends. But she was also curious, open to new people and experiences, and accustomed to young men joining her circle of admirers. Because she was nice, smart, and pretty, she would have been a "nerd magnet" at Penn State, Kliphuis said. She didn't mind. They were like her—smart students, good people. Except when they only seemed to be.[5]

Nor did Kliphuis believe she would have readily shared with the people around her that she was having problems with an admirer. "She was not going to let you know what was going on in her head," he said. Betsy wrote letters that fall to Jan Sasamoto, Peggy Wich, and Olga Lozowchuk, but none of them could remember any references to problems with a young man. "Betsy and I wrote frequently," Lozowchuk said. "I remember Betsy writing me that she had met a fellow by the name of Guy. I thought, 'What an unusual name.' I assumed he was a fellow student, but I can't be sure." Her friend Linda Marsa could remember nothing about any threats. David L. Wright either, although it might well have been awkward for her to tell him that she was worried about some guy she had gone out with once or twice. The hectic life of a graduate student didn't leave much time for long, leisurely conversations with friends in any case.[6]

Much of what we know about Rick Haefner's interactions with Betsy comes from statements he reportedly made to a state trooper, Ken Schleiden, during the early days of the murder investigation. As reported by *State College* magazine writer Sascha Skucek, he told police that he had met Betsy outside Atherton Hall not long after she'd first arrived on campus in September. During October, they went for ice cream at the Creamery, a Penn State institution, dinner at the Nittany Lion Inn on campus, and bowling at Bellefonte Lanes, which suggests that he had a car, since the bowling alley is nine miles from Atherton Hall. Rick recounted that Betsy told him (as she told others) that she had come to Penn State because of the Coed Killer at the University of Michigan. According to Skucek, the state police also heard from Sharon Brandt, Betsy's roommate, that she had seen Betsy and Rick together. And around 2010–11, Trooper Leigh Barrows, assigned to the Aardsma case, talked to Charles Hosler, retired dean of the College of Earth and Mineral Sciences, and mentioned to him the encounters Rick had had with Betsy during a long conversation about the case.[7]

Betsy's brief friendship with Haefner ended badly after about four weeks. She told her family in Michigan that she considered Rick to be "a creep." Ominously, she began to have premonitions of her own early death. More than once that fall, she expressed those thoughts to her family. Both verbally and in letters, she said that she had to accomplish many things because her time on Earth was limited. She wrote, "Time has already run out on me, even before I start. It matters little how long the time really is. It just has to be used." About a month before her death, she told her mother that she didn't know why she was at Penn State, that she had a "weird feeling" about being there. Her family dismissed the premonitions.[8]

David L. Wright did sense, at least vaguely, that something was wrong. After Betsy had been in State College for a month, around the time she stopped spending any time at all with Haefner, she told David that she wanted to move down to Harrisburg permanently and enroll at the branch campus of Penn State there. She told him more than once how "ridiculous" it was to be apart. "In retrospect, when I thought about that, I'm wondering if she was worried about something up there. My wife's theory is that she just wanted to move things along and be closer." She and David made plans to spend Thanksgiving together. Holland and home were five hundred miles away. It was just too far to travel, and of course, she had no car.[9]

In the meantime, Betsy became more involved in the antiwar and civil rights movement at Penn State. On November 14, 1969, she joined in teach-in activities on the Penn State campus, part of a nationwide protest that weekend, the Moratorium to End the War in Vietnam, organized by some of the same people who had organized Senator Eugene McCarthy's campaign for president. The main event was a march by a half-million people in Washington, DC, demanding that President Nixon end the war. They were led by folksinger Pete Seeger in singing a new song by John Lennon, "Give Peace a Chance." Nixon put out word that he watched sports on TV at the White House while the mass protest went on nearby.

At the Penn State campus that day, the protests were on a smaller scale but no less fervent. Betsy led a one-hour discussion at 3:30 p.m. in Room 215 of the Hetzel Union Building on "The War and Black Authors," then yielded the microphone to a math student who led a discussion on "Science and the War." Betsy had been truly captivated by the black authors she had read in Davis's course, marveling at their take on the American experience that was so different from her own.[10]

In their letters, Betsy and Jan Sasamoto had discussed the possibility of Betsy traveling to Charleston, West Virginia, over Thanksgiving, but in truth, Charleston was 330 miles from State College, well over half the distance that Holland was, and would have been a complicated weekend trip from Penn State for someone like Betsy, without a car. She dropped the idea and looked forward to seeing David. She and David had not yet become formally engaged but were looking at engagement rings. Everyone assumed an announcement would come at Christmas, perhaps with a wedding the following summer.[11]

On Thanksgiving morning, Betsy took the bus to Harrisburg, and David met her at the station on Market Street. During the twenty-minute drive to Hershey, they talked about their plans for the day. Some of the female medical students were cooking Thanksgiving dinner for themselves and a few of their men friends from the class. Between six and eight people were at the dinner that afternoon, including David and Betsy. He recalled it as "just a real nice time." There was no hint of any quarrel between them, any problem in the relationship. Betsy phoned her family in Holland and assured them everything was fine, and that she would be home for Christmas. Afterward, they talked about whether she would stay for the weekend. In the end, their studies won out. David had finals coming up, and Betsy had a paper due for Professor Meserole. According to him, it was her choice to go back to Penn State. David drove Betsy to the bus station that night, kissed her good-bye, and never saw her alive again.[12]

CHAPTER 20

Murder

On November 28, 1969, the final morning of her life, Betsy Aardsma awoke late, showered, dressed, put on her contact lenses, and then wrote a letter to David, as she did nearly every day. It had been a late night. After the bus ride back to State College, she had stayed up talking to Sharon Brandt, her roommate. She folded the sheet of stationery neatly, placed it in an envelope, licked and applied a six-cent stamp, and dropped the letter in the dorm mailbox. She had a paper to write for English 501.

Betsy decided to grab some lunch. She set off walking up the gently curving path that traversed the ground between Atherton Hall and the HUB. The sidewalk hugged the edge of a broad lawn that Penn State University had so far spared from its building boom. The air was cold, a little over 30 degrees, but there was no snow on the ground. Perhaps feeling girlish and happy that morning, Betsy had put on a red, sleeveless dress over a white cotton turtleneck sweater—she could have passed for a Holland High School cheerleader with those clothes and those colors—plus panty hose to provide a modicum of warmth to her legs. Old habits died hard. Holland High had not allowed girls to wear slacks to school even in the dead of winter, even if there was deep, drifting snow. Girls there were about a year away from protesting the gross unfairness of that policy and getting it changed. She also wore a winter coat, scarf, and gloves, which were found in Pattee Library after her death.[1]

The campus seemed empty. Hardly anybody was in the dining hall. Most students, unless they were from foreign countries or distant states, or were graduate students like herself with papers to finish, had gone home for the Thanksgiving holiday. Her paper for Professor Meserole was due in less than two weeks. Betsy went through the line and then sat down at a table with her tray.

Her English 501 assignment was to write a critical study of a manuscript from the Pattee Library rare books room, or of one of a number of photocopies Meserole had made of early American manuscripts in the collections of the American Antiquarian Society in Worcester, Massachusetts, or the Massachusetts Historical Society in Boston. Betsy had chosen one of Meserole's photocopies from the Massachusetts Historical Society for her term paper. It was an American transcription of an anonymous English satirical poem from around 1670, "New Instructions to a Painter." She needed to transcribe the text of the manuscript, establish authorship—the most likely suspect was Andrew Marvell—and date, reconstruct its historical context, and explain anything that would not be clear to a modern reader. It was difficult detective work, and it made the English 501 students crazy.[2]

Nearly everyone in the English 501 class, including Betsy, would be in the Level 2 stacks at Pattee Library that afternoon. A little before 4:00 p.m., Betsy Aardsma and Sharon Brandt left Atherton Hall for the library, where they each had work to do. It was a ten-minute walk. They went out the side door of Atherton and followed the sidewalk leading across the lawn and between the Henderson buildings. Then they traversed the lawn in front of Old Main, site of so many demonstrations over the past two years, before finally reaching the Mall and turning right toward Pattee Library, still nearly a quarter-mile away, walking beneath the majestic elm trees that the university went to so much trouble and expense to protect. At the library, they said good-bye, promising to meet for dinner at seven o'clock and then go see a movie.

After Sharon went inside to her carrel, Betsy was about to go downstairs to Professor Meserole's office but remembered at the last minute that Professor Joukovsky had asked to see her. She wasn't sure how late he would be there, so she headed back down the library steps and over to the Burrowes Building, which was perpendicular to the library at its eastern end, and was the home of the English Department, or at least most of it. Henry W. Sams, the department chairman, had his office there. Joukovsky's office, Room 31 [now Room 13], was easy to find. After Betsy went through the south-door entrance off the Mall, it was the first office on the right. She sat down with a couple of other English 501 students in the waiting area.[3]

Joukovsky needed to see one of the source books she had used for her paper about Dr. Arbuthnot, which she had written for him earlier in the term. He did not know Betsy well. As always, she tended to be the quiet girl who studied hard and got good grades, blending into the mass of her fellow students. He asked her if she still had the book. "It was very important," Joukovsky recalled more than forty years later. "I wanted to see that to evaluate her paper." Betsy said she had already returned it to Pattee Library, but offered to retrieve it and bring it to him after she went to see Meserole about her current paper later in the day. It was about 4:15 p.m. when she walked back to Pattee Library, where Meserole had his office.[4]

Despite the holiday weekend, there were quite a few students in the library. Some have claimed the library was nearly empty, but the statistics don't show that. The total for the day was 3,148, compared to 4,632 the previous Friday, according to library statistics in the Penn State Archives. Betsy went down to the Level 2 stacks and left her coat and scarf at her carrel; then she went briefly to look for a book in the Core, possibly the book that Professor Joukovsky wanted to see, before her 4:30 appointment with Dr. Meserole. Dean Brungart, the assistant stacks supervisor, saw her between two rows of books toward the middle of the Core when he went downstairs to retrieve a book shortly before his shift ended at 4:30 p.m.[5]

Betsy didn't tarry long in the stacks, moving on through the library maze to Meserole's office, where members of the English 501 class had been coming and going all afternoon. One of them, David R. Johnson, was just leaving to pick up his son at the babysitter and greeted Betsy as they passed in the doorway. Priscilla Letterman, Meserole's secretary and later his wife, complimented her on the red dress she was wearing. She spent about fifteen minutes with the professor discussing "New Instructions to a Painter" and the paper she planned to write. They talked about what else she needed for her paper. All of that material, it seemed, was in the Level 2 stacks. Betsy left Meserole's office around 4:45 and returned to the main floor to use the card catalog, where she was observed by a member of her class, who was never publicly identified by the state police. Was it Marilee Erdely, who told police she saw Betsy not long before the murder? In any case, Betsy found the cards for the books she needed and made notes of their call numbers. Then she walked to the nearby door, opened it, and descended the narrow staircase into the gloomy and dimly lit stacks. It was about seven or eight minutes before 5:00 p.m. No one was following her, Sergeant Keibler believed.[6]

Dean Brungart had seen something else during his brief foray into the stacks: Two young men were talking to each other at the western end of the Core. "There was no one else in the Core," he told Mike Lenio of the *Daily Collegian* in 1987. One of the two young men was later identified by Brungart as Larry Paul Maurer, who was in English 501 and would later admit to state police investigators that he was in or near the Core around the time of Betsy's murder. But Brungart didn't or couldn't identify the other young man.[7]

From all that is known today, the author concludes that the killer of Betsy Aardsma was Richard Charles Haefner, the geology graduate student who was obsessed with her. Why was he there? He had no known reason to be in the English literature section of the library. Was he stalking her? Had someone else from English 501 told him she would be there? Many of the answers may never be known. What set him off in the stacks? Had Betsy stumbled upon him as he leered at the Dutch porn magazine found near the murder site, perhaps while masturbating? He was a devotee of pornography. In 1992, police in Chincoteague, Virginia, would find a large collection of "fairly disgusting" porn in Haefner's van after they arrested him in connection with taking an underage boy to the shore without his mother's knowledge. Ample evidence of someone's masturbation was found in the area of the crime site the following day by Mary Willard, the forensic chemist from the Penn State faculty. Perhaps it was not Haefner's first visit. And as would be evident throughout his life, Haefner had a scary, volatile temper when it came to women—especially women who crossed him.[8]

Betsy would have recognized Haefner instantly and might well have let her disgust show on her face. Perhaps she said something sotto voce, unheard even in the stillness of the stacks by anyone but him. Certainly, neither Erdely nor Uafinda nor Richard Allen, the third witness, heard any verbal unpleasantness, but perhaps it occurred seconds before they moved into auditory range. More likely Betsy did not confront Haefner and moved quickly away from him, intent on finding the book she needed so she could get out of there. But the damage was done, as far as Haefner would have been concerned. "Rick would never have allowed anyone to upend his career," said his cousin, Christopher Haefner.[9]

Haefner's rage toward Betsy could have been fueled by a mixture of fear and anger. She had rejected him, and now might report him to the university for the porn and maybe for masturbation in a public place. In his mind, and possibly in reality, that could have been enough to get him kicked out of Penn State on moral grounds and denied the master's degree he had earned in geology. He was well aware of the danger he faced from this sort of accusation. There would be no PhD, no career in the field, geology, in which he believed himself destined for greatness. Everything he had worked for was at risk.[10]

Because there are no known living witnesses, we can only speculate about what happened next, filling in between the known facts. It probably went something like this:

Haefner felt his anger surging. In a rage, he reached into his jacket pocket for the homemade shiv that he had carried since McCaskey High School and removed the ball of tape on the tip. Jumping to his feet, he followed Betsy into the Core. Absorbed in looking at the Library of Congress call numbers on book spines, she did not immediately react when Rick Haefner approached. She believed him to be a creep but probably considered him relatively harmless. Then she saw his eyes and was terrified. He was tall and powerful, six-foot-one, five inches taller than her, and 195 pounds to her 125 pounds. Before she could scream or run, Haefner had his hand over her mouth. He raised his other hand and she saw the weapon. In a blind panic, Betsy climbed backward onto a shelf, which only made her a better target. In an instant, he slammed the blade horizontally into her chest about midway between the bottom curves of her breasts. It was an angry blow, delivered with no hesitation, powerful enough to penetrate the sternum and pierce her heart (which is directly behind the breastbone). Nearby in the maze of the stacks, Joao Uafinda heard a sound like a fist hitting a chest, but no scream. Haefner saw the life go out of her eyes. Suddenly spent, he let go of her and the weapon, briefly appalled at what he had done. Betsy seemed to clutch a shelf but then fell hard to the floor. Her weight caused the shelf to give way, spilling scholarly books around and on top of her body. One of her feet was still propped up on a lower shelf from that last, desperate effort to escape.[11]

Haefner then probably tried to pull the shiv loose. There was almost no blood, but it was firmly implanted in her breastbone. He wiggled it until it came out, in the process slightly widening the exterior wound and making it appear as if it had been made with a larger blade. Where was all the blood? There was nothing on his hands. He had to get out of there. Gingerly placing the weapon in his jacket pocket, he took off on a run, intending to go up the nearby staircase.

Haefner slowed when he saw Erdely and Uafinda. "Somebody had better help that girl," he said, pointing back at the Core. But it would not be him. The Dutch pornography lay abandoned on the carrel, soon to be found by George Keibler's investigators, and Betsy was quite dead.

CHAPTER 21

The Night Visitor

A little after 6:00 p.m. on the evening of Betsy Aardsma's murder, Professor Lauren A. Wright and his wife, Myrtle, had just sat down to dinner in their modern home at 219 Ronan Drive in a woodsy development on the outskirts of State College. Wright was a geology professor and chairman of the Department of Geology and Geophysics, a post he had held since 1963. She had been a secretary in the department, and he met her soon after arriving at Penn State from California in the fall of 1961. They were a gentle and cultured couple. He was forty-three when he met her and she was forty-two. It was his first marriage but her second, and she had a son from her first husband. Myrtle, a devout Quaker, spent her days in private study of the Greek language, Greek mythology and history, or playing the recorder. Wright spent time away each year mapping and studying Death Valley, the great desert wilderness in California that was his life's work. He would leave almost every year in late September, often accompanied by a graduate student, and come back just before Christmas.[1]

When the doorbell rang, Professor Wright got up to answer the door and came face-to-face with Rick Haefner, who was one of his graduate students. They had spent the fall terms of 1967 and 1968 together in Death Valley. Wright considered him to be a "pretty good" geologist, "very diligent in his work," and had signed his master's thesis about six weeks earlier, giving it his official stamp of approval. Haefner, who was twenty-five years old, was out of breath and disheveled. A kind man who tried to see the best in everybody, Wright instinctively invited Haefner inside. Thus began one of the strangest episodes in the Betsy Aardsma case, and one that may have been a significant factor in the failure to solve her murder.[2]

Some have suggested that Haefner literally ran from Pattee Library to Wright's home, fleeing in panic from his murder of Betsy Aardsma. But Wright's house was in the southwest corner of State College, exactly three miles from Pattee Library. While walking that distance in an hour would have been theoretically possible—indeed, Google Maps helpfully calculates the walking time at fifty-five minutes—it just doesn't seem likely. Wright himself didn't think that Rick walked.

After eluding Joao Uafinda, the Mozambican student who had followed him, thinking he was going to help a girl, Rick probably walked briskly to the less visible and less trafficked West Entrance of Pattee Library, went through the doors, and out into the enveloping darkness. Rick may have been the young man seen running from the front of Pattee Library minutes after the murder, but no one could give a good description of whomever it was they saw. He had the dumbest of luck. It seems exceedingly doubtful Haefner would have risked a return to his room in Atherton, even to grab his things, given that he had to expect the police soon would be in the building, poring over Betsy's dorm room. And indeed, they were. Those two students—he did not know their names to be Erdely and Uafinda—had seen him coming out of the Core. Maybe they knew who he was. It is much more likely that Rick made his way to his car, wherever it was parked, and drove around for a time, deciding what to do.[3]

Haefner that afternoon and evening exhibited some traits of a *piquer,* or girl stabber, a rare form of sadism. As described in 1958 by Dr. J. Paul de River in his book, *Crime and the Sexual Psychopath,* a piquer often stabs a young woman in places associated with her femininity, such as a breast or thigh, for the thrill it brings. A photo in de River's book shows the entry wound in the breast of a young woman, the caption noting that the weapon reached the heart, which is directly behind the breastbone, and killed her almost instantly. "Many of them desire to see blood, if possible, but they often become frightened and disappear without viewing the results of their actions. . . . Frequently such individuals will watch the newspapers to see if their acts have made the headlines," de River wrote. He said piquers are "psychopathically tainted" but legally sane.[4]

Once in his car, Haefner probably stopped somewhere and disposed of his homemade shiv, which has never been found. Perhaps he even drove out of State College for a few miles and then turned around, doubling back to Wright's house. He might have parked a distance away, fearing the police were already looking for his car, and then walked quickly through the darkness, perhaps running across the broad field at the end of Ronan Drive and then moving among the trees and shrubbery, which abounded in Wright's neighborhood. That would account for him being out of breath.

Rick had been to Wright's house before but was not a frequent visitor. He was disturbed that night, Wright remembered, asking if there was any news in the papers about a girl he knew, Betsy Aardsma, being killed in Pattee Library. In fact, the *Centre Daily Times,* which was then an afternoon paper, had gone to press hours before the murder. No media outlet, whether newspaper, radio, or television, is known to have had any news about Betsy's slaying before eleven o'clock that night. Wright sat him down at the dinner table and talked with him. The professor had heard nothing about the murder, but almost nobody had at that point. Haefner stayed about an hour and then left.[5]

Professor Wright found Rick to be "puzzling," never completely open when they conversed. He wondered later if his student knew more about the murder than he was letting on, and he claimed in 2010 that his concerns prompted him to go to his dean, Charles Hosler, the very next day—a Saturday on a holiday weekend—to report his suspicions. But he did not, Hosler said, not for nearly seven years. "No, had that happened, it would have been quite a different story," Hosler said. In fairness to Wright, at the time he made that claim, he was within three years of his death and had already begun slipping into mild dementia that would grow worse with time. We can be confident that Rick's visit happened that night because Wright told the story a number of times over the years, when he was in robust health.

Where Rick went after he left Wright is unknown. He probably drove to his parents' house at 217 Nevin Street in Lancaster. At some point, if not that weekend, then later, he told a version of what happened in the stacks to his mother, Ere Haefner. A sharp-nosed and sharp-tongued woman, she adored her son and helped to inflate his sense of self-importance. She would have done anything for him. As Christopher Haefner put it so pointedly, if Rick had brought home Betsy in the trunk of his car, Ere would have helped him bury her body. She would never be his conscience, only his security guard. Even so, one wonders if Rick shaded the truth in what he told Ere, perhaps calling it a foolish accident so as not to come off as a cold-blooded killer. We will never know. All we know is that she did not turn him in.[6]

Haefner returned to campus after Thanksgiving, perhaps worried that his absence would draw unwanted attention. The state police were indeed on the lookout for students who had abruptly dropped out of Penn State after Betsy's murder. He was looking forward to receiving his master's degree in geology on December 14 and had already begun work on his doctoral degree. What plausible excuse could he make for suddenly dropping out now?

Within a week of the murder, Rick was summoned for a routine interview at the state police command center in the Boucke Building. Sharon Brandt had reportedly mentioned Rick's interest in Betsy to investigators. Because of Professor Wright's silence, Trooper Ken Schleiden had no reason to suspect that Haefner was anything more than a concerned acquaintance of Betsy's. He talked about his dates with her and of learning about her death—he claimed it was on Saturday, November 29—while eating a meal in the HUB.[7]

Schleiden has little or no memory of the report he wrote forty-five years ago. Other retired troopers say he has beaten himself up over not being more suspicious of Haefner. But he ought to be forgiven. Schleiden had no idea that Haefner was a pedophile, or that he had made that visit to Professor Wright an hour after the murder, because Wright didn't tell anyone. Rick had never been arrested. The odds were slim that anyone could have unearthed Rick's background minus a good tip, especially at a time when the state police were interviewing thousands of students and professors. On the other hand, Larry Paul Maurer, who did set off alarms, seemed bound and determined to come across as a plausible suspect. The continuing interest in him by the state police was as understandable as the decision not to probe more deeply into Haefner's past. Investigators go with their instincts, barring anything else. And sometimes, like human beings everywhere, they are wrong. And too, Haefner was a clever psychopath accustomed to lying to cover up his secret life. There was much to conceal, but he was good at it. [8]

Part IV: Flight from Justice

The Earth has not managed to swallow me into the abyss
Nor has the sea engulfed me with its raging storms
I have fled from the law and escaped the arena
I've even stained my hands with blood
Only to end up here, destitute, exiled from my country, abandoned.

—Opening lines, *Fellini: Satyricon*, 1969

CHAPTER 22
Bad Seed

When he died in 1916 after a long illness, the German immigrant Joseph Haefner, owner of the Haefner Empire Brewing Co., was a business aristocrat in his adopted hometown of Lancaster, Pennsylvania. The *Intelligencer Journal* newspaper memorialized him as a "progressive, straightforward business man and a good citizen in every respect." His life had been a tribute to the American dream. Son of a brewer from the city of Bamberg in Bavaria, Haefner had arrived in America in 1872 at age twenty-four. He spent the next fourteen years as a journeyman, perfecting his knowledge of the beer business. He worked for a succession of breweries in New York City and Reading, Pottsville, Philadelphia, and Lancaster, in Pennsylvania. Finally settling in Lancaster in 1886, he acquired a brewery at the corner of Lime and Locust Streets and expanded it over the years to three times its original size. He sold beer in the region under brands that included Kaiser, a pale ale, and Muenchener, a dark Bavarian ale, all delivered in horse-drawn wagons. And he prospered.[1]

In 1874, Joseph Haefner married a young widow and single mother, Margaret M. Fisher, whose father was the proprietor of the Reading Depot hotel in Lancaster. She had been married to Henry Bauman, who died at age thirty-one in 1869, a year after the birth of their son, Henry C. The son always went by Harry, and was the direct ancestor of Rick Haefner. News stories never mentioned Margaret's first marriage, always asserting that Joseph married "Miss Margaret Fisher." He gave Harry his family name, which suggested he had adopted him, but referred to Harry as "my stepson." The couple, who were Catholic, went on to have seven more children, of whom five survived to adulthood. In 1890, to house his large family, Joseph built a redbrick mansion at 134 Locust Street, across from his brewery and set amid the average row houses of the working class. It was gabled and Victorian but decidedly unfancy on the outside, a product of his practical German outlook.[2]

Not everything he touched turned to gold. By the time he died in 1916, Joseph Haefner was beset by financial woes brought on by his investment in the Union Irrigation Co. of Opelousas, Louisiana, a venture that joined Southern dreams and Northern capital. Founded in 1903 as the Union Rice & Irrigation Co., the venture aimed to open up five hundred thousand acres of rich, clay soil roughly sixty miles west of Baton Rouge for rice cultivation. What happened to push the company into bankruptcy around 1914 is unknown, but Haefner's obituary observed that "he was a large loser financially" as a result of its downfall.[3] His will made equal provision for his five children with Margaret and his stepson, Harry, who was accounted for separately in the will. Each received $10,000, the equivalent of more than $210,000 today.[4]

When Prohibition finally ended on December 5, 1933, the Haefners went back into the beer business, producing 46,800 barrels of Pilsener-type beer during 1934. But they and the other three remaining breweries in Lancaster were hobbled by old and inefficient production facilities. None of them had modernized in the years running up to Prohibition. Haefner Brewing Company, as it was then known, went out of business in 1945, too small to compete with the large national brands and decades before the advent of microbrews. In 1946, the same year of Harry C. Haefner's death, the brewery filed for bankruptcy and was no more.[5]

Harry left behind six sons, Francis J., Henry C., Paul A., Leon J., Joseph G., and George P. Haefner, who was the youngest, born in 1908. In the late 1930s, George married Ere Seaber. Leon J. Haefner, his brother and the grandfather of Chris Haefner, married one of Ere's sisters. That bound the two families even closer. Ere bore George two sons, George P. Jr. in 1938 and Richard Charles, who came along in 1943.

In the spring of 1951, George Haefner moved his family to 217 Nevin Street in Lancaster, in a working-class neighborhood of older homes. The house, on the end of a row of long, narrow houses with nearly identical front porches, was a far cry from the mansion his father and grandfather had inhabited. But he was not a prosperous businessman, just an average Joe who sold insurance. The wealth of the Haefner family ancestor was long gone. Only the prestige of the name remained, and even that was fading with time. The house adjoined an alley that intersected Nevin Street, and the kitchen door opened to a small landing and steps that led down to the ground. Across the alley was an old four-stall garage with heavy wooden doors that belonged to one of the homeowners around the corner on Chestnut Street.

Farther up Nevin Street in the other direction was Sacred Heart Catholic Church and its parish school. George and Ere Haefner were nominal members of the church but rarely attended Mass. When Rick was born, they did not have him christened or baptized, a priest there would later say, referring to the traditional Christian ceremony by which an infant is admitted to the Kingdom of Heaven and absolved of all sins. Nor did they send him to Catholic school.

There is the Lancaster County of tourist imagination and a somewhat richer and darker reality. On one hand, it was a place of agricultural abundance, supposedly the second-richest farming area in the United States. Here lived the Amish, offshoots of the Anabaptists in Europe, a sect of Plain People who wore nineteenth-century clothing and shunned electricity, land-line telephones in their houses, and automobiles. They spoke an ancient form of German, and in the mid-twentieth century became a nearly irresistible tourist attraction.

The vast majority of Lancaster County residents were not Amish and not farmers. But many, like the Haefners, were of German descent, although they had long since dispensed with the German language. As a general rule, German Catholics tended to live in the city of Lancaster, where the Catholic churches originally were, while the German Protestants—of many denominations—lived everywhere but dominated the rest of the county.

Yet despite its churchiness, and for reasons that remain unclear, Lancaster County is also known for its strange and brutal murders and murderers. Every locale has murders, but these were far from the ordinary: adults killing children, children killing children, children killing adults, and adults killing adults out of sexual dysfunction. Author Richard Gehman wrote about one of the latter in his 1954 book, *Murder in Paradise.*

In 1950, Edward L. Gibbs, a senior at the then all-male Franklin & Marshall College in Lancaster, got to know Marian Baker, a twenty-two-year-old secretary in the bursar's office at the college. Gibbs, who was unhappily married, took Baker, who was engaged to be married, for a ride one day and bludgeoned and strangled her to death. He hid the body and returned to campus, where he showered and went out to dinner with his wife. For the next few days, tormented by guilt, Gibbs thought of going to the police and confessing. He asked two fellow students, sons of undertakers, how long it took a body to decompose. He even went to a funeral director and asked if a strangler's fingerprints could be recovered from the neck of his victim, saying he needed the information for a criminology class. After Marian's body was finally discovered, Gibbs took to appearing each night at the Lancaster *Intelligencer Journal* to buy the paper when it came off the presses in the wee hours of the morning.

Lancaster police detectives eventually heard of Gibbs's questions about bodily decay and made further inquiries at the college. One day, Gibbs appeared at the office of F&M president Theodore Distler and confessed to the murder. An aide to Distler then took Gibbs on a remarkable walk across campus to his own office, where detectives were waiting. They took Gibbs for a ride, and he showed them where he dumped his weapon and some of Marian's belongings. They asked him about a number of other unsolved murders around the state, including that of student Rachel Taylor at Penn State University in 1940. Gibbs was of no help in that regard.[6]

Psychiatrists who examined the F&M student portrayed him—this was in 1950—as the son of an overprotective, smothering mother and a weak, ineffectual father. They didn't call him a homosexual, but their account today reads like a description of a deeply closeted and repressed gay man who also hated women. Gibbs dated women and eventually married one, but only because that was what he thought he was supposed to do in life. District Attorney John Milton Ranck found the psychiatric testimony incredible or irrelevant. He believed Gibbs simply had made a sexual advance to Baker and killed her in a rage after she rejected him and threatened to tell the college, or his wife. "Gibbs was not insane," Ranck told Gehman. "He was devilishly clever. It is frightening to think how close this fellow came to getting away with this crime." The jury agreed, and Gibbs was sentenced to death. He died in the electric chair at the State Correctional Institution at Rockview on April 23, 1951.[7]

What is notable here is that Franklin & Marshall College, its staff and students, had helped the police solve the Marian Baker murder in ways that counted. No one in the community protected Gibbs or looked the other way, and he paid the price for his awful crime. The college moved on, having done its civic duty. Penn State University would have done well to take note.

Rick Haefner was intellectually gifted and pursued the college preparatory course at J. P. McCaskey High School in Lancaster. He was active in high school theater, playing the role of the boss's son, Tony Kirby, in *You Can't Take It With You,* and worked on the student newspaper. His grades were good enough to gain him admission to Franklin & Marshall College when he graduated in 1961. By then, he knew he wanted to become a geologist, and F&M had one of the better undergraduate geology programs in the country. He had worked at the college's North Museum, a natural history museum, as a volunteer guide, lecturer, and researcher—his description—since the age of twelve or thirteen. The curator, John W. Price Sr., became his friend and mentor and fired his passion for museum work. Rick's house at 217 Nevin Street was close enough to the college that he could walk there in fifteen minutes, so he lived at home. He was a dedicated student and did well in his classes, but made few lasting impressions on his classmates. Lane Schultz, a geology major who was a year behind Haefner, recalled little beyond Rick being a sharp dresser and wearing khaki pants nearly all the time.[8]

Psychologists tend to believe today that pedophiles are born that way, comprising 1 to 5 percent of the male population. Rick may well have seemed normal for a long time. He went through the public schools in Lancaster, but by the time he reached McCaskey, he had begun to set himself apart from other boys. They considered him to be gay, although cruder terms were probably employed. He was harassed mercilessly, according to his cousin, Chris Haefner, and, as noted, began carrying a homemade knife for protection.[9]

Rick first became known to police at age nineteen in the fall of 1962, when he solicited a boy from Wharton Elementary School for sex. At the time, he was a sophomore at Franklin & Marshall College and working as a counselor in the Grey-Y program at the Lancaster YMCA, where the crime occurred. All we know about the incident is contained in a one-paragraph document in the files of the Lancaster Police Department, which says they were informed of the incident after it reached the attention of District Attorney Alfred Alspach. Why he wasn't arrested is unknown.[10]

Although Rick did not attend Mass at Sacred Heart Catholic Church, barely a block from his parents' house, he did participate in the parish's Boy Scout troop, which had been in existence since 1913. Sometime after he enrolled at Franklin & Marshall, he became an assistant scoutmaster of Troop 24. Handsome and clean-cut, Rick was the picture of a Boy Scout leader.

He may well have molested boys throughout his time with the troop, but the crisis came early in the summer of 1965, when Rick's sexual recklessness seemed to peak. Michael D. Witmer, who was in Troop 24 when Haefner was an assistant scoutmaster, remembered Rick on one hand as "a really cool, smart guy" who would do anything for him or his friends. He also sought to endear himself to their parents, sometimes simply showing up at the front door to visit their sons, other times volunteering to drive them places. Anyone who has been in Boy Scouts will recognize the type, at least as it was supposed to be. The boys gravitated toward him because he was closer in age to them than their scoutmaster—more like an older brother who seemed to know a lot about the world and was totally into the outdoor Boy Scout life.

Today, what Haefner did would be called grooming, meaning to befriend the boys, to give them things their parents would not or could not, and in so doing, to lessen their resistance to the sexual activities he envisioned. It also meant easing the concerns of their parents about a young adult male spending time alone with their preteen sons, much easier in 1965 than in today's justifiably cynical world. Like so many pedophiles, he had them completely fooled. Witmer recalled vividly his shock on the day when his best friend, Dave S., told him how Haefner had reached into his sleeping bag on one of the troop's campouts and fondled his genitals. His story poured out in a torrent of fear, confusion, and self-loathing.[11]

Dave S. today recalls Haefner with anger and bitterness, believing that his former Scout leader stole an important part of his childhood. He said Haefner molested him four or five times in 1963 or 1964, usually at either Camp Chiquetan, a former Boy Scout camp in Lancaster County near the confluence of Conestoga Creek and the Susquehanna River, or on private land along Chesapeake Bay in Maryland, where Troop 24 sometimes camped. Dave S. suspects that Haefner picked him because his father, a disabled, one-armed World War II veteran, seemed nonthreatening. Witmer urged his friend to check with other members of the troop to see if any of them had had similar experiences with Rick. When several admitted they had, Witmer urged Dave to tell his parents or somebody in authority what had happened.[12]

Word eventually did reach the parents, who in turn complained to the scoutmaster and Father John S. Paukovits, the priest at Sacred Heart Catholic Church. Father Paukovits, who was popular and respected among the boys (they called him "Father Jawbreaker" for the treats he gave them in school), called Haefner in for a meeting. Whether or not Rick confessed isn't known, but Paukovits concluded that the accusations against him were valid. Witmer remembers a parent telling him and the other boys in the troop, after meeting with Paukovits, that the priest believed Rick was sick beyond help. "As I recall, after our church pastor investigated, Haefner was relieved from his assistant scoutmaster position and, incredibly, that was the end of it," Witmer said. Actually, it wasn't. The troop leadership reported Haefner to the regional Boy Scout Council, which in turn reported what had happened to the national headquarters of the Boy Scouts of America. Haefner was banned from Boy Scout work for life.[13]

But no one informed the police, and Rick continued to work his summer job as a day camp supervisor at Camp Optimist for the Lancaster Recreation Commission. An application he filled out on January 4, 1965, to work as a summer playground supervisor for the Lancaster Recreation Commission still listed the Boy Scouts as a reference, suggesting that his activities had not yet come to light at that time. He received the second-highest rating for his leadership that summer, meaning he was considered good but not outstanding. Interestingly, the one area in which Haefner didn't measure up on the evaluation form was in the category "Demonstrates mature judgment; common sense," in which he received a middle rating of "Fair; usually shows good judgment." It seems amazing that Rick was able to end the summer with a generally good performance rating. How someone could work well with accusations of child molestation hanging over his head is a mystery. He seemed to be able to disassociate himself from his crimes, in part by explaining them away in his own mind.[14]

The strange thing was that he was allowed to work at a day camp at all, but there was no Internet then, and it was much easier for misdeeds to stay hidden. He had worked summer jobs for the Lancaster Recreation Commission since at least the summer of 1961, and had come back in the summer of 1965 after graduating from Franklin & Marshall and before starting his graduate work in geology at Penn State in the fall. Because this job was ultimately with the Lancaster School District, Rick was required to obtain a temporary teaching certificate from the Pennsylvania Department of Public Instruction, today the Department of Education, before he could take the job. The one he obtained in July 1962 was issued before the YMCA incident that November, but the renewal the following summer came months afterward. G. Wayne Glick, dean and acting president of Franklin & Marshall, even signed the application form attesting to Rick's "good moral character." What this says as much as anything is that Rick had no arrest record, that word of his pedophilia was confined to a very small group of people, and that he was good at deceiving the world.

In late August 1965, Rick persuaded a trusting single mother in Lancaster to let him take her sons, ages ten and eleven years, on vacation with him for five days to Ocean City, Maryland. Ocean City was a popular vacation spot for central Pennsylvania residents, three and a half hours from Lancaster by car. They were boys he had gotten to know during his day camp work that summer. After plying them with more spending money than their mother ever could, and providing plenty of good times on the beach and boardwalk, Haefner evidently molested them both. The boys did not go to the police, or even to the motel desk clerk, but on the day they returned, they did tell their mother. She angrily confronted Haefner and then unloaded on Philip Bomberger III, chairman of the Lancaster Recreation Commission. What she didn't do, as far as can be determined, was call the police.[15]

Bomberger, to his credit, tried to assess what had happened, and also tried to help Rick deal with his demons. After a one-on-one meeting on August 30, 1965, Bomberger wrote that Rick "appeared very nervous and shaken about the reaction of the victims' mother. . . . Richard said he felt only compassion for this mother, and if he had done anything wrong, he wasn't aware of what it was." He explained to Rick that he had sexually assaulted both boys, but his words seemed to go over Haefner's head. "He said he was only trying to do something good by taking the boys on a vacation before they [went] away to school. Richard said the boys never complained about anything, so he didn't realize anything was wrong." It was classic pedophile behavior: groom the boys with money and good times to the point where they'll reluctantly submit to molestation for fear of angering their sugar daddy.[16]

At the time, Haefner seemed mainly to be concerned with the impact on his brother, his parents, and himself if the mother's complaint became public. "Richard's immediate response was that he had only two alternatives—to run away or to commit suicide," Bomberger wrote. His brother George, about to graduate from Penn State with an engineering degree, planned to work in the defense industry and could possibly lose his security clearance. His parents might have to leave town, or could even die from the shock, Rick said. And it might lead Penn State to rescind his acceptance to graduate school in geology, a legitimate fear if not an unwarranted outcome. Given Rick's later history, it is possible that all of the fears he expressed were a con job to defuse the problem with Bomberger.

In fact, Bomberger consulted with two medical professionals who had different opinions on whether Rick should be reported to the police. Dr. Charles H. Kurtz, the family physician of the two boys, told him that he was leaning, albeit reluctantly, to the idea that Rick's crimes should be reported to the police for his own good, but that he first wanted to consult a psychiatrist, Dr. Robert J. Kurey, to get his opinion. Kurey, a member of Sacred Heart Church, where he was head usher, was adamantly opposed to involving the police. "Dr. Kurey's opinion was that we have no legal obligation to report this person to the police, and that we should make every effort to protect this boy's reputation and future. Dr. Kurey also warned that this individual was sick and needed help immediately," Bomberger wrote in his report.[17]

Bomberger then arranged for Rick to get immediate psychiatric help, from Dr. Kurey, which he was supposed to continue with a local practitioner in State College in late September, after he reported to the Penn State campus. Rick did see Dr. Kurey on September 13. But early in 1966, Bomberger made follow-up calls to both Kurtz and Kurey. Neither, it turned out, had checked to see whether Rick had continued receiving psychiatric care at Penn State. They had just passed him along.[18]

In the 1960s, the dominant belief was that pedophilia was more of a civil offense against decency than a criminal offense that destroyed a young, innocent soul. It was bad, yes, but something to be worked out, perhaps with a stern admonishment to the perpetrator to get counseling and sin no more. Philip Jenkins, author of *Moral Panic: Changing Concepts of the Child Molester in Modern America* and coincidentally a Penn State professor of history and religious studies, writes that America has swung back and forth in its attitudes toward pedophiles. Between the Progressive Era and the end of World War II, the country saw child molesters as "malignant sex fiends," but after the war embarked upon twenty-five years of a more nuanced and libertarian view of pedophilia, including, among some, the belief that it was an innocuous offense. Jenkins writes that during the 1960s, the orthodoxy was that "molestation was a very infrequent offense unlikely to cause significant harm to the vast majority of [victims] . . . and molesters were confused inadequates unlikely to repeat their offenses." He wrote that child victims in those years were "often regarded as seducers" who bore a share of responsibility for what happened to them. In the 1960s, no one seemed inclined to ask the police to arrest Rick.[19]

But there may have been another reason Rick stayed out of jail. Professor Roger Cuffey at Penn State, who employed Rick as a geology teaching assistant for three semesters, from January 1969 to June 1970, said Haefner came to him in the spring of 1969 and told him a story about how the district attorney of Lancaster County had tried to bring molestation charges against him several years earlier, based on a complaint from two teenagers who had worked with him and with his mentor, Professor John W. Price Sr., at the North Museum at Franklin & Marshall College. The case described by Cuffey doesn't sound like either the Boy Scouts or the Ocean City case, so perhaps it was yet another example of Haefner accosting and molesting boys in his community. According to Cuffey, Rick went to Philadelphia and obtained help from Arlen Specter, then an assistant district attorney in Philadelphia and, later, a United States senator. Cuffey said Rick talked to him at length about how Specter had helped him. Could it have happened? Yes, although there is no known proof that it did.[20]

Assistant district attorneys in Philadelphia at that time were allowed to have private law practices on the side. When Specter left the Philadelphia law firm today known as Dechert, Price & Rhoads in 1959 to become an assistant DA, he also organized a private law practice and accepted any number of cases over the next several years. He would take private cases even when he was heavily involved in something else. On Election Day in November 1965, for example, when Specter was on the ballot as the Republican candidate for district attorney, he voted and then went to federal court to represent a client in a product liability case. If Specter did help Haefner, it might have been because he was intrigued by Haefner's claim of law enforcement corruption in Lancaster County. Those kinds of cases drew Specter like a dog to a fire whistle. In his autobiography, Specter made much of his "truth-seeking" and fights against government malfeasance. Did he make a few phone calls to Lancaster and head off charges? Maybe; maybe not.

CHAPTER 23

Death Valley

Rick Haefner's mentor in the rigorous and research-oriented graduate geology program at Penn State was Professor Lauren A. Wright, who taught Geology of North America and was chairman of the Department of Geology and Geophysics from 1963 to 1971. Wright joined the faculty in 1961 from the California Division of Mines and Geology, where he and his nearly lifelong research partner, Bennie Troxel, had prepared geologic maps of the southern half of Death Valley National Monument. Later in life, he became known as the "dean of Death Valley geologists." Wright returned to the hot, beautiful, and dangerous desert nearly every fall, usually taking a student or two along with him, and always staying in a house trailer he owned in the desert crossroads of Shoshone, California. He would have gotten to know Rick one way or another as chairman of the department, but for whatever reason, they hit it off.[1]

It was Wright who suggested to Haefner that he might want to consider Death Valley as a good locale for his own research, and agreed to be his master's thesis advisor. He invited Rick to accompany him to Death Valley during the fall and winter of 1967 to do the field research for his thesis. That made it easier for Wright, because it was Penn State's practice to send the thesis advisor to verify the fieldwork and surveys of a geology graduate student to make sure the measurements were right. Most graduate students went out on their own to do research, but it wasn't unheard of for both the professor and the student to be out together.[2]

Rick did reasonably well in his graduate studies at Penn State. He had a rough start, earning a C in a nonmetallic crystal chemistry course and withdrawing from a physical chemistry class (typically a move to avoid a poor grade), which he took again the following year, and likewise earned a C, the minimum passing grade for graduate students. In his geology and non-math courses that first year, however, he scored straight As.[3]

One thing Haefner didn't have to worry about at Penn State was the draft, despite the river of induction notices going out to feed the Vietnam War military. Indeed, draft calls doubled in 1965 over 1964, and rose more than 50 percent again in 1966 before settling down somewhat in 1967. But Haefner, like most college students of the era, had received the 2-S student deferment, available to both undergraduate and graduate students, first at Franklin & Marshall College and then at Penn State. (New graduate deferments were ended in 1967, but those who already had them, like Rick Haefner, were usually allowed to keep them, so he had little chance of being drafted into military service.) Nor was there any necessity for him to confront his sexual attraction to boys. Whether that would have been unearthed in the psychological or moral fitness examinations if he had been called for his draft physical is hard to say, but because of congressional policy, he was deferred from the draft while he pursued his studies, provided he kept his grades above a middling level, which he did.[4]

Wright eventually figured out that Haefner was not a normal heterosexual male, although the extent of that knowledge may have been his observation that Rick was uncomfortable around women and rarely seen in their company. He even commented on it to other students who worked around Rick, saying on one occasion that he "wasn't sure Rick really liked girls." Those who knew Wright, who died in 2013, universally labeled him as someone who tried to see the best in people. "He never gave me a hard time," said Joe Head, an undergraduate geology student at Penn State when Rick was there. "I was not a good geology student, but we hit it off personally. He was a person who seemed to want to think the best and believe the best and encourage you, rather than being critical." Geology professor Roger Cuffey, who occasionally counseled gay students and employed Rick as a teaching assistant, took a different view, believing him simply a socially inept young man. "Rick fit into what we nowadays would call a geek kind of position. He got up the courage occasionally to ask a couple of girls out here and there."[5]

Haefner and Wright left by car on their research trip to Death Valley around the start of the fall term on October 1, 1967. Their field work could only be done between late September and the middle of May, because the brutal heat in Death Valley regularly soared past 110 degrees in the summer months. Accompanying them was Joe Head, who on a whim had signed up as Haefner's field assistant after seeing the job posted on a bulletin board in the Deike Building, where the geology department was located. Head later learned it wasn't typical for graduate students to have field assistants—that they usually did all the work themselves. Did Wright want a third person along as a buffer between himself and Rick's weirdness, or even because of nagging doubts about Rick's sexuality? Perhaps he worried about gossip.[6]

Wright and Haefner did most of the driving on the 2,400-mile trip from State College to the professor's double-wide trailer in Shoshone, following a meandering route across the West. In Missouri, they picked up US Route 160 and followed it across southern Colorado, passing Mesa Verde, the ancient Native American cliff dwellings, and stopping at Four Corners, where Colorado, New Mexico, Arizona, and Utah come together. Like nearly every tourist did at Four Corners, Rick had his picture taken in a crab squat with his feet in two of the states and his hands in the other two, which allowed him to claim he was in four states at once. Then it was on to the Grand Canyon, Hoover Dam, and, finally, to Las Vegas, the jumping-off point for Shoshone, still eighty-five miles distant. At the time, Las Vegas was the last vestige of civilization before Death Valley, the place for car repair or medical care or to load up on supplies at a more reasonable price.[7]

They emerged from the desert into the lights and glitter of the Las Vegas Strip, where they stayed overnight and went to a "rather risqué" show. "It was kind of like a chorus line," Head said. "They may even have been topless, I can't remember." In the morning, the trio got back on the road, quickly leaving the city behind and entering the red rock desert moonscape. They saw only sporadic signs of human habitation until they reached Pahrump, Nevada, then much smaller and less commercially developed than today. In the middle of town, they made a left turn onto a lonely, two-lane highway that took them back out into the desert.

Founded in 1910 by Ralph J. "Dad" Fairbanks, Shoshone once served as a home for the men who worked in the borax mines in the surrounding desert. Some of the miners even dug their own caves and lived in them, receiving free, natural air-conditioning during the sweltering summers. Fairbanks and later his descendants owned nearly everything in the town. If you lived in a house, it was rented from the family. If you owned a trailer, as Wright did, you still paid ground rent to whichever member of the family happened to be in charge. Fairbanks's daughter Stella and her husband, Senator Charles Brown (he served in the California Senate from 1938 to 1962), took over Shoshone in 1927. Their daughter, Bernice Sorrells, and her husband, Maury, took over in 1942. Bernice was still in charge the day Wright, Haefner, and Head pulled into town. Her husband had died in a plane crash in 1965. Wright knew her well.[8]

During the ten weeks they were in Shoshone, Head spent most days in the field with Rick, helping him to conduct research for his master's thesis. This consisted mainly of driving Haefner to the site of his research about ten miles northwest of Shoshone in the Greenwater Range near Deadman Pass and driving him back to the trailer at day's end in the four-wheel drive Ford Bronco that Penn State kept in Shoshone for Wright's use. Only toward the end of the trip was Head allowed to do some mapping on his own. Haefner was investigating the location and cooling history of a rhyolite unit, a huge, thick mass of volcanic rock that might run for miles. At his research site, the rhyolite was exposed in layers of pink, yellow, and gray. Professor Wright was usually off in a different location doing his own research, sometimes accompanied by his old friend, Bennie Troxel.[9]

Life was not all work in Shoshone. The three of them would sometimes go swimming in the municipal pool after dark, letting the warm, volcanic water ease muscles tired from a day in the desert. One time they drove 240 miles to the Los Angeles area. Rick's brother, George Haefner Jr., was an electrical engineer for Hughes Aircraft and lived in Huntingdon Beach. Once a year, Hughes would take over Disneyland in Anaheim for a night and treat its thousands of employees and their families to a free evening of fun at the storied amusement park. Head remembers driving to Huntingdon Beach, having dinner with George and his family, and then spending the night there after they returned from Disneyland. "Rick's family—his brother seemed nice, and I didn't feel awkward or uncomfortable," Head said. "They seemed like they were really good friends as brothers." That would prove to be an understatement; George Haefner, like his parents, would prove to be a fierce defender of his brother against those who would hold Rick responsible for his sex crimes.[10]

On Thanksgiving weekend, about two weeks before the end of their stay, Professor Wright, Rick, and Joe Head were invited to Bernice Sorrells's home for dinner. Her daughter, Susan, who was a senior English major at Smith College in Northampton, Massachusetts, had flown home for the holiday weekend and was at the dinner. She was attractive, with brown eyes and dark hair cut in a bob. Head did not recall any noticeable interaction between Rick and Susan that night, but it marked the start of Rick's infatuation with her. She was serious, smart, and eager to engage the world. Sorrells, whose classmates at Smith included Catherine MacKinnon, the feminist legal scholar, and Diana Kerry, sister of former senator and Secretary of State John Kerry, eventually would do a tour in the Peace Corps in Liberia. She was a lot like Betsy Aardsma, but different, too, especially in hairstyle. The three men left Shoshone around December 10 to drive back to State College. Susan was quite done with Rick, but he was not done with her.[11]

Rick may have seen in Susan what he would see in Betsy and other women later in his life: unwitting cover for what he was. There is no evidence any of them understood the role he planned for them in his life. In the spring of 1968, he drove six hours and nearly four hundred miles from Penn State to Smith College and knocked on Susan's door in Morrow House, her dorm. When she answered and expressed astonishment at him being there, he said he had a crush on her, or words to that effect.

That didn't go over well. Susan asked him to leave, finding his presence bizarre and a little threatening, and he slunk away. She complained to her mother, who complained to Lauren Wright, who depended on Bernice Sorrells's good graces to remain welcome in the tiny town she owned, and where he leased a trailer space from her. They must have worked out an accommodation, because in the fall of 1968, Rick was back in Shoshone with Lauren Wright and a new field assistant, Dan Stephens. Stephens remembers that Wright seemed to be paying close attention to Rick's interactions with Susan, who had graduated from Smith by then. Rick was on his best behavior. The three of them went to dinner at the Sorrells house more than once that fall, Stephens said.[12]

Like Joe Head, Dan Stephens served as Rick's driver. After cooking breakfast for Rick and Professor Wright, he would load up the Ford Bronco and drive Haefner out to the spot in the desert where his mapping for the day would begin. Rick was working on his doctoral dissertation, doing further research on the same rock formation he had studied for his master's thesis. He called this formation the "Shoshone volcanics." Wright and Bennie Troxel, when he was there, went off on their own. At day's end, Stephens would pick up Rick at a predesignated location. They spent little time together during the day, because Stephens would be given mapping assignments of his own elsewhere in the lonely desert, often miles away from Haefner. At night, back in the trailer in Shoshone, Stephens would cook dinner for Rick and Professor Wright, and afterward they would compare notes on what they had done that day and perhaps test some of the rocks. On many nights, Dan and Rick listened to Wolfman Jack's raspy voice as he played rock and roll and Motown hits on station XERB-AM out of Tijuana, Mexico, more than three hundred miles away. It was about the only entertainment available out in the desert.[13]

Stephens didn't really care for Rick, considering him nerdy and annoying. "He had these glasses which, at first, made him seem like he was looking down his nose at you," Stephens remembered. "Dark-rimmed glasses. And he always seemed to wear those baggy, khaki pants." Rick was also a neat freak, he said, an odd characteristic for a geologist. Geologists are forever getting dirty. "He always had a clean shirt," Stephens said.

"That's a little odd for a geologist." Rick could be moody or he could be giddy, giggly, and bubbly, he said. Wright, he said, referenced his graduate student's "troubles with girls" a couple of times during the trip, once even commenting that he wasn't sure Rick even liked girls.

Toward the end of October, sensing that Dan was near the breaking point with Rick, Wright invited him to accompany him and Bennie Troxel on a weeklong field trip. Stephens jumped at the chance, and Rick was left alone with the Ford Bronco. He went back alone into the desert, where he is likely to have encountered no one, unless . . .

Among the intriguing but ultimately unanswerable questions in this story is whether Rick briefly came under the spell of his desert neighbor, Charles Manson, during his week alone. Manson and his nominal second in command, Paul Watkins, were roaming Death Valley in dune buggies that fall, looking for the mythical "Hole in the Desert" where the Family was supposed to hide out during Helter Skelter. The women in the Family, including Susan Atkins, sometimes panhandled in Shoshone. Who better for Manson to stop and ask about a weird geological formation than a geologist? And maybe invite him back to the Barker Ranch for some drugs, sex, music, and listening to Charlie rap about life and death. Manson did this with a number of young men he saw as potential recruits. But there is no proof that this ever happened with Rick, even if Haefner did develop several Manson-like characteristics. The most notable was the casual, philosophical attitude toward murder and death he would voice in later years. Manson taught his followers that it was not wrong to kill a human being. To Charlie, according to Vincent Bugliosi, the prosecutor at his trial, murder and death were no more important "than eating an ice-cream cone." Rick's philosophy was much the same. Not that Manson was the only possible source for that. But it is, as they say, food for thought.[14]

CHAPTER 24
Left Behind

One night in May of 1970, Louis C. Cotts, Betsy's uncle, had a terrifying nightmare about her death. The terror ended only when Betsy came to him in the dream and told him that she was okay, that things were okay. She told him she was happy in Heaven and had no desire to return to the living. He awoke sobbing and continued to express emotion for several hours. About two weeks later, according to Dennis Wegner, Betsy's brother-in-law, Cotts died when a pulmonary aneurysm burst in roughly the same spot where the killer's knife had nicked Betsy's pulmonary artery. She had been his favorite niece, he had urged her to go to Penn State to get away from the Coed Killer, and he never got over her murder.[1]

Neither did any other close family members. Dick Aardsma, her father, sank back into alcohol and bad driving, not necessarily together. A gentle man who liked to read history, his alcohol problem predated Betsy's death. Jan Sasamoto, Betsy's friend, recalled that she thought him a little different, a little silly at times. And a terrible driver, which she did not connect with his drinking until much later. On February 20, 1971, a Saturday, Dick Aardsma was driving north on M-40 around 8:40 a.m. when his car collided with another car on wet pavement near the big curve in the highway at East 48th Street, a mile or two from his house. Aardsma, who was fifty-five years old, was admitted to Holland Hospital with injuries to his nose, chest, and right arm. Two teenagers in the other car, both members of the Holland Christian High School wrestling team, were treated for cuts and bruises.[2]

Esther Aardsma descended into deep depression after her daughter's death but coped with it largely on her own. Therapy was not a realistic option in Holland at that time. She and Dick kept to themselves. Bernice Kolenbrander, a neighbor for years on East 37th Street, said she didn't know them very well. "They were quiet people," she said. Neither parent phoned for updates on their daughter's case, according to Sergeant George Keibler, the lead investigator of the murder. For the first three or four years after 1969, Keibler made a point of calling them once a year, or more often if he thought they might have seen something in the media about the investigation. There wasn't much news coverage after the spring of 1970, though, just anniversary updates that reported the murder was still unsolved. Keibler told his men that any call to the Aardsmas had to be cleared through him. He didn't want them bothered about something minor.[3]

David L. Wright, Betsy's boyfriend and unofficial fiancé, says he grieved for "two or three months" after her murder, a period that was "pretty bleak." Then he started dating again, first with a nursing student, according to his medical school friend, Ian Osborn, and then, according to Wright, with the roommate of Osborn's girlfriend at Elizabethtown College near Hershey. She eventually became his wife and was described by a friend as "very, very nice, but very different from Betsy." Their friends had always wondered about the ultimate staying power of a relationship between a liberal, artistic, free spirit and a politically and socially conservative physician. Wright, over the years, has projected Hamlet-like ambivalence about Betsy, whether or not he actually felt that way. "I'm never sure if you're 100 percent certain when you get engaged if that's the right person," Wright said. "I'm sure we would have gotten engaged that Christmas and married the next summer, but then you kind of go back and forth. Then I'm thinking, 'Gee, now I'm totally free and I can look around.' It's just a weird feeling."[4]

Ian Osborn, who believes David was serious about Betsy and intended to marry her, says his friend "handled it all very well. He was a very hard-working, fast-talking, somewhat nervous guy who often cracked funny jokes." Osborn says Wright threw himself into his schoolwork and dealt with Betsy's death by avoiding thinking about it too much. As close as the two of them were, Wright never spoke to Osborn about the murder. "I never pressed him," he said. "I spent a whole summer with him working at a hospital in Chicago, and the whole affair was never broached. I was always curious, of course, but I didn't think it appropriate to question him about any aspect of it."[5]

Dennis Wegner returned to Madison, Wisconsin, after the funeral. His wife, Carole, Betsy's older sister, stayed behind for a time to help her parents. Dennis resumed his graduate studies in medical microbiology, but he never got over her murder. Temporarily alone in their apartment, he found himself in emotional hell. He tried to pretend Betsy had never existed, or that her murder was a bad dream and she would be coming home soon. "I managed to use these forms of denial successfully for short periods of time," Wegner wrote in an essay, "Coping with Unexpected Death." "Unfortunately, hearing her name mentioned, seeing her picture, looking at her paintings and writings, or hearing certain reminiscent songs on the radio would snap me back to reality and plunge [me] back down to the bottom." He eventually found a degree of peace through spiritual counseling he received from a former Hope College roommate, Reverend Warren Bovenkerk, and in providing help and counseling to others who had lost loved ones.[6]

In January 1972, Dennis and Carole Wegner made headlines when they sent a letter to US Supreme Court Chief Justice Warren Burger, asking him to strike down the death penalty and spare the life of whoever killed Betsy, if he was ever caught. The letter was written and signed by Dennis but had the full support of Carole and the rest of the Aardsma family. The letter went in the mail to Burger a few days before the Court heard arguments on January 17 in *Furman v. Georgia*, a major death penalty case. Copies went to several newspapers around the country, as letters to the editor. The UPI version of the story that ran in the *Holland Evening Sentinel* quoted Dick and Esther Aardsma as saying they knew Dennis was writing to the chief justice. They "concurred with the spirit" of the letter but had not seen the entire text.[7]

Wegner's letter to Burger pleaded for the life of Betsy's killer and the lives of other condemned prisoners. He portrayed his late sister-in-law as a martyred saint. "Betsy loved America, and the fact that many were without food, medical attention, warmth, and understanding were sources of great pain to her. Her only real concerns in life dealt with the preservation and improvement of human life. Therefore, the execution of her murderer would be a glaring contradiction of everything she lived for," Wegner wrote. He reminded Burger—anticipating the biblical "eye-for-an-eye" argument—that Jesus Christ had stopped the stoning execution of a prostitute with the words, "Let he who is without sin cast the first stone." Finally, Wegner argued on behalf of the families of condemned prisoners, saying that the death of a loved one is doubly traumatic if they are murdered or executed. He did not want them to experience "the emotional hell that I did."[8]

Several months later, the Court ruled, five to four, that the death penalty was unconstitutionally cruel and unusual punishment under certain circumstances. Wegner's letter didn't have the hoped-for effect on Burger, who was one of the dissenting votes. Most convicts under sentence of death across America, including Charles Manson and several members of the Manson Family, had their sentences commuted to life imprisonment because of this and later decisions.

Keibler continued to investigate the murder, despite ever-dwindling resources and interest from his superiors. By the end of May in 1970 he was down to six investigators, but he considered that to be an ideal number, easy to manage. At the end of 1970, he turned back the rooms in the Boucke Building to Penn State and moved the investigation back to Rockview. Penn State needed Room 109, which was large, for a classroom. University officials told Keibler he could have other space on campus, but he decided it was time to go. He told Ken Silverman, a reporter for the *Daily Collegian,* that he and his investigators had talked to at least five thousand people during that first year after Betsy's murder.[9]

Asked why the case had not been solved, Keibler always came back to the one-hour delay between the time Betsy was found on the floor of Pattee Library and the discovery by Dr. Elmer Reed that she had been stabbed to death. That, and the slow, disorganized response by Colonel Pelton and the Campus Patrol had allowed evidence to be inadvertently contaminated or destroyed, some during the library mop-up, some by gawkers who tromped through the crime scene, touching books and bookshelves, unrestrained by the Campus Patrol. The delay also provided plenty of time for the murderer and potential witnesses to leave the library and vanish into the darkness.[10]

"We know there were more than twenty persons in the Core area at the time Betsy was stabbed," Keibler told Silverman. "Only eight of them have been located—and some of them were brought back from other states so we could talk to them at length. We believe the twelve or more we have never located might have information that could help us." Taft Wireback, in his 1972 article on the Aardsma case, wrote that Keibler blamed "student apathy" in part for the state police failure to solve the murder.[11]

Larry Paul Maurer dropped out of Penn State not long after his questioning in the Aardsma murder and returned to his parents' farm, where he stayed for a short time before enlisting in the army. Why he did this has been the subject of much speculation. Was he running from speculation that he was somehow involved in Betsy's murder? Had his father, furious at the spectacle his son had made, forced him to enlist to straighten out his life? Or did he simply want to trade the academic life for the army life? It could happen, even with the Vietnam War still raging at the beginning of 1970. Maurer had been in the Naval Reserves, assigned to the State College Reserve Center until November 4, 1969. For whatever reason, after 1970 he disappeared into the army, probably (based on his APO address) to one of the American bases in West Germany and, later, into the super-secret National Security Agency.[12]

In the spring of 1973, a Federal Bureau of Investigation memo quoted a state police investigator as calling an unnamed man matching Maurer's description "a prime suspect in this killing, even though there is no strong evidence to support his contention." It was an odd statement, and Sergeant Keibler today, while acknowledging that the redacted memo referred to him and Maurer, flatly denies that he considered the student a prime suspect. He admitted that Maurer was surrounded by a lot of smoke, but that the polygraph results had eliminated him as a real suspect. Then Keibler added, "I think Maurer made a lot of the smoke by wanting to appear important to the people there. He wanted to let his buddies know that, hey, the state police are still talking to me."[13]

Just like the fictional character David Parker, the attention-seeking young actor who taunted police in the movie *The Boston Strangler,* a film that played at a theater in State College in the month after the murder, Maurer was, to borrow a phrase from Winston Churchill, a riddle inside a mystery wrapped in an enigma. What did he know about Haefner, his former roommate? Why did he behave in the way that he did? The state police kept him at the center of their thoughts, while, unbeknownst to them, the real killer was still on the Penn State campus, finishing the work for his PhD.

CHAPTER 25

Hiding in Plain Sight

After returning from Christmas break early in 1970, Rick Haefner slipped back into his daily routine at Penn State. This sort of behavior is not unusual, according to Dr. Stuart W. Twemlow, a retired professor of psychology at Baylor College of Medicine in Texas. He was talking about the Boston Marathon bombers to a *New York Times* reporter in April 2013, but the principle is the same. He said going back to the old routine helps someone who has committed a horrible crime "blot out the horror." Twemlow called it "a normal, dissociative response" that helps the criminal to deny and compartmentalize what he has done. Rick was hiding in plain sight, and with the state police tending to believe that Larry Paul Maurer was the most likely suspect, it seemed unlikely he would be caught, short of an error on his part or a decision by Lauren Wright to reveal to the authorities what happened on the evening of November 28, 1969.[1]

There seemed little chance of that. Rick continued to work with Wright on his doctoral dissertation. He did on-campus research in the winter and spring terms of 1970, then passed his comprehensive examination, a rite of passage for doctoral students. Beginning in the fall term of 1970 and continuing through the summer term of 1972, he was off-campus, most likely in Lancaster, writing his dissertation and working toward receiving his PhD in geology on September 16, 1972.

When he did come up from Lancaster to consult with Professor Lauren Wright, he often brought young boys with him, according to Charles Hosler, who was dean of the College of Earth and Mineral Sciences. He would take the boys to visit the Earth and Mineral Sciences Museum, which at that time occupied parts of three floors in the Steidle Building. The museum was a popular attraction for schoolchildren, where they could see such things as the museum's collection of fluorescent minerals glowing under a black light. Everett Tiffany, Hosler's assistant, was the first to notice that Haefner was bringing a lot of boys to the museum. He didn't know that Rick was a pedophile, but something about the visits set off alarms. For a time, Tiffany didn't say anything.[2]

But then the curator position at the museum came open and Rick applied for the job. He had enough experience from his years of volunteer work at the North Museum at Franklin & Marshall to warrant serious consideration. He loved museum work and saw it as his favored career. Now Tiffany went to Hosler with his suspicions about Rick's friendships with boys, and Hosler decided the prudent option was to hire somebody else. "We were very suspicious," Hosler said. "To tell you the truth, one of the reasons we didn't even consider it was that we felt he would have used it as an access to boys."

It is doubtful Rick was ever told exactly why he had been turned down, and not much else changed for him at Penn State. He was allowed to finish his dissertation, and he continued to bring boys to visit the museum, including his young cousin, Chris Haefner, who was then ten or eleven years old, and a boy named Mark who was about twelve years old. Mark was from Aberdeen, Maryland, an area where Rick spent a lot of time, and Chris Haefner came to believe Mark was in a long-term relationship with Rick.[3]

Confronting men about their unacceptable sexual or other behavior was not the Penn State way, in the early 1970s or for many years afterward. If an involuntary exit from Happy Valley was necessary, it more often occurred in some quiet way that did not alert the public—or, at least, very much of the public—to what had happened. "What I'm saying is . . . the things that would be tolerated here would not be tolerated elsewhere," Hosler said. Looking at what has happened at Penn State over the years helps when it comes to understanding why Rick Haefner was not expelled or, at the very least, questioned about his apparent attraction to boys, and even why Lauren Wright stayed silent for so long about what had happened at his house the night of Betsy's murder. There was the scholarly community of Happy Valley, with its moral relativism, and there was the world outside, with its unyielding laws and morality. That contest was really no contest. How Penn State handled Rick Haefner was less an aberration than part of a sad continuum. Was it "policy"? No. It was more business as usual, the way things were handled in this academic community.[4]

Take the case of Antonio C. Lasaga, a geochemistry professor at Penn State from 1977 to 1984, who was lauded by his peers for his brilliance. His field was chemical kinetics, the study of how quickly or slowly a chemical reaction proceeds. Hosler, who was his dean, considered him a good friend. Tony Lasaga's professors at Princeton, where the young Cuban émigré obtained his undergraduate degree in 1971, and Harvard, where he subsequently completed his graduate work, could barely find enough superlatives to describe his intellect. Apparently unknown to anyone who mattered, Lasaga was a pedophile. Like Rick Haefner and, later, Jerry Sandusky, he was particularly attracted to prepubescent boys. Even when the truth became impossible to deny, some could not reconcile Lasaga's desperate pedophilia with the fact that he had a lovely wife and children. They could not comprehend how a man with a wife, or who, like Rick Haefner, claimed to want a serious relationship with a woman, could pursue boys on the side.[5]

On August 27, 1981, Lasaga, then thirty-one years old, was arrested by police in Patton Township, one of the municipalities that abut State College, and charged with fondling the penises of two boys, ages nine and eleven, at the Park Forest Pool, where he was a member. Park Forest Village was a housing development on the outskirts of State College. The arresting officer, John R. Dodson, persuaded Lasaga to appear voluntarily at the police station for questioning. The Penn State professor admitted to holding the boys upside down—disturbing behavior in and of itself—but denied fondling them.[6]

Dodson asked Lasaga to take a polygraph exam, which he initially agreed to do. But a few days later, he called back and said he had changed his mind, according to police records. Lasaga told the officer, "Couldn't we get this thing cleared up?" He argued that he had no criminal record, which may have been more due to luck than virtue. There had been an incident earlier that month reported in the *Centre Daily Times* in which a boy was molested by an unknown adult male at Holmes-Foster Park in State College, but the perpetrator got away. Lasaga told Dodson he could provide numerous character references and asked him to approach the parents of the two boys about dropping the charges, according to police records. The officer agreed to make the calls, but the families wanted nothing to do with a deal. Lasaga then agreed to a polygraph examination and passed, although the accuracy of the test was later questioned. Whatever happened, it seems to have softened opposition to a deal.[7]

Lasaga's claim that he could provide character references was probably true. Hosler says the professor was much admired and loved by everyone in the department. Indeed, the deal that got him off may have been brokered by C. Wayne Burnham, the Geosciences Department chairman, who worshipped his talented junior colleague. The charges were eventually dropped. Hosler heard that Lasaga paid the parents $500 to back off. That was a low price for pedophilia even in 1981, but perhaps after the polygraph result he was in a better bargaining position. Carol Vonada, the departmental secretary, said Burnham referred to one of the parents as "a welfare mother in it for the money." Not long afterward, Professor Roger Cuffey was standing near the chairman in a hallway, waiting for the start of a faculty meeting, when he overheard Burnham say, "I got Tony off this time."[8]

Lasaga stayed another three years at Penn State before accepting a position at Yale University. He could not keep his hands off young boys. His world collapsed in 1998 when he was arrested by the FBI on federal child pornography charges. Investigators concluded that Lasaga had downloaded as many as 150,000 child pornography images via the Yale computer system. A month later, New Haven police accused Lasaga of sexually assaulting a thirteen-year-old boy he had met through an inner-city mentoring program. He had been a volunteer in the program since 1992. Some of the child pornography items were videotapes Lasaga made of himself having sex with the boy when he was as young as seven years old. In 2002, he pleaded no contest to the charges against him.[9]

His colleagues at Penn State were horrified—not at Lasaga's crimes, which they tended to disbelieve, but at the possibility of a brilliant scholar being lost to science. Two of his former colleagues in the Geosciences Department at Penn State, Hiroshi Ohmoto and Hubert Barnes, testified as character witnesses at his sentencing hearing on the state charges in 2002, pleading for leniency. "He is in his most productive years," Barnes told the court. "When you penalize Tony for his indiscretions, you also penalize society." The *Hartford Courant* reported that when Barnes referred to Lasaga's crimes as "indiscretions," some in the audience gasped. Superior court judge Roland D. Fasano was having none of it. "Even the defendant's magnificent scientific achievements pale in comparison to the destruction of a young life," he said. Fasano called the evidence against Lasaga "overwhelming" despite what his friends and family wanted to believe. State's Attorney David Strollo said he had "never heard people deliver comments so disconnected with reality."[10]

Fasano sentenced Lasaga to twenty years in prison, to run concurrently with the fifteen-year sentence he had received on the federal child pornography charges. Lasaga was placed in the federal system to serve his time there first. Barnes and Ohmoto visited him at the federal prison in Beckley, West Virginia, where he served much of his sentence. Barnes says he persuaded the prison authorities to give Lasaga some computer access. Barnes called Lasaga a "Mozart of chemical kinetics" who has remained productive even during his years behind bars. "I continue to visit and interact with Dr. Lasaga to cooperate in producing research papers that I believe are important to advancing our science," he said. In 2013, a paper of which Lasaga was senior author was said by Barnes to be under review for publication by a leading, peer-reviewed chemistry journal. It all seemed like something out of *Alice in Wonderland* and puts Professor Lauren Wright's moral failings in some perspective.[11]

Hosler, who eventually rose to the position of acting provost at Penn State in 1987 before retiring in 1991, related stories about a number of other professors and officials at Penn State who committed egregious acts. One story concerned a manic-depressive geochemist in the College of Earth and Mineral Sciences, John Weber, who sexually harassed his female graduate students. Parents complained, but he basically was allowed to continue on his merry way. He kept guns in hollowed-out books in his university office, played around with explosives, and threatened to kill Hosler at one point. Weber later killed himself by drinking 200-proof laboratory alcohol.

When Penn State *did* crack down on bad behavior by its staff, there often seemed to be a lesbian in the mix. Hosler told the story of a dean who was hired, with much fanfare, by the Penn State president. Within two weeks, he said, the university was trying to get rid of her, having discovered she was a bad alcoholic. Her greater sin, though, appeared to be that she was disruptive to the existing lesbian social order. As Hosler put it, she found lovers by breaking up lesbian couples on campus. The dean was eventually paid as much as $400,000 over five years to leave, he said. Then there was the woman at the university press who allegedly sexually harassed women who worked for her—for example, by leaving candy vaginas on their desks. "And these country girls, born-again Christians, were just going up the wall," Hosler said. Her boss fired her, she sued, and she eventually won a $50,000 settlement on grounds of antigay discrimination, and a job in another department of the university.[12]

There certainly was no Penn State official policy to tolerate faculty misbehavior—just incident after incident of looking the other way.

CHAPTER 26

Downfall

Haefner spent the year after he received his PhD looking for work. His first professional job was an adjunct position as a visiting assistant professor of geology at the State University of New York at New Paltz during the 1973–74 school year. That was followed by another adjunct position during 1974–75 as an assistant professor of geology at the College of Charleston in South Carolina. Michael P. Katuna, chairman of the department when Haefner was there, said Rick did not cause any problems, and students thought he was a good professor. "A very likable but quiet individual," Katuna remembered. Haefner could put on the charm when he needed to.

Yet he found he didn't really like teaching, and he searched for employment in the field he really loved, not entirely for legitimate reasons: museum work. At the same time, beginning in the early 1970s, Rick owned and operated a rock shop in a rented, four-door garage on the other side of the narrow alley adjoining his parents' house at 217 Nevin Street in Lancaster. The shop, which had no sign or name, was not the kind that caters to rock hounds looking to buy colorful minerals or fossils to add to their collections. It was more like a little factory, manufacturing boxed sets of mineral specimens. Rick had originally assembled collections of Pennsylvania minerals, which he sold to museums such as the Franklin Institute in Philadelphia, for resale in their gift shop. After not too long, he began making sets of specimens from a wider territory and sold them to the Smithsonian Natural History Museum in Washington, DC, for resale in their gift shop, a relationship that continued for more than twenty years. The Smithsonian, because of record destruction, could not verify the business relationship, but there seems little doubt that one existed. Chris Haefner, Rick's cousin, described accompanying Rick when he made deliveries of the rock boxes to the Smithsonian.[1]

Rick employed neighborhood boys to help him crack mineral specimens into smaller pieces and assemble the boxed sets paying them $30 to $40 a week for part-time work, much more than they could have earned most other places in the early 1970s. During the summer, when work was at its peak, the old wooden garage doors would stand open for ventilation and Rick would flit in and out of the building "like a fly," one neighbor observed. It seems to have been a profitable business. He charged a wholesale price of five dollars for one of the boxed sets, and sold between a thousand and two thousand per year. Every couple of months, on a Saturday, he would load up a trailer with hundreds of the boxed sets and make the two-hour drive to the Smithsonian, usually with one or more of the boys coming along as helpers.

Often that included his young cousin, Christopher L. Haefner. Actually, Chris's father and Rick were first cousins. That made Chris a first cousin, once removed, of Rick, but because of the age difference, Rick seemed more like an uncle. Chris was thirteen years old when he started working for Rick, who was then twenty-nine years old, in the summer of 1973. He worshipped his cousin, thought he was cool, but eventually came to wish he was four or five times removed from Rick instead of once.[2]

Chris went to Sacred Heart Catholic School, about four blocks from his family home at 131 North Pine Street. Coming home after school, he would often use the alley that ran between Nevin and Pine Streets, which passed the garage where Rick and his workers made the boxed sets. At the time, he did not realize that the people in the house on the other side of the alley were Haefner relatives. Chris saw bits of unusual and colorful rocks next to the garage and began to pocket the ones he fancied. An "old lady"—Ere Haefner, Rick's mother—sometimes saw him take the rocks and yelled at him from the nearby house. Chris would hurry away with his treasures. One day she came out and confronted him. He protested that the rocks dumped by the alley were no one's property and were worthless. Ere agreed but chastised him anyway. At that moment, Rick stepped out of the garage and intervened. He figured out that Chris was a Haefner relative, and this seemed to calm his mother down. The two families had drifted apart. His parents and George and Ere rarely socialized, and he was unaware until that day that the woman who yelled at him was related to him. Rick invited Chris into the rock shop and had him try on a pair of cracking gloves. He showed him how to break rocks for the boxed sets and put him to work that very day. Soon, he was earning $1.65 per hour, or $30 to $40 per week—enough to keep him well supplied with candy, Tastykakes, and comic books.[3]

Rick's world fascinated him. Chris was thrilled to work at the rock shop and to hang out with his cousin. "I loved it," he said. "It was a great feel. Rick recognized the fact that I was interested in geology, and became a mentor to me." Chris considered his cousin to be a genius, pure and simple, albeit one who could come off to the unaware as sort of an Andy Taylor country bumpkin.[4] Late in the summer of 1973, before he headed off to SUNY New Paltz to teach geology, Rick invited Chris and his brother to go camping with him at the entrance of an old silver mine near Pequea, ten miles southwest of Lancaster. As they roasted hot dogs over a fire, Rick explained that the mine had been opened in the Colonial era and had been flooded for nearly a hundred years, ever since miners in 1875 had broken into a pocket of water. Chris was fascinated by the nearly forgotten mine and the prospect of finding a precious metal. The following February, he met the new owner of the mine, and after the shaft was pumped dry, he lowered himself down the hundred-foot shaft by rope and eventually found the veins of silver that had first attracted the Colonial-era miners. Rick disapproved, but he did it anyway. In 2009, Chris self-published a novel, *The Silver Mine,* a lightly fictionalized account of those halcyon days, minus the bad parts.[5]

Rick and his teenage helpers traveled far and wide to collect the minerals that went into the boxed sets or were sold to retail rock shops. It was like playing nature's own lottery, searching for free treasure and having teenage boy fun while doing it. They went up to Bancroft, Ontario, to collect purple lepidolite and down to Calvert Cliffs along Chesapeake Bay for fossils. Some of the collecting was done in Lancaster County.

They found amethysts in a stream near Strasburg and goethite crystals in a farmer's field near Columbia after a rainstorm. In Chester County, some forty miles from Lancaster, Rick knew a secret place to gather blue quartz. Retail buyers would press Rick for the locations where he collected these fine specimens, but he put them off, giving them different, not-as-good places to hunt. He was good at keeping secrets.[6]

In the Cedar Hill Quarry near the Maryland border, which he knew from a paper he wrote while a student at Franklin & Marshall, Rick found two blue minerals (dubbed "Blue One" and "Blue Two") that appeared to be unlike any known to science. He began the process of obtaining recognition for his discoveries, one of which he intended to call Haefnerite. This required him to analyze and then synthesize the minerals, which involved growing crystals in the laboratory. He did this in the geology laboratories at Penn State, where he was still welcome, of course, despite Dean Hosler's concerns. He took Chris along, as he had taken other boys before him, and introduced him to Lauren Wright and his other old professors. But before he could complete his research and proof of discovery, he was beaten to the punch by Japanese geologists who had found Blue Two and worked harder to prove it was unique. They named it Nakauriite. Blue One was eventually named McGuinnessite in honor of the collector in California who had first discovered it. Rick sputtered in helpless fury, certain he had found Blue Two first, but there was nothing he could do. As Chris remembered it, his cousin was involved in many things and did not spend enough time in the laboratory to prove his find.[7]

"It wasn't just like he lives in a house and goes to a job," Chris Haefner said of Rick. "He had an interesting life. There were things happening in his life, and especially if you liked rocks and gems and minerals and fossils and the outdoors and all that. It was a great life. And he would pay your way for everything. You never had to spend a dime. He spent thousands of dollars on me and my brother, and everybody. Probably tens of thousands on the kids he was sexually involved with."[8]

Rick's urge to have sex with boys seemed to grow ever stronger after leaving Penn State. He finally turned to Chris, his own cousin. It was in the late spring of 1975, probably in May or June, after Rick had returned from the College of Charleston for the summer. His mother had warned Chris of rumors about Rick's behavior with another neighbor boy, but he had brushed her off, not willing to see his hero tarnished. He did notice that his cousin liked to rub the shoulders of the boys who worked for him, but he passed it off as an affectionate gesture. The inevitable finally occurred when he and Rick and another boy were on a collecting trip to Plum Point, Maryland, on Chesapeake Bay. They were staying in a motel, and it was Chris's turn to share the bed with Rick. Just as with Dave S., and no doubt with the boys in Ocean City in 1965, Rick's hand crept over and grabbed his crotch. Chris flinched and turned away, then sweated in terror the rest of the night. Rick did not try again, nor did he speak of it. "It was horrible," Chris said.[9]

In subsequent days, Chris began to distance himself from his cousin. "That ruined everything for me with him," Chris said. Yet he did not break away entirely, or really much at all, when you came right down to it. Chris was unwilling to give up the good parts of his relationship with Rick, or the money he received, and continued to go to the rock shop to work on the boxed sets with the other boys in the family Rick had created for himself. Chris found Rick's world too interesting to leave. It was the classic victim response to the pedophile who had groomed him. Asked if he was ever frightened of Rick, Chris said he was scared only that he would try to molest him again. Yet he never really forgave Rick, and as he grew older, what had happened weighed on him ever more.[10]

If one boy rejected Rick, he moved on to others. On June 30, 1975, he hired two more boys, Kevin S. Burkey, twelve, and Randy K., fourteen, to work in the rock shop, the first act in a long-running tragedy that would handcuff these youths to Haefner for many years. The Burkey family had lived a few doors down from the Haefners on Nevin Street until around 1974, when the parents had split up, and Kevin now lived with his father near St. Mary's Cemetery on the east side of Lancaster, almost two miles away. Randy K. lived in the same neighborhood as Burkey. Rick would claim he fired Burkey for incompetence and attitude three days later and that the molestation complaints were pure retaliation, but the Lancaster police didn't believe him. Indeed, they accused him of molesting the twelve-year-old during the first week of July 1975 in another garage he rented along an alley, just east of the 300 block of Nevin Street. Rick likely took him to the garage, one of three he rented to store mineral specimens, on the pretext of work. He partially undressed Kevin and then rubbed him with Bismoline Medicated Powder, a brand of talcum powder made in Lancaster. Then he performed oral sex, police said. Burkey kept quiet for more than a month, confused and embarrassed about what had happened. He told no one. Not until Randy K. was molested around August 11, during one of Rick's out-of-town collecting and camping trips, did he come forward.[11]

Randy must have told his parents upon returning home that night. Upon hearing what had happened, Kevin then told his older brother, Jimmy, what Rick had done to him. Jimmy urged Kevin to tell their mother, who went straight to the police and filed a complaint. Police records, the few that still exist (more on this in a later chapter), show the complaints were filed on August 12, 1975, and that Haefner was arrested on August 15 and charged with two counts of corrupting the morals of a minor and one count of involuntary deviate sexual intercourse. These acts went beyond the groping to which other boys had been subjected.[12]

The Lancaster police and county prosecutors would not always comport themselves well during the subsequent investigation and trial, bending the rules in an attempt to get the result they so desperately wanted. They probably knew to some extent about the previous accusations against Rick, dating back more than ten years, and saw it as their duty to get him off the street and into prison. Had they succeeded, other boys would have been spared Rick's sexual predations, and his involvement in the Betsy Aardsma murder might well have come to light decades earlier. As it was, their tactics sometimes crossed the line. So did those of Rick. It was a deadly serious battle of wits. Rick was a monster, but he was a smart monster, and he could and did bite back.

Detectives Jerry P. Crump and Edward H. Smith came to 217 Nevin Street around noon on Friday, August 15, and asked Rick to accompany them to the police station to answer questions. They said they wanted to question him away from his mother. Rick initially refused, but went along after the officers threatened to arrest him. At the station, the detectives interrogated him at length, asking, for example, if he had ever been alone with the boys or touched them below the waist. He insisted he had not but acknowledged taking Randy K. camping overnight that week. They took him to another room in the station where he was photographed and fingerprinted. His shoes, belt, watch, and wallet were taken from him, and he was patted down for weapons. Rick asked if he was being charged with something. He received no answer but was placed in a holding cell. It was his first time behind bars, but it seems to have done little to reduce his sense of self-importance and arrogance. It is a fair assumption that Haefner was scared, and soon would be even more so.[13]

Around 3:00 p.m., Crump and Smith removed Rick from the cell and took him to the evidence room, where he saw brass knuckles and knives on a table. Rick claimed in 1981, in a remarkable complaint to the FBI about his arrest and prosecution for the child sex offenses, that one of the officers stood in the corner with his back turned. The other shook his fist at him and told him the parents of Burkey and Randy K. were very angry, and that if Rick had molested *his* child, he would have "beat the living shit" out of him. According to Rick, the officer told him he "could get hurt in this room." The other officer then turned around and continued the interrogation. He told Haefner that the only way to clear this up was to take a polygraph test. Rick agreed, fearing physical harm if he refused. He also would claim that the detectives had promised to free him if he passed the lie detector test.

Around 4:00 p.m., they took him to the polygraph room and the operator hooked him up to the machine. The operator supposedly told him he passed, although we have only Haefner's word for this. Afterward, Crump and Smith did not release him, returning him to his cell. He asked one of the officers if he would be charged, and his response was that he was "doing the paperwork." Around 9:45 p.m., he was taken from the cell to another room, where he talked to Crump and Smith about the lie detector test. Rick reminded them of their agreement to free him if he passed the test. They denied there was any such agreement and took him to night court for arraignment at 10:00 p.m.[14]

George and Ere Haefner, after consulting with George's brother, Henry Haefner, who was a lawyer in Lancaster, hired James F. Heinly, a prominent Lancaster criminal defense attorney, to represent their son. Heinly met with Rick at the district magistrate's courtroom and reviewed the charges against him. His uncle Henry the lawyer was there, too. Rick waived a formal arraignment, which meant among other things that the charges did not have to be read in open court. He signed the waiver form, "Richard Haefner, PhD." Rick thought the PhD honorific set him above other men, but it is doubtful the police even gave it a second glance. Increasingly, Rick would cling to that honorific like a talisman, demanding with no small amount of arrogance to be referred to as *Doctor* Richard Haefner. Rick's parents put up their house for his $12,000 bail, and he was released around 11:00 p.m. He went home to the only house he would ever truly call home, to his rear second-floor bedroom at 217 Nevin Street.[15]

Did the Lancaster police violate Rick's rights? Did they break an "agreement" to free him if he passed a lie detector test? It seems obvious that Crump and Smith had legitimate reasons to arrest Rick that day. The questioning, even as related by Rick in his own, highly subjective account, does not seem to have been out of bounds. As far as the implied threats of violence, police interrogators have always used psychological tricks against suspects, and even in Rick's one-sided account, they did not actually hit him.

As far as the supposed agreement to free him if he passed the polygraph test, it seems doubtful Crump and Smith would have agreed to this, especially knowing as they did the limitations of the test. Polygraphs can sometimes be beaten, especially by intelligent psychopaths firmly believing they did nothing wrong. It is up to the police how much credence to give the results, which in any case cannot be introduced in a court proceeding. When Larry Paul Maurer passed his polygraph examination during the hot phase of the Aardsma investigation in early 1970, he was allowed by the Pennsylvania State Police to go on his way. Whatever the results were of Haefner's polygraph exam, the Lancaster police were not convinced of his innocence, based on what the boys told them. And they may well have been aware of the previous molestation accusations against

Rick and not given him the benefit of doubt. Perhaps they said something vague to get him to agree to the test, or perhaps they intentionally deceived him. In the end, it didn't matter.

The next day, both the morning and afternoon Lancaster newspapers ran news briefs about his arrest. The story in the morning *Intelligencer Journal* was placed among the obituaries, a fitting choice for something that ought to have doomed him to a life of scorn and obloquy. But for Rick Haefner, it instead marked a new beginning. His dream of a legitimate career in geology or as a museum curator was over, although he did not know this yet. His new career as a menace to society would continue until his death. Rick Haefner had killed Betsy Aardsma. He had sexually molested any number of young boys. And now those two roads to Hell were about to merge.[16]

CHAPTER 27

Kill Me the Way You Killed Her

Ere J. Haefner was sixty-three years old in the summer of 1975, a diminutive, stern, overbearing mother who had raised two well-educated sons. Her eldest, George P. Haefner Jr., was a successful aerospace engineer in California who seemed to have lived a relatively trouble-free life. Her other son, Rick, had many problems, but she ignored or disbelieved them. Ere worshipped both of them, but especially Rick, her golden boy. He was the distinguished *Doctor* Haefner, and if the world did not recognize his genius, his superman status, they were fools. Ere would have done anything for him, anything at all. Appearances, not morality, were everything to her. So when Rick was arrested on August 15, 1975, and charged with molesting the two boys, her world fell apart. How could he be so stupid?

On Saturday, August 16, Ere was agitated because of what had happened to her son, but even more so because of the small article about Rick's arrest in the morning *Intelligencer Journal* newspaper. After the story appeared, Rick began receiving obscene telephone calls at home, some twenty-eight in all, he would later claim. No doubt Ere answered some of those calls. When the afternoon *New Era* arrived—she took both editions—Ere saw the story again and erupted in anger and frustration. Looking out the kitchen window, Ere saw Rick emerge from the rock shop into the alley, where he was blithely attending to his rock boxes as if nothing had happened. She stormed outside to confront him.[1]

Her husband and Rick's father, George P. Haefner Sr., who was sixty-seven years old, was absent from this drama, although we can imagine he must have been as upset as his volatile wife. Chris Haefner described George Sr. as an honest man of integrity, although he seems to have taken no more action than his wife did to rein in Rick. Chris argues that Rick's father knew nothing of his dark side, even if that is hard to accept. Mostly retired, he sometimes helped his son in the rock shop and occasionally conducted fire insurance inspections. He had been an independent insurance agent for many years. For whatever reason, he wasn't home that afternoon. This drama directly involved only Rick and his mother, but it was overheard and observed by Chris Haefner, who was gluing rock samples for the boxed sets inside the building a few feet away.[2]

Chris was unaware that his cousin had been arrested the previous day. He had arrived after lunch and gone straight to work, as he often did on weekends. He did not see Ere before he began cracking rocks, but he did see Rick. And then he saw Ere go after Rick. Out of control with anger, she backed her son into an outside corner of the garage and began to scream at him. Chris heard every word. "She was saying, 'You did this again! Why did you do this again?' She accused him of having killed some girl at Penn State, in a way that [made it obvious] he had admitted it to her back then. And she was very clear about that. 'You got out of that,' Ere screamed. 'And now, here you are doing this [breaking the law] again. You might as well have killed me the way you killed her.'" Chris, who was fifteen at the time, said it was "very, very clear" to him that Ere was saying that Rick had once murdered a girl at Penn State and then confessed to her. Betsy's name was not mentioned during the argument. She was always "that girl." But no girl other than Betsy Aardsma had been murdered at Penn State since 1940, three years before Rick was born.[3]

Rick did not deny his mother's accusation about the murder, or even try to defend himself. He listened for two or three minutes, then ushered her back into the house. Then he went back to the rock shop, but he couldn't work. He didn't say anything to Chris, just paced the floor for what seemed like minutes before abruptly leaving and walking back to the house. The kitchen window, which had a screen, was open, and Chris heard everything. In a fury, Rick laid into Ere, telling her she should never have said those things out in the alley. Chris was in the rock shop and heard her, Rick said. He was showing the side of himself that women who angered him would see throughout his life. In a frightened, timid voice, she confessed she hadn't known Chris was there. And then the confrontation ended as quickly as it had begun. Rick came back to the garage and still seemed angry. Chris assumed he was angry toward him for having overheard the conversation. But Rick said nothing.[4]

Aunt Ere did not treat Chris differently after the alley incident, going completely silent on what had happened. "My world with her was about chocolate cake, and did I want chocolate milk, did I want hot dogs or hamburgers for my lunch. No, she never spoke with me." Nor did Chris tell his parents or priest what had happened. It had been a bad moment, and he wanted to put it behind him. Chris, at fifteen, was worried about keeping his job at the rock shop and the money that came with it. "None of this meant anything to me," he said. "My whole life was about protecting what was mine." Was Ere telling the truth when she accused Rick of murder? Chris didn't know. Maybe it was just one of the crazy things adults did. So he shrugged it off, or tried to.[5]

Rick saw the danger, and for several weeks after the August 16 incident, sought to pull Chris back into his camp. Chris believes he was worried that Detective Jerry P. Crump, the young Lancaster police officer in charge of the molestation investigation, would come nosing around and begin talking to Haefner family members. Rick had to have feared that Chris would tell Crump what he'd heard Ere say that day. He also wanted Chris on his side for the molestation trial if they could not get the charges dismissed. So he tried to make Chris believe that he had not heard what he thought he heard—that Rick was guilty of the murder of a female student at Penn State University.[6]

One day that fall, Rick invited Chris to accompany him on a collecting trip. Their destination was a farmer's field in western Lancaster County, not far from Columbia, where they could find goethite crystals. They drove up Indian Head Road, stopping before it began snaking up the mountain. If you went all the way to the top, it was possible to look down on the old Columbia drive-in theater, Chris remembered. They parked the car and began their search.

Before too long, Rick began talking about what Ere had said that day in August. He was nervous, and his hands were in his pockets. "You know, I know who did it," Rick said. Chris asked him what he meant. "You know, what happened in the garage when your aunt came out and [talked] about that girl that was killed," Rick said. "I know who did it, and that's why she's all upset. I told her about it."

This was not exactly a confession, if you took him at face value: Rick was saying he knew who had killed the coed, and it wasn't him. It all happened a long time ago, he said, when he was in graduate school at Penn State. Chris "shouldn't worry about it." Why his mother had brought it up that day, he had no idea. Rick said his mother believed he was going to get in trouble for knowing who killed the girl, meaning Betsy Aardsma. He didn't tell Chris who killed the girl, just that it wasn't him. Someone was with him at Pattee Library that day. He was trying to shift the blame for Betsy's murder to someone else. He wasn't the killer. But, according to Chris, that wasn't what his mother had been screaming at him in the alley.[7]

A few days later, when they were back in the garage and working on the boxed sets, Rick again began talking about the girl who was killed at Penn State. He told Chris that the dead girl was not who people thought she was. She wasn't a big deal, Rick said, and she was never going to be anybody. All that she was trying to do at the school was get with a guy, to have a life, and that's why girls went to college. To Rick, she was no different than any other college coed. "He was pretty much downplaying the relevance of her as a person, saying that she was really not important," Chris said.[8]

These were astonishing statements. Rick sounded exactly like a bitter, rejected suitor who had been thrown over—although his status with Betsy was entirely in his mind—for a medical student, meaning David L. Wright. Chris spent many hours working in the rock shop that fall, in part because Rick needed the help now that Kevin Burkey and Randy K. were no longer working for him. One wonders whether other parents stopped their sons from working at the shop in the wake of Rick's arrest. Chris says all his friends knew about the arrest and some were already teasing him about it the night of Aunt Ere's outburst.[9]

It was later in the fall of 1975 that Rick began to voice chilling, Charles Manson–like soliloquies on the unimportance of individual life. He told Chris that God does not look upon the death of one person as such a bad thing. After all, when Cain killed Abel, God didn't kill Cain. He put a mark on him as a murderer. And so what if someone is killed by a latter-day Cain? Or, as Chris remembered it: "We were all going to die—you're going to die, I'm going to die, everyone's going to die—and everybody makes too big of a deal about it. So if we're all going to die, and God intended this plan of death upon everybody, then what's the big deal?" Rick could have been Charlie Manson preaching to the other Family members around a fire at the Barker Ranch, deep in Death Valley in the fall of 1968. Perhaps he *had* spent a night with the Family during the fall of 1968—or perhaps he had merely heard of Manson and read the recently published (1974) book, *Helter Skelter: The True Story of the Manson Murders,* by Vincent Bugliosi with Curt Gentry. Either way, it was warped and twisted, the product of a psychopath's mind. [10]

Chris, who accepts that Rick killed Betsy, believes his cousin's attitude toward death was why he could live with himself after the murder and not be wracked by guilt. In Rick's view, what he had done with his knife was merely to hasten the inevitable end of Betsy's life.[11]

CHAPTER 28
Miscarriage of Justice

During the five months between his arrest on molestation charges in the summer of 1975 and the start of his trial, Rick Haefner could not simply sit back and let his attorney, James F. Heinly, handle all the preparations. That would not do for *Doctor* Richard Haefner, as he had begun to insist that people call him. He set out on his own to gather incriminating evidence against the two boys who had leveled the accusations against him and caused his arrest.[1]

He rigged one of his older cars with a tape recorder, concealing it in the back of the passenger-side front seat. Then he instructed two of the older teens among his growing posse of fanboy followers, Steve Groff and Willie Bise, how to use it. Their job was to drive twelve-year-old Kevin Burkey around and record any incriminating statements he might make, ideally a confession that he made up the whole thing. Bise, the only black among Rick's followers, thought Rick was cool. When the tape recorder in the seat didn't function properly, Bise concealed it on his person. They made many tapes of Burkey talking in the car. "I think there was something in there, because he did have the lawyers listen to them," Bise remembered.[2]

Whatever they contained, the tapes would have been inadmissible in court because they violated the Pennsylvania wiretapping law, which, like similar laws in some other states, outlaws secret taping. "I'm not sure what came of it, because I was just a pawn," Bise said. "I was just out there getting them to talk, and I'm not sure what they said because I was just having fun." He thought it was possible that Rick was guilty of child molestation because of the way he messed around. By that, he said he meant that Rick was much friendlier to the younger boys, like Kevin Burkey, than the older ones, like himself. "I never seen him doing it, so I can't judge him on that," Bise said. "He never tried anything with me."[3]

Haefner pursued other measures against the two boys. In his complaint to the FBI in 1981, he says he went to Lincoln Junior High School in Lancaster, where one of the boys was a student, and demanded information about him from the school principal, who notified the police. The police, in turn, threatened to arrest Rick for harassment if he ever returned to the school or tried to speak to the principal again. Haefner would cite this incident as an example of police harassment of *him,* which suggests he didn't know or care how his actions might be perceived by the public.[4]

Rick's brother, George P. Haefner Jr., a thirty-seven-year-old electrical engineer, arrived from California in early October to help with his brother's defense. Almost immediately, George ran into trouble with the Lancaster police. On October 6, 1975, he was walking in downtown Lancaster not far from the police station when he was confronted by two plainclothes officers who asked him to show some ID. He told them he would not do so unless he had an attorney present. There was a scuffle and George was arrested. He was held for about four hours and was eventually told that the officers thought he looked like a forgery suspect they had been watching for. He was charged with disorderly conduct, a summary offense carrying a $10 fine and $11 in court costs. George fought it at the district magistrate level, lost, then appealed to the Common Pleas Court, where he lost again. The judge, annoyed, raised the fine to $25 and the costs to $62.50. No one ever accused the well-educated Haefner brothers of having much common sense. The family was circling the wagons, not urging Heinly to cut a deal to get Rick out of a jail term. Or urging Rick to get professional help, for that matter.[5]

It is possible that George had come to Lancaster with a check to help pay for Rick's defense. In 1996, he told the FBI that he had loaned his brother $10,000 back then, the equivalent of about $43,000 in today's money. More than twenty years later, George thought he had loaned the money in 1972 or 1973. But it is hard to imagine that Rick would have needed that big of a loan in those years, when he was living at home or teaching at SUNY–New Paltz and living in a motel. Was he contemplating fleeing the country if the investigation of Betsy's murder came too close and he needed money to start a new life? That didn't happen, of course. It seems more likely that the loan was actually made in 1975 and used to pay Heinly. Rick's parents were not wealthy, and their house was already encumbered for the $12,000 bail. More than twenty years later, the loan from George had still not been repaid by Rick.[6]

A preliminary hearing on the molestation charges was held on November 7 and continued on December 3, 1975. After he was ordered to stand trial, Rick's court date was scheduled for the last week in January in 1976. Heinly petitioned the Lancaster County court to separate the charges related to Randy K.'s complaint and to try those later. He argued that the Randy K. and Burkey incidents were unrelated, arose from different events, and had occurred more than a month apart. Judge Anthony R. Appel agreed. He barred testimony relating to Randy K., only later conceding that this posed a problem, since Burkey had come forward only after hearing from Randy K. about Rick's actions on the camping trip. This freed Heinly to mount an attack on the credibility of Kevin Burkey, who was the more problematic and less sympathetic of the two boys. Burkey died in 2011 at age forty-seven, before he could be interviewed for this book.[7]

The emotional pressure of Rick's impending trial took its toll on his mother, Ere Haefner. Her carefully constructed world, her delusion of grandeur in which her son was a golden boy, a professor of geology admired by his peers, was falling to pieces—although she, like Rick, believed it to be the result of a conspiracy. It must have required a great deal of mental effort on her part to rationalize or dismiss everything her son had done, whether to Betsy Aardsma, to the boy at the YMCA, the Boy Scouts, the boys in Ocean City, or the two boys from his rock shop. For whatever reason—perhaps worrying that the stress of watching her son on trial would kill her, or contemplating suicide, or just coincidence—Ere went to lawyer Henry Haefner on January 25, a few days before Rick's trial began, and wrote out her last will and testament. She left everything to her husband, or if he was not alive, to George Jr. and Rick, divided equally.[8]

Jury selection began on Tuesday, January 27, in the historic old county courthouse in downtown Lancaster, the same place where F&M student Edward L. Gibbs was tried, convicted, and sentenced to death in 1950 for the murder of Marian Baker. Assistant District Attorney John A. Kenneff was the prosecutor. One of the people in the jury pool, Richard Peters, remembers being asked whether he had any children or was related to anyone in law enforcement. He answered "yes" to both questions. Peters had two sons, ages nine and eleven, and his brother was a state trooper. Despite that, he was picked for the jury. The jury was comprised of three women and nine men, all of them white.[9]

The trial would hinge on the credibility of young Kevin Burkey. Peters recalls that the youth was visibly embarrassed at having to repeat the details of the sexual assault, dwelling at length on Rick rubbing him with Bismoline powder. "Then what happened?" prosecutor Kenneff asked. "He blew me," the boy replied. Peters remembers Kevin as being a highly credible witness. "I was not prejudiced, I'm sure," he said. "I tried very hard not to be." But he had boys of his own and four brothers and did not believe a twelve-year-old would say such things in court if they were not true. "He would not do that," Peters said. "Too embarrassing."[10]

Rick's father, George P. Haefner Sr., testified that the accusations by Kevin Burkey were retaliation for things he had told police about Kevin's older brother. He abruptly stopped the proceedings at one point, claiming to be having chest pains and making groaning noises. He was taken out of the courtroom for medical treatment, but it turned out he was not having a heart attack, and he returned in subsequent days. Peters thought both Haefner parents seemed old. He wondered if they had raised Rick as a spoiled brat. They seemed totally devoted to their son, no matter what he was accused of doing.[11]

Rick followed the proceedings closely, consulting a stack of note cards and a notebook from time to time. The defense sought to make Kevin Burkey out to be a bad street kid who had been into all sorts of trouble. To prove this, Heinly called as a witness a teacher from the boy's school, asking him to describe how Kevin had made fun of his name, turning it into a sexual reference. Judge Appel soon put a stop to the humiliating questioning. "But it was things like that—they were [grasping] at straws continually to present that this guy was innocent, and the kid was lying; this is a great man, and he shouldn't be persecuted," Peters said.[12]

The defense called a long list of character witnesses who testified that Rick had an excellent reputation and was known to be "a peaceful, honest, and law-abiding citizen." They included Orville Snoke, a retired teacher, who said Rick had been a day camp counselor for him for eight summers at Camp Optimist—the job where he had met the two boys he molested in Ocean City—and three other prominent former Lancaster educators, Edward C. Kraft, retired assistant principal at McCaskey High School; Harry E. Langford, retired principal of Reynolds Junior High School; and Tomkins B. Smith, retired assistant superintendent. Also taking the stand were John W. Price Sr., curator emeritus at the North Museum at Franklin & Marshall College, and a longtime friend and mentor of Rick's; Harold Banks Jr., an F&M classmate who was now a geologist for the Smithsonian Institution; and Alexander James Barton, a scientist with the National Science Foundation. If nothing else, the parade of character witnesses showed how good Haefner had been at deceiving those around him. He truly led a dual life.[13]

The first unusual incident during the trial occurred on Friday, January 30, when Steve Groff, one of Rick's young friends, was called to the stand. Groff testified that Kevin Burkey had made incriminating statements—statements that supposedly indicated he had fabricated the charges against Rick—during long car rides with himself and others. When he mentioned that he had secretly recorded these conversations using the tape recorder Rick had installed, Judge Appel stopped the trial and threatened Groff with arrest for violating the state's wiretapping statute. The following Monday, he informed the jury that all of Groff's testimony had been stricken from the record, and that they should likewise "erase the testimony of Steve Groff from their minds" and not consider it during deliberations.[14]

On Monday, February 2, Rick Haefner testified in his own defense. He denied having told Detective Jerry P. Crump that he had "massaged" Kevin (denying it was a sexual act). He accused Crump of having concocted the statement, then fell back on religion. "My religion does not condone things like he was talking about, namely homosexual activities," said Haefner, a Catholic who rarely—if ever—went to church. He testified that he could account for every minute of the time Kevin Burkey worked for him between June 30 and July 3, 1975, claiming that all the boys were eating hamburgers in his mother's kitchen at the time the molestation supposedly occurred. Haefner said he had fired both boys for their attitude on July 3, but then implied in further testimony that he might have had other, more pressing reasons for getting rid of them.[15]

Rick said that at the close of work on Wednesday, July 2, 1975, he took the boys to Good's Ice Cream Barn for ice-cream cones and some air-conditioning. While there, he overheard Kevin tell the other boys that he and his brother "were approached by a queer at the railroad station," meaning the Amtrak passenger terminal in Lancaster. Did this mean that Kevin would also talk about Rick when out of earshot? Haefner testified that he was disturbed by the comment and tried to change the subject. He and his parents decided that evening that Kevin had to go because his behavior supposedly "was not very good. He never smiled . . . he fought with the other kids . . . he always did things contrary to what you wanted him to do [and] he had a short attention span." Rick says he phoned Kevin's mother and told her his job would end the following day.[16]

But during much of his time on the stand, Haefner took the jury on a rambling tour of his victimhood, how the police had persecuted him for no reason at all. Juror Peters says Rick was not likable and seemed full of himself. He went on and on about his eight hours of interrogation in the police station, as if no one else suspected of a serious crime had ever been questioned for so long a time. At one point, Haefner said, "I digress," and Judge Appel interjected, "Yes, you do." Rick risked being convicted of annoying the court if nothing else.[17]

Before the trial, Haefner and his lawyer, James F. Heinly, had discussed many times how they wanted to somehow introduce the results of his polygraph examination in the Lancaster police station at trial, believing it would help the case. At the beginning of the trial, however, Judge Appel had warned them not to mention it in any way, a standard warning, since the results of polygraphs, or whether they were taken or not taken, may not typically be introduced in court. Surprisingly, prosecutor Kenneff was open to the idea of discussing the polygraph exam in open court. Whether he planned to lay some sort of trap is unknown. But Judge Appel would have none of it. During cross-examination, Kenneff asked Haefner to discuss his appearance before the district magistrate on the night of August 15, 1975. He specifically wanted Haefner to say whether he had made any complaint to the magistrate, and, if so, about what. Kenneff was asking Haefner to violate the judge's order, and he walked right into it. "I complained . . . that I had agreed to take a lie detector test from Detective Jan Walters, and Detective Walters told me I passed the test," Rick testified. "We had an agreement that if I passed that test, they would not bring any charges, and they brought them anyway." Haefner argued in court that he had no choice but to answer Kenneff's questions.[18]

Judge Appel didn't agree and sent the jury out of the courtroom. "I remember everything stopped," Peters said. There was discussion among Judge Appel and the two lawyers about allowing more questioning about the polygraph exam now that the subject had been broached, but the judge refused. He recalled the jury, ordered the testimony stricken from the record, and directed them, just as in the Groff testimony about the surreptitious taping of Kevin Burkey, to disregard what they had heard. After his final comments to the jury the following morning, Judge Appel cited Haefner for contempt of court and scheduled a hearing on the penalty for two days hence. At 11:52 a.m. on February 3, the jury retired to begin its deliberations on a verdict after hearing the final words of defense counsel Heinly that Kevin Burkey was "a proven malicious boy who can't tell the truth."[19]

Most of the jurors weren't buying it. Kenneff had said in his own closing remarks, "You believe one side, or you believe the other." Most of the jurors believed Kevin Burkey. At the beginning of their deliberations, Peters recalls, the jurors were split about evenly on Haefner's guilt or innocence. No one firmly believed him guilty, although many were leaning that way. Most of the jury believed *Doctor* Richard Haefner to be incredibly annoying.

"I remember the foreman said, 'Please—we cannot allow his personality to get in the way of justice,'" Peters said. "'We need to look at all the facts.' And we did. I think everyone tried to give him a fair assessment." As they reviewed the testimony in the trial, doubts began to fall away. "The thing that came down in my mind, what made me realize he was guilty, was the boy's testimony," Peters said. Before too long, the jury was eleven to one for conviction. The holdout was a man who found Haefner's story of police persecution to be credible. This juror said he had once been arrested by the Lancaster police for speeding and had been ill treated in the process. "He was very much prejudiced. You could tell," recalled Peters, who thought the juror was a nice guy nonetheless. "It very much upset the rest of us. . . . We talked about all the evidence. And this guy was not budging."[20]

At 5:10 p.m., the jurors returned to the courtroom and informed Judge Appel they had not been able to reach a decision, and might not be able to. He sent them back to continue deliberating. At 6:35 p.m., the jury sent out a written question asking to be read the testimony of two police officers about events during the questioning of Haefner at the police station. Appel told them to rely on their recollections. At 9:15 p.m., Judge Appel called them back to the courtroom, only to be informed that they were still deadlocked. The foreman thought they could still reach a unanimous decision, but such was not the case. Shortly after 10:00 p.m. on February 3, the jury came back and reported that it was hopelessly deadlocked. Judge Appel declared a mistrial, thanked them for their service, and sent the jurors home. Everyone believed there would be another trial, but declaring a mistrial so soon would prove to be a critical legal misstep by Appel.[21]

On February 5, Judge Appel dismissed Haefner's arguments in defense of disclosing the polygraph test and sentenced him to a $500 fine and thirty days in the county jail for contempt, sentence to begin immediately.

Haefner was handcuffed and taken into custody by the county sheriff and processed into Lancaster County Prison at 6:30 p.m. that evening. For most people with no prior exposure to the criminal justice system, entering prison is a slap in the face, a quick and brutal confirmation of how low they have fallen. Haefner was no exception. Rick told the intake officer that he was an unemployed geologist but refused to say what his religious preference was. The officer typed "None" on the intake form. Asked for the names and addresses of his parents and brother, Rick again refused, saying it was unnecessary information. As all prisoners were, he was ordered to strip naked and surrender his clothing, including a pair of brown pants, a brown belt, a yellow shirt, a tie clip (but apparently no tie), brown loafers, a houndstooth sport jacket, and a brown overcoat. The items in his pockets, also surrendered to the prison, included his wallet and $6.30 in cash, five plastic cards in the wallet that apparently were organizational membership cards, four keys, two felt pens, and a book of stamps. Haefner was given a prison jumpsuit to wear, which he complained was too small.[22]

According to prison records, Rick was then placed in medical quarantine for forty-eight hours, another standard procedure. At the time, the prison was dealing with a scabies and a body lice outbreak that it believed it had under control, and was trying to forestall a flu epidemic. Haefner, in his overly dramatic, self-pitying tone, says he was marched to "the hole," meaning solitary confinement, a small, windowless cell containing only a toilet and no bed or chair. He claimed that one of the guards deliberately made the toilet overflow, flooding the floor with water, then shut the door, turning off the light from the outside. The guard allegedly told Haefner that he would be kept there for the entire thirty days, and when his sentence was up, they would find a way to keep him there longer. If any of this was true, it was likely a rough attempt to make him cooperate with the guards.[23]

"I was in total darkness, except for a crack of light at the bottom of the door," Haefner told a reporter for the Philadelphia *Evening Bulletin*. "I couldn't find a dry spot to sit down. I thought I was suffocating. I was down on my hands and knees. I was crying, trying to gasp for air at the crack at the bottom of the door." At that very moment, if Rick is to be believed, *Doctor* Richard Haefner was supposed to be lecturing at Drexel University's Academy of Natural Sciences in Philadelphia. "They had a Chinese dinner planned and all," he told the *Bulletin*. "You know how they treat guest lecturers." After several hours, according to Rick, the guard let him out and took him back to the intake room, where he now provided the names and addresses of his parents and brother and answered any other question they posed to him.[24]

Haefner was then taken to a regular cell, which he had to himself. He contends he was kept locked up for the next five days, fed his meals in his cell, and allowed no visitors. His new home had a toilet, a mattress and a blanket, but no washcloth, soap, or towel—or shower. What Haefner never knew was that one of his former Boy Scouts from Troop 24 at Sacred Heart Catholic Church, one who knew about the sex accusations that got Rick removed as an assistant scoutmaster of the troop ten years earlier, was working as a guard at the prison. Michael D. Witmer was in his first job after leaving the military and thought it strange to encounter Rick in this setting. "I don't think I ever talked to him," he recalled. "I knew what he was in for, and thought about bringing something up." But Witmer thought better of the idea and remained silent, probably saving Rick from the violence prison inmates are said to dole out to those who molest children.[25]

During his second week in prison, he was allowed visitors and received seven of them, including his parents, John W. Price Sr., who was the former curator of the North Museum and one of Rick's character witnesses, and Bob Freiler of Lancaster. Another visitor, not recorded on the log, was his lawyer, James F. Heinly. He told Rick that he would have to provide a retainer of $2,500, the equivalent of more than $10,000 today, before he would file an appeal of his contempt sentence. Apparently, the Haefner family did pay. Under Pennsylvania law, such an appeal went directly to the Pennsylvania Supreme Court, bypassing the state Superior Court, the intermediate appellate court for criminal cases. Justice Robert N. C. Nix Jr. held a bail hearing on February 17 and ordered Rick freed while the appeal of his contempt sentence was determined. Bail was set at $1,000, and he was let out of prison immediately.[26]

He had lost fifteen pounds and contracted body lice. He had also caught the flu, and there was worse to come in his personal life. But for now, Dr. Richard Haefner was a free man.

CHAPTER 29

The Philadelphia Lawyer

Within a day of his release on bail, Lancaster police and the county prosecutor were making plans to retry him. Ominously for Rick, they served a subpoena on Philip Bomberger III, executive director of the Lancaster Recreation Commission, who had tried to sort out Rick's Ocean City molestation crimes in 1965. The subpoena asked for Rick's employment, counseling, and investigative records, which would surely give Detective Jerry P. Crump more ammunition than any police officer needed to destroy the credibility of a suspect who proclaimed himself innocent of molesting Kevin Burkey, and who had testified that his Catholic beliefs would have prevented him from committing such a crime.

After springing Rick from jail at least temporarily on the contempt charge, James F. Heinly resigned as his lawyer. Whether he thought Haefner needed a different lawyer for the appeals or was fed up with his client's behavior is unknown. Rick set out to find a new champion. He went to Philadelphia early in the spring, possibly to look up Arlen Specter. If so, he was disappointed. Specter had been back in private practice for three years since losing his bid for a third term as district attorney, but during the late winter and spring of 1976 was in the throes of running for the Republican nomination for US Senate in the May primary.

Nevertheless, Rick found the tough guy he wanted, eventually hiring one of the best criminal *prosecutors* in Philadelphia to mount his defense. Richard A. Sprague had won fame for convicting the men who plotted and carried out the 1969 murders of United Mine Workers reform candidate Joseph Yablonski and his wife and daughter. During Sprague's fifteen years in the Philadelphia DA's office, he tried sixty-six people accused of homicide, and all but one was convicted of first-degree murder. Senator Arlen Specter, in his memoirs, called him "a courtroom master." When Rick Haefner went looking for representation, Sprague was in private practice with the David Berger law firm in downtown Philadelphia.[1]

Sprague's switch to criminal defense work had been notable enough to command a story in *Time* magazine the week of May 17, 1976. He told the magazine that he was able to make the switch mentally by seeking out defense cases, often appeals, that stirred his blood because of the alleged unfairness shown by a prosecutor to the defendant. He loved the role of activist lawyer defending the downtrodden. "Each side has a right to have its interests vigorously defended," he told the magazine. Sprague mentioned several cases he was handling at the time; one of them was the Rick Haefner case. Rick was described by *Time* as "a geology professor in Lancaster County's Mennonite community who is accused of sodomizing two boys." Rick was no more a Mennonite than he was Chinese, but the description in the magazine reflected the popular perception in much of the country that Lancaster County was populated mainly by Amish and Mennonites.[2]

At their first meeting on April 13, 1976, Haefner told Sprague that he was "fighting for his life," and that going to prison terrified him. Sprague later told the Philadelphia *Evening Bulletin* that when Haefner first appeared in his office and told his story, he was dubious. His inner warning system told him that things just didn't happen that way. As much as Sprague liked fighting for the little guy, he had to have known that most claims of police conspiracies are hogwash. But after looking into it more, Sprague agreed to take Rick's case. "This man was fighting the establishment, and everyone decided to stand together against the upstart," Sprague told reporter David Runkel. "It was really unbelievable." He should have listened to that inner warning.[3]

Sprague told the *Philadelphia Inquirer* that Haefner's case met all his tests for criminal defense work, namely "fundamental issues worth fighting for" and "a heavy presumption that his client is innocent." The reporter, Mike Leary, included the remarks in a longer story about Rick's case that included a brief mention of how Rick had been about to start a prestigious position at the Los Angeles County Museum of Natural History before his arrest wrecked everything.

Beginning in January 1974, when Rick was still teaching at SUNY–New Paltz, the Natural History Museum of Los Angeles County approached him about becoming their next curator of Mineralogy-Geology. The man dangling this plum and potentially lifetime job was Theodore Downs, chief curator of the Earth Sciences Division and a giant in his field. Downs was best known for overseeing the spectacular fossil finds in the La Brea Tar Pits in Los Angeles, and for founding the Page Museum in 1962 to house the reconstructed dinosaur skeletons and other finds from the pits. Haefner was coy at first, but after more entreaties from Downs, finally applied for the job in June 1975, less than a month before the incident involving Kevin Burkey. There followed the usual round of interviews. On November 26, 1975, Downs phoned Haefner to offer him the job, and Rick immediately accepted. Downs then sent a letter putting the offer in writing on November 28, six years to the date after Betsy Aardsma's murder. Rick had also agreed to Downs's request to teach geology at UCLA and do research part time.[4]

By that time, of course, Haefner was out on bail from his arrest on the child molestation charges of August 15, 1975, and was five days away from his second preliminary hearing. He knew, or should have known, that he was going to trial in a few weeks. Yet somehow, he forgot to mention any of this to Downs. This may have been his psychopathic belief that he had done nothing wrong, or perhaps it was pure calculation, reasoning that since Downs had no effective access to the Lancaster newspapers in Los Angeles, he wouldn't find out. Perhaps it was a little of both. And of course, Rick expected to be fully exonerated, after which his problems would go away. He didn't seem to understand that in the eyes of society, an arrest for child molestation was nearly as damning as a conviction—that the taint could almost never be fully erased. We also see here, once again, Haefner's ability to compartmentalize his life, packing away on a shelf the trauma of facing trial on child molestation charges.

The new job was not intended to start until March 1, 1976. But in the interim, Downs gave Rick several projects to complete, including leading the search for his own assistant, reviewing the plans and blueprints for a new gem and mineral hall being built at the museum, including a high-security gem vault, and visiting gem shows in the Mid-Atlantic states to search for specimens for the museum. Rick may have reasoned foolishly that he could do all of that while out on bail without Downs ever being the wiser.[5]

It was the contempt sentence and immediate jailing that spoiled his calculations. Representing the museum, Haefner was supposed to give a talk at the Tucson Gem and Mineral Show on February 15, 1976, a night when he was still sitting in his orange jumpsuit in his cell in Lancaster County Prison. He had not been allowed by prison officials to make a phone call to museum officials to let them know he had been unavoidably detained and could not make the speech.

This was no ordinary rock show he missed. Tucson was, and still is, one of the premier gem and mineral shows in the world, held annually since 1955 and attracting visitors and professionals from many countries. Most big museums with gem, mineral, or fossil collections sent representatives. Marion Stuart, a member of the Natural History Museum's board, hosted an annual dinner at the show, and it was probably this dinner at which Rick was expected to speak. Not only was Stuart an influential member of the museum board and the museum foundation, but her philanthropy was also paying for the new gem and mineral hall that would be Rick's domain once he became curator. The hall would be named the E. Hadley Stuart Jr. Hall of Gems and Minerals after her husband, whose family had founded, and at that time still owned, Carnation, the food products company. We can only imagine her annoyance when Haefner, the geologist who would be in charge of the glittering new wing, neither showed up at the dinner nor called.[6]

During the rock show, Stuart learned of his arrest for allegedly molesting the two boys in Lancaster. Who told her is unknown, but one suspects that someone broke the news to her after Rick failed to appear for the dinner. She then told Los Angeles museum officials that Rick was morally unfit for the curator job and should not be hired. On February 17, 1976, a letter went to Rick from the museum informing him that he was no longer being considered for the curator position. No explanation was given, but seeking to smooth the waters, Haefner was allegedly told verbally after the letter arrived that he would be considered for other significant employment at the museum. We have only Rick's word on that, but it is what he believed. Downs soon reached out to another candidate, Peter J. Dunn at the Smithsonian, telling him that Haefner "was dishonest" and had deceived him by not informing him that he had been arrested for sex crimes involving children. He told Dunn, who did not take the job, that the offer to Haefner had been withdrawn. Metaphorically at least, they had locked the door of the museum and thrown him into the La Brea Tar Pits.[7]

Rick was as devastated and bitter as anyone who loses a dream job he thought was his. Being a museum curator or director had been a lifelong dream for him. He had talked about it to Joe Head, his field assistant during his Penn State research in Death Valley in 1967. He had worked at the North Museum on the Franklin & Marshall College campus, a short walk from his home in Lancaster, from an early age. That was where he had gotten to know Dr. John Price, the museum curator who had been one of the character witnesses at his trial. Price would conceive of new exhibits and, at least when Rick was in college, would give him the responsibility of designing and then building the exhibit, helped by high school students employed by the hour.[8]

Officially, he had no idea the job offer was withdrawn because of his child sex arrest and assumed it was because he was sitting in prison and couldn't give the speech. He poured out his tale of woe to Sprague, and a tiny bit of it made its way into the *Philadelphia Inquirer* article. Rick added the Natural History Museum to his enemies list, biding his time until he could strike back. How could they promise him the job in writing in November and then withdraw the offer in February without even so much as a partial explanation? But part of him also hoped they were telling the truth about hiring him if another curator job opened up.[9]

Sprague's job as Rick's new lawyer was to stop a retrial, but also to prepare in the event he lost that fight. Chris Haefner remembers accompanying Rick to Sprague's ornate Philadelphia office three or four times to prepare his own testimony. He marveled at a beautiful fireplace mantel that Rick told him was made of serpentine, a dark green mineral that was mottled like a snake's skin.

One of Rick's friends, Terry Lee Hess, had come forward with a claim that during the trial, he had been in a courthouse men's room and overheard Detective Jerry P. Crump offering a bribe to Randy K. to testify as a rebuttal witness in a way that would help to convict Haefner. The story was problematic for a number of reasons—first, because Randy K.'s case had been separated from Burkey's before the trial started, and second, because of how Hess claimed to have observed them. If police were bribing witnesses, what point did they have in bribing Randy K. when Judge Appel had barred any testimony about Rick's alleged assault on the boy? But it was the second problem that proved more serious. Hess claimed to have heard Crump and Randy K. talking about the bribe in the restroom, but also to have seen them reflected in the mirror over the sink.

A suppression of evidence hearing had been held on March 10–11, 1976, highlighted by testimony from Hess about the alleged bribe. On May 3, Lancaster police arrested Hess and charged him with perjury, in part because a college physics professor brought in as an expert witness concluded that Hess could not have seen the mirror reflections of the detective and boy. The arrest created a problem for Sprague, because if Hess feared anything he said in court could be used against him in the perjury case, he would probably refuse to testify. In October 1976, Haefner hired Sprague to represent Hess, and the perjury charge was eventually dismissed.[10] The retrial was scheduled to begin May 19.

As the second trial approached, Sprague filed motions seeking a suspension of the proceedings against Haefner until the Hess case was resolved. He also petitioned for a change of venue and suppression of some of the evidence. Sprague demanded court-ordered psychiatric testing of Kevin Burkey, accusing him of having made false accusations in the past about homosexual activities. Sprague was doing what any lawyer would do to defend his client, but that was scant comfort to the alleged victims.[11]

After analyzing Haefner's case, Sprague believed that invoking double jeopardy might stop a retrial altogether. The concept of double jeopardy—that no one shall twice be put in jeopardy of life or limb for the same offense—is found in the Fifth Amendment to the US Constitution, adopted by Congress as part of the Bill of Rights in 1789 and ratified by the states in 1791. The framers of the Constitution drew the right from English common law. But until 1969 and the US Supreme Court ruling in *Benton v. Maryland*, double jeopardy protection was guaranteed only in federal courts for federal crimes, such as bank robbery, kidnapping, and counterfeiting. Many states, including Pennsylvania, had double jeopardy clauses in their state constitutions, but they typically applied only to death penalty cases. The Benton ruling in 1969 applied the protection against double jeopardy to all criminal proceedings in all courts, federal and state, eliminating the requirement that "life or limb" be threatened. Prosecutors could not try a defendant twice for the same offense, no matter what it was.

But with mistrials, it got tricky. Some mistrials triggered double jeopardy protection and some did not. Sprague set out to show that Judge Appel should not have declared a mistrial after only eight hours—that he should have required the jury to deliberate longer, even put them up for the night (they were not sequestered) and bring them back the next morning to try again. The fact that he did not, Sprague argued, made a retrial a violation of Haefner's right not to be tried twice for the same offense. Judge Appel's declaration of a mistrial was, in effect, a directed verdict of acquittal. The juror Richard Peters scoffed at the idea that Appel didn't try hard enough, remembering considerable pressure from the judge to bring back a verdict. But Sprague and his associates had studied the case law carefully.[12]

At a proceeding in Lancaster County Court of Common Pleas on May 19, 1976, which was packed with local lawyers hoping to see their famous Philadelphia colleague in action, Sprague persuaded Judge Wilson Bucher that Haefner's retrial should be postponed at least until September to deal with pretrial motions, especially his demand that a retrial be barred entirely on double jeopardy grounds. Prosecutor Kenneff argued that Judge Appel had been within his rights to declare a mistrial when he did, but Judge Bucher granted Sprague's request and reserved a full discussion of double jeopardy for early in June. Possibly reacting to the *Time* magazine article in which Sprague mentioned the case, he ordered both sides not to make public statements.[13]

In his brief on the double jeopardy issue on June 2, Sprague argued that a judge cannot declare a mistrial unless the defendant gives consent, an exception being if there is an instance of "manifest necessity" requiring discharge of the jury over defense objections. He cited a number of appellate decisions.[14]

Kenneff, in his own brief, argued that Appel had declared a mistrial over the objections of the prosecution, and that defense counsel James F. Heinly had, in fact, urged the judge to do so. He further argued that the jury was not split over issues of law or fact, but over whom to believe, Rick Haefner or Kevin Burkey. Moreover, Kenneff said, the Pennsylvania Supreme Court had ruled in *Commonwealth v. Campbell* (1971) that it was up to the judge to determine how long of a jury deliberation was enough.[15]

Judge Wilson Bucher sided with the prosecution, ruling on June 25, 1976, that Judge Appel's declaration of a mistrial had been prudent and not premature. The decision meant that Haefner would be retried in September. Two weeks later, Sprague began a round of appeals. He lost in the state Superior Court but won in the Pennsylvania Supreme Court. On June 3, 1977, the state high court sent the appeal back to superior court for decision. That court heard arguments on December 6, 1977, and more than two years later ruled that retrying Haefner would be double jeopardy and ordered him released.[16]

Rick had been free since his release from the contempt sentence three years earlier. Now he no longer had to worry about the sex charges, and his parents were released from their $12,000 bail obligation. Nor did he have to worry about the contempt sentence, since the Pennsylvania Supreme Court had ruled long ago that he should not have been charged and jailed by Judge Appel. Indeed, they called the whole contempt affair "preposterous." Rick proclaimed forever after that he had been "exonerated" of the sex charges, which wasn't true at all. Thanks to employing Sprague and his associates, who seemed vastly more skilled than the county judge and prosecutor, he was indeed a free man. He had gotten off, beaten the rap.

But no one who looks at the case today with an open mind would agree that he was actually innocent, as he claimed. Just damned lucky. Or perhaps damned *and* lucky, depending on one's perspective.[17]

There was a postscript to Rick's victory. Beating the rap was not enough for him. He was upset that the stain of the child molestation arrests seemed permanent. He applied for jobs at other museums, hoping to find one who hadn't heard he was a pedophile, or about the debacle in Los Angeles. But it was a small world he had sullied, and they all knew, even in the years before the Internet exposed a man's life to easy scrutiny. It didn't matter that Rick had been, as he put it, "exonerated" of the charges. Boards would not take the chance of putting a man with that kind of arrest record in charge of museums that by their very nature drew large numbers of boys among their visitors. There was no way you could explain someone like Rick Haefner to the public, especially at a time, the mid-1970s, when public attitudes in America were returning to the old view that child molesters should be harshly punished, not understood. He had many of the qualifications of a good museum curator or director, but it just didn't matter.

Penn State geology professor Roger Cuffey, Rick's most ardent defender, said the rumors about his arrest and trial in Lancaster would get reported secretly to museum hiring committees, who would then drop him from consideration. Cuffey, who had served on hiring committees at Penn State, said mere arrests are not supposed to be considered in evaluating job searches, only criminal convictions. "In my letters of recommendation for him, I tried to counter these prejudices, but hiring committees then were among the most cowardly in the world—the merest whiff of anything scandalous and they'd cut off possibilities, no matter how good the student was," he said. He remembered running into Rick at a professional meeting in the mid-1970s and asking him how the job search was going. "He said, 'Same as always; they all find out about things.'"[18]

Rick became convinced that if he could make the records disappear, his troubles finding a museum or university job would also vanish. So with Sprague once again as his champion, Rick set out to rewrite history.

In a petition to expunge Haefner's criminal record filed in the Common Pleas Court of Lancaster County on August 9, 1979, Sprague described his client as "an individual of unblemished reputation, never before having been arrested or criminally prosecuted in his life." This meant before the Lancaster arrests in 1975. Sprague clearly didn't know about the molestation accusations from the early to mid-1960s, for which Rick had managed to avoid arrest, or else disbelieved or discounted the stories. He asked the court to order the Lancaster chief of police to destroy Haefner's fingerprints and photographs, to remove the record of his arrest from departmental files, and to ask the FBI and state police to return any records forwarded to them. They should be destroyed, too. Moreover, Sprague asked that the deputy court administrator in Lancaster County be ordered to remove all references to the arrest from the dockets and indexes of the Court of Common Pleas and the district magistrate.[19]

Rick testified at a subsequent hearing that the arrest record had damaged his reputation and made it impossible for him to get a teaching or museum job. He swore to the court that he was actually innocent of the molestation charges but provided no evidence to back up his claim, which Judge Paul A. Mueller Jr. noted with disapproval. Surprisingly, prosecutor John A. Kenneff Jr. did not attend the hearing, telling the court he was neutral on the petition and would leave it up to the court's discretion. It was a remarkable move, almost as if he was running up the white flag in the face of Sprague's legal blitzkrieg.

But Judge Mueller wasn't convinced. He based his opinion on a Superior Court decision two years earlier, *Commonwealth v. Mueller* (no relation), in which the expungement decision hinged on whether the prosecutor had made a *prima facie* (on the face of it) case against the defendant. In the Haefner case, he said, the prosecution *had* made a prima facie case—at his trial. The subsequent mistrial, he said, established neither guilt nor innocence. So the record could not be expunged until Haefner disproved the prosecution's prima facie case at another hearing. He criticized Haefner for presenting no evidence to rebut the Burkey charges and said his personal declaration of innocence was not enough. It was different in the Randy K. case, which had never been brought to trial and which had just been *nolle prossed*, or dismissed as unwinnable by the prosecution. Judge Mueller denied Haefner's petition to expunge the Burkey records, but approved destruction of the Randy K. file. He gave the police and court record-keepers four months to comply.[20]

At the police and courthouse level, there were few illusions about Haefner's innocence. Rick sent a letter to Judge Mueller on October 8, 1980, complaining that nothing had been done about destroying the Randy K. records. Meanwhile, Sprague appealed Judge Mueller's decision on the Burkey records to Superior Court, and on October 30, 1981, they won. Judge John P. Hester, writing for the majority, saw the situation quite differently than Mueller had. In his view, the mistrial had proven that the prosecution had failed to convince a jury of Rick's guilt (although it had deadlocked eleven to one for conviction, which Hester didn't know). So that didn't create a prima facie case. Compounding the matter, he said, the prosecution had failed to present any evidence at the hearing in favor of preserving the record. Hester then extolled Haefner's testimony in favor of expungement and indicated that he didn't care that Rick presented no evidence to back up his claim of innocence. Hester directed Judge Mueller to order the destruction of the records.[21]

Mueller complied with the order, but once again, court officials in Lancaster didn't act. Six months later, Haefner went to the Clerk of Courts office with a notary public as witness and found a thick file of documents from the Burkey case still publicly available. He complained bitterly to the Clerk of Courts, but it did no good. A friend, Bob Freiler Sr., one of the people who visited him when he was in county prison on the contempt citation in 1976, went back a day later and found them still quite available. It is believed the records were not destroyed until around 1989, when Haefner submitted a new petition to the court.[22]

CHAPTER 30

Penn State Drops the Ball

Rick came to believe that his thesis advisor and most important professor, Lauren A. Wright, was not doing enough to help him get a museum job, and must have wondered if his arrest and trial on the molestation charges had anything to do with it. Wright would admit years later that Rick "was commonly in the company of younger boys, but those of us who knew him at the time didn't think of the pedophile aspect here. He seemed to be interested in just encouraging young men to acquire an interest in natural history." This seems a remarkably clueless attitude, especially given that Charles Hosler, the dean of the College of Earth and Mineral Sciences, had rejected Rick for that very reason when he applied to run the Penn State geology museum. Another interesting possibility is that Wright was indeed holding back on helping Rick, but because of the Betsy Aardsma murder, not the pedophilia. Regardless of which it was, Haefner's anger grew and festered. At some point—probably in the late summer of 1976, after his legal problems began to disappear, thanks to Sprague's brilliant lawyering—Rick went to Penn State to confront Lauren Wright.[1]

If Wright shut his eyes to the pedophilia, he harbored deep suspicions about Rick and the murder of Betsy Aardsma. He knew his old student regularly carried a homemade knife for protection. Yet he had remained silent about that, and about Rick's strange visit to his house on the evening of November 28, 1969. He said nothing to Penn State officials in the seven years after Betsy was stabbed to death in Pattee Library, and certainly nothing to the state police, who were everywhere on campus in the wake of the murder. We will never know exactly what motivated him.

Many have spoken about how he supposedly saw the best in everybody, but this doesn't excuse his silence about Rick's strange behavior that night. Not when the stakes were this high. Was there something in his personal life he feared Rick might disclose? Wright may simply have been following a long Penn State tradition of looking the other way, but he certainly knew his duty as a citizen, a duty that was not obviated by the hoary traditions of academia. His long silence begs the question of whether Rick knew something about Wright that the professor didn't want anyone else to know. That is a question that cannot be answered now.

Rick's visit in 1976 ended his silence, at least in part. We don't know exactly what Haefner said, but it left Wright frightened. After he left, Wright went immediately to see Hosler, who had an open-door policy and allowed faculty to come in without an appointment if he wasn't talking to someone else. Wright walked in and shut the door behind him. "Lauren was really fearful of him," Hosler said. "He actually was visibly shaken." He knew Wright to be "a pussycat. . . . He was always a mild, meek guy. He would never speak ill of anybody. So he must have felt pretty threatened to come down and talk to me about it," he said. But it wasn't just Rick's threatening behavior that the professor wanted to talk about.[2]

The dean listened in shock and astonishment as Wright described how Haefner had appeared unexpectedly at his house at 219 Ronan Drive on the evening of Betsy Aardsma's murder, not much more than an hour after she died. Rick was out of breath and agitated. He wondered if the *Centre Daily Times* had come and whether there was anything in the paper about a girl being killed in Pattee Library. Hosler said Wright described "in detail" the weapon Rick typically carried, referring to it as resembling a sharpened screwdriver. At that point, Hosler understood that Wright was telling him that Rick Haefner had probably murdered Betsy Aardsma.

"I was pretty shocked," Hosler said. "Immediately, a whole lot of things came together when he told me about what happened." Late in life, Wright would claim that his meeting with the dean took place the morning after Betsy's murder. But Hosler said that wasn't accurate, that it took place years later, after Rick's arrest and trial in Lancaster. "Had he done that [reported his suspicions immediately], we could have really done something," Hosler said. As it was, the dean knew he had to report what Wright had told him. But to whom?[3]

Hosler went not to Penn State president John Oswald, who had succeeded Eric Walker in the summer of 1970, but to someone who was arguably even more powerful and influential—the university's outside general counsel, Delbert J. McQuaide. McQuaide, a name partner in McQuaide Blasko, the largest law firm in State College, filled that role for twenty-seven years, from 1970 until his death from cancer at age sixty in 1997. He devoted much of his life to Penn State, his only significant client, yet was not a Penn State graduate. McQuaide had grown up in New Kensington, Pennsylvania, and had graduated from Juniata College in Huntingdon, Pennsylvania, where he was president of the board of trustees late in life, and from NYU Law School. McQuaide was an outsider at Penn State, yet at the same time, a consummate insider.[4]

Steve Garban, who would resign as president of the Penn State board of trustees in 2012 in the wake of the Sandusky scandal, told the *Centre Daily Times* in 1997 that McQuaide was not just a lawyer but "an integral part of the institution." Penn State president Graham Spanier, another victim of the Sandusky scandal outcry, said McQuaide had "a great legal mind, and was party to all of Penn State's most important progress and decisions for years and years." Hosler, who later in his career was a senior vice president and the provost of Penn State, said there were no important meetings that McQuaide did not attend. Carol Herrman, a senior vice president for administration at Penn State and a neighbor and friend of the university lawyer, was quoted by the State College newspaper as saying that McQuaide told her he could have made more money working as a lawyer in New York than in State College but felt he had made the right choice, "because I work for an institution that was concerned with doing the right thing."[5]

So, Hosler went to McQuaide, revealed what Wright had told him about Rick Haefner and the Betsy Aardsma murder, and told him he ought to pass the information along to the state police. But McQuaide did not seem interested. "I didn't feel he took me terribly seriously," Hosler said, speculating that McQuaide was thinking, "Yeah, this is another professor who's got weird ideas." Sometime later, he happened to see McQuaide and asked him whatever became of the matter. And the university general counsel said, "Oh, the police said they'd already looked into that. And that was the end of it."[6] Hosler now believes he should have gone to Penn State president Oswald, "but I figured the university lawyer would know these people and how to approach them."

Sergeant George Keibler was still the head of criminal investigation at the state police Rockview barracks in 1976, and still lead investigator of Betsy's murder, although it was basically just him now. He did not recall the general counsel speaking to him about Rick Haefner. "I can't recall him ever giving any information on the Aardsma case," Keibler said.

By 1976, he had little hope left that Betsy Aardsma's murder would be solved. On November 3, 1976, Keibler was quoted in "Pennsylvanians Here & There," a feature of the Associated Press, in which newspaper readers wrote in with questions. One reader, who identified himself as having been a Penn State student in 1969, wrote to ask what had ever become of the investigation of the murder of a coed in the school library. Keibler's bleak reply: "We are no closer to solving the Aardsma case than we were the night the murder occurred." Even given Keibler's normal reticence, that does not sound like the response of an investigator who had been handed a hot tip, and it is probably safe to conclude that McQuaide did not go to the state police with the information about Rick Haefner.[7]

Professor Roger Cuffey, Haefner's defender, speculated that McQuaide looked into what Hosler told him and concluded that while the story told by Professor Wright *did* point to Rick as Betsy's killer, there was nothing that could be prosecuted. He speculated that perhaps the Penn State lawyer decided that it was just better to let the Aardsma investigation die.[8]

Outsiders were beginning to become interested in the unsolved case. Less than a week after Keibler's comments to the Associated Press on November 3, 1976, Frank W. Merritt of Bucknell University in Lewisburg, Pennsylvania, wrote to Charles Ness, assistant director of libraries at Penn State. He described himself as a retired English professor who "had often thought that the details of the [Aardsma] case would provide the foundation for a detective story." Whether Merritt envisioned fiction or nonfiction, he didn't say. He inquired whether Pattee Library had materials about the case that would be available to him and whether he would need to travel to State College [about 55 miles] to look at them. Finally, Merritt wondered how long it would take to go through the collection.[9]

Ness replied a week later that "regarding the Aardsma incident of Fall 1969," he guessed that the most comprehensive files from the case were in the custody of the Pennsylvania State Police. He said nothing about the large number of documents that Penn State itself must have generated during the murder investigation, when forty state troopers were swarming the campus and interviewing thousands of students and faculty. Instead, Ness said that Pattee Library had "a small file of information" that he could probably examine "in two or three hours." If this was the same file of news clippings and press releases from the Aardsma case available at the Penn State Archives today, it would not take nearly that long. Merritt, perhaps discouraged by the response, never published a book about Betsy Aardsma's murder.[10]

Late in February of 1977, a crude, taunting, and anonymous postcard about the failed Aardsma investigation arrived at the office of the Campus Patrol at Penn State bearing an Atlanta, Georgia, postmark. It said, "We killed the cunt in the library; you'll never solve it." Members of the Campus Patrol passed the letter around amongst themselves for five or six days, Keibler recalled, then decided maybe they ought to tell Colonel Pelton, the director of security. He was furious, Keibler said, and immediately turned the postcard over to the state police. There were no fingerprints on it beyond those of the Campus Patrol officers who had passed it around. Nor did the handwriting yield any clues. Haefner's movements at that time are unknown. Was it sent on behalf of one person, or two, as the wording suggests? One thinks of the two young men librarian Dean Brungart saw in the Core shortly before Betsy's murder. Keibler found it interesting that the postcard was mailed to zip code 16802, for University Park (Penn State's postal location), rather than to 16801, the State College zip code. That suggested to him that someone with a connection to Penn State, possibly a former student, sent the spiteful message.[11]

Keibler inquired of Colonel Pelton how many Penn State alumni lived in the area served by the Atlanta mail-processing facility and was told, after consultation with the Alumni Association, that the number was too large for any kind of practical investigation to be carried out. The postcard, like the one sent in 1969, urging police to "look for the guy in the work pants in the library," remained a mystery. Both seem to have been sent by someone who knew Haefner and the circumstances of Betsy's murder quite well. Maybe the postcard writer simply enjoyed taunting law enforcement.[12]

Among Penn State students, the murder of Betsy Aardsma had already become an urban legend. At the beginning of 1979, Nancy Bertram, a student, conducted a remarkable survey of her fellow students at University Park, asking them what they knew about the murder in the Pattee Library stacks. She had no trouble getting responses. One coed said that a friend who worked in Pattee had been told the story by the head librarian when he was about to go work at the spot where Betsy had been killed. In this version, a girl was in the stacks around midnight, "way back in the catacombs of the library, where very few people go or even know about, and someone stabbed her." And she wasn't found for a day or so, but they thought she had fainted. There was a "little trickle of blood" coming out of her mouth, which supposedly sometimes happens when people faint. But they figured out she was dead, and when they did the autopsy, they found "a tiny hole left by a penknife in her left breast." She had been stabbed directly in the heart, but there was no blood on her clothes. "So they think that she was killed by an expert, and he probably had something to do with the Mafia or a drug ring or something. But the fact that the penknife was placed perfectly makes them suspect that experts killed her."

Bertram heard several versions in which the victim was a policewoman or narcotics agent who was both raped and murdered. In nearly all versions, the body was not found for at least a day, or even several days. In a different version, a female student had fallen asleep in the library and woken up to noise and "this guy in there." She ran into the stacks, but her killer caught up to her, stabbed her, and dismembered her body. Another student Bertram interviewed had heard a version of the Robert Durgy story, without knowing Durgy's name or that he had been an English professor. The student told Bertram that it was "really weird," because her husband knew Betsy and also knew a guy who was also from Michigan who was "having some real emotional problems right around that time. And shortly after that murder, he went back to Michigan and committed suicide." That would have been Durgy, who police eventually concluded had nothing to do with Betsy's murder.

Bertram asked many other students if they had heard about the murder in the stacks, and most of them had, although they didn't know the details. "The story has become part of Penn State's lore," she concluded, "and I'm certain it will be kept alive for many years [to come]."[13]

Part V: Monster

Let them hate, so long as they fear.

—Lucius Accius, Roman poet and playwright (170–86 BC)

CHAPTER 31

Revenge

After Charles Hosler's failed attempt to get Penn State interested in Lauren Wright's story, Rick would never again come close to being exposed as Betsy Aardsma's killer, even as he engaged in reckless and criminal behavior. He spent the rest of his life in a vain quest to regain his professional respectability, to be *Doctor* Richard Haefner to the world, but no one would have him. He pursued boys for sex with the same abandon that he pursued unique mineral specimens. And he wrecked people's lives with frivolous lawsuits. In so many ways, he was a monster.

In his own mind, Rick had been "exonerated"—a word he frequently misused—by the legal skills of Richard A. Sprague, his talented defense counsel from Philadelphia. He believed himself innocent, believed that he had never molested those boys, and couldn't understand why the rest of the world didn't believe him. It made him angry, and when Haefner got angry, he tended to behave in crazy, scary ways. You didn't want to cross him, Chris Haefner recalled. As a former editor of the Lancaster *New Era* newspaper put it, Rick was "persistent and unrelenting. You could never win an argument with him."[1]

For a long time, even as he slid deeper into mental illness, Rick kept a lid on the volcanic rage that the author believes had left Betsy Aardsma dead on the floor of Pattee Library. But even at a simmer, he was dangerous. His weapon of choice became the lawsuit. Sometimes lawyers handled these for him, but it eventually dawned on Haefner that it was really pretty simple to fill out the legal paperwork and represent himself *pro se.* It wasn't brain surgery, or at least, so he thought. Because Haefner claimed he was a pauper—without income—he was often excused from the costs paid by most litigants. He could sue the world and incur no legal fees, often not even filing fees. This was meant to be a protection for the legitimately poor, a way to allow people of no means, especially prison inmates, to gain access to the legal system. Haefner tried and often succeeded in getting pauper status in his lawsuits. It was an easy lie, and too often, judges didn't roll the log away to see if there was a snake underneath. Nor was there any point to suing him back—he had no *known* income or assets to attach. The targets of his revenge—the Natural History Museum of Los Angeles County, the police officers who arrested him in 1975, municipalities who employed the officers, or average citizens who crossed him—incurred thousands of dollars in legal fees and untold hours of time and mental anguish in dealing with Haefner's revenge lawsuits, which they could not simply ignore. While they suffered, Rick boasted of his courtroom prowess.[2]

Neil Albert, a lawyer who defended the City of Lancaster from some of the lawsuits, commented sardonically that he had "the pleasure of knowing Mr. Haefner for many years." Albert said the amount of legal paperwork generated by Haefner's litigation was staggering. "If my memory serves me, one piece of litigation went on for eighteen years before the final defendant was dismissed. And there were others." Asked to assess Rick's abilities as a pro se litigant, Albert said he found Haefner to be very bright, with an excellent memory, when it suited him—he had a way of deliberately misremembering details—and very energetic and focused. But he also found Haefner to be difficult for no reason, deeply suspicious and hard to deal with. Part of this seemed due to his personality, Albert said, and part of it was due to his unfamiliarity with the legal process. Asked about the total costs incurred by the taxpayers to defend Rick's lawsuits, at least the ones involving his client, Albert said it was a difficult question to answer because of the multiplicity of defendants. "I am sure the costs were over six figures," he said.[3]

The same guaranteed access to the legal system that protects good people, giving them their day in court, also grants nearly unfettered access to those whose motives are less pure. American judges have historically been reluctant to bar any but the most flagrantly frivolous of litigation, meaning that a defendant can be forced to pay thousands of dollars in legal fees just to get to dismissal. It mattered little to Haefner that he lost nearly all of his revenge lawsuits. The point was to inflict pain on his perceived enemies or to massage his easily bruised ego, and filing a lawsuit accomplished both quite nicely, even if he lost.

In fact, the only significant revenge lawsuit that Haefner pursued in which he was conventionally victorious was against Los Angeles County as owner of the Natural History Museum of Los Angeles County, and against certain officials of the museum. This lawsuit was in court in the early 1980s. Rick's grievances were many, dating back to February 17, 1976, when the museum terminated its offer to hire him as curator of mineralogy-geology. That occurred after Marion Stuart, a member of the museum board and a major donor, learned of his arrest on the molestation charges in Lancaster. Haefner didn't disclose the arrests when he was being interviewed for the position, or when it was finally offered to him. Although he claimed that museum officials told him he would be considered for other positions, three years later, when Rick applied for the position of chief curator of Earth Science, he received a summary letter of rejection. They wanted nothing more to do with him.[4]

Deciding to fight back, Rick and his mother, Ere Haefner, flew to Los Angeles in February 1980. They showed up at the home of Leon G. Arnold, who was acting director of the museum and chief of personnel, and confronted him. According to Chris Haefner, who was told the story by Rick, Arnold admitted that Rick was qualified for the curator positions but would never be hired because of his arrest on the child molestation charges. Haefner claimed he was told that he would forever have a "black mark" against him, and that his presence at the Museum of Natural History would be bad for the museum's image. Chris Haefner says Rick secretly recorded the conversation and that it proved crucial to his case, although, again, it should be noted that only Rick's interpretation of this meeting is known.[5]

Haefner made other accusations in his complaint. He revealed that he had applied for a job at the Smithsonian Institution in October 1981 and that the official who did the vetting was his old F&M classmate, Harold Banks Jr. Banks phoned Arnold and was told, according to Haefner's lawsuit, that the museum didn't hire Rick in 1976 because of his arrest on the molestation charges. Banks can't have been totally surprised, since he was a character witness for Haefner at the trial, but regardless, Rick didn't get the Smithsonian job. Rick would also claim that Marion Stuart urged that he not be hired by the US Geological Survey when he sought a job there in 1983. She told a USGS geologist that she had Rick checked out thoroughly, and that he was a repeat sex offender.[6]

One of Haefner's stronger arguments in his litigation was that the museum's decision to deny him employment based on an arrest, rather than a conviction, violated the California Labor Code. But there was more to it than that. The law simply didn't allow a California employer to treat a job applicant in the way the museum had treated Haefner, even given his background. Part of the lawsuit was thrown out in 1982, but the rest lived on and was later modified to incorporate the allegations regarding the Smithsonian and USGS jobs he had sought. US District Judge Mariana R. Pfaelzer denied a defense motion for summary judgment on July 12, 1984. This ultimately led to settlement talks and to a payment by the museum to Haefner of damages said by Chris Haefner to have been upward of $250,000. He hid the money from his creditors, especially from Richard A. Sprague, his lawyer, and lived on that for years, according to Chris. He never won another significant lawsuit, even though he filed many and caused considerable pain to the targets of his wrath.[7]

In the first blush of their professional relationship, Rick Haefner and Richard A. Sprague agreed that because of the nature of the criminal charges filed against him in 1975—child molestation—there might be a strong civil rights case for damages against the Lancaster Police Department. It is no surprise that Haefner thought so. He spent nearly every waking minute obsessed with his victimhood. Sprague, who did not respond to several requests for an interview for this book, believed in Rick's innocence, and the case was the kind he loved. Seemingly, it was about a little guy inexplicably persecuted by a small-town legal system run amok. It is no surprise he thought it might yield a strong civil lawsuit for damages.[8]

There was no doubt he was a skilled litigator; in assessing the winnability of Haefner's case, though, Sprague was at a disadvantage. It is doubtful Rick ever told him about the other boys he had approached for sex over the past fourteen years, ever since that first reported incident in 1962. Nor, we can imagine, did Rick seem mentally ill. Indeed, he could come off as charming, intelligent, and normal, according to Chris Haefner. Rick and Sprague would spend seven years together as client and lawyer, until Haefner's anger and paranoia got the better of him.[9]

When Sprague filed the lawsuit on March 9, 1981, the defendants were, in order, the County of Lancaster, Lancaster County Prison, the City of Lancaster, Lancaster Police Department, Detective Jerry P. Crump and Sergeant Edward H. Snyder, Jimmy Burkey, because of his role as a concerned older brother in encouraging Kevin's accusations against Haefner, Kevin Burkey himself, Thomas Dommel, captain of the guard at the county jail, and Randy K., the other victim. The defendants who were government employees were also sued as individuals in case the court ruled they had immunity in their public roles.

Haefner demanded compensatory and punitive damages in excess of $50,000. He accused the defendants of engaging in a conspiracy that resulted in him being denied his right to a fair and impartial criminal trial. His prosecution was "malicious," he said, intended to inflict emotional distress. He accused the Lancaster police of having a policy or practice of condoning false testimony. He specifically accused the Burkey brothers and Randy K. of knowingly providing false testimony to Detectives Crump and Snyder, intended to result in his arrest. His standard complaints about the polygraph and the supposed deal the police ignored were also included.

In dismissing the lawsuit on August 11, 1981, US District Judge E. Mac Troutman zeroed in on the statute of limitations, saying Haefner should have filed the lawsuit before February 1978. Troutman ruled that it didn't matter whether his complaint had merit. Nor, under federal law, could Haefner claim malicious prosecution, because his trial had ended in a mistrial. To seek damages for malicious prosecution, he would need to have been convicted.[10]

Rick was furious, believing that Sprague, the lawyer who had saved him from prison, must have filed a "defective" lawsuit. Sprague filed an appeal on Rick's behalf to the US Third Circuit Court of Appeals, and later, to the US Supreme Court, but neither luck nor law was with him. He also filed a second civil rights lawsuit that he hoped would evade the statute of limitations problem by adding later events that Haefner claimed were part of the alleged conspiracy. Judge Troutman did not agree. He dismissed the new lawsuit but transferred parts of the case back to Lancaster County Common Pleas Court, the last place Haefner wanted to be. Rick was beside himself with anger.[11]

He would continue to harass some of the defendants with further lawsuits that he filed himself, especially the various members of Kevin Burkey's family. If Rick Haefner hated anyone more than the Lancaster police or the Lancaster Recreation Commission, it was the Burkeys—David, Jimmy, their parents, Harry and Eileen, in addition to Kevin. They had once been his neighbors on Nevin Street but had moved away after the parents divorced. Between 1981 and 1995, Kevin Burkey was tied up in one lawsuit after another. David and Jimmy were in some of them, especially after 1989.

It was a remarkable instance of one psychopathic pedophile's misuse of the legal system to ruin the lives of his accusers. No judge seemed able to stop it. No sooner would one of Haefner's lawsuits be thrown out of court than he would be back with another, or so it seemed. Too often, the judges in Lancaster County seemed to be on autopilot, unable to see the harm that was occurring before their very eyes. Rick was relentless, without pity, and he forced his victims—the Burkeys were not alone—to worry endlessly and pay money to lawyers to defend themselves and avoid a default judgment. They had no choice. Rick would have destroyed them if he could. The Burkeys were not angels, and they used questionable tactics at times to get back at Haefner. But they were the real victims, and their agony lasted for twenty years, beginning the day Rick took Kevin Burkey to the garage until 1995, when the last of the lawsuits involving the brothers was dismissed.

CHAPTER 32

Paranoid and Agitated

Rick Haefner became convinced that the police and prosecutors in Lancaster and Lancaster County were entirely corrupt and were engaged in a conspiracy to deprive him of his civil rights. The lawsuits stemming from his 1975 arrest, beginning with the one filed by Richard A. Sprague, were only part of a broad effort by him to persuade the world that he, Dr. Richard Haefner, a distinguished professor of geology, was a victim of a relentless, sordid conspiracy.

At first, he thought that if he went to federal law enforcement outside of Lancaster County, he would get an objective hearing and could make his case that what he said was true. Late in 1976, or early in 1977, not long after a private detective he hired to look for dirt on his accuser, Kevin Burkey, allegedly was hassled by the Lancaster police, Rick went to the offices of crusading US Attorney David W. Marston in Philadelphia and told his story. But Marston wasn't interested, much to Haefner's dismay. This should have been no surprise. No one who approaches a prosecutor—or a newspaper reporter, for that matter—and claims that the entire local law enforcement system is corrupt is going to get a good reception unless they have some really solid evidence. They've heard it all before, and it never seems any less paranoid. But such were Haefner's delusions of grandeur that he thought *Doctor* Richard Haefner, PhD, would automatically be believed.[1]

Haefner had little trouble attracting sympathetic coverage from the Philadelphia newspapers. Stories about potential police or government corruption and the little guy fighting back were an easy sell to journalists in those post-Watergate days, especially in Philadelphia. It was no surprise, and little reflection on them, that they went for Haefner's story. He was white, handsome, well educated—a college professor! He told a good story, and the renowned Richard A. Sprague was his lawyer. What more was necessary? No one knew of his earlier pedophilia incidents. The *Philadelphia Inquirer* wrote a story in 1976 when Sprague first took his case, and on March 18, 1979, a week after the double jeopardy ruling, the Philadelphia *Evening Bulletin* weighed in. Then on its last legs (it would cease publication in 1982), but still turning out quality journalism, the *Bulletin* published a long story and sidebar by David Runkel about Haefner's quest for vindication.

"My career has been in limbo," Haefner lamented to Runkel. "My interest is in Death Valley. I haven't had access to it, or to any laboratory equipment or computers that are essential for my research. I have read articles, but have not been able to pursue my research, or teaching, or my museum work." No one would hire him, he complained. Rick told the *Bulletin* that the arrest and trial had ruined his parents and brother financially, leaving them "destitute." They would all leave Lancaster if only they could. Not wanting to miss an opportunity, he leveled a blast at the legal system in Lancaster County. "The courts operate directly contrary to the way I've been trained," he told Runkel. "In science, we assume the integrity of the other side and organize the facts around that. In Lancaster County law, you attack the integrity of the other side and ignore the facts. Logic has no part in the legal system of Lancaster County." It was a remarkable portrait of how Haefner thought. He assumed that the criminal justice system outside of Lancaster County operated like a genteel academic debate in the Deike Building at Penn State. "I shudder to think of where I would be if it weren't for Mr. Sprague," said Rick, concluding his remarks to the *Bulletin*. "He unlocked the truth."[2]

But despite his good press, the harassment continued—at least as he saw it. Rick claimed in one of his lawsuits that on June 11, 1979, and October 4, 1979, he was accosted by Lancaster police officers in a parking garage in downtown Lancaster and threatened with arrest unless he produced identification. And that on March 5, 1980, he was stopped by police on the street and advised to plead guilty to the Randy K. charges, about three weeks before they were withdrawn by the prosecution. And that on March 25, 1980, the police photographed him on the street. Were the police messing with him? It's hard to say, but it would not be entirely surprising.[3]

Brilliant, yet too obtuse to understand the consequences of what he was doing, Haefner tried to turn the tables on the police, helped by his brother George when he was visiting from California. George would watch from a parking garage across the street from the city police station and try to obtain video evidence of the Lancaster police mistreating Rick when he went downtown and, apparently deliberately, strolled past the station. Chris Haefner remembers that George got in trouble once when police accosted him in the parking garage and took his videotape. But he continued to watch them, sometimes helped by their mother, Ere Haefner. This went on for years, and one has to wonder whether George, in particular, and perhaps even Ere had their own mental health issues.[4]

Late in 1980, Rick took his accusations about corrupt law enforcement in Lancaster to the FBI. On November 24, he phoned the Public Corruption Hotline run by the Philadelphia Field Office of the FBI to state his concerns, but he apparently received no reply, or at least no reply that satisfied him. So off he went to Washington, DC, appearing at the office of US Senator Richard Schweiker of Pennsylvania, where the staff inexplicably referred him to US Senator Barry Goldwater of Arizona. Goldwater's staff referred him to FBI Headquarters. Haefner then was referred to the Washington Field Office of the FBI to make his complaint. He described who he was and why he believed the entire police department in Lancaster to be corrupt, along with the district attorney's office in the county. He alleged that "certain judges" were also involved in a conspiracy to deprive him and others of their civil rights. Rick told the FBI that he never molested anyone and that the accusations against him were concocted by Harry Burkey, Kevin's father. The FBI agent took careful notes on everything he said, telling him they would send an agent to interview him at home in Lancaster.[5]

An agent did visit him at his house on December 22. Haefner later complained bitterly to the Harrisburg Field Office of the FBI that the agent "excused himself early that day and did not finish taking the complaint from me." The agent had apparently promised to return "after the notes he had taken thus far were typed up." And of course, he had not returned. Rick knew a blow-off when he saw one. In a February 6, 1981, letter, Haefner protested that the agent had requested him to make his statement in detailed, chronological order, and that he was far from being finished when the agent abruptly excused himself and left. Like some other people of a paranoid bent, Rick could not stop talking about his perceived victimization.[6]

In a memo to William Webster, the director of the FBI in 1981, the Special Agent in Charge of the FBI Philadelphia office explained that Haefner had spoken to at least seven agents during the course of making his complaint. He noted pointedly that Haefner "considers himself" exonerated of the molestation charges against him in Lancaster. "It is believed that further contact with Haefner would be both counterproductive and unnecessary," the agent wrote. "Both in personal and telephonic contacts, Haefner has adopted an adversary posture." In a reply memo from headquarters, he was advised to inform Haefner that his complaint had been reviewed by the Civil Rights Division at the Department of Justice, and that "no further investigation has been requested by the Department." Like every agency that dealt with Rick Haefner, the FBI seemed under no illusion that he was blameless in what had happened to him.[7]

On the same day he mailed the letter to the FBI complaining of the truncated interview, Haefner, now thirty-seven years old, appeared in an agitated state at the downtown offices of the Lancaster *Intelligencer Journal* and *New Era* newspapers. In a subsequent lawsuit against the City of Lancaster and the police officers who arrested him, Rick said he went to the newspaper offices to arrange for publication of a news story about his belief that the city and its police department were engaged in a corrupt conspiracy against him. He was probably upset, too, because the FBI had shown no interest in his case. That was why he had sent the letter that morning. Rick's visit to the newspapers did not go well.[8]

The subsequent police report doesn't fill in all the details, but suggests that Haefner was denied permission to enter the newsroom and began yelling at the reception staff and acting aggressively. They urged him to use the lobby phone to talk to a reporter. Ernest Schreiber, the reporter for the *New Era* who spoke to him, recalls the incident today but not what they talked about. Meanwhile, the staff phoned the police and three officers arrived. They talked Haefner out of the phone booth—the lobby phone was in a phone booth for privacy—and away from the receptionists. Officer John Wertz asked for identification. Rick insisted he didn't have to provide it. He began pacing the lobby, moving back toward the reception desk, and became boisterous. Finally he reached over the counter into the cashier's area, almost inviting a police response.[9]

Wertz grabbed Haefner by his arms and pinned him against the counter. He arrested him, handcuffed him, and took him to the police station. There, Rick went wild, according to the official report, offering "considerable resistance" to being placed in a holding cell. He took a swing at one of the officers. They finally had to manhandle him into the cell. That afternoon, he was charged with disorderly conduct, a summary offense, arraigned before a district magistrate, and released on ten dollars' cash bail. Rick hired Sprague to represent him at the hearing on the citation, and the law firm ran up more than forty-two billable hours on his behalf. That resulted in total fees and costs of $4,106, but Sprague got the case dismissed.[10]

Schreiber dealt with Rick Haefner for many years, first as a reporter and later as editor of the newspaper. He recalled another incident in which Haefner did indeed reach the newsroom and became "quite voluble." More often, he said, Rick would call to complain about a story that had been in the newspaper or which he believed was about to be published. "He was persistent and unrelenting, and you could not win an argument with him," Schreiber said. "You could only try to reassure him." At the time, Schreiber did not think Haefner seemed paranoid. "I saw him as a really intelligent guy who was doing his own defense work and who was vociferous about himself. He wanted to make sure we followed the rules of journalism."

But clearly, Haefner also benefited from his social class. "He came from a respected family and was well educated," Schreiber said. "He was accorded the respect that you would give to a college professor." That would have been true at almost any newspaper, where class distinctions among news subjects are parsed carefully, if often unconsciously. It was thus understandable, but it allowed Rick Haefner to get away with a lot. He was never treated as just another nut on the street.[11]

CHAPTER 33

Suing His Own Lawyer

In June 1983, the Sprague firm dropped Rick Haefner as a client. Neither side ever said why, at least publicly. At that point, Rick had run up $72,034.06 (at an apparently discounted rate of $75 per hour) in legal fees and expenses on the Burkey charges, $18,957.39 in fees and expenses on the Terry Hess case, for which Haefner had assumed responsibility, and $4,106.22 on the newspaper incident, for a total of $95,097.67. It isn't clear whether this total included fees and costs from his first and second civil rights lawsuits against the Lanaster County defendants. His brother, George, had loaned him just under $30,000 toward his total debt to Sprague, but that left more than $65,000, or more than $130,000 in today's money. Sprague never did collect on the balance, despite suing Rick in 1987. Haefner wiped out the debt with a Chapter 7 bankruptcy filing in 1993.[1]

The summer of 1983 went badly for Rick. In addition to being dropped by Sprague, Judge Troutman in June dismissed a third civil rights lawsuit that Rick had filed pro se, seeking damages from the City of Lancaster and the police officers who arrested him in the lobby of the Lancaster Newspapers on February 6, 1981. Why Sprague didn't handle the case is unknown. Perhaps Rick's tab had gotten too high, or perhaps they had a falling-out. Then, on July 21, Haefner was arrested for shoplifting in a Kmart store in Manheim Township, a suburb of Lancaster, after a store clerk saw him switch the price tag on a seat cover. He was released with a citation and presumably paid the fine, no longer having Sprague to fight his petty arrests. It was not his first offense. He had been arrested at another store in Manheim Township back in December 1981, which suggests Rick had as much of a problem with theft as he did with pedophilia.

And then, on August 9, 1983, consumed with misplaced anger toward the lawyer who had saved him from a long prison term, but who had been stymied in his efforts to win damages from the authorities, Haefner filed a pro se lawsuit against Sprague, his law firm, and several other lawyers in the firm, seeking damages for, among other things, loss of reputation. He accused them of mishandling the two lawsuits filed over his arrest in 1975 by missing the statute of limitations deadline. Rick swore to the court, again quite falsely, that he was a pauper.[2]

Did the lawsuit induce a certain amount of mirth in Sprague's ornate offices off Rittenhouse Square in Philadelphia? If so, it was premature. At first, it is true, Rick did not seem particularly attentive to this lawsuit, being repeatedly warned by Judge Alfred J. DiBona Jr. about the consequences of "non-prosecution." His lack of focus may have stemmed from the death of George P. Haefner Sr. His father died at age seventy-five on December 28, 1983, succumbing to a heart attack as he drove home one afternoon, crashing into a neighbor's garage. At the time, he was working as an insurance inspector for the Mutual Inspection Company and still helped out frequently in the rock shop, making the boxed sets.[3]

By the time Rick filed his second lawsuit against Sprague on April 16, 1984, he had his crazy back, and he gave the lawsuit his full energy and attention. It quickly became a sort of medieval battle in which the catapults hurled legal papers instead of boulders or boiling oil. He matched Sprague and his lawyer, Ms. Gene E. K. Pratter, then of the large Duane, Morris LLP law firm in Philadelphia, now a federal judge, brief for brief over the next five years. But his pretrial behavior in and out of the courtroom annoyed the judge and opposing counsel and frightened their staff.

The case was assigned to Judge Louis G. Hill, who had been a Democratic state senator from Philadelphia from 1969 to 1978 before being elected a judge. Hill had run unsuccessfully against Mayor Frank Rizzo for the Democratic nomination for mayor in 1975. He first encountered Haefner on October 30, 1985, when Rick abruptly appeared in Hill's chambers and filed an emergency petition for documents from Sprague's lawyer, who had apparently told him he couldn't have them right then and there. Ms. Pratter had to drop everything and file an affidavit explaining why they were unavailable. On March 11, 1986, Haefner did the same thing. This time, Hill ordered Pratter to make immediate arrangements for Rick to inspect and, if necessary, copy thousands of documents. On another occasion, Haefner submitted a court order to a deposition by Pratter but left before it was finished, saying he had to catch the train home to Lancaster. Despite his self-taught knowledge of judicial language and procedure, Rick seemed unaware of the normal, almost scripted pas de deux by which opposing lawyers maintain a thin veneer of civility during contentious legal battles.[4]

Haefner harassed Pratter, according to Judge Hill, and on one occasion caused an uproar in her office. A receptionist at the Duane, Morris law firm said in an affidavit that she was "quite frightened" of Haefner. This, by the way, was neither the first nor the last example of Rick's hostile or threatening behavior toward women, whether lawyers, secretaries, or waitresses; there are numerous examples throughout his life. In response, Hill issued an order directing Rick to avoid prolonged discussions with Pratter's staff and to behave himself in her offices. "Dr. Haefner demonstrated that he was an assertive, willful, and, at times, abrasive individual who was uncooperative and difficult," the judge wrote. Rick complained that Hill had called him "a manipulative liar." Hill denied using that exact phrase, conceding only that he had termed Haefner "a manipulative individual," who in the past had "not been candid with the court." There was a touch of humor in that, but much of Rick's behavior was simply scary.[5]

Some of the sharpest arguments in the pretrial phase came from Pratter's ultimately successful attempt to subpoena two sets of documents relating to pre-1975 sexual offenses attributed to Haefner. She believed, no doubt correctly, that they would undermine Rick's claim to have had a good reputation before the 1975 arrests and the doomed lawsuits. Her investigators may have heard about the incidents from the Lancaster police, who apparently learned of them from the Lancaster Recreation Commission, even though there was never any prosecution. In 1986, Pratter subpoenaed a confidential file on Rick maintained by Franklin & Marshall College.

Early in 1988, she also went after Haefner's personnel file at the LRC from his work as a day camp counselor at Camp Optimist. The pretrial hearings on this issue brought out some of Rick's more menacing behavior. The court reporter, who sat less than five feet away, told Judge Hill he was uneasy. So did the court crier and law clerks. Somewhat nervous himself, Hill requested a deputy sheriff to be present during the rest of the pretrial hearings. He considered Rick to be "explosive, unpredictable, and impulsive." Few who dealt with him over the years would disagree.[6]

Haefner fought to keep the accounts of his alleged sexual misdeeds out of the court record. When he heard that Sprague's lawyer was going to subpoena the personnel file, which included information about the Ocean City and Boy Scout scandals, Rick made frantic efforts to get the file from the Lancaster Recreation Commission. But what he might have been able to do a few years earlier was now impossible. In January 1988, he twice went to the Recreation Commission offices and demanded the documents, but on the advice of counsel, Susan E. Abele, the executive director, would not turn them over, or even let him see them. Haefner said the file was "possibly embarrassing, and has no influence on this case." The first part was true, the second quite false, which was why Rick was trying so hard to toss it in the fire.[7]

With the trial date of his lawsuit against Sprague approaching, Haefner hand-delivered a letter to the LRC on April 25, 1988, demanding that the records subpoenaed by Sprague be removed from his file, or that at the very least, a hearing on his request be held. Donald Lefever, the commission's lawyer, advised Abele that Rick was just making "hot air threats." But Haefner, who was in his *Terminator* mode, would not be denied. There was a hint of menace in his words and actions. He appeared at the office on April 26 and asked to see Abele, who was not in. On April 28, he returned and again asked to see Abele. Told once again that she was out, he asked the secretary for the addresses and phone numbers of the Recreation Commission members, which she refused to provide. Rick demanded a response to his previous letter by the end of the day, or he would deem his request for a formal hearing denied. He didn't get it. Not long afterward, Rick asked for and received a continuance of the trial until October.[8]

By that time he had a new lawyer, Kenneth W. Richmond, of Philadelphia. Rick had apparently lost confidence in his own legal skills, or perhaps he realized that the mighty Sprague would be too tough of an adversary. In addition, his financial situation had changed in a surprising way, and he now had the money to pay, even though he was still claiming to Judge Hill that he was a pauper. Haefner had already offered another lawyer a $10,000 retainer to take his case but was turned down. Some lawyers he had approached looked at his case file and refused, or signed on and then quickly resigned when they realized what they were up against. Anthony P. Ambrosio, a New Jersey lawyer who represented him briefly in 1988, told the court that Rick had made "material misrepresentations" that might require him to violate the Rules of Professional Conduct. He said Rick refused to take his advice and persisted in taking matters into his own hands. Ambrosio called Haefner "deceitful and dishonest."[9]

One day in the summer of 1988, Richmond had been preparing to go home from the courthouse after finishing a trial. Haefner, who had observed him in action, approached and asked if he would represent him. Surprised, Richmond asked what the case was about. When told it was a lawsuit against Richard A. Sprague, and that Judge Hill was in charge of the case, Richmond told Rick that he "didn't stand a chance." Haefner said he didn't care. "I have to have an attorney," he said. "I just can't go on by myself." Richmond told him it would cost a lot of money, because he would have to put everything else aside. Rick asked how much and was told the retainer would be $25,000.

Haefner didn't blink. Soon afterward, he appeared at Richmond's office in downtown Philadelphia and handed him a shoe box. Inside was $25,000 in small bills for the retainer. Taken aback, Richmond asked to see the case file. Haefner had his helpers—presumably his usual posse of young male admirers—carry up seven or eight file boxes full of pleadings and videotaped depositions Rick had conducted of Sprague and other parties to the case. Richmond groaned when he realized that the videotaped depositions had not been transcribed, a requirement before anything in them could be used in court. But when Richmond watched the videotape of Haefner's deposition of Sprague, he was transfixed. It was

Richard C. Haefner

ORIFLAMME YEARBOOK, 1965, FRANKLIN & MARSHALL COLLEGE

Ere S. Haefner, Rick's mother
COURTESY OF CHRIS HAEFNER

George P. Haefner, Rick's father
COURTESY OF CHRIS HAEFNER

Haefner's Pilsener Beer label
COURTESY OF BOB KAY

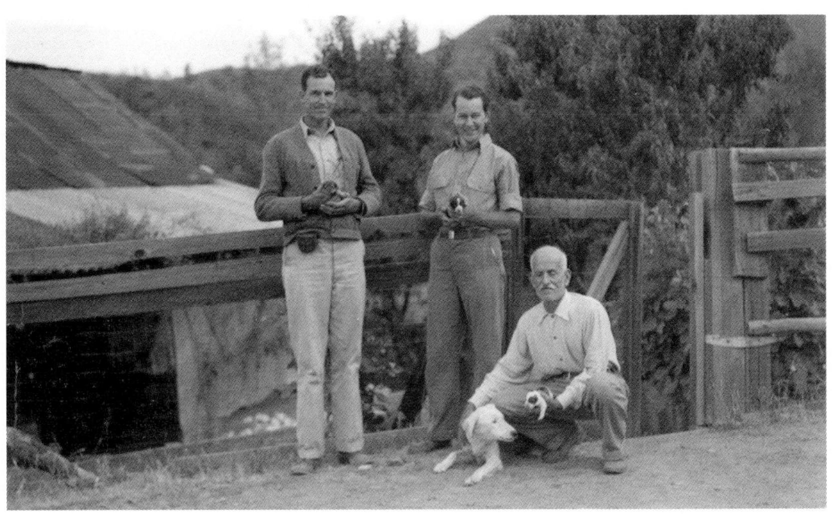

Lauren A. Wright, center, with friends, 1942
BENJAMIN PAGE COLLECTION, STANFORD UNIVERSITY LIBRARY

Charles L. Hosler, dean of Penn State College of Earth and Mineral Sciences
COURTESY OF CHARLES L. HOSLER

Lauren A. Wright and Rick Haefner, 1968
COURTESY OF DAN STEPHENS

Rick Haefner in Death Valley, 1968
COURTESY OF DAN STEPHENS

Rick Haefner's former rock shop and Christopher L. Haefner, 2010
DAVID DEKOK

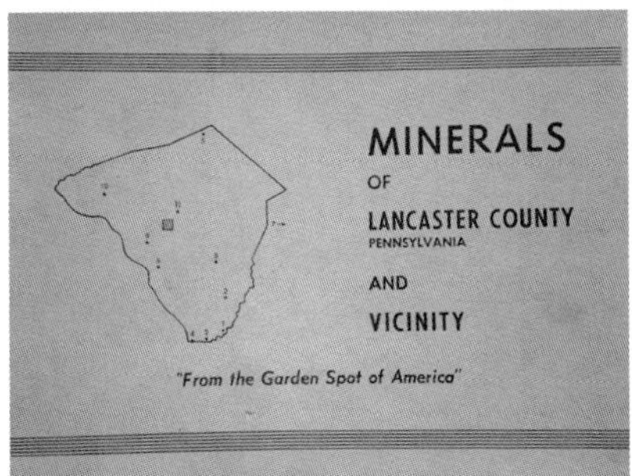

MINERALS
OF
LANCASTER COUNTY
PENNSYLVANIA
AND
VICINITY
"From the Garden Spot of America"

Rock box prepared by Rick Haefner for sale in museum gift shops
COURTESY OF CHRIS HAEFNER

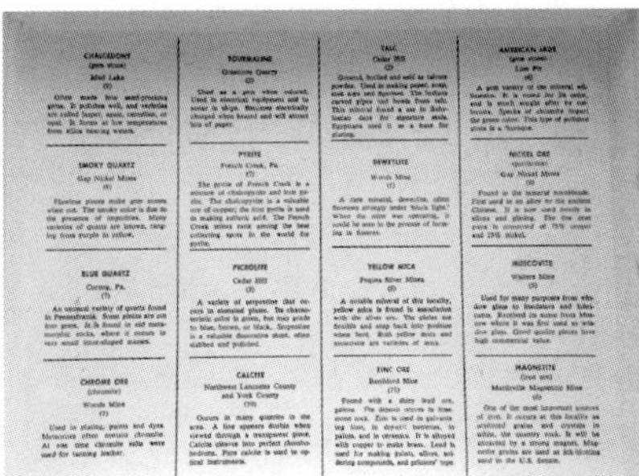

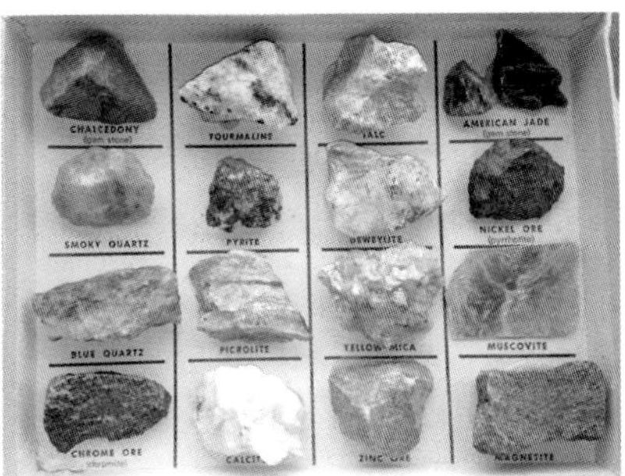

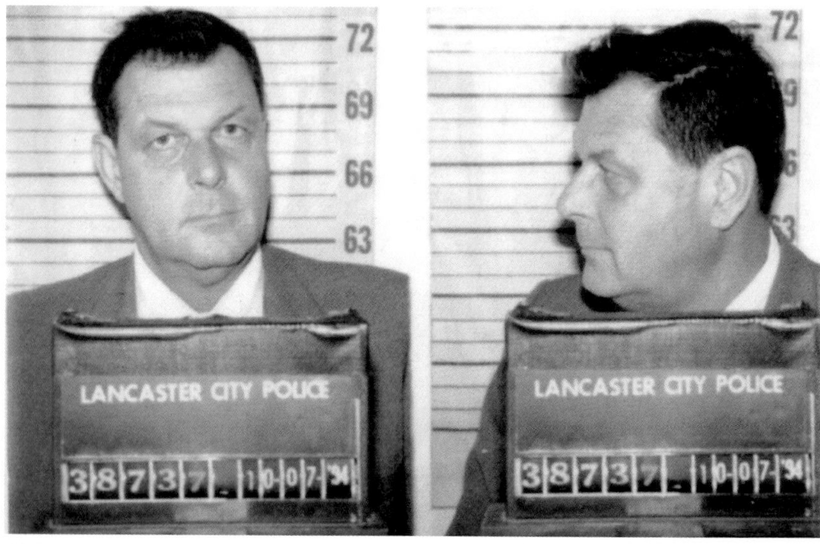

Rick Haefner's mug shots from his October 5, 1994, arrest in Lancaster
COURTESY OF THE CITY OF LANCASTER

Catherine R. Schuyler, savagely beaten by Haefner in 1998
COURTESY OF PETER SCHUYLER

Robert G. Durgy, who was investigated in Betsy's murder but cleared
COURTESY OF MARTHA DURGY

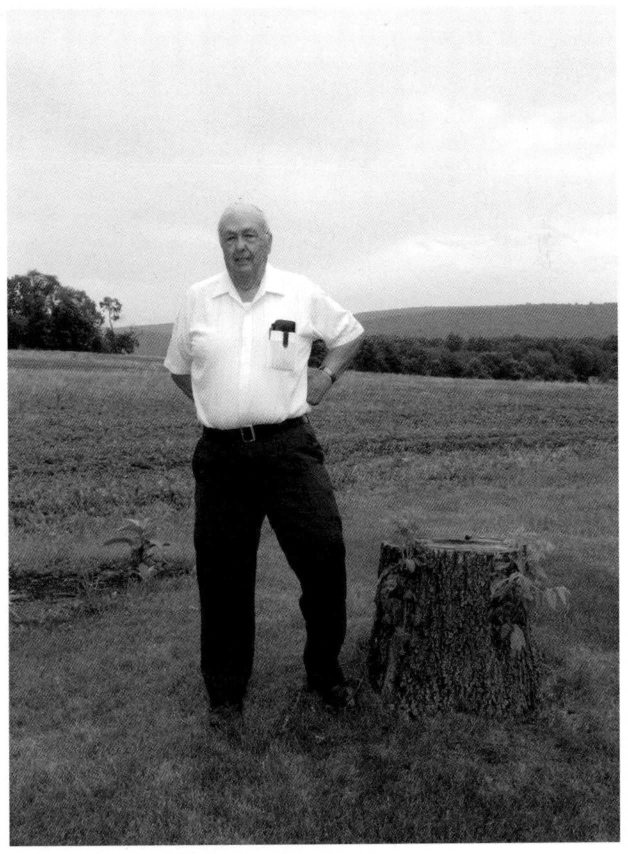

Sgt. George H. Keibler at age eighty-two
DAVID DEKOK

Richard C. Haefner's grave, St. Anthony's Cemetery, Lancaster, Pennsylvania
DAVID DEKOK

Remains of the house in Tecopa Hot Springs that Rick Haefner stole from the Parmeters, and his car. It has been largely undisturbed since his death in 2002.
DAVID DEKOK

"astonishingly good, amazing," Richmond said. "I was flabbergasted at how well he pulled it off." He dealt with objections and with Sprague's lawyer, Gene Pratter, a skilled litigator. "She's a really elegant sort of woman, kind of impatient, well-educated, very sharp, and excellent at repartee," he said. "Yet he handled all that with perfect aplomb." Richmond decided to represent Haefner.[10]

One issue that had to be resolved in the litigation was Rick's claim that he had lost income because of the failed civil rights lawsuits. Pointedly asked how he was paying his lawyers if he was as poor as he claimed, Haefner said his brother, George, had loaned him $25,000; the amount of George's loans to him varied in the retelling. But that didn't strike Richmond as being the whole story. "I insisted on knowing where the money was coming from. There were flea markets of some sort [actually gem and mineral shows he ran]. It wasn't adequate to explain the shoe boxes." Richmond demanded that Rick tell him the whole story about where he was getting his money. He did, and it was a shocker.

Rick was a trained gem expert, particularly when it came to emeralds. In the mid-1970s, after he left Penn State, he had taken courses in gem grading and appraisal offered in the United States by the Gemmological Association of Great Britain. That turned out to be a marketable skill. Haefner admitted to Richmond that his money came from appraising emeralds used "in huge, illicit drug transactions." He told his lawyer that one emerald could equal a suitcase full of cash. Colombia mines 60 percent of the world's gem-grade emeralds, and between 1984 and 1989, Colombian drug lord Pablo Escobar and his Medellin Cartel waged a bloody, if ultimately unsuccessful, war for control of the emerald trade. They used emeralds to launder drug money.

Now the shoe boxes full of cash made sense. Rick had worked for drug dealers. "Yes, that was the source," Richmond said. Haefner was not selling illegal drugs, but he was aiding and abetting the drug trade by appraising emeralds so his clients did not get cheated. That disclosure was "a very, very large mistake," Richmond said, because if he had been called to testify about how Haefner was paying him, he would have had to disclose the real source of Rick's money. But fortunately for Rick, the court never went beyond his earlier claim that his brother, George, had loaned him $25,000. George, who attended the trial, had to explain where he got the money. Everyone moved on, and Richmond and Haefner exhaled.[11]

Richmond kept Rick on a short leash during the trial, commanding him not to say or do anything. He considered him to be one of the more intelligent clients he had ever represented but also found him "super-controlling and wanting to micromanage everything." That all changed after the drug emerald revelation. Haefner stayed on his best behavior. He paid his fees on time and did what his lawyer told him to do. Richmond recalled that the color would visibly drain from Rick's face if anyone called him a sexual deviant.

Sprague claimed in his testimony that Haefner had given him permission to wait to file the first civil rights lawsuit for strategic reasons. When Pratter, on November 8, 1988, made a rarely successful motion for a *nonsuit,* or a judicial declaration that a case is over and won't go to the jury, she said that Haefner giving Sprague permission to wait was undisputed. "Well, it was disputed," Richmond said. "It was disputed by Haefner's testimony. Nevertheless, Judge Hill jumped on that. You could see his eyes light up." Hill declared a nonsuit the following day. In his opinion, the judge noted that Sprague was allowed by Haefner and Richmond to have "free rein" to tell his own side of the controversy for three days, in testimony running to 426 pages.[12]

Haefner appealed to Superior Court, alleging that Judge Hill was biased against him. Several months after the trial ended, he appeared unannounced in Hill's chambers and requested the judge's pretrial notes of testimony. At that time, Hill was analyzing them because of the appeal and refused to hand them over. Rick became argumentative, Hill said, to the point where Hill told him not to come in again without an appointment and that if he did not leave immediately, a deputy sheriff would remove him.[13]

A year after Judge Hill stopped the trial, Haefner sent a coldly worded letter to the Lancaster Recreation Commission demanding that his personnel file be removed and destroyed. Given his history, they had to know a lawsuit was coming. He was again in *Terminator* mode, aggressive and relentless. Susan E. Abele, the LRC executive director in 1989, wasn't sure what to do. She asked Donald E. Lefever, their lawyer, for help in drawing up a list of conditions under which the commission would consider destroying the file. But LeFever stood firm: Abele should *not* destroy the file or turn the originals over to Haefner, he said—not when there was still the threat of litigation. He said Haefner could place a letter in his file to address any perceived inaccuracies and could be provided with photocopies of its contents, but that was it.[14]

Haefner filed a pro se lawsuit on March 19, 1990, demanding that Lancaster County Common Pleas Court issue a writ of mandamus—a court order to a public official to carry out a legally mandated duty—ordering the Recreation Commission to destroy his personnel file from twenty-five years earlier. What is truly fascinating—and disturbing—about the complaint is what Haefner said, and the way he said it. For example, he said that the LRC, meaning Bomberger, accused him, in his own words, of "behavior that was *thought* to be immoral [*emphasis added*]." So masturbating preteen boys wasn't really immoral? Rick couldn't bring himself to drop the qualifier. It was the same attitude he had expressed to Bomberger when he was summoned, late in the summer of 1965, to explain his actions with the boys. "Richard said he felt only compassion for this mother, and *if he had done anything wrong, he wasn't aware of what it was* [*emphasis added*]. He said he was only trying to do something good by taking the boys on a vacation before they go away to school." That he would make a similar claim in the lawsuit shows he was still in denial about the real nature of what he was.[15]

In the spring of 1991, the Lancaster Recreation Commission and the City of Lancaster responded to the lawsuit and challenged the legal underpinning of Haefner's request for a writ of mandamus. They argued that Haefner had not demonstrated that the city or the LRC had any legal duty to expunge his personnel file and asked that his "frivolous" lawsuit be dismissed. It finally was, on June 19, 1991.

CHAPTER 34

Thinking about Ted Bundy

In 1982, Sergeant George Keibler, then nearing the end of thirty years of service with the Pennsylvania State Police, received a phone call from a woman in State College who had read *The Stranger Beside Me,* a nonfiction book by Ann Rule published in 1980 about serial killer Ted Bundy. The caller knew that Keibler was the lead investigator of Betsy Aardsma's murder. She wondered whether Bundy might have killed Betsy Aardsma. This call launched Keibler on his last major effort to solve Betsy's murder.[1]

Keibler was less than two years away from retirement, planning to call it quits on December 31, 1983. It had been many years since Betsy had been found on the floor of Pattee Library at Penn State, and despite much sound and fury, the state police were no further along in figuring out who had murdered her than they were on November 28, 1969. Keibler had told reporter Taft Wireback in 1972 that Betsy's murder would probably not be solved unless the killer sought psychiatric help or was apprehended in connection with another crime. Bundy seemed to fit into the second part of his prediction.

What Keibler saw in Ann Rule's book intrigued him. Officially, Bundy had killed at least thirty young women in six states, although he famously boasted that thirty was one digit too few. The tall, dark, and handsome Bundy killed young women as predictably and casually as most people go to the grocery store. Some were teenagers, some in their early twenties. Often, he killed women on or near college campuses. Bundy had spent his earliest years in Pennsylvania. His mother, Eleanor Louise Cowell of Philadelphia, had been left pregnant by Lloyd Marshall, who supposedly was a student at Penn State University. Marshall didn't stay in the picture, and Eleanor gave birth to Ted at a home for unwed mothers in Burlington, Vermont. Moreover, Rule described how Bundy, beginning in early 1969, came back to Pennsylvania from Seattle looking for information about his birth father. He seemed to be killing women everywhere, Keibler mused. Why not at Penn State? As a theory, it had promise, although he learned only later that Ann Rule had erred in saying Lloyd Marshall attended Penn State. He had actually attended the University of Pennsylvania in Philadelphia, if he existed at all.[2]

Bundy stayed in Philadelphia for the first six months of 1969, even enrolling at Temple University. He was back in Seattle in the fall, attending the University of Washington and meeting with a female friend, one he didn't kill, on September 26, 1969. Yet much was still unclear. Not every week, or even every month, in Bundy's life was accounted for. Rule wrote in the updated edition of her book in 2000 that there could have been many other victims of Ted Bundy. She called it an impossible task to determine precisely where he was on a particular date. "Ted was always a traveler," Rule wrote. "He would say he was going one place, and head somewhere else. He hated to be made accountable for his whereabouts." So yes, he was in Seattle on September 26, 1969, but did anyone really know where he was on November 28?[3]

Keibler set out to learn as much as he could about Ted Bundy and his time in Pennsylvania, making numerous phone calls to Ann Rule, who was cooperative and even mentioned a "Pennsylvania homicide detective" who was clearly Keibler in the 2000 edition. Even so, she got the story half wrong, writing that he was investigating the murder of "a beautiful dark-haired young woman" who was stabbed to death in the stacks of a library, but at Temple University in Philadelphia, which is jarring to see in print. Detective Robert D. Keppel, who had investigated several of Bundy's early murders for the King County Police Major Crimes Unit in Seattle, was less friendly, Keibler said, but did answer his questions.[4]

Keibler believed that Ted Bundy fit the description of the man seen running out of the Core seconds after Betsy was struck down. "He's five foot, eleven [actually six feet tall, according to records], he's a young guy, he's dressed up. You look at Allen's statement. . . . He's dressed better than a student. He has a tie and white shirt on. Students don't dress like that normally," Keibler said. He readily acknowledged that no one knew where Bundy was on November 28, 1969. Could it have been Pattee Library? Maybe; maybe not.[5]

But in the end, Keibler believed Bundy's pornography addiction was the key to linking him to the Aardsma murder. "The key to this case, as I've told you before, are those [Dutch porn] books in the corner," he said. "That's the key. Either that son of a bitch [the man who was reading the porn book] is her murderer, or else he witnessed the whole thing." And if it was Bundy, it was safe to assume he didn't go there to work on an English paper. Ann Rule told Keibler that she knew Bundy liked porn at the time they worked together answering phones in 1971 at a crisis hotline in Seattle. Keppel told him that when they searched Bundy's residence, he observed a lot of porn lying around. What if it was Bundy who had abandoned the expensive porn book in his rush to flee Pattee Library?[6]

If it was, Bundy's fingerprints should have been all over it. So Keibler requested copies of Bundy's prints from the warden of Raiford Prison in Starke, Florida, where Ted was on Death Row. He received Bundy's fingerprints, palm prints, and toe prints. When he contacted the state police crime lab in Harrisburg—where the Aardsma evidence was supposed to be stored, since it was part of an active criminal investigation—he was told that sometime between 1970 and 1980, it had been shipped to Troop G headquarters in Hollidaysburg, with no notice to anyone involved in the case. There was no record of the transfer.

Upset at not having been notified, Keibler went to Troop G and asked the Bureau of Criminal Investigation lab to retrieve the book and see if they could find Bundy's prints. They agreed to do so. "For a month, I'm after them," Keibler said. They finally came back and told him that Bundy's prints were not on the book. But it wasn't just that. They claimed that nobody's were. Keibler found *this* hard to believe—that a porn book found in a library would have no fingerprints at all. "If that's Ted Bundy sitting there with that book, son of a bitch's prints *have* to be on that book. It's that simple."[7]

Still hoping to save his investigation, Keibler wondered whether Bundy would talk to him. He again called down to Raiford Prison, where they warned him that Bundy was nuts. "He may tell you to come down, and you come down, and he may tell you to go screw yourself, or he may talk to you," Keibler remembers being told. But the commanding officer of Troop G, Captain Vincent Fiorani, would not let him go to Florida, unconvinced that the trip would be worthwhile. Keibler argued that Bundy might spill information about other unsolved murders or disappearances in Pennsylvania. "I could have gone higher than him and around, okay?" he said. But he did not. "That is a tragedy, that the state police didn't do that," Keibler said. Seemingly, his investigation of Ted Bundy was over. He wrote a report saying that Bundy was a suspect, but that he could not prove his involvement.[8]

Now the question became, with Keibler retiring at the end of 1983, who would take over the Aardsma investigation? He was fifty-two years old and had been head of criminal investigation at the Rockview barracks since 1965. The Aardsma case had been his responsibility since Lieutenant William Kimmel handed it off to him in December 1969, three weeks after the murder. During those fourteen years, Keibler saw no reason to hand it off to anyone else.

His last day on the job, Keibler burned the hypnosis tape of one of the Nittany Mall rapist victims of 1969, keeping a promise he had made to her parents all those years before, when Corporal Dan Brode had insisted on devoting time and resources to his theory that the rapist—who was believed to be a working man from the country and had probably never been on the Penn State campus—was the most likely suspect in the Aardsma murder. They had pursued the idea much longer than they should have.

In January, Keibler phoned Captain Fiorani and asked him who he was going to assign to the case. To his dismay, Fiorani was noncommittal. "I said, 'Captain, you have to have someone sitting on top of it.'" Fiorani, who clearly didn't agree, said he just didn't have an answer for him. In his typically plainspoken manner, Keibler said, "Well, make up your mind. I should have a month to talk to him, back and forth." Fiorani questioned whether that was necessary, saying the new man could just read the report. Keibler snorted. "I said, 'C'mon; there's sixteen or seventeen hundred pages, plus fourteen years.'" It would take anyone a serious amount of time to get up to speed on a case like this. It also might have been worthwhile to have a new set of eyes go over the information that had accumulated over fourteen years. But it wasn't to be.[9]

"No decision was ever made," Keibler said. "I retired and did my thing. I became aware that nobody was assigned to follow it up." Eventually, a cold case officer was assigned to the Aardsma case, but neither he nor any of his successors ever went to Keibler for a briefing about what had happened, he said.

A big part of the problem, as it had always been, was that Betsy Aardsma was not from Pennsylvania. She had no family in the state to pressure legislators for action, to complain to the state police regularly about the lack of an arrest, or simply to be angry. No legislators are known to have asked pointed questions about the Aardsma case to the state police commissioner at the annual budget hearings in Harrisburg over the years, a common occasion for questioning heads of agencies about their failures. Nor were Penn State's presidents questioned by legislators. Betsy was nobody's constituent in Pennsylvania, so why would they? Keibler and the original investigators cared deeply about the case, and still do, but the university and nearly everyone else, even her family, had moved on.[10]

Keibler and his wife, Beverly, were on a bus trip in 1989 when he heard on the radio that Ted Bundy was about to be executed in Florida's electric chair. Trying to stave off the inevitable, Bundy was talking to investigators from around the country about girls he had killed and where he had buried their bodies. On the night before his execution, he was interviewed over the telephone by James Dobson, the conservative religious commentator from Colorado Springs who headed the group Focus on the Family. Dobson pushed Bundy to say that he had gotten into murder through pornography, and the condemned man was eager to oblige. He told Dobson that pornography put the Devil in his head, and that he had killed those young women because he read pornography. Keibler, a conservative man, liked Dobson and considered him a straight shooter. He thought the pornography admission strengthened his case against Bundy. But in the end, the interview didn't change anything. On January 24, 1989, Bundy was put to death.[11]

The arguments against the idea that Ted Bundy killed Betsy Aardsma outweigh those in favor of the notion. Bundy preferred to strangle or bludgeon his victims to death, not stab them, although he would sometimes use knives to carve them up or behead them after death. "To go up to a girl and just stab her, that is so non-Bundyish," psychologist Art Norman told reporter Ted Anthony of the Penn State *Daily Collegian* for a story about the twentieth anniversary of Betsy's murder. "None of his needs would be fulfilled." Norman, who was part of Bundy's defense team and interviewed him extensively, cautioned, however, that Bundy could have broken from his pattern, especially early in his killing spree. And he did like to murder women on college campuses.

It hardly seemed possible that nearly twenty years had passed since Betsy was found on the floor of Pattee Library with a single stab wound in her heart, and equally hard to believe that her killer was still unknown, still free, and not serving a life sentence in a Pennsylvania prison. Esther Aardsma, Betsy's mother, told reporter Phil Galewitz of the Harrisburg *Patriot-News* in 1988 that she hadn't heard from the Pennsylvania State Police in more than a decade and had accepted that Betsy's murder would likely go unsolved. A year later, she was quoted in Anthony's *Daily Collegian* story, lamenting, "It's such a cold trail, such a long time. I can't imagine what they could do." Once again, there was an Aardsma cold case officer. Corporal Jeff Watson, ironically the son-in-law of Corporal Mike Mutch, one of the original investigators, said there was "a good possibility this was a random act." Like Mutch, he said Betsy's sterling character made it hard to find a motive for her murder.

The Aardsma murder had rarely been mentioned in the *Holland Evening Sentinel* after the first year. Dick and Esther Aardsma did not place memorial tributes in the newspaper on the anniversary of Betsy's death, as some in Holland do for a year or two after loved ones die. One of Betsy's high school beaus, Luke Kliphuis, didn't even find out about her death until the early 1980s, even though he lived in Holland. (They broke up well before high school graduation, and he had been in the army, stationed in West Germany, when it happened.) At some point in the early 1980s, he found out in the worst possible way. Kliphuis ran into Dick Aardsma, Betsy's father, at an Alcoholics Anonymous meeting, remembered him from years earlier, and asked how Betsy was doing.[12]

CHAPTER 35

A Life Destroyed

By the end of the 1980s, when he had passed his forty-fifth birthday, Rick Haefner's regular companions were boys who ranged in age from preteen to late teen. Other than Chris Haefner, his cousin, they were often from struggling families, from broken homes. To them, Rick was cool, a source of money and good times. They worked in the rock shop, went with him on collecting trips, or just hung out.

Often the activities were innocent, even fun, but inevitably, for those he deemed ready, the bill came due. Rick would sit in the car with his arm around his favorite of the moment or disappear with him to his bedroom for an hour or two. Chris, who had rebuffed his groping hand in 1975, saw it all. But like the others, he kept quiet, not wanting the good times to end. In truth, Rick had so cowed the Lancaster authorities in the early 1980s with his aggressive lawsuits that even if one of these wayward boys had gone to the police, it seems unlikely the authorities would have rushed to intervene.

Perhaps Rick was less Charles Manson and more Fagin, the nineteenth-century fictional character in *Oliver Twist* (he was known as a *kidsman*) who schooled poor London boys in the ways of crime and shrugged if they were caught and hanged. In the end, it was all about his needs. Rick led his boys into a moral netherworld where there were only Rick's rules and where the innocence of youth was merely a delight for him to pluck. How much the boys knew about his activities on the wrong side of the law is debatable, but they had to see him as an authority figure who got away with a lot. Several of them acquired extensive criminal records as adults. Some, as teenagers, even stole from him.[1]

One of the few women in his life was his mother, Ere Haefner, who had fiercely defended him and possibly covered up his involvement in Betsy Aardsma's murder. After she died on June 2, 1991, whatever Rick did at home was now his business alone.

There was actually another woman, however, with whom he claimed to have "an intimate relationship." His courting of Harriet Sandomer and the grooming of her son, Bruce, who was nine years old when they first met, seemed to come straight from Pedophile 101. A single welfare mother, Harriet was deformed by spina bifida. Attorney Kenneth W. Richmond, who represented Haefner at the time, described Harriet as somewhat overweight and practically bent in half from her condition. She also had a Valium dependency problem. Harriet had grown up a few blocks from Rick but was nine years younger. They would meet at a nearby coffee shop. Rick added Bruce to the crew of boys at the rock shop and gave Harriet between $100 and $150 a month toward her living expenses. In addition, Rick brought her food and took Bruce to places she could never afford to take him on her own. "Rick feels sorry for me," Harriet told Richmond. "But he's a bastard, too." She did not elaborate.[2]

Haefner fooled few into believing that his relationship with Bruce was completely innocent. Jimmy Burkey certainly didn't think so. He had referred derisively, in Haefner's presence, to Rick's "little pussy Bruce." But it was not until after Ere's death in June 1991 that a confrontation with the outside world began to gather steam. According to Haefner, Lancaster County Children and Youth Services, the county's child welfare agency, began "slandering" him to his neighbors around that time, calling him a sexual pervert and dangerous. Of course, what is "slander" to a psychopathic pedophile may simply be an agency doing its job and inquiring whether neighbors had observed anything bad going on. Kevin Burkey even paid a visit to Harriet Sandomer to warn her about Haefner's true nature and what had happened to him.[3]

Bruce, who had attention deficit disorder, struggled in school and received help from the Lancaster-Lebanon Intermediate Unit, known as IU 13. Intermediate units in Pennsylvania are regional public education entities that provide special education and other services to school districts in their territory. On December 3, 1991, Rick was summoned to the offices of IU 13 outside Lancaster and informed that Bruce, then twelve, was going to be arrested for aggravated assault, possibly against a girl student, although the details are incomplete. Bruce was a small boy, just five-foot-two and weighing a hundred pounds. Before he was read his Miranda rights by the police, a parent or adult guardian needed to be present. Rick was already well-known to the IU staff.[4]

Haefner claimed in his subsequent lawsuit that Monica Steward, a teacher for IU 13, became agitated when she saw him walk into the room. She pointed and accused him of assaulting the staff and said the IU was preparing to file charges against him. She urged the police officers who were there to remove Haefner and not allow him to stand in for Bruce's mother or to take him home. Rick says he demanded that Steward either explain or retract the accusation, but she would not. The details of Haefner's assault on IU staff members remain shrouded, but he was often accurate, at least to a point, in describing the "false" accusations against him in the many lawsuits he filed. He didn't agree with the accusations—that was the point of the lawsuits—but his descriptions were usually accurate, allowing for some hyperbole. What was important here was that a woman, Monica Steward, had criticized and challenged him, and he was in a rage. He might get angry at men, such as his lawyer Richard Sprague, but against women who crossed him, he displayed pure, acid, scary rage.[5]

Later in the day, Rick went to see Dr. Richard Sherr, the director of IU 13. He complained about the "slanderous statements" by Steward and demanded that she write a letter retracting the accusation. Sherr told Haefner he would look into the matter and give him a response. When it was not forthcoming after several days, Rick began telephoning Sherr's office, demanding a retraction. There was still no response. On December 18, 1991, Haefner and Harriet Sandomer had a meeting at the IU offices about Bruce. Steward was there, and when the meeting was over, he asked her point blank whether she would withdraw her accusation. "I won't," she said and strode out of the room.

Haefner's pro se lawsuit against the Intermediate Unit veered into *Alice in Wonderland* territory. He wrote that "Dr. Haefner is a good, true, honest, and virtuous inhabitant of this Commonwealth." He had never been "arrested for assault," which was true, though not for long, and "has never been convicted of a crime," also technically true. As a result of Steward's accusation, Haefner wrote, "Dr. Haefner has been greatly hurt and injured in his good name, fame, and reputation aforesaid, and has been brought into disgrace and disrepute among his neighbors." It was all true, except that it wasn't Steward who was responsible, it was Rick himself. The lawsuit dragged on for two years at a cost to the taxpayers of thousands of dollars in legal fees before it was finally settled on undisclosed terms on May 31, 1994.[6]

Bruce ran away from home in early May 1992. When questioned a few weeks later by police in Chincoteague, Virginia, he claimed he stayed "with friends" after leaving home but didn't know their names. He may well have been staying with Haefner. In an affidavit four years later, Bruce said he went to Rick's house after a few days and asked to go to the seashore. "Rick did not kidnap me or get me to try to run away from home," he said in the affidavit, sounding like a Soviet-era prisoner writing a self-criticism. "From the age of about nine, Rick Haefner helped raise me as a father would. We were very close."[7]

Oddly, Harriet did not report him missing until May 16. Five days later, without informing her, Rick took Bruce to Chincoteague Island, Virginia, the southern half of a windswept barrier island in the Atlantic Ocean (the northern half, which is in Maryland, is called Assateague Island). He had a trailer in Tom's Cove Campground. There they stayed, working on Rick's boat and repairing the trailer. According to Bruce, Rick had a word processor in the trailer, and they worked together, writing up a lawsuit against the Lancaster police. "I wanted to help him to criticize the police and do something to bring them under control, even though I was just a kid," Bruce wrote in his 1996 affidavit. On what turned out to be their last day together, May 28, Rick drove Bruce to Ocean City, Maryland, a distance one-way of fifty-two miles. They spent a few hours on the boardwalk, riding the rides and having fun, before returning toward dusk.[8]

How the Lancaster police learned he was with Rick in Chincoteague is unknown, but the information probably came from an upset and worried

Harriet. She had let Bruce go there with Rick several times before. At 1:00 p.m. on May 28, Detective Raymond Dimm of the Juvenile Bureau phoned the Chincoteague police and asked them to be on the lookout for Bruce. He believed Bruce was with Rick in Tom's Cove Campground and provided two possible license numbers for Haefner's vehicle, a beat-up Dodge or Chevy van with a white camper top. Shortly before 3:00 p.m., Dimm called back with another detail, that the van was brown or bronze in color. He also provided a more detailed description of Bruce, saying he was five feet, two inches tall, weighed a hundred pounds, and had medium-length brown hair and brown eyes.[9]

Around 11:45 p.m., officers knocked on the door of Haefner's trailer. He answered and acknowledged that Bruce was there. They awakened him and took him to the Chincoteague police station, with Rick in hot pursuit. At the station, Haefner demanded to see the documents faxed by the Lancaster police and demanded to talk to a lawyer. "Mr. Haefner was informed he was free to talk to any attorney he chose and that we just needed to talk to [Bruce] and not him," the Chincoteague police wrote in their report. Chief Willis Dize then escorted Bruce into his office. Haefner yelled after the thirteen-year-old, as any loving father figure would, "Bruce, keep your mouth shut!" About what? Bruce knew.

The conversation went like this, according to the official police transcript: "Q: Did anything happen between you and Mr. Haefner while you were with him? A: No, and I don't want to talk about it. Q: Talk about what? A: Every time we get around the police, they like to accuse Rick of doing things. He's not like that."

Dize phoned Harriet Sandomer, who told him she did not want Bruce released to Rick's custody and, in fact, wanted Haefner arrested. They let Bruce speak to his mother before taking him to Lighthouse Ministries, a church-run shelter, where he was to stay pending the arrival of a caseworker from Children and Youth Services in Lancaster.[10]

They arrested Haefner the next day on a warrant from Pennsylvania, charging him with interfering in the custody of a child. Dimm had warned Dize to do everything by the book when he arrested Haefner. "He's sued us a number of times, and he will sue you, too," Dimm said (and he did). Rick was taken into custody after his van was pulled over and placed in the Accomack County Jail pending an extradition hearing. The police towed and impounded the van and then searched it. In a compartment in the van, they found a large collection of pornography, which they laid out on a table and photographed. Dize described the sex magazines as "fairly disgusting." They subsequently searched the trailer and discovered more porn mags, but also a vibrator and rubber "butt plugs" intended for anal sex.[11]

After learning Haefner had taken Bruce to Chincoteague, Lancaster County Children and Youth Services moved quickly. On June 2, while Rick was still in jail, the agency obtained an emergency court order, removing Bruce from his mother's custody and placing him in the Fulton Shelter in Lancaster. Harriet attended the emergency hearing and agreed to the placement to prevent Rick from taking him away again. And there he stayed, with Haefner barred from visiting.

By the time of Rick's preliminary hearing on July 24, on the interference charge, Harriet was back under his sway. She testified that Rick had her permission to take Bruce to Chincoteague, even if she hadn't known he was taking him on this particular trip. And she had been "relieved" to find out that Bruce was with Rick. Harriet had completely changed her story. As a result, the district magistrate threw out the charges. But a few days later, she went in a panic to the YWCA Sexual Assault Prevention and Counseling Center and told a supervisor that she feared her son *had* been molested. She refused, though, to have the Center open a case file, apparently afraid of Rick's reaction.[12]

Bruce reached his eighteenth birthday in 1996, and Haefner filed a petition in Inyo County, California, to adopt him. Why he did this is open to speculation. Bruce was old enough to decide with whom he wanted to live, but perhaps Rick feared someone would still make trouble for them. The petition, which was signed by both of them, said they intended to move from Pennsylvania to California in November 1997. Inyo County, which is huge, includes both Death Valley and Shoshone, Rick's home base when he did geological research for his master's and doctoral degrees in 1967 and 1968. But something happened along the way and the adoption never went through. Perhaps Bruce had grown tired of Rick and wanted his youth back, or perhaps he simply matured to the point where he was no longer the pliable child Rick wanted. Bruce stayed in Pennsylvania and soon drifted into crime.[13]

CHAPTER 36

Neighborhood Menace

Rick Haefner was also a physical menace to adults around him, or a threat to their property. In the early 1990s, he began losing any pretense of civility. By the end of the decade, he would show that it was quite plausible he had killed Betsy Aardsma so many years before in a temporary, blinding rage.

The earliest incidents had to do with Haefner's ill-mannered cocker spaniel named Dudley, to whom he was devoted. Three days after Haefner turned fifty on December 13, 1993, he was issued summary citations for disorderly conduct and "dog-at-large" by the Lancaster police. Dudley had been running loose in the Nevin Street neighborhood, getting into garbage cans and making a mess. The dog's rambles drew a third citation on February 10, 1994. Two of Rick's neighbors, Lori D. Miller and Tony Freeman, who lived at 221 Nevin Street, testified against him at a preliminary hearing on June 29.

Perhaps eight hours after the hearing ended, and not long after midnight, Eric Smith, who lived across the street from Haefner, heard someone coughing outside. He looked out his second-floor window and had a clear view of Rick walking with Dudley, who was unleashed, back and forth in front of the row houses on the other side. Streetlights made it easy to see what was happening. Rick stopped in front of the Miller/Freeman residence, two doors down from his own house, and trampled the small flower garden in front of their home. Then he turned to Dudley, who was lying on the sidewalk, and appeared to mumble something to him. Then he picked up Dudley and carried him to his house and put him inside before returning to the porch.

Smith observed Haefner walk toward the Miller/Freeman car, a blue Pontiac. He leaned down by one of the rear tires with one hand on the car trunk, then went back to his house. By now, Smith had called Freeman and Miller and told them what was going on. They went outside, saw their trampled garden and its mangled wire fence, which Haefner had also ruined, and heard a hissing sound coming from one of their rear car tires. Freeman placed soapy water on the punctured area and saw bubbles as air escaped the tire. Miller called the police and Haefner was arrested for witness retaliation, a serious offense. The jury found him guilty, and Judge Lawrence Stengel sentenced him to twelve months of probation, a $100 fine, and about $200 in costs and restitution. It was a comparatively light sentence.[1]

A more violent incident occurred at Rick's house a little over three months later, and it was a wonder that Rick, and especially his brother, George, were not shot by the police. George, who was fifty-six years old and heavyset, was visiting from California. He was in poor health, having suffered a stroke and two seizures the previous summer. Late in the morning of October 5, he had another seizure, collapsing outside but managing to make it back to his brother's front steps. A passerby, observing him shaking and in a bad way, ran home and called 911, then came back to meet the ambulance crew from St. Joseph Hospital. Officer Christopher DePatto of Lancaster police arrived around the same time. Rick met them at the door and said his brother was up on the second floor. He led the crew inside and up the stairs, followed by Officer DePatto. Spotting the officer, Rick leaned over the second-floor railing and yelled, "Get the fuck out of my fucking house. No city cops allowed in my house." DePatto told Rick he would leave and began backing down the stairs.[2]

George's seizure was over, but he was dangerously agitated. As the three ambulance attendants came up the stairs, he sprayed them with Mace. They hollered for help and DePatto raced upstairs, only to be sprayed in the face himself. He managed to help two of the attendants downstairs, but the third had locked himself in the bathroom. DePatto ran back inside and up the stairs to rescue the third medic. George once again hit him directly in the face with a blast of Mace. Amid the burning pain and profuse tearing, the officer opened his own can of pepper spray and emptied it back at George and Rick, who were standing next to each other. He retrieved the third medic and got him safely outside. Barely able to see, DePatto frantically radioed for assistance. Police cars began screeching to a halt outside. Officer Michael Corso and Sergeant Gary Metzger were told that George might have a rifle. They entered the house, which was filled with a choking cloud of Mace and pepper spray fumes that made their eyes and skin burn and left them coughing and gasping for air. At that point, Rick Haefner started coming down the stairs and demanded again that the police get out of his house. Corso told Rick that he had to arrest George for spraying Mace at the ambulance crew. "You're not getting anyone!" Rick shouted, and abruptly pushed the officer, knocking him to the floor.[3]

Sergeant Metzger yelled to Rick that he was under arrest and grabbed him from behind. Rick struggled to free himself and then lurched backward. Metzger lost his balance and pulled Haefner down with him. They fell against a small table, which broke under their weight. Rick continued to struggle, trying to break free. Officer Timothy Goodson, who wrote in his report that Rick "continued to behave like a wild man," managed to get a handcuff on one of Haefner's wrists. They dragged Rick off of Metzger, forced him out onto the porch, and then facedown on the ground. In that position, they were able to get the second handcuff on him.

They took Rick to the police station, where he was allowed to call his lawyer of the moment, Roy Shirk, telling him, "This is Richard Haefner. I'm in jail again." Meanwhile, police set up a defensive perimeter. They were worried about the firearms George was said to have access to in the house. For the next two and a half hours, they heard George yell things like, "You're the Gestapo." Eventually, he was talked out of the house and arrested. At St. Joseph Hospital, it took ten men to force George into the mental health holding room. Goodson found and removed a .22 caliber rifle from the house. It was amazing that no one was seriously injured or killed during the fracas.[4]

Rick Haefner was charged with obstructing law enforcement, resisting arrest, simple assault, and disorderly conduct. The first three charges were dropped and he pleaded guilty to disorderly conduct, receiving twelve months of probation. Rick's brother George was charged with four counts of simple assault and one count of disorderly conduct (fighting). He was released on $25,000 cash bail. George subsequently jumped bail and returned home to California. His bail was ordered forfeited on January 19, 1996.

Rick had another face that he showed to the world—namely, that of the smiling, friendly proprietor of the Lost Dutchman Gemboree, an annual rock and mineral show that included exhibits of gold and jewelry from New York gem dealers and was billed as fun for the entire family. He presented himself as a sort of homespun Dr. Geology, offering gold-panning trips, visits to an iron mine in Morgantown, a quarry in Gettysburg, a site near St. Clair that was world-famous for fern fossils, even a visit to what appeared to be the same farm in Lancaster County where he had taken Chris Haefner in 1975, to collect goethite crystals, and where he had begun talking about Betsy Aardsma. Rick had run the show since 1986, first holding it in Strasburg and then moving it to the Lebanon Valley Exposition Center outside of Lebanon, Pennsylvania. The dates for the show in 1996 were August 14 through 18.[5]

But on Saturday night, August 17, thieves broke into the North Hall of the Expo Center and made off with more than $838,000 in gold jewelry and precious stones from exhibitors. Their haul included Colombian emeralds, Burmese rubies (the most valuable of gems), and sapphires. Security, which had been promised to exhibitors on a twenty-four-hour basis in the contract they signed, led most of them to leave trays of gems in their booths overnight, while they slept at motels or in a campground. The thieves supposedly broke a window to gain entry, although some of the exhibitors didn't believe this was the real means of entry.

Lester F. Rittle, the head of security, says Haefner did not want the guards in the building overnight. Haefner claimed that was Rittle's rule. Whichever it was, Rick hired two brothers he met at the Orange County Fair in New York in July to sleep overnight in the Expo Center in front of the locked doors between Center Hall and North Hall. "So if anybody tried to get in the lockup room, they'd have to crawl over them," Haefner later testified. That assumed the thieves would come in the front door. Even if the brothers had heard or seen something, they didn't have keys to North Hall. And they were out with Rick having dinner at a nearby Ponderosa Restaurant from 8:00 p.m., when the building was locked up, until around 11:00 p.m.[6]

The eight gem dealers who were robbed were devastated, and one collapsed upon discovering his losses. The proprietors of Gems & Jewelry Palace, Inc., of New York, told the FBI that they lost more than $275,000 worth of gems, wiping out their life savings. Most did not have insurance because of the high cost of a policy, depending instead on the security guarantee in the contract. One of them called the Harrisburg *Patriot-News* that Sunday and complained bitterly about the lack of security. The author was the reporter who took the call. Using a phone number supplied by the caller, he reached Haefner, who denied security was lax. "We had good security. We always had good security," Haefner said.[7]

From the start, police, the FBI, and Cincinnati Insurance Co., which had sold a $500,000 policy to Haefner for the Lost Dutchman Gemboree, wondered if it was an inside job. They of course didn't know Rick appraised emeralds for international drug dealers, which presumably would have given him the connections to move the stones without too much difficulty, if he indeed had masterminded the heist. North Cornwall Township Police checked the NCIC and discovered that one of the brothers hired by Rick for nighttime security had a criminal record in New York for grand larceny and weapons possession.[8]

FBI suspicion soon fell on George Haefner. Rick's brother had managed the Lost Dutchman Gemboree for the past several years, but he had stayed in California in 1996. Agents learned that Rick owed George about $30,000 but didn't know for what (most likely it was legal fees paid to Sprague). They finally reached George on the phone on November 18, 1996. He became agitated when questioned about why he had not run the show this year and made reference to an arrest in which the Lancaster police had supposedly used excessive force. George danced around the truth and never quite sat down. What no one in the FBI apparently picked up on was that George was a bail jumper; that was why he was back in California. UFAP, or unlawful interstate flight to avoid prosecution, is what the feds would have called it. He had forfeited his cash bail of $25,000 and would never get it back.[9]

Rick brushed off the FBI after initially telling agents that Colombian gem gangs stalked shows like his. He told them they should go after the criminals, not waste time talking to him. The FBI deemed him "uncooperative." Rick said he felt sorry for the victims of the theft, but it was not his fault. His behavior had been strange from the beginning, notably when he tried to stop jewelers from calling the police, and remarkably insensitive, demanding that the show open on Sunday after the thefts were discovered, even though many of the dispirited vendors wanted to go home. He tried to shift the FBI's attention to a gypsy fortune-teller and a couple of supposedly swarthy Hispanics seen at the show on Saturday. The thefts were never solved, and the FBI closed the case on September 25, 1997, saying there were no more leads and no suspects.[10]

George Haefner's son Keith, speaking nine months after his father died in late 2009, believed—from family conversations he had heard—that Rick had been implicated in the Lebanon gem theft, although he had no personal knowledge of that involvement. Keith said Rick was always borrowing money from George. No matter how it may have appeared, he said, relations between his dad and Rick were not warm. "They just never got along," Keith insisted. "I know there was no real love for Richard. At least in my family."[11]

Rick began planning the 1997 Lost Dutchman Gemboree almost before the police had left the building, seemingly oblivious to the ramifications of what had just occurred. He blithely advertised the show and took deposits from exhibitors while ignoring the demands of the Expo Center board and North Cornwall Township for better security. In the end, they refused to grant permission for the 1997 show to be held.

Many exhibitors who had been willing to come back to the show even after the large heist in 1996 lost their deposits, generating an enormous amount of ill will toward Haefner. One of them phoned a few weeks later and accused him of fraud and stealing exhibitors' money. In February 1998, another disgruntled exhibitor publicly confronted Rick at the big Tucson Gem and Mineral Show, and accused him of cheating many people and personally defrauding him of over $900. A fight broke out and Haefner was arrested by show security, but nothing came of it.[12]

Rick was experiencing increasingly volatile mood swings, in part because of the antidepressant Paxil, which he was supposed to be taking for depression but sometimes didn't. He had always had a volatile temper—the author believes Betsy Aardsma was a victim of one of his rages—but now things seemed to be getting worse. And women, as always, were the ones who set him off.

He was mainly living in California now, in Tecopa Hot Springs, a tiny community near Shoshone. But he periodically came back east and was outside of Wilmington, Delaware, on January 6, 1998, when an incident occurred that made it seem quite likely that he could have attacked Betsy Aardsma in a volcanic rage. Dudley, his by-now nearly blind, fifteen-year-old cocker spaniel, was with him as he pulled into the parking lot of Liquor World at 1325 McKennans Church Road in the Milltown Shopping Center, about fifty miles from his home in Lancaster. He was there to buy a bottle of Jameson Irish Whiskey.

The problem was that Haefner was off his meds. Paxil, an SSRI drug (Selective Serotonin Reuptake Inhibitor) that had come on the market in 1992, was in the same class of antidepressants as Prozac and Zoloft. But Rick's prescription had run out several days before he called in a refill on January 5, 1998. Aggression and violence are two well-known symptoms of Paxil withdrawal (or from any SSRI drug), and they don't take long to appear after the last pill is taken. Rick had stayed "on the couch" for two days and then gotten himself to the drugstore, only to be told by the pharmacist that his doctor thought his dosage was too high and that it was being cut down. Everything was in place for a tragedy.[13]

Catherine Rachford Schuyler, who was about six miles from her home in Hockessin, Delaware, had also gone to Liquor World that day. It was where she typically bought wine and spirits for herself and her husband, Peter A. Schuyler. Catherine was forty-nine years old. She had been born a year after Betsy Aardsma and, like her, was slender and on the tall side for a woman, five-foot-ten and 150 pounds. A Cincinnati native, she was of Irish descent, had red hair, and had been a competitive swimmer in college. She loved to cook and entertain. Peter was an executive in the plastics industry, and they had lived in many places. His father, Roy L. Schuyler, had been a three-time football letterman for Penn State in the 1930s.[14]

Haefner had left Dudley in a shopping cart outside the store. When Catherine walked up to the door of Liquor World, the cocker spaniel was barking and whining. She saw the cart start to roll toward the parking lot, so she grabbed and steadied it. By the time she came out with her purchases, Dudley was still there, evidently quite unhappy. She cared deeply about dogs and noticed that Dudley was shaking and had severe cataracts in his eyes. Two other women soon joined her, and they discussed among themselves whether Dudley had been abandoned. One said she would take the dog to her own veterinarian and attempt to locate the owner from the tag on its collar. She went to her car to get a leash.[15]

They lifted Dudley from the cart and began walking him away. At that moment, Haefner emerged from Liquor World with his purchase, saw what was happening, and freaked out. He began screaming at Schuyler and the leash woman. Catherine told Haefner, "Maybe some people shouldn't have a dog," which infuriated him all the more. Schuyler got in her Isuzu Trooper to leave. Haefner began banging on the left rear quarter panel of the SUV with the glass bottle of Jameson, leaving noticeable dents. She rolled down her window and demanded he stop. Rick turned and walked across the parking lot to his van. Then Schuyler made a big mistake. She drove her SUV close to Haefner's van and parked, intending to write down his license plate number. Her doors were unlocked.[16]

Rooting through her purse for a pen and a piece of paper, she didn't see Haefner approach. Suddenly, her door was yanked open and she felt his hands encircle her neck and drag her out of the vehicle. She screamed. Rick was only a couple of inches taller than her but outweighed her by at least fifty pounds. Pushing her against the SUV, Rick struck her several times in the face and again wrapped his hands around her neck. A witness, who wondered if this was a domestic dispute, saw him try to slam her head against the SUV roof. Schuyler managed to break free long enough to kick Haefner in the groin, but it only made him angrier. Another witness saw him grab her by the hair and punch her in the face. Rick was out of control, and Schuyler feared for her life. There is no telling how far things might have gone if the driver of a Tastykake delivery van had not rushed to intervene. Haefner saw him approaching, let her go, and ran to his van and drove away.[17]

Schuyler had significant facial injuries but could still speak, and she called 911 to report the incident. She was treated by her family doctor and received three stitches in her upper right lip, where Haefner's punch had landed. But there was much more damage inside her mouth. Haefner's punches and banging her head on the SUV during his violent rage had loosened teeth and caused other dental damage. Her jaw had been badly dislocated to the point where she could not chew solid food; she would lose thirty-two pounds after the assault. She needed five dental implants and faced two years of restorative dental work that would cost nearly $45,000, fortunately covered by the couple's insurance.[18]

On January 16, 1998, Sergeant Joseph P. Aviola Jr. of the Delaware State Police telephoned Haefner and told him he was going to be arrested for assault and criminal mischief. Rick had an explanation ready: He had hit Schuyler to protect himself, because she was assaulting him. He told the sergeant that he had a disability, asthma, and that if he was hit in the head he could possibly die. It was a fantasy story only Rick Haefner could write. No one believed him. Aviola persuaded Rick to come to Wilmington to give himself up, and, amazingly, Haefner did.

Judge Jay Paul James was unsympathetic to Rick's claim that Paxil withdrawal had led him to assault Schuyler, especially after Rick said he knew there would be problems when he let the prescription run out. But he was livid about Rick's fantasy tale of Schuyler assaulting him, of how she was supposedly "arrogant" toward him. He testified that he only "tapped" on her SUV with the Jameson bottle to get her attention so he could explain why Dudley was not a mistreated dog.

Judge James: *"The court frankly finds the defendant's testimony absolutely incredible."*
Haefner: *"But it was true, Your Honor."*
Judge James: *"You may say that, sir, but I'm finding that you were not telling the truth throughout your entire testimony. I watched your actions. I watched your conversation. I watched your inflection. And I am absolutely amazed at how absolutely dishonest you were."*[19]

Rick told Judge James that he hated being dependent on Paxil and wanted to stop taking it. His psychiatrist—never identified—had told him that a change of lifestyle would be beneficial. Rick said he had moved to California, back to the area where he had researched his thesis. "And it turns out that my former thesis advisor [Lauren Wright] and his field partner [Bennie Troxel] are still there. They are about eighty years old now, but they spend every winter out there," he said. Haefner said he was hoping to get a teaching job at the University of Nevada–Las Vegas. "And I've started to do research out there. I've tutored a graduate student. I've [guided] classes on trips in the area. And I'm getting back into my profession. And if I can do that, then hopefully the general level of my mood will be high enough that I can have the doctor slowly take me off that medication."[20]

Judge James stared at him in incredulity. "You stand up here, sir, and tell me that you're working toward getting off medication that keeps you from becoming a loose cannon," he said. "That scares me to death."

After the jury found Rick guilty, Judge James sentenced him to one year in prison, of which eleven months would be suspended after he served thirty days. That would be followed by one year of probation and payment of restitution to Schuyler. And he ordered Rick to get anger management counseling and continue seeing a psychiatrist.

The story was not over. Haefner served his month in jail and completed twelve months of probation. He then requested a hearing to determine the amount of restitution he would be required to pay to Schuyler for her injuries. Rick testified that his only income was a Social Security disability check of $548.30 per month, a check he received because of his asthma and depression. It was a convenient fiction, since he had always been able to wring much more income out of his other activities, unless his gem appraisal services were no longer in demand by the Medellin Cartel. He said he lived rent-free in the house at 217 Nevin Street, which was owned by his brother. The court ordered Rick to pay $100 per month in restitution, which meant it would take him more than thirty years to pay the full amount. It was his latest joke on the public in a lifetime of financial comedy for Haefner. Schuyler subsequently received $1,920 from the Delaware Violent Crimes Compensation Board. Rick had told the court he accepted responsibility for his actions, but in truth, he had nothing but hatred and contempt for Catherine R. Schuyler. He paid no more than a few hundred dollars in restitution, her husband said.

His feelings toward Schuyler became evident on April 11, 2000, when Haefner filed a pro se lawsuit in federal court against her, charging her with assault, battery, intentional infliction of emotional distress, negligent infliction of emotional distress, damage to property, and fraud and abuse of legal process. It was a voyage into the bizarro world of Haefner's brain, in which everything that he had done to Schuyler, things that had been observed by witnesses, were transformed into things she supposedly had done to him. Peter Schuyler said their umbrella liability policy covered the cost of defending the lawsuit. The lawyer provided by the insurance company proposed a quick $10,000 settlement to make Haefner go away. Catherine Schuyler refused. She wanted to fight. The couple even came to believe that Haefner was stalking their house. Catherine was sure she saw Haefner's beat-up brown van, he said. She had done a lot of research on Rick and knew about his child molestation arrests in 1975. She also found out that he had apparently beaten up another woman in Las Vegas, Nevada. Catherine was affected permanently by the beating she received from Haefner. "She was a very strong woman," her husband said. "He took her pride and strength. She suddenly realized she was vulnerable."[21]

Judge Roderick R. McElvie made quick work of Haefner's claims, dismissing them because they were the same claims he had tried to make in his trial, which the court had rejected. Schuyler's lawyers asked the court to sanction Haefner for filing a meritless lawsuit "for an improper and harassing purpose." Judge McElvie wrote in his opinion that "Dr. Haefner should be aware that his filing in this case borders on frivolous, and that his intent to harass Ms. Schuyler is clear." And if he ever did that again, McElvie said, there might be trouble. But as for now? He was unwilling to sanction Haefner, although Schuyler could submit testimony as to the costs and attorney fees she had paid. It was the same old story of judges bending over backward to give an abusive plaintiff like Haefner his day in court. Except in the most extreme cases, it was up to the jury to determine whether there was a case; that was how the system worked. Any other judge might have done the same.[22]

And given Rick's record, it seems unlikely that the threat of future sanctions would stop him from doing anything. Even after completing his month in a Delaware prison and the anger management program, he had gone right back to his old ways. On October 29, 1998, he gave a deposition for his lawsuit against the Lebanon Valley Exposition Corporation over their refusal to allow the 1997 Lost Dutchman Gemboree to use the Expo Center. A lawyer for North Cornwall Township said something that disturbed Rick, and he began to argue with him "in a loud and angry manner." But he took out his anger on the nearest woman, court reporter Lisa A. Snyder. He slammed a court order on the table in front of her, "and in a loud, angry, and physically intimidating manner ordered me to mark the order as an exhibit." Snyder refused, and was "so scared and intimidated by Mr. Haefner" that she started crying and could not continue. Defense lawyers terminated the deposition and Rick left the building, but he remained in his car in the parking lot. Snyder was afraid to leave the building until Haefner finally drove away.[23]

CHAPTER 37

Hole in the Desert

Rick had always wanted to go back to the desert, to the dusty crossroads of Shoshone, California, where he had stayed with Professor Lauren Wright while doing research on volcanic rocks in Death Valley in 1967 and 1968. Here he hoped to find his own Hole in the Desert, to borrow an obsession of Charles Manson, a refuge from the helter-skelter outside world. He had spoken about California to the boys who surrounded him in Lancaster. Rick told them about George's home near the sea and about the mines he owned in the desert between Shoshone and Tecopa Hot Springs. One mine was called George and one was called Ere, after his parents.

The desert culture around Shoshone was tolerant, and no one asked too many questions. As one resident put it, "You can blend in here as long as you stay low-key." Here Rick could pretend to be an eminent geologist who was just doing his own thing. Here he could pretend that he would soon be teaching geology at the University of Nevada–Las Vegas. Here he could tramp the desert with Lauren Wright.[1]

Wright still had his trailer in Shoshone and was frequently joined during the winter months by his longtime friend Bennie Troxel. In 1976, Wright had gone to Charles Hosler, the dean of the College of Earth and Mineral Sciences, and told the strange story of Rick coming to his house on the night of Betsy's murder and how he thought Rick might have had something to do with that murder. Although he had not changed his opinion over the years, he had done nothing more. Even Ted Anthony's story about the twentieth anniversary of the Aardsma murder in the Penn State *Daily Collegian* in 1989 had not prompted him to reach for the telephone and call the state police.

In the early 1990s, possibly during the first fall or winter after his wife, Myrtle, had died on January 2, 1990, Wright ran into Dan Stephens during a tour of the Nevada Test Site, where atomic weapons are exploded underground. Stephens had been the field assistant when Wright and Rick Haefner did research in Death Valley in the late fall of 1968. When they recognized each other, they immediately began to talk about old times. Stephens eventually asked how Haefner was doing. Wright hesitated, his face took on a strange expression, and then he began describing how Haefner had come to his house the night of Betsy Aardsma's murder, out of breath and out of sorts. Stephens was agog. He had heard nothing about the murder. "And he was relaying this murder to me and how he thought Rick did it," Stephens said. "All the circumstances upon which this occurred, and how he just knew right away that it was Rick." Wright also talked about Rick's problems with the Natural History Museum of Los Angeles County and his continuing difficulties in finding a job in his field.[2]

Yet despite all this, Wright, who was in his early seventies, continued to associate with his former student. Haefner didn't know that Wright had gone to Hosler in 1976. At what point does Wright say, "Oh, well, I guess they aren't going to do anything, so let's just pretend nothing happened"? Or does it continue to fester in his soul? He and Troxel had been coming to Shoshone since the early 1950s. It was their town, not Rick's. But it was also a very small town, and avoiding him would have been difficult if that is what Wright wanted to do.

Perhaps Haefner *did* know something about Wright that the professor did not want to become public knowledge. Why else would someone keep a dreadful secret like that? That Wright used Dan Stephens as a confessor—someone whom he had not seen in years—suggests that he desperately needed to share his guilty secret with someone. Had the death of his wife in January 1990 made him more willing to risk talking about Haefner? But even then, more than twenty years after Betsy was murdered, Lauren Wright remained unwilling to go to the state police.

Kathy Nixon, manager of the Tecopa Hot Springs County Park, knew Haefner as well as anyone toward the end of his life. He lived in a trailer in the campground for a time. She said the region is a geologist's dream and that Rick seemed "genuinely happy" there and wanted to share what he had with others. His dream was to put in a geology study center devoted to Death Valley. Rick made his money, she believed, by conducting faceting classes—instruction in cutting stones—at the big rock and mineral shows in Tucson and Quartzite, Arizona. Two of Nixon's sons accompanied Rick to the shows on two separate occasions. "They never had any issues with him," she said, adding, "A mother would know." But she did remember her sons saying that on both trips, Rick got them all kicked out of a restaurant after flying into a rage at the waitress. Did Nixon like him? "He was okay," she said.[3]

Nixon remembered Dudley, his aged, nearly blind cocker spaniel, and how he was nearly deaf, too. Because of that, he wore a blinking collar. Dudley died before Rick moved out of the county park, Nixon recalled. Bennie Troxel, Lauren Wright's friend, also remembered Dudley, and so did Fred Bachhuber of Boulder City, Nevada, who was chairman of the Department of Geology at UNLV from 1997 to 2001, at the time Rick was trying to get a job there. He even brought Dudley with him once to a meeting at the school.[4]

In a number of affidavits filed in his lawsuits that were active at the time, including one dated July 3, 1997, Haefner presented himself as a working geologist who was involved in ongoing research in Death Valley. In his own description, he was sought out by geology classes and other groups, "some from as far away as Germany," some of whom regarded him as "the world's leading expert on rhyolitic lava flows," the subject of his master's thesis and doctoral dissertation. "I conduct my own research in Death Valley. Two collaborators, Dr. Lauren A. Wright and Bennie W. Troxel, retired geologists, also live in the area. We regularly do field work together." This was verifiably true at least in the case of Troxel. He and Haefner cowrote a paper, "A Petrologic Paradox in Central Death Valley, California," that was presented to the Geological Society of America at its annual meeting in 2002, a few weeks after Rick's death. Lauren Wright is mentioned in the acknowledgments as having provided some basic data needed to complete the research.

Bachhuber, who listened to Rick's appeals to be hired as a lecturer at UNLV, and who was surprised when he brought Dudley to his office, considered him to be a rather strange person. "He wanted a formal relationship," Bachhuber said. "He was willing to come in to give symposiums. He might have given one talk. But he was interested in things that didn't fit our program. He was more a technician than a real geologist." Told that Haefner claimed to have been supervising a geology graduate student, Bachhuber was dubious. "I rather doubt he was on anyone's committee," he said, referring to the university group that supervises a graduate student's research work. "He would have to submit his résumé and be approved by the graduate college. I don't think there was any attempt to get him certified." But what perplexed Bachhuber the most was Haefner's relationship with Wright and Troxel, "who had very, very good reputations. Why is he doing field work with those two? Things didn't fit very well."[5]

Rick Haefner eventually sued UNLV, but not for failing to hire him as a geology lecturer. The lawsuit was for towing his car. He had asked Bachhuber if he could leave his "field car"—the car he drove out into Death Valley when he did his research—at his home from May to October 1999, when he would be in Pennsylvania. The department chairman said no. According to Haefner, the Geology Department then asked UNLV Parking Enforcement to issue Rick a parking permit for the summer, which they did. Because of a bureaucratic mistake, no renewal application was sent at the end of the summer, and his car was deemed abandoned. On September 12, 1999, it was towed and impounded by a private Las Vegas towing company. The lawsuit, which generated more than a hundred court filings of greater or lesser size, was dismissed after Haefner's death in 2002.[6]

As comical and ridiculous as Haefner's court activities might seem—Bennie Troxel remembered telling Rick he should have been a lawyer, because he was always talking about suing people—we know by now that his lawsuits often hurt innocent people, either directly or as collateral damage. The last years of Haefner's life were spent in litigation with Cliff and Marge Parmeter, an elderly couple from Henderson, Nevada. Their sin? They sued *him* after he defrauded them in a real estate transaction for a small house they owned in Tecopa Hot Springs. So, of course, he sued them right back. Their plucky lawyer, Dana Crom, was a woman, and that triggered all of Rick's worst instincts and craziest behavior. If he was trying to show the world one last time what kind of a sociopath he was, he accomplished it with his treatment of the Parmeters and Crom.

Rick began thinking about buying a house in California at the same time he started thinking about adopting Bruce, who had turned eighteen at the end of 1996. He heard that a house and lot were for sale in Tecopa, or technically Tecopa Hot Springs, a sort-of suburb of Tecopa. Located about six miles south of Shoshone, Tecopa Hot Springs is mainly trailer parks and a motel surrounding a natural hot springs where visitors can bathe. It is set in a dry, dusty, but starkly beautiful desert landscape where a few mesquite trees provided the only shade from the baking sun. You could reinvent yourself here. Paul Watkins, a one-time follower of Charles Manson (he was an active member of the Manson Family but had not been involved in the Tate-LaBianca murders in 1969), was Tecopa's unofficial mayor until his death from cancer in 1990. In the distance are the mountains in Nevada where Las Vegas mobsters are said to have disposed of bodies. The great casino city of the desert is only seventy-seven miles away, but there is almost nothing in between unless you take the long way around, through Pahrump. The Parmeter house wasn't anything fancy, and it needed some work, but it was clean and tidy and the price was reasonable. There was plenty of space on the lot to put a house trailer where Rick could stay while his new home was being renovated, and to use as a guesthouse later.[7]

He met with Cliff and Marge Parmeter at their home in Henderson on March 12, 1997. Both Parmeters were in their early nineties and in poor health. Rick and the couple came to a verbal contract. They agreed to a discounted price of $42,500 and to do a seller-finance deal if Rick would make a down payment of $5,000 and then pay off the balance by December 15, 1997. At their age, they couldn't wait forever for their money. The Parmeters put the oral agreement in writing when the deal closed on May

9, signing and notarizing it and mailing it to Rick. But their efforts to get him to sign proved fruitless. Every time they raised the issue, he would call and get them to reaffirm the oral terms and then not sign anything.[8]

Things began badly. Rick was supposed to make the down payment in ten days, but he didn't do so until late August. He told the Parmeters he hadn't been able to pay on time because he supposedly had been the victim of an assault. Whether this actually happened cannot be verified. In a letter to Rick of November 12, 1997, the Parmeters offered their sympathy. "It is a sin how some people have no respect for others," they wrote. "Hope you recover with no aftereffects." They told him to stop by their Nevada home to pick up the keys.[9]

Rick didn't pay off the balance by December 15. In early January 1998, around the time he beat up Catherine Schuyler, he renegotiated the deal with the Parmeters. Now he would pay interest of 11 percent—in effect, rent of approximately $400 per month—and pay the annual property tax on the house and land. He would make principal payments at least annually. In return, they let him take possession of the property, even giving him a letter of introduction that he could show to the neighbors when he moved in. But Rick's promises this time were no better than the ones he had made before. He paid nothing at all until May 1998, when he sent them $3,000, then another thousand dollars the following month. Then nothing more. Not the property taxes, not the monthly interest payments, not anything. The Parmeters fumed at his betrayal.[10]

On December 26, 1998, a telephone conversation occurred between Haefner, Cliff Parmeter, and Parmeter's daughter, who was not named in Rick's subsequent letter. She said the property was no longer for sale to him and called him a "con artist" They wanted him out. He took offense at being called a con artist and said in a subsequent letter that he would not be sending the Parmeters the $5,000 check he had planned to mail if the house was truly no longer for sale to him. Nor could he move his trailer and belongings from the property until he arrived from Pennsylvania toward the end of January. The call terminated when Cliff Parmeter began having chest pains.[11]

The arrest of Bruce for armed robbery in State College on February 23, 1999, and his sentencing later that spring to two to four years in state prison for the robbery and a string of other crimes, ended any possibility of him being adopted by Rick, if either still even wanted it by that point. Haefner claimed to have begun working with two adoption agencies around this time, seeking to adopt a boy somewhere else. Whether this was true or merely a ploy to gain sympathy from the Parmeters is impossible to say. In March 1999, Rick hired Kirk Livermont, a lawyer in Independence, California, the county seat of Inyo County, to formalize his purchase of the house and land. He may have talked the Parmeters down from the ledge with an offer of a $15,000 down payment, which is referenced in a letter Livermont sent to the Parmeters on March 29, 1999. Around the same time, Haefner hired a local contractor, Dan MacBrohn, to make repairs to the Parmeter house, which suggests he expected to be staying there for the long term.

But on May 20, 1999, Livermont sent the couple a letter informing them that Rick could pay neither principal nor interest at that time, and he asked them to accept a promissory note. Cliff Parmeter angrily refused and sent the papers back to Livermont. There was no further correspondence until November, when Parmeter sent a bitter letter to the lawyer summarizing what he now viewed as a complete fraud. Moreover, he had just inspected his property, accompanied by an Inyo County sheriff's deputy, and found it in deplorable condition, which greatly upset his wife. He told Livermont he planned to evict Rick from the house and land. But things could never be that simple. On January 7, 2000, Haefner won a temporary restraining order against the Parmeters, staying the eviction after arguing, among other things, that it would disrupt his plans for adopting a child and make it impossible for him to earn a living. Then, acting as his own attorney—Livermont had apparently resigned beause he wasn't getting paid—he filed a lawsuit against the Parmeters. They in turn sought out a lawyer and hired Dana Crom of Bishop, California, who had just gone into private practice after working as a government lawyer, handling family and dependency law.[12]

To Crom, it seemed like a straightforward case. Haefner didn't own the property. He hadn't paid the Parmeters, and now they wanted him out. She received a cold dose of reality at her first meeting with Rick after laying out in no-nonsense terms what he needed to do. This apparently triggered all of his resentments toward women. He began screaming at her and saying nasty things about the Parmeters. Nearly every time they met he would scream at her, to the point where, for the first time in her career, she requested a court officer be present at any meeting they had. "He would become enraged, absolutely enraged over the littlest of things," Crom said. "It was ridiculous. It was a slam-dunk case: Either pay for it or give it back." He wouldn't do either. She had a great deal of sympathy for the Parmeters. "I know he scared my clients," Crom said. "He was very threatening to them. He had written them very nasty letters. Anyone who read them would consider them threatening."[13]

Haefner conducted depositions of the Parmeters in Nevada, and they went off without a hitch. To make it cheaper and more convenient for Rick himself to give a deposition to her, Crom agreed to do it while she was in Philadelphia visiting her brother-in-law, who was a lawyer for Pepper Hamilton LLP in downtown Philadelphia. "It was he [Haefner] and I and the court reporter," Crom said. "He wanted to talk settlement." She completed her questioning and was escorting him out of the building at 2 Logan Square when he suddenly became enraged, in the same manner as before. "He was really agitated and upset," she said. "It was so loud my brother-in-law and husband came running. I was looking at the receptionist during this and said, 'Please call security.' I wouldn't respond to him. I was shaking like a leaf." When Rick heard security being called, he ran out of the building. Crom thought it odd how Haefner could be so levelheaded for a period of time, then just explode.[14]

The case dragged on into 2001. In April of that year, Crom filed a motion for summary judgment, and the judge said he would grant it. That forced Rick to settle. The terms were surprisingly favorable: He got to keep the property and paid a reduced price to the Parmeters. Unlike before, he did keep his word.

How does a murderer die? How should he die? In Rick Haefner's case, it began without drama. He and Bennie Troxel had been out on a long hike in mid-March 2002 in the area up behind Shoshone that Rick had named the Shoshone Volcanics. They were investigating a peculiar geologic formation, and Lauren Wright may have been with them. Bennie and Rick had collaborated on a paper that would be presented later that spring at the annual meeting of the Geological Society of America. "I should have known something was going on," Troxel said. "He tired out before me, and I was in my eighties." Haefner was only fifty-eight years old. But nothing else happened during the hike.[15]

Not long afterward, Rick was at, or near, home when he experienced chest pains and reached out to his neighbor, Kathy Nixon. He told her he thought he had indigestion, the first indication of so many heart attacks. He was taken by ambulance to Valley Hospital in Las Vegas. By the time he arrived, he indeed was having a heart attack, but the emergency room physicians stabilized him. He seemed to be getting better, Nixon said, and his brother George and George's wife, Margaret, came to visit him at the hospital. But on March 19 around 5:08 a.m., he suffered complications and died. According to the information on his Nevada death certificate, the cause of death was ventricular rupture. Cardiologists say this means that the soft, immature scar tissue, which had begun to form on the front wall of Rick's heart after the first heart attack, blew out like a bike tire from the pressure created by the heart, the blood pump, when it contracts. This happens in a small percentage of heart attack patients, typically during the critical third to fifth day after the initial attack. Even with immediate surgery, say cardiologists, ventricular rupture is very difficult to survive.

Haefner died in the same way Betsy Aardsma had died—from blood pouring out of an injured heart into the chest cavity. What was different, of course, was how the injury had occurred. What had been done to Betsy with a knife had now been done to Rick by God.

George had Rick's body cremated; what became of the ashes is unknown. There is a bronze marker for Richard C. Haefner next to his parents in St. Anthony's Catholic Cemetery in Lancaster, but Chris Haefner says the cremains aren't there.[16]

CHAPTER 38

The Road to Rick Haefner

After Sergeant George Keibler retired in 1983, the Aardsma investigation became an orphan for a few years. Captain Vincent Fiorani, the commander of Troop G, saw no need to assign a new shepherd after fourteen years and rebuffed Keibler's offer to train his replacement. After Fiorani left, the officers eventually given charge over the cold case didn't approach it in the same way. For Keibler, it had been a personal crusade, a promise to keep to the Aardsma family. For his successors, it was just one assignment among many. Trooper Jeffrey Watson, who was the son-in-law of Corporal Mike Mutch, one of the original investigators, had the case for a time in the late 1980s, followed by Trooper Bill Madden, followed by Trooper Sally Brown, who had it on her desk until around 2005, when she retired and Trooper Kent Bernier took over. He had the case until 2009, when he was promoted to corporal and transferred and Trooper Leigh Barrows took over. Even as late as 2001, Brown told Keibler that she had never read the entire, voluminous case file, which was comprised of a 1,700-page main report and several boxes of other material, including Keibler's card file. And it was all on paper, not in searchable digital form. There was no executive summary. Nor had any of the later investigators actually gone to Pattee Library to get the lay of the land until Bernier did so in the late 2000s.[1]

We look back now and think, Why didn't they go after Rick Haefner? But the exit onto that road had been obscured by the long silence of Professor Lauren Wright and aggravated by the failure of Penn State general counsel Delbert MacQuaide to do anything with Wright's information in 1976, when the professor finally went to Charles Hosler, his dean, and broke his long silence. Keibler never heard any of that.

The other problem was that when the state police thought about anyone in connection with Betsy Aardsma's murder, it was usually Larry Paul Maurer, who had been in the English 501 class with Betsy Aardsma and had lived in Atherton Hall. When stories about the twentieth anniversary of the Betsy Aardsma murder in 1989 reminded everyone that the crime had never been solved, it was Maurer they began looking at once again, not Rick Haefner, who was unknown to them beyond the brief interview conducted by Trooper Schleiden in 1969. Around 1989, the Pennsylvania State Police created the Criminal Investigative Assessment Unit (CIA), an attempt to formalize and improve their approach to cold cases. The CIA officer in a troop, as he or she became known, studied cold cases to see if they could be solved by using modern methods and technology, including DNA testing and psychological profiling.

In Troop G, the CIA officer was Trooper Roger Smith in Bedford, Pennsylvania, who began to read through the Betsy Aardsma case file around 1990 as one of his first assignments. He did not replace Trooper Sally Brown, who was still the investigator assigned to the case, although she felt increasingly marginalized. Smith was an extra set of eyes. His initial goal was to find references in the Aardsma file to a particular individual, who he hinted was Maurer. One of the original investigators, probably Trooper Tom Jones, by then deceased, had always been interested in Maurer. He and Trooper Tom Shelar were the ones who picked him up at his father's farm near what is now Line Mountain High School in Mandata, Northumberland County, in January 1970, and drove him across the Susquehanna River to his polygraph examination at the state police barracks in Selinsgrove. Jones had always thought Maurer ought to be interviewed again. Smith's job was to understand why.[2]

His task was daunting. There was the report itself, which was so long that no investigator since George Keibler had ever finished reading it. The case file was old enough to have a musty smell. Smith couldn't imagine what he could get from the report that all the other investigators had missed over the years. But he discovered that facts and connections and interesting angles do get overlooked. "There's a lot of different things you find when you look through the old cases," he said. "Even though somebody's looked at it twenty-five times before you did, I've always found something in there." And he did.

He began writing down the names of anyone in the report who had a connection with Betsy Aardsma, no matter how small. They might have been fellow classmates or someone who went out for coffee with her. One of the names he wrote down was Rick Haefner, Smith recalled, although it didn't lead to anything. He would try to figure out what had happened to them in the intervening years. Had they gotten in trouble? Were they arrested for other crimes? He found himself making voluminous notes. Frustration overwhelmed him at times. "You would be reading the pages and it would look like this is going to go somewhere, and it fizzles out. That's over and over again, throughout the whole report." Smith would find himself interested in someone on page 300, but by the time he got to page 600, he knew he had wasted his time. He never found any indication that the state police had ever been close to solving the Aardsma murder, even if some investigators disagreed. And he found nothing to warrant a new interview of Larry Paul Maurer.[3]

Some other troopers with an interest in the Aardsma case remained firmly in Camp Maurer. It was not hard to understand why. As already noted, he seemed to wear guiltiness on his sleeve, even though he passed a lie detector test. Afterward, he had abruptly quit Penn State and gone into the army, and from there into the supersecret National Security Agency, a part of the Department of Defense that conducts communications surveillance in the name of US national security. They tried to be more secret than even the Central Intelligence Agency. The joke was that NSA stood for "No Such Agency." Was it any surprise they could not put Maurer out of their thoughts?[4]

Tom Shelar spent the last thirteen years of his career working in the Bureau of Criminal Investigation for the Pennsylvania Attorney General in Harrisburg, beginning in 1989. He tried to interest his bosses in starting a grand jury investigation of Maurer, but to no avail. "I think they felt it was a dead horse," he said.[5] Shelar did place a notation, or "stop," about Maurer in the National Crime Information Center (NCIC) database.[6]

In 1994, Maurer returned from an overseas posting for the National Security Agency and was due for the background examination required every five years to keep his top-secret clearance. Maurer's background investigator would mainly look for questionable contacts with foreign nationals, but also for criminal activity. By chance, the NSA investigator assigned to do his background check was John Shambach, a retired investigator for the Pennsylvania State Police. He had not worked on the Aardsma case but knew some of the men who did. Shambach, who retired from the NSA in 1998, was not permitted to say exactly what Maurer's NSA job was, commenting only that he "had assignments and worked with a group." Shambach said Maurer did a couple of tours overseas. "He had just come back when I interviewed him," he said.[7]

In conducting a routine check in the NCIC, he found the "stop" that Shelar had placed on Maurer. Shelar was an old friend, so he called him up. He told him about Maurer and the Aardsma investigation. Armed with that information, Shambach set out to see if he could get a confession from Maurer that he had killed Betsy Aardsma. Shambach had a reputation as a tough questioner. Three other NSA investigators observed the interview through a one-way mirror.

"He never did [directly deny] that he [had done] it," Shambach said of Maurer, who has declined to be interviewed about the Aardsma case. "And I put that to him in different ways over the course of two interviews." By the time of the second interview, Maurer had contacted an NSA lawyer and was not cooperating. What struck Shambach was that when he asked about Betsy Aardsma, Maurer would not look him in the eye. "And he sort of sloughed it off with a laugh," he said. Instead of denying the crime, as most people would, Maurer would say, "Why would I kill her? What would I kill her for?" He was still toying with them, a quarter-century later. To which Shambach would reply, "She brushed you off, didn't she? You were trying to hit on her, and she brushed you off." He was hoping for an angry reaction, but Maurer only smirked, Shambach said.

Maurer had already passed a routine polygraph exam about his contacts with foreign nationals, but Shambach wanted to run a "criminal" polygraph on Maurer, in which he would be asked questions about possible criminal activities. His superiors refused. One supervisor asked, "What if he fails? What do we do then?" To Shambach, it was simple: You turn him over to the Pennsylvania State Police and let them take it from there. But he had reached a dead end.

Maurer has always been a problematic figure in the Aardsma investigation, generating thick clouds of smoke but no fire. He has never been arrested for anything connected to Betsy Aardsma, despite interest by the Pennsylvania State Police going back to December 1969. Maurer knew Haefner—they had briefly been roommates—and knew that Betsy would be at Pattee Library that afternoon, because everyone in English 501 would be there. Could he have mentioned that to Rick Haefner, upset as he had to be about Betsy's intentions toward David L. Wright? There is no evidence that he did, nor any that he had advance knowledge that Rick planned to kill her. Maurer admitted to being nearby in the Core when the murder occurred but always denied that he participated. He did not match the description of the running man who emerged from the Core moments after Betsy's body collapsed to the floor in a cascade of books, the one who said, "Somebody had better help that girl." We come back again to the fact that he obviously enjoyed toying with the state police, giving them tantalizing hints that perhaps he was their man. It is little wonder that some in the state police found it impossible to give up on the idea that he indeed *was* the killer of Betsy Aardsma.

Oddly, by the mid-1990s, there seemed to be almost as much investigation of the Aardsma murder being conducted by state police retirees like Shelar and Shambaugh, and by citizen investigator Bill Earley, as by the state police themselves. Maurer was a particular obsession of Earley's, a 1969 Penn State graduate who stayed on to get a master's degree in 1972. A resident of Philadelphia's Main Line, he had been vice president of technology and marketing for the New York Stock Exchange and a sales manager for Xerox Corporation before heading off into financial consulting. But the Aardsma case was his passion, and he spent many hours and many dollars on his personal quest to learn who might have killed her. His intention was to write a book. Earley seemed convinced that Maurer was the killer, and that he had been aided and abetted by two Penn State friends who will remain nameless here. He worked closely with a number of the original investigators after they retired, particularly Mike Simmers, although they eventually had a falling-out. It was Earley who brought John Shambach and his interrogation of Maurer in 1994 to the attention of Roger Smith. The book never materialized, however. He told the *Philadelphia Inquirer* in 2008 that it was unfinished, and that he had no plans to publish it. Nonetheless, Earley continued to telephone the original investigators to share his theories.[8]

As the investigation reached its thirtieth year, police were no closer to finding the killer than they had been in 1969, when Sergeant George Keibler returned early from his hunting trip to lead the investigation of the most brutal on-campus crime in Penn State's history. Betsy Aardsma was not completely forgotten. She resided in the memories of the men who had been the original investigators and, it turned out, one of their children.

In 1999, Kim Simmers, the daughter of (now) Captain Mike Simmers, had completed her undergraduate degree at Penn State's main campus. She was now working on her master's degree in applied psychology at Penn State Harrisburg and needed an internship. She had discovered that clinical work was not to her liking, and when her father told her about a paid summer internship available with the state police in the Criminal Investigation Assessment unit, she took the position. After she had settled in, her supervisor asked what she wanted to work on, apart from the things she needed to do for her degree. The first thing that popped into her mind was the case she had heard so much about growing up: the unsolved Betsy Aardsma case.[9]

"That was one of the most amazing things, one of the most memorable stories that my dad had always told us. Being a young female and having to go into that library, knowing what happened—it just always kind of intrigued me," she said. "But I'll tell you, every time I did go into the stacks, into the Central Core, it was get in and get out. It was just kind of an intimidating place. It was very dark. Even if you didn't know what happened, if I had to get a book for research that was really far deep in there, it was like, I really don't need that book."[10]

She told her supervisor at CIA that she would like to see if there was anything helpful she could glean from the thirty-year-old Aardsma case. He was surprised, but let her look at the most recent supplementals to the case file, if not the entire 1,700-page report. Her deeper immersion in the case came four years later after she was hired as an analyst for the CIA unit and began attending monthly meetings held to review cold cases. Troops from the western half of the state sent their CIA officers to a meeting in Punxsutawney, and those in the east to a meeting a week later in Harrisburg. Each month a CIA officer from a different troop would bring a cold case to the meeting, review the details, and talk about suspects, if there were any. The group then asked questions and perhaps would profile the suspect and suggest an approach to interviewing him or her.

The Aardsma case finally had its day in 2005. In advance of the meeting, Simmers was allowed to read the entire case file at her cubicle, not just in bits and pieces. "The coolest thing for me was reading those first couple of reports that were turned in by Trooper Simmers," she said, referring to her father, who in 1969 had been her age, in his early twenties. But what struck her as an analyst was the lack of forensic evidence collected at the crime scene in Pattee Library, which, of course, had been due to the failings of the Campus Patrol and the library staff. Simmers remembers no particular buzz about the Aardsma case. By then, it was just one among many unsolved crimes from across the state.

On February 20, 2006, Trooper Smith submitted a Freedom of Information Act request to the National Security Agency, seeking copies of records in its files pertaining to Maurer and the interviews conducted by Shambach in 1994 about Maurer's possible involvement in the Aardsma murder. A month later, Smith received a letter from the National Security Agency informing him that a thorough search had been conducted, and that no relevant records had been found. A week later, Smith filed a FOIA appeal, laying out the reasons he believed the NSA had the documents he wanted. Six months later, on October 30, 2006, the NSA informed Smith that it did indeed have records relating to Maurer and the Betsy Aardsma case, but that he couldn't see them. The reason? They were personnel files, and to the NSA, that would "clearly" infringe upon Maurer's right to privacy. After Smith retired in January 2008, a new FOIA request was submitted, this time under the name of the state police commissioner, Jeffrey Miller. The new request was written to more precisely define what it was they needed from the NSA. Smith believes this FOIA request did yield at least some material about Maurer but doesn't know what was released.[11]

There was also talk in 2007 and 2008 of asking the Centre County district attorney, Michael T. Madeira, to convene a grand jury to investigate the Aardsma case and to force Maurer to provide a blood sample for DNA testing. Simmers convened a meeting at his house that included citizen investigator Bill Earley; John Shambach, who flew up from his home in Florida; Roger Smith; and Dave Aiello, who succeeded Smith as CIA officer in Troop G. The grand jury idea was still active in the fall of 2008, when the author was working on his series about the Aardsma case for the Harrisburg *Patriot-News* that preceded his work on this book.

At the time, Sergeant George Keibler declined to be interviewed for the stories. Later, he changed his mind, and he began the first interview on January 4, 2011, by explaining that his refusal to be interviewed in 2008 was because Trooper Kent Bernier, then the Aardsma cold case officer, had told him that Madeira was going to take the Aardsma case to a grand jury. He told Keibler that he wasn't telling him not to be interviewed, "but we'd sort of like you to just cool it."

Corporal Roger Smith said he met with Madeira late in 2007, just before he retired, to talk about getting a body search warrant in Maryland, where Maurer resides. Bernier confirmed the talks with Madeira but said the grand jury idea died because "you need some evidence and/or a suspect. I had neither—or at least, not enough at that time." Once again, the state police had rushed to Camp Maurer only to find the smoldering remains of nothing.[12]

In 1986, Pamela West, a novelist then living in State College, became interested in writing a nonfiction book about the unsolved Betsy Aardsma murder and approached Sergeant Keibler, by then two years retired, for an interview. Keibler agreed, but says he first made West promise not to contact the Aardsma family. During her research, she was told by a young professor, whose name she does not remember, that on the night of the murder, a "geography" graduate student had shown up at the home of his professor and inquired breathlessly whether he had heard about a girl being murdered in Pattee Library. Poking into it further, West learned that the student's name was Rick Haefner, that he was actually a *geology* graduate student, and that the professor was Lauren A. Wright. But at the time, it was little more than rumor. She eventually gave up the idea of a nonfiction book because she could not prove her suspicions and feared getting sued. Instead, she wrote a science-fiction novel, *20/20 Vision,* about a police archivist who sends a clue back in time to a detective to help solve the mysterious stabbing death of a beautiful college girl in the music building of her university. Parts of it read exactly like the Aardsma case, while other parts are, well, science fiction. It was published in 1990, and is out of print, but can be acquired from online used book dealers.[13]

West came to the attention of Sascha Skucek, an adjunct lecturer in the Penn State English Department at the main campus, who had written five articles about the Aardsma case for *State College* magazine between 1999 and 2010. He and his associate, Derek Sherwood, extensively researched the original murder, although they never had access to Keibler. West told them about Haefner, and they set out to learn more. Sometime in 2009, Sherwood placed a notice on the Internet that he and Skucek were looking for anyone in Lancaster who had known Richard C. Haefner.[14]

Chris Haefner, Rick's younger cousin, was forty-nine in 2009. He was a supervisor at the M&M Mars candy plant in Elizabethtown, Pennsylvania, and in his spare time was a novelist, writing books based on his life and adventures with Rick. His favorite, *The Silver Mine,* about his adventures exploring the old silver mine near Pequea that Rick had first showed him in 1973, was published in 2009. In January 2010, Chris was surfing the Internet, looking for information about Rick, when up came "Reward:

Offer for Information about Richard C. Haefner from Lancaster." Chris thought it must be a joke. Why would anyone offer a reward for information about Rick? Out of curiosity, he e-mailed Sherwood, who told him about the murder of Betsy Aardsma and how they suspected Rick might have been involved. It was the first time he had been able to put a name to some disturbing old memories.[15]

Reeling, Chris did more searching online and found a story about Betsy that someone had put on Myspace, the social media website. He also found an Internet page where Rick was profiled in the way someone might profile the Zodiac Killer. He stayed at it for several days, and everything he had suppressed for so long began coming back: the angry words in the alley between Ere and Rick, Rick's attempt in the goethite field to justify Betsy's killing, and all the bad things his cousin had done to him and the other boys.

Chris had always had a good memory. He remembered the good times with Rick, too, but after several days of reflection, he had a clear picture in his mind of his cousin and the damage done. He believed that Rick had killed Betsy Aardsma. What clinched it for him was the official state police description of the running man in the Core. It fit Rick almost exactly. He contacted Skucek and Sherwood and agreed to an interview. The two researchers later played the tape for Trooper Leigh Barrows, the Aardsma cold case officer.[16]

Barrows treated Chris with a cold professionalism that came off as disrespect, doubt, and disbelief. She did not go to interview him in Lancaster but instead traded e-mails. She criticized him for putting up his own Myspace page about how Rick was the killer of Betsy Aardsma. She finally turned off Chris completely by asking him where the murder weapon was. He thought it a ridiculous question, and told her so. He didn't have any idea, and besides, he would say, Rick was too smart to have left it lying around for forty years. He either ground it down to dust or threw it in the Susquehanna River.

After that, he said, Barrows seemed to lose interest. "So what the hell did [the state police] do for the last forty years except have somebody officially assigned to the case who did nothing?" Chris said. "And then, when they find someone like me, all they're after is, 'Do you have the murder weapon?'" He was disgusted.[17]

Barrows insisted in an e-mail to the author that she had interviewed Chris and did not "turn my nose up at him." She said he had provided the author with wrong information, but was not specific. Chris was "full of BS," Barrows said, and was likely angry because she had told him to take down his Myspace page about Rick.[18]

Yet despite the friction, Barrows came to accept that Rick Haefner most likely had killed Betsy Aardsma. She mentioned it to several people, including Charles Hosler, the retired dean of the College of Earth and Mineral Sciences, to whom Lauren Wright had finally come in 1976 with his story about Haefner's visit to his home on the night of Betsy's murder. "She came here and I talked extensively to her, and she was pretty convinced that all the evidence pointed to Haefner," he said. Barrows arranged for Skucek and Sherwood to give a PowerPoint presentation on the case to a group of present and former troopers, some of whom, like Mike Mutch, had been involved in the original investigation. Mutch said Barrows was enthusiastic about the PowerPoint and believed Haefner was the killer.[19]

Even more importantly, Barrows told the Aardsma family in the summer of 2010 that the case appeared to have been solved, and that Rick Haefner was Betsy's killer. Kathy Aardsma, Betsy's younger sister, was in Holland for her high school class reunion and told several of her friends. One of them mentioned it to her hairdresser, Angela Wich, the sister of Peggy Wich, Betsy's old friend from Holland High School. Angela, knowing of her sister's interest in the case, told Peggy that one of her customers had informed her that the case had been "solved." Peggy was excited and wanted to know more. She e-mailed the author, who began contacting his other sources. One of them said that the Aardsma family was relieved that the identity of Betsy's killer might finally be known. Trooper Barrows said that a meeting was being held regarding Haefner that very afternoon.[20]

But then the Pennsylvania State Police pulled back. When the author called Barrows again after the meeting, she said she could not comment and referred him to Trooper Jeff Pettucci, a spokesman for Troop G.

Pettucci put a damper on speculation about Rick Haefner, saying, "We're not close to solving the Aardsma case" and that he "didn't know what was told to the family." He acknowledged that Rick Haefner's name came up at the meeting the afternoon of August 19, but only in the sense that he might "possibly have [had] more information about the crime." He said Haefner "is not a suspect," but said the state police would never call someone a suspect unless charges had been filed, and they could not indict a dead man.

But why not say as much publicly? Especially with the Aardsma family being told that Haefner killed their Betsy. "I don't know what the family was told," Pettucci repeated. Barrows, in a later e-mail exchange with the author, reacted defensively to questions about why she didn't close the case if she was certain Rick Haefner had murdered Betsy Aardsma. "I just don't need to explain myself to anyone," she said. "I have to follow the policy of the Pennsylvania State Police."[21]

It was an odd turn of events, suggesting that the state police could not see beyond procedure and/or felt humiliated by the fact that civilians had developed Haefner as a suspect, and not themselves. A bewildered Sascha Skucek told Chris Haefner in an e-mail on September 14, 2010, that the state police think they know who did it now, and they were going to make some arrests in the next couple of months. That didn't happen. It was just another diversionary gambit in a forty-five-year-old murder case with a long history of diversions and false hopes.[22]

Epilogue

Betsy Aardsma's family never truly recovered after her murder.[1] A neighbor, JoAnn Pelon, remembered seeing Dick Aardsma, Betsy's father, taking long walks. "He just looked very sad and very lonely," she said. Peggy Wich ran into him years later in a support group for overeaters. He remembered her from the old days as a friend of his daughter's, and told Peggy that no one in his family would talk to him about Betsy. She was always his favorite, and he cherished the memory of her sunny personality. He died of a stroke in 1997. His obituary asked for memorial contributions to Alcoholics Anonymous.

Esther Aardsma died in 2012 at the age of ninety-three, living long enough to hear of Trooper Barrows's belief that the murderer of her daughter had finally been identified, even if her superiors then, strangely, disavowed her. Esther had long since given up hope of the murder being solved, and had many years to think about it. The women in her family tended to be long-lived. Her sister, Anna Ruth Cotts, who had accompanied Esther to State College in 1969 to bring back Betsy's body, lived to the age of one hundred, dying in 2008. Betsy's murderer may have stolen at least seven decades of life from her, not to mention a lifetime of accomplishments now lost in the mist of might-have-beens.[2]

Carole Aardsma, Betsy's older sister, and her husband, Dennis Wegner, divorced in 1985. She had been an art teacher for several years after they married but had been a stay-at-home mom after their oldest son, Lorin, was born. After the divorce, she became a Reformed Church minister, serving as associate pastor or director of Christian education at a number of churches before settling into a long career as a prison chaplain. She continued to live with her parents in the family home on East 37th Street. Dennis, who remains deeply affected even today by Betsy's death, felt a need to fill the void her death created. Betsy had planned a life of service to people, and he did the same, switching from microbiology research to clinical work, with a more direct impact on suffering people.

He remarried and has lived for years in Ottumwa, Iowa. Dennis and Carole had one further tragedy to endure: the accidental death of their son Lorin in 2006.[3]

"I guess you never really recover," Dennis said, speaking of the deaths of Betsy and his son. "The pain is less intense, but you never fully recover. That passage from 'not okay' to 'okay' is a kind of zigzaggy line. You never quite get there, to the point where it is totally gone. For a long time afterward there are little things that happen that put you into the meltdown phase. Just out of the blue."

No one from the Aardsma family ever phoned Sergeant George Keibler to find out how the investigation was going or to encourage him to continue. Kent Bernier, who was the investigator of the Aardsma case from 2005 to 2009, and who took the first serious look at the case in many years, said members of the family largely refused to talk to him, which he found hard to understand. "Why would they not be more responsive to the police when their daughter was murdered?" he said. "I know it was forty years ago, but still."

Perhaps the reopening of old wounds was simply too painful, but their reticence, combined with the fact that none of Betsy's family lived in Pennsylvania, removed pressure on the Pennsylvania State Police to bring the investigation to a successful conclusion, especially after Keibler retired in 1983. For the original investigators of her murder, the desire to bring closure to the family and justice to the murderer never went away, but they weren't in charge anymore. Even as old men, they would gather periodically over lunch to discuss the case and, once again, go over the theories of who and why. For a long time, they never had a good answer to either question. Some believe they still don't. Of the originals, George Keibler, Mike Simmers, Ken Schleiden, Ronald Tyger, and Tom Shelar are still alive at this writing. Bill Kimmel, Tom Jones, Bob Milliron, Mike Mutch, and Dan Brode have passed.

Trooper Tyger did not learn of Dennis and Carole Wegner's 1972 letter to Chief Justice Warren Burger, opposing the death penalty for Betsy's killer, for many years. Tyger had gone to work in security for Lockheed Martin Corporation after retiring from the Pennsylvania State Police but had never mentally let go of Betsy Aardsma's murder. He would periodically search online for news about the case. "You've gotta love that girl," he said of Betsy. "I can shut my eyes and see that girl's face, just so vivid. That's the downfall of a criminal investigator. You can't let it alone; it's always tugging at you." In 2001, Tyger came across an article about the Wegners' letter to the chief justice. Disgusted, and taking it as a personal affront, he gathered up all his personal files on the Aardsma murder and left them at the Rockview barracks.[4]

Keibler is in his early eighties and seemingly quite healthy. His tidy home in Zion is bordered by a soybean field, and he has a good view of Mount Nittany, the holy mountain of Penn State University. He and his wife, Beverly, still travel when they aren't attending their grandson's Little League games. He keeps a copy of the letter she typed for him as a young trooper, requesting permission from the State Police Commissioner to marry her, a long-ago requirement that is now part of history.

Sitting back on his basement sofa, Keibler reflected on the Aardsma case and his own role in it. He acknowledged, first, the criticism that his men spent too much time on questionable theories, notably Corporal Brode's Mall rapist. He agrees with the criticism to a point, but argues that in a murder investigation, all halfway-credible leads must be followed. He levels his own criticism toward those responsible for the damaged crime scene his men inherited from the Penn State Campus Patrol, who were there during the critical first ninety minutes after Betsy was murdered on November 28, 1969.

"We had a crime scene that for all practical purposes had been taken away from us," he said. "It had been cleaned up, things had happened. We had no good crime scene." Yet he is unstinting in his praise of the late Colonel William B. Pelton, who was in charge of the Campus Patrol, calling him a very moral man. The state police in 1969 did not have the advantage of the crime scene investigation techniques and technologies that are well known to anyone who watches *CSI* or *Law & Order* on television. There has always been DNA, but in 1969, they didn't have the slightest idea how to test for it or use it. They had Mary Willard, the Miss Marple of Penn State, but she was too little, too late.[5]

Keibler said Penn State did not put up roadblocks during the investigation—unless the probe was steering toward a member of the faculty. "But the wall wasn't such that you couldn't go around it," he said. He was never involved in investigating Jerry Sandusky, the disgraced Penn State assistant football coach and pedophile, but followed the investigation avidly in the *Centre Daily Times* and told this author that people at all levels of authority in the university and Centre County were aware of Sandusky's activities long before the scandal was exposed by the author's former newspaper, the Harrisburg *Patriot-News*. Keibler said this more in a conspiratorial whisper than an authoritative voice, but one suspects much of what he said was dead on.

The Sandusky scandal has no known link to the Betsy Aardsma murder, but both affairs displayed the regrettable instinct of Penn State University to place the fortunes of the university above all else—above saving the boy victims of Jerry Sandusky or allowing justice to prevail for the family of a slain coed. Professor Lauren A. Wright, who flunked a serious legal and moral test when he stayed silent for seven years about Rick's visit to his home the night of the murder and never called the state police at all, died early in 2013. He made several bequests in his will, some large, and left his double-wide trailer in Shoshone to Susan Sorrells, the woman who was briefly and involuntarily an obsession of Rick Haefner's in 1967–68, when she was still a Smith College coed and her mother owned Shoshone. Sorrells did not respond to multiple requests for an interview. She and others organized a memorial service for Wright in Shoshone on March 23, 2013, that was preceded by a field trip to view some of the geological anomalies the professor studied during his long years in Death Valley.

Chris Haefner ruminates about his cousin, Rick Haefner, and the sexual abuse he suffered at his hands. He will tell you in one breath how Rick was a genius, a truly great geologist, and in the next, provide yet more evidence of what a monster he was. His cousin scarred so many lives, most of all those of Betsy Aardsma's family and friends, but also the lives of his boy victims, who had their innocence stolen. Chris seems to regret having come forward, saying that many in his family remain furious at his betrayal. Yet his brave act finally made it possible to bring some closure to the Aardsma family.

Penn State University and the Pennsylvania State Police owe the public, especially the Aardsma family, an in-depth postmortem of what went wrong in the investigation of Betsy's death. No family should have to worry that if something happens to their child at Penn State, the public image of the university will be the paramount concern. With the death of so many of the key players, such as former Penn State president Eric A. Walker, this will necessarily require full access to the vast number of documents generated by the investigation. Penn State is almost certainly keeping a large number of Aardsma administrative documents out of public view, if it has not shredded and burned them. No university can expect anything but incredulity when it claims that a single folder of documents—mostly old press releases—and one or two scattered, irrelevant pages elsewhere comprise the sum total of administrative documents it ever generated about what, at that time, was without argument the worst crime in its history, when forty state troopers were on the campus for weeks, questioning thousands of students and faculty. Are we to believe that Penn State president Eric Walker, who wrote memos to the file about the weather and detailed accounts of student demonstrations, had no thoughts about the murder trauma engulfing his campus? Only the files in the Penn State Archives of the university library—not directly mentioning Betsy Aardsma but quite relevant to the story—escaped the apparent purge.

The files of the McQuaide Blasko law firm ought to be explored as well, so that the question of what, if anything, Penn State counsel Delbert McQuaide did with the information about Rick Haefner he allegedly received from Charles Hosler in 1976 might finally be answered. Sergeant George Keibler says the state police knew nothing about that, and the author believes him, because Keibler made a point and provided examples of how he followed up on every halfway-credible tip he received, even implausible ones. He yearned to solve this murder but needed Penn State's full cooperation—when it counted—to do so.

"There is nobody in the administration, in the [campus] police department, working at the library, or in any kind of position here who could respond to any of this speculation or claims about an event four decades ago," said Penn State spokesman Bill Mahon.[6]

Anyone who reasons that all colleges and universities might behave this way under similar circumstances should look at the example of Franklin & Marshall College in Lancaster, Pennsylvania, which in 1950 fully cooperated with local police in their investigation of the murder of Marian Baker, a college employee. They did so even when tips from students and others began to point to one of their own students, Edward L. Gibbs, as her killer. Gibbs confessed to the murder, was tried, sentenced to death, and executed in the electric chair. F&M administrators had to have realized early on that that might be the grim outcome of their cooperation, but they did their civic duty.

So, too, should the state police open their own large Aardsma archive to outside researchers so their handling of the case over forty-five years can be fully assessed. In some states, though admittedly not all, at least some of these records would have long ago become available. Pennsylvania has made them all secret forever, unavailable under the state's Open Records Act, no matter whether the investigation is open or closed. Even the federal government limits secrecy of national security documents to twenty-five years, with agencies allowed to petition to keep specific documents secret longer if they are still demonstrably sensitive. This seems like a workable solution for granting access to state police documents from old cases. Thanks to lobbying by former Penn State president Graham Spanier, the Pennsylvania Legislature also exempted most Penn State documents from the reach of the Open Records Act, which it came to regret after the Sandusky scandal broke. That broad an exemption from public scrutiny is nearly unheard of for public universities in other states. A full airing of what happened to Betsy Aardsma, and all the reasons the investigation failed, could finally lay this tragedy to rest.

Had she lived, Betsy Aardsma would be the same age as Hillary Clinton. They were born just a couple of months and about two hundred miles apart. She might have had an equally distinguished career, or she might be a comfortable unknown, just another grandmother enjoying her grandchildren. What Betsy did not deserve was a grave in Pilgrim Home Cemetery at age twenty-two, a victim of the wicked hands of a man who despised women.

Acknowledgments

The love of family makes it possible for a writer to spend the enormous amount of time it takes to research and write a book. I am indebted to my wife, Lisa W. Brittingham, and my daughters, Elizabeth and Lydia DeKok, for surrendering me to my third-floor office and the passion that drove me to research and write this story.

I could not have written this at all if not for the cooperation of George H. Keibler, the retired sergeant and senior criminal investigator of the Pennsylvania State Police, who tried for fourteen years to discover the identity of Betsy Aardsma's killer. That he could not was an enormous source of frustration to him. Now in his early eighties, he sat patiently for numerous interviews and answered most of my questions, reserving answers only when he had promised anonymity to a source. His sharp memory helped me to re-create for the first time what really happened in Pattee Library on November 28, 1969, and to dispel many myths about Betsy Aardsma's murder. My other invaluable source among the original investigators was Mike Simmers, a retired captain who at age twenty-three was the first state trooper to arrive at the murder scene. Mike tapped his extensive network of friends and colleagues to open doors for me that might otherwise have remained closed. He and his wife, Emily, were always hospitable and friendly.

As I noted in the introduction, Betsy Aardsma and I both grew up in Holland, Michigan, and graduated from Holland High School. She was six years older than me and I didn't know her, but we had several teachers in common. When her friends talked about how much she admired Olin Van Lare, the eccentric but inspiring English literature teacher, I could envision my own hours in his class. I owe a special debt to Betsy's many friends at Holland High School, Hope College, the University of Michigan, and Penn State, who talked to me at length, sharing their recollections about her and how much they still grieve her senseless death. From Holland High, I was particularly helped by Jan Sasamoto Brandt, who was her closest friend, Phyllis "Peggy Wich" Vandenberg, Margo Hakken

Zeedyk, Judi Jahns Aycock, Leslie Nienhuis Herbig, Sandy Vande Water Oosterbaan, and Vicki Sparks Miller, who all knew her as a fellow Dutch Dancer and good friend. Three boys she dated in high school, Luke Kliphuis, Tom Bolhuis, and Jeff Lubbers, also shared their recollections.

Other people from Holland who helped me included Deb Noe Schakel, who provided early and continuing encouragement, especially when I was researching and writing the two-part series in the Harrisburg *Patriot-News* in 2008 that preceded this book. That series was written just before the involvement of Rick Haefner in her murder became known, which took my book in an entirely different direction. JoAnn Pelon Wassenaar, my own high school classmate and friend who grew up a couple of doors down from the Aardsmas, shared her recollections of the family. There was also one friend from Holland who asked not to be named but knows how I feel. My former next-door neighbor on Graafschap Road, Jim Reidsma, who had a long career in the Michigan State Police, helped me to track down his colleagues who assisted the troopers sent from Pennsylvania in a fruitless search for something in Betsy's life that would tell them why she was murdered.

Randy Vande Water, the former city editor of the *Holland Evening Sentinel,* shared his recollections of publishing the news of Betsy's death, which occupied a significant part of his front page for several days. I valued as well his vast knowledge of Holland people, churches, and history. His various books on Holland history, especially *Tulip Time Treasures* and *Heinz Holland: A Century of History,* proved useful as background when I was researching this story. We also swapped newspaper yarns, a bad habit of former journalists.

I cannot say enough about the regional history collection of Herrick District Library in Holland, which helped my research in so many ways. I have used and enjoyed that library ever since, as a boy, I helped to carry boxes of books from the old library in Holland City Hall to the shining new library building donated by the Herricks. My thanks also to Catherine Jung at the Holland Museum Archives for unearthing Betsy Aardsma's high school transcript from among their holdings. At the Joint Archives of Holland, I found the oral history interviews of Chaplain Bill

Hillegonds, Al Vanderbush, and J. Cotter Tharin, which provided many details about Hope College when Betsy was there. Another great source of information for that period was the Hope College *Anchor,* where I began my training as a journalist as a freshman in 1971.

Among Betsy's friends at Hope College, I extend special thanks to her freshman-year roommate, Linda DenBesten Jones, who told me many things about her friend, and George Arwady, the former publisher of the *Newark Star-Ledger,* who dated her once or twice. My brother Dan's University of Michigan alumni guide helped me to find Terrie Andrews Newman, who along with Andrea Yunker Marchand and Olga Lozowchuk Kraska shared the apartment at 441 South First Street with Betsy. It was Olga who offered up the priceless anecdote about author Kurt Vonnegut Jr.'s visit to their apartment in January 1969. Olga had Masses said for Betsy for many years after her death. The staff at the Bentley Historical Library at the University of Michigan was always friendly and helpful. Dr. David L. Wright, Betsy's boyfriend/fiancé, agreed to an interview in 2008 when I was working on the *Patriot-News* series, but then would not respond to my requests for a second one after I began writing the book in 2010. His friends, Dr. Ian Osborn, Jim Schoolmaster, Dr. Nick and Joann Lekas, and Dr. Steven Margles, offered their own perspectives on his relationship with Betsy Aardsma.

From the three months Betsy spent at Penn State University before her death, I am indebted to her good friend Linda Marsa, a fellow author, for sharing memories. Jeffrey Berger, the president of Students for a Democratic Society at Penn State in the fall of 1969, described the political landscape of the campus in a long and delightful conversation. Pam Farley talked about the birth of the feminist movement in Happy Valley in 1969, and how the Women's Liberation Front was forced to meet in a restroom in the HUB because the university, at first, would not grant them a proper meeting room. Although Professor Roger Cuffey and I disagreed about the essential nature of Rick Haefner, his former teaching assistant, he answered all of my questions and helped me to understand the process of pursuing graduate degrees in geology. Professor Nicholas Joukovsky, who taught Betsy in the fateful English 501 class and was among the last to see her alive, was endlessly helpful. Joe Head and Dan Stephens, Rick Haefner's field assistants in Death Valley in 1967 and 1968, respectively, provided valuable information. Penn State University archivist Jackie R. Esposito helped to find material I wanted to see. I believe the purging of the archives of nearly all administrative documents (if they ever arrived there) related to the Aardsma investigation occurred well before her tenure.

Chet Davis, who is an artist and former art teacher at Shamokin Area High School, deserves my particular gratitude. Hearing I was working on this book, he remembered and unearthed from his basement a copy of a nearly forgotten magazine, *Focus Fall: Penn State's Fountain of Truth,* published in 1972 and containing an article, "Murder in the Stacks," written by his roommate, Taft Wireback. I had never heard of this article, and it proved to contain a wealth of important information about the Aardsma case, especially about the events in Pattee Library that preceded the murder.

I cannot say enough about Christopher L. Haefner, the young cousin of Rick Haefner who came forward at no little personal cost to expose his relative for the monster that he was. He was an enthusiastic guide to the better history of the Haefner family in Lancaster and its one-time brewery. Ken Richmond, a Philadelphia lawyer who represented Haefner in his lawsuit against his former lawyer Richard A. Sprague, had an endless store of anecdotes and provided important insights on several matters. Peter Schuyler, whose late wife, Catherine, was savagely beaten by Rick Haefner in a Delaware parking lot in 1998, shared many painful details. He believed that her death from alcoholism in 2012 was the end result of that assault. I also thank Michael Witmer and Dave S. for coming forward and relating how Rick Haefner sexually assaulted boys in Troop 24 in Lancaster when he was an assistant scoutmaster. Dr. Bill Apollo answered my cardiology questions, and Jean Callahan researched the etymology of the word *stacks* in a library context.

Most of the Aardsma family chose not to be interviewed. I suspect they had bad experiences with one or more of the self-styled citizen investigators of their daughter's murder before I ever arrived on the scene to write this book. Two who did talk to me were Ron Cotts, Betsy's cousin, who flew her parents and uncle and aunt in his own plane from Holland to Chicago on the first leg of their sad journey to bring Betsy's body back from Penn State, and Dennis Wegner, the ex-husband of Carole Aardsma, who described the horror in the Aardsma house when Reverend Gordon Van Oostenburg brought the news of Betsy's death. I have tried to be fair to the late Reverend Van Oostenburg, whose sermon about God's will at Betsy's funeral was disliked by many of her friends.

It is impossible to understand Betsy Aardsma without understanding the Dutch-American and Calvinist culture from which she sprang. I lived in Holland from birth in Holland Hospital in 1953 until I left after graduating from Hope College in 1975 to pursue a newspaper career. Betsy Aardsma and I had much the same sort of childhood. Each of our parents were Hope College graduates. We both marched in Dutch costume with our fellow elementary school students in the annual Tulip Time parades, before throngs of tourists, and thought it entirely normal. I listened to WLS radio from Chicago, heard the news, and had the same aspirations to escape from 1960s Holland and its stifling conservatism, lily-white blandness, and conventionality as she did. The outside world beckoned. Betsy dreamed of James Baldwin and the Peace Corps and Africa, but she never expected to be diverted from that path by others and to encounter Rick Haefner lurking in the Penn State library, among her beloved books. As her onetime boyfriend Luke Kliphuis noted, Holland left her innocent and unprepared for a psychopath like Haefner.

She would have been delighted to know that a changing Holland in 2008 cast a narrow majority of its presidential votes for Barack Obama. I still find it almost inconceivable, however delightful, and I'm sure she would, too.

Notes

The following abbreviations are used in the notes for this book:

CLH: Christopher L. Haefner
CPCLC: Common Pleas Court of Lancaster County
FOIA: Freedom of Information Act, a federal law
GHK: Sergeant George H. Keibler, lead investigator of the Aardsma murder for the Pennsylvania State Police from 1969 to 1983
IJ: *Intelligencer Journal,* a newspaper in Lancaster, Pennsylvania
JSB: Jan Sasamoto Brandt, Betsy Aardsma's friend
LRC-RTK: Lancaster Recreation Commission Right to Know request filed by the author.
Museum Suit: Rick Haefner's lawsuit against the Natural History Museum of Los Angeles County over their withdrawal of a job offer
PSA: Pennsylvania State Archives, the official archives of the Commonwealth of Pennsylvania in Harrisburg
PSU: Penn State University
ULAD: University Library Administration Documents in the Penn State Archives
USDCEDP: United States District Court for the Eastern District of Pennsylvania

Epigraphs (book and Part I)
1 - "Every unpunished murder": Daniel Webster, in *The Trial of John Francis Knapp as Principal in the Second Degree for the Murder of Captain Joseph White,* before the Supreme Judicial Court of the Commonwealth of Massachusetts, at a special session commenced at Salem, July 20, 1830 (Boston: Dutton & Wentworth, 1830), 35. Webster was the prosecutor in the case.
2 - "That place was a jungle": Sergeant George H. Keibler (GHK), Pennsylvania State Police, retired. Interview by the author, January 4, 2011. Keibler was the lead investigator of the murder of Betsy Aardsma between 1969 and 1983.

Chapter 1: The Library in Happy Valley
1 - "something terrible was about to happen": Howard Taft Wireback, "Murder in the Stacks," *Focus Fall: Penn State's Fountain of Truth* (1972): 13–14; Memo, W. Carl Jackson to Paul M. Althouse, December 3, 1969, ULAD.
2 - Penn State: The university began its history as Pennsylvania Farmers High School in 1855 from empty fields in the middle of nowhere. The name was changed to Agriculture College of Pennsylvania in 1862, when it became one of the early Land Grant colleges under the Morrill Act, and to Pennsylvania State College in 1875. That name survived until 1953, when Penn State president Milton S. Eisenhower, brother of Dwight D., changed the name to The Pennsylvania State University (the definite article always seemed

faintly pretentious). Eisenhower also petitioned the post office for a separate postal designation for the university, which duly became University Park on letters parents sent to their children on the sprawling campus. State College borough officials reacted by proposing to change the name of the town to Mount Nittany, after a beloved local landmark, but voters rejected the idea. Eventually the main campus became known as the University Park campus in State College, a confusing bifurcation if ever there was one.

3 - "equally inaccessible from all parts of the state": This bit of humor is attributed to Edwin E. Sparks, the eighth president of Penn State (1908–20); *an underground nuclear explosion:* "Blast Proposal Gains Momentum," *Centre Daily Times,* State College, PA, April 19, 1967. The kicker on the headline was secrecy shrouds project.

4 - "a village lost in the mountains": J. Marvin Lee, *Centre County: The County in Which We Live* (State College, PA: Self-published by J. Marvin Lee, 1965), 226.

5 - "Pattee Library": Pattee Library was named after Fred L. Pattee, a late-nineteenth-century professor at Penn State who was an early advocate of the study of American literature as a distinct discipline from its English cousin. He also wrote the Penn State Alma Mater, still sung at football games and other occasions.

6 - "Pattee's stacks . . . were open": Letter, William Wisely to Eric A. Walker, president of Penn State University, "Proposed Opening of the Stacks at Pattee Library as a Controlled Experiment during the Summer Term 1964," May 15, 1964, ULAD; Laurie Devine, "Pattee to Retain Open Stack Plan," *Daily Collegian,* September 29, 1964.

7 - "gloomy underworld of the stacks": Douglas Harper, in his authoritative *Online Etymology Dictionary* (www.etymonline.com), says the first attested use of *stacks* to describe "the set of shelves on which books are set out" was in 1879, but offers no other details. The *Compact Edition of the Oxford English Dictionary,* 1971, on page 758, dates the term to 1888 in Jacobi's *Printers' Vocabulary,* where it was defined as "paper or printed works arranged in stacks." One monumental work in which the term does not appear is Edward Edwards's two-volume study of the world's libraries, *Memoirs of Libraries* (London, 1859), which instead refers to "shelf rooms." But beginning in the late nineteenth century and continuing to the present day, *stacks* became the word of choice to describe the rooms where libraries kept their books.

8 - "the building was dark": Carole L. Stoltz, interview by the author, June 18, 2012.

9 - "another odd word": The term *carrel* was even more ancient than *stacks,* dating to the 1590s and *carula,* "a small study in a cloister," although the Online Etymology Dictionary says its definition as "private cubicle in a library" is more recent, dating to 1919 (www.etymonline.com).

10 - "Pattee's inadequacies": Lois Nagy, "Library Inadequacy Remains," *Daily Collegian,* Penn State University, University Park, July 24, 1969.

11 - "only the fourth-largest library in Pennsylvania": Rodney Hughes, "Pattee, Fred Lewis," spring 2006, http://pabook.libraries.psu.edu/palitmap/bios/Pattee__Fred_Lewis .html, accessed January 11, 2012. Pattee Library's collection size and how it compared to other libraries is drawn from the American Library Directory for 1970–71, the edition which best reflects where things stood at the end of 1969. Among academic libraries in the East and Midwest, Pattee was smaller than some and larger than others. Ohio State's library, for example, had 2.24 million books, while that of the University of Maryland in College Park had 1.09 million. The three larger libraries than Penn State's in Pennsylvania were: 1) the Free Library of Philadelphia, with 2.53 million books; 2) University of Pennsylvania–Van Pelt Library in Philadelphia, with 2.18 million; and 3) Carnegie Library in Pittsburgh, with 2.07 million. The Library of Congress in Washington, DC, dwarfed all other American libraries, with its 14.8 million books.

12 - "in the mid-30s": Joan A. Kurilla, "Research Library Dedicated," *Centre Daily Times,* State College, PA, July 5, 1969.

13 - "Reverend Ralph David Abernathy": Paul B. Foreman, "What Penn State Students Asked Dr. Ralph Abernathy," March 11, 1969. Charles Davis Papers, Beinecke Memorial Library, Yale University, New Haven, CT.

14 - "bus driver's son": Jeffrey Berger, interview by the author, February 28, 2013; *generally orderly behavior:* Op. cit., Kurilla, *Centre Daily Times,* July 5, 1969.

15 - "One of the first memos": Francis E. Hooley to Charles H. Ness, et al., July 12, 1969, ULAD, PSU Archives.

16 - "They were not a bona fide police department": Howard "Buzz" Triebold, interview with the author, November 3, 2011.

17 - "He was generally respected": GHK, interviews by the author on January 4, April 15, and October 10, 2011. Keibler discussed the Campus Patrol and Pelton during each of those interviews, as did Trooper Mike Simmers, PSP retired, interview by the author, October 3, 2008, and Raymond O. Murphy, PSU vice president of student affairs, retired, interview by the author, September 12, 2008; *"Pig Pelton":* Jeffrey Berger interview, February 28, 2013.

18 - "a library memo": Francis E. Hooley, budget assistant, University Library, to James A. Rhodes, Dean of Students staff, January 9, 1969, ULAD.

19 - "spectrum of people": Charles Hosler, dean of the Penn State College of Earth and Mineral Sciences, retired. Interview by the author, November 8, 2011, which was a few days after the arrest of former Penn State assistant coach Jerry Sandusky and two university administrators in a child sex scandal and alleged cover-up that rocked the university.

20 - *"Garfield Thomas Water Tunnel":* The navy had built the high-speed water tunnel on the Penn State campus in 1949. It was named after Garfield Thomas, the first Penn State graduate killed in World War II.

21 - "an admirer of FBI director J. Edgar Hoover": On December 12, 1964, according to a memo in the FBI file on Walker, the Penn State president made a speech in which he claimed to have been warned by the FBI of a supposed plot by Communists to bring in bogus students and bogus faculty—the long-feared "outside agitators"—to disrupt American universities. Walker's speech went viral, to use a modern term, and his quote was cited by numerous other college presidents. Hoover wrote to several of them claiming that the FBI had never said that. But in many ways, the two men were a mutual admiration society. Hoover wrote to Walker on January 28, 1971, praising him for a commencement speech he had delivered recently, and which had been reprinted in *Popular Mechanics.* On the same day, Hoover recommended Walker's speech to Vice President Spiro T. Agnew. Walker replied to Hoover in a letter of February 12, 1971, thanking him for his remarks. "I am sure that you know that many of us are conscious of the work you have done to help us protect our way of life," he wrote. FBI FOIA Request #116295, Eric A. Walker.

22 - "Jerry Rubin": Larry Reibstein, "Rubin Leads 'Happening' in HUB," *Daily Collegian,* February 14, 1969; *During a seven-hour sit-in:* Allen Yoder and Marge Cohen, "Students Hold Old Main Sit-In, But 400 Avoid Police Confrontation," *Daily Collegian,* February 25, 1969. *"Bring out the coons!":* Pat Gurosky and David Nestor, "The Scene Outside—Hecklers Protest Occupation of Old Main," *Daily Collegian,* February 25, 1969; *to welcome President Richard Nixon:* The visit to State College by the Nixons is described by Jim Dorris in "President Nixon Attends Uncle's Funeral Service" in the March 7, 1969, edition of the *Daily Collegian; Walker, who despised student protesters:* The bill to penalize student protesters on Pennsylvania college campuses was introduced by Senator Robert Fleming (R-Allegheny) and cosponsored by forty of the fifty members of the Pennsylvania Senate. It is described in "Proposed Bill Outlaws Student Disruption" in the *Daily Collegian* of February 26, 1969.

23 - "a blaze was set": Letter, Stephen A. McCarthy, executive director, Association of Research Libraries, Washington, DC, to directors of ARL member libraries, March 10, 1969, ULAD; *The arsonist struck again:* News release, Department of Public Information, Penn State University, March 14, 1969, ULAD; *Additional small fires:* Memo, W. M. Carr Jr. to W. F. Christoffers, Controller, July 7, 1969, ULAD.

24 - "especially among gay teenagers": Simmers interviews, October 3, 2008, and February 22, 2011.

25 - "ordered him to put them back": GHK interview, January 4, 2011.

26 - "otherwise molesting female students": Memo, W. Carl Jackson, director of libraries, to Paul M. Althouse, vice president for resident instruction, December 3, 1969, ULAD.

27 - "the girl would be so upset": Wireback, 14.

28 - "impossible to have a patrolman everywhere": Denise Bowman, "Security Improved at Library: Guards Could Not Have Stopped Murder," *Daily Collegian,* January 21, 1970; *"had a manpower problem":* Wireback, 14; *Jackson used library funds:* Memo, W. Carl Jackson to All Library Staff Members, March 14, 1969; *in an especially tight year:* letter from Stanley F. Paulson, dean of the College of Liberal Arts, Penn State University, to Charles Davis, professor of English, Penn State, July 2, 1969, Charles Davis Papers, Beinecke Rare Books and Manuscripts Library, Yale University, New Haven, CT.

29 - "fifteen thousand copies of a pamphlet": "Minutes of the Penn State University Safety Council Meeting of September 17, 1969," PSU Archives; *unattended hot plates:* "Minutes of the Penn State University Safety Council Meeting of November 19, 1969," PSU Archives.

30 - "playing with himself": "Coeds Report Peeping Toms," *Daily Collegian,* December 2, 1969.

31 - "den of iniquity": GHK, January 4, 2011.

Chapter 2: Somebody Had Better Help That Girl

1 - "At five minutes before five o'clock": GHK interview, January 4, 2011. Keibler was certain that the stabbing took place at 4:55 p.m., not at 4:30 p.m., as has often been stated over the years.

2 - "one of thousands of workers": Obituary of Edward G. Erdelyi, *Beaver County Times,* Beaver, PA, July 31, 1994.

3 - "Harrison T. Meserole": Nicholas Joukovsky, interview by the author, January 13, 2012.

4 - "she had spotted Betsy Aardsma": "Two Men Sought in Coed Slaying," *Philadelphia Daily News,* December 2, 1969; *They had two classes together:* This conclusion comes from examination of the official Penn State transcripts of Betsy Aardsma and Marilee Erdely.

5 - "a logical place to go": Pattee Library attendance figures for November 28, 1969, are found in the Statistics subgroup of the ULAD record group in the Penn State Archives. They show that 2,630 people went through the turnstile when leaving Pattee through the main entrance that day, the day after Thanksgiving, compared to 3,906 the previous Friday. Records for Exit 2, which was in the West Wing of Pattee, showed that 518 left by that door, compared to 726 the previous Friday; *to go on a slow day:* Op. cit., Joukovsky interview.

6 - "a refugee from the war of independence against Portugal": E-mails from Dr. Mario J. Azevedo, dean of the College of Public Service, Jackson State University, Jackson, MS, April 11 and 13, 2011. Azevedo and Joao Uafinda fled Mozambique for Malawi around the same time in 1964, and subsequently became friends after they landed in the United States. Uafinda's date of birth and physical description are found on the visa issued to him on April 26, 1965, by the US embassy in Zomba, Malawi. The original document is in the University of Rochester Library in Rochester, New York.

7 - "He was visiting his son Robert": Robert B. Allen, interview by the author, February 21, 2012. Allen was a professor of architectural engineering at Penn State for a number of years; Joe Nelson, "Celebrated Covered Bridge Writer Passes," *Vermont Bridges.com,* posted July 27, 2008 (www.vermontbridges.com/index.htm), accessed February 21, 2012. Richard Sanders Allen also wrote books on the early history of American aviation.

8 - "began walking toward Erdely": GHK interview, January 4, 2011.

9 - "Allen thought he heard something": GHK interview, January 4, 2011; *Uafinda heard a thump:* Thomas H. Shelar, Pennsylvania State Police, retired, interview by the author, March 7, 2011.

10 - "victim's silence hard to explain": Dr. Steven W. Margles, interview by the author, November 11, 2008. Margles was a classmate of David L. Wright's, Betsy Aardsma's boyfriend, at the Penn State College of Medicine in Hershey in 1969.

11 - "better dressed than the typical student": GHK interview, April 15, 2011: *a white shirt and tie:* GHK interview, July 23, 2012.

12 - "Somebody better help that girl!": News release, December 1, 1969, Department of Public Information, Penn State University; *headed back in the opposite direction:* GHK interview, January 4, 2011.

13 - "Uafinda followed the running man": GHK interview, January 4, 2011.

14 - "It was Betsy Aardsma": *Daily Collegian,* December 2, 1969; *with whom she had*

spoken so recently: GHK interview, January 4, 2011; *red, sleeveless dress:* Dr. Thomas J. Magnani, Autopsy report, Betsy Ruth Aardsma, December 11, 1969, Centre County Hospital, Bellefonte, PA, Department of Pathology.
15 - "she began smoothing Betsy's hair": James Severs, husband of Marilee Erdely Severs, interview by the author, October 25, 2011. Erdely died in 2002.
16 - "a breakdown that would mystify": GHK interview, October 10, 2011.
17 - "Martin began mouth-to-mouth": Wireback, 1972.
18 - "thought he detected a faint pulse": Quarteroni, "10 Years Later: Woman's Death Still a Mystery," *Centre Daily Times,* State College, PA, November 28, 1979.
19 - "they were met by Dr. Elmer Reed": Dr. John A. Hargleroad, director of University Health Services, interview by the author, November 14, 2008; *an ear, nose, and throat specialist:* Hargleroad, "The Ritenhour Health Center Annual Report, 1969–70"; *Two registered nurses:* Jane M. Galas, RN, interview by the author, June 12, 2012. Galas was one of the two nurses on duty that night.
20 - "Maybe there was a pulse": Op. cit., Hargleroad interview; *The closest real hospital:* Dr. Thomas J. Magnani, Centre County pathologist, interview by the author, January 17, 2012.
21 - "pronounced her dead": Op. cit., Hargleroad interview, November 14, 2008; *as if in a trance:* Op. cit., GHK interview, October 10, 2011.
22 - "It was up to Murphy": Raymond O. Murphy, interview by author, September 12, 2008.
23 - "two bedrooms down": Dennis Wegner, interview by the author, November 13, 2008.
24 - Michigan weather statistics for the month of November, 1969, are collected in the local history section of the Herrick District Library in Holland, Michigan; *Holland Evening Sentinel,* November 29, 1969, for the time the Aardsmas were notified.
25 - "were visiting from Madison": *Holland Evening Sentinel,* December 1, 1969; *somber expression:* Dennis Wegner, interviews by the author on October 29, 2008, and March 30, 2011.
26 - "very cold and short": Wireback article, 1972. Taft Wireback interviewed Dick Aardsma, Betsy's father; *Koch Funeral Home:* Raymond O. Murphy interview, September 12, 2008; *"but none of us slept very well":* Dennis Wegner, e-mail to author, February 12, 2012.

Chapter 3: The Long Night
1 - "Around 6:00 p.m.": GHK interview, March 14, 2012.
2 - **The Pennsylvania State Police had been created:** "History, Pennsylvania State Police," Pennsylvania State Police Historical, Educational, and Memorial Center website (www.psp-hemc.org/history/psp.html), accessed June 17, 2012; *fewer than 3,000:* the official complement in early 1967 was 2,350, although Governor Raymond P. Shafer intended to raise that to 3,550 by the end of his administration in 1971, according to a news release of March 4, 1967, found in the Governor Raymond P. Shafer Papers, PSA.
3 - "We did everything": Eugene Kowalewski, retired Pennsylvania State Police corporal, interview by the author, July 16, 2012.
4 - "a much shakier hand": GHK interview, July 23, 2012.
5 - "It was around 6:30 p.m.": GHK interview, March 14, 2012.

6 - Not that Simmers was the only person working undercover on the Penn State campus; the FBI also had an informer in President Eric Walker's office. Never identified publicly, the informant had access to Walker's personnel files, and had informed the FBI that Walker, who was an engineer by training, had traveled to a UN engineering education conference in Paris a little over two months earlier. The informant's identity was redacted from a February 28, 1969, memo released by the FBI under the Freedom of Information Act (FOIA). The informant's "identity should be protected," the memo said.
7 - "Simmers tangled with SDS protesters": Mike Simmers, Pennsylvania State Police, retired, interview by the author, October 3, 2008, and Simmers interviews of February 22, 2011 and March 1, 2012, and e-mail of January 2012. Simmers was a trooper at the time of the Westmoreland incident, but retired as a captain after a long career on the force.
8 - "WELCOME A MASS MURDERER": Marc Klein, "Police Break Up Protest: Westmoreland Visit Stirs SDS Sit-in," *Daily Collegian,* Penn State, November 7, 1968.
9 - "He got his ass kicked: Simmers interview, February 22, 2011.
10 - "descended to the Level 2 stacks": Simmers interview, October 3, 2008.
11 - "out of his depth": Simmers interview, February 22, 2011, and e-mail, January 2012; *The desk man reached Brode:* No one alive today could recall the names of the desk man or the shift supervisor the night of November 28, 1969. There was some thought that Trooper Bob Etters was the desk man, although no one could say with certainty. Etters was on permanent desk duty as a result of an injury, but obviously did not hold the position 24/7. He is deceased.
12 - "ordered him to stay with Betsy's body": Jan Hoffmaster, Pennsylvania State Police, retired, interview by the author, October 16, 2008.
13 - "was certain he knew": GHK interview, January 4, 2011.
14 - "unable to match": GHK interviews, January 4, 2011, and October 10, 2011; *widespread computerization:* Emily Simmers, interview by the author, February 22, 2011. Emily Simmers is the wife of Mike Simmers, and was a police fingerprint expert for many years.
15 - "Forty-five minutes had elapsed": GHK interview, October 10, 2011, and *Daily Collegian,* January 15, 1971; *high-ranking university administrators:* GHK interview, March 14, 2012.
16 - "They were just milling around": Kowalewski interview, July 16, 2012.
17 - "ordered a janitor": GHK interview, January 4, 2011; *Books that had tumbled:* Kimmel interview, November 2, 2008; *thoroughly contaminated:* GHK interview, January 4, 2011.
18 - "remained open for business": Hourly usage statistics for Pattee Library, November 28, 1969, ULAD.
19 - "Brode ordered Simmers to accompany": Simmers interview, February 22, 2011; *who practiced in Altoona:* Mike Mutch, Pennsylvania State Police, retired, interview by the author, February 17, 2012.
20 - "Brown didn't know Dr. Magnani": Judge Charles Brown, interview by the author, January 30, 2012; *"mad as a hornet":* Dr. Thomas J. Magnani, interview by the author, January 17, 2012; *In an alternate version:* GHK interview, October 10, 2011; *"too big of an ego":* Magnani interview, January 17, 2012.

21 - "Neff . . . told the reporter": "Dead Girl Found in Library," *Altoona Mirror*, November 29, 1969.
22 - Dr. Thomas J. Magnani, "Autopsy Report, Betsy Ruth Aardsma," Pathology No. A-69-41. November 28, 1969. Office of the Prothonotary, Centre County Courthouse, Bellefonte, PA.
23 - "She was not raped": W. Robert Neff, Centre County Coroner, quoted in the *Centre Daily Times,* State College, PA, November 29, 1969.
24 - "from the front": GHK interview, April 15, 2011, and Simmers interview, October 3, 2008; *from behind:* Mike Mutch, Pennsylvania State Police, retired, interview by the author, September 17, 2008, and Ron Tyger, Pennsylvania State Police, retired, interview by the author, September 23, 2008.
25 - "no defensive wounds": GHK interview, January 4, 2011; *any skin of the killer:* Mutch interview, September 17, 2008.
26 - "drove the blade": Simmers interview, February 22, 2011. Physicians throughout history have commented on knives and breastbones. Dr. B. F. Joslin wrote in the New York *Lancet* in 1842 about a woman stabbed three times by her husband, including a fatal thrust through her breastbone. He marveled that "it must have required powerful muscles, called into vigorous action under the influence of rage, to drive such a weapon through this barrier of bone placed before the heart for its protection." In this case, the victim lived for nine minutes and was able to stagger to a neighbor's house, where she collapsed on a settee and died.
27 - Sherman B. Nuland, MD, *How We Die: Reflections on Life's Final Chapter* (New York: Alfred A. Knopf, 1994), 123–24, 128–29, 132.
28 - President Reagan ultimately lost even more blood than Betsy Aardsma—almost 3.75 quarts—after he was shot by John Hinckley Jr. in 1981. But the bullet didn't quite reach his heart, and he arrived at George Washington University Hospital in minutes and was hooked up immediately to a replacement blood supply. That, a better understanding of trauma care in 1981, and skilled surgeons available the moment he arrived, saved his life. D.Q.W. Wilber, *Rawhide Down: The Near Assassination of Ronald Reagan* (New York: Henry Holt, 2011), 170, 188.
29 - "just a slit": Magnani interview, January 17, 2012. Dr. William K. Heydorn, a thoracic surgeon and former medical director of Letterman Army Hospital in San Francisco, looked at the facts of Betsy Aardsma's wound, and in an e-mail to the author offered the same rationale for the lack of much external bleeding. "The wound of entry was very small." Heydorn said that for Betsy Aardsma to have been resuscitated would have required drainage of the blood out of the pericardial and pleural spaces via a chest tube, and immediate closure of the heart wound followed by blood replacement. "It would be a difficult situation even today, and would need attention in a good emergency room with skilled physicians," he said.
30 - "Maybe you stretch things": Wireback article, 1972.

Chapter 4: Trying for a Do-Over
1 - "She was in their dorm room": Sharon Brandt, e-mail to the author, September 7, 2011; *Detective Cornelius Shovlin:* According to Sergeant Keibler, Detective Shovlin was

the brother of Dr. John P. Shovlin, the superintendent of Farview State Hospital for the Criminally Insane in Waymart, Pennsylvania. Dr. Shovlin and the hospital would be engulfed in controversy in 1976 when the *Philadelphia Inquirer* exposed the brutal treatment and deaths of inmates there in a Pulitzer Prize–winning series. Dr. Shovlin was indicted in four of the deaths, but ultimately acquitted.

2 - "They told him to get dressed": Dr. David L. Wright, interview with the author, November 10, 2008; *twenty minutes questioning him:* Kevin Cirilli, "Betsy Ruth Aardsma: 40 Years Later," *Daily Collegian,* Penn State University, State College, PA, November 20, 2009. Sergeant Keibler, questioned about Wright's assertion that Detective Shovlin kept him in the dark for twenty minutes, was doubtful but did not rule it out. He said Shovlin was a good detective and might have had a reason for doing that, but found it difficult to imagine how he could subject Wright to all those questions without telling him why he was there.

3 - "wanted to scream": Op. cit., Cirilli.

4 - "roused the other occupants": Dr. Steven Margles, interview by the author, November 11, 2008; In 1981, Misiti, as a physician for the National Institutes of Health, would care for one of the first known AIDS patients. *See,* Dennis Rodrigues and Dr. Victoria Harden, interview with Dr. Thomas Waldmann, March 14, 1990, from, *In Their Own Words: NIH Researchers Recall the Early Years of AIDS* (http://history.nih.gov/nihinownwords/docs/waldmann1_01.html), accessed March 6, 2012. Margles became a well-known boxing hand doctor, repairing damaged fists. One of his patients was Micky Ward, whose life was fictionalized in the Academy Award–winning 2010 film, *The Fighter:* Op. cit, Margles interview.

5 - "medical precision": Op. cit., Margles interview.

6 - "called his father": Op. cit., Cirilli; *He thought it was the state police calling:* Op. cit., Wireback.

7 - "ordered Trooper Ken Schleiden": Trooper Kent D. Bernier, interview by the author, September 30, 2008; *first coed dormitory:* GHK interview, January 4, 2011; *Room 5A, was in a corner:* Sharon Brandt, e-mail to the author, January 13, 2013; *Brandt was long gone:* Op. cit., GHK, January 4, 2011; *would stay with friends in Atherton:* Sharon Brandt, e-mail to the author, February 12, 2013; *Schleiden opened Betsy's desk:* Ken Schleiden, interview by the author, March 31, 2011; *but no formal diary:* GHK, October 10, 2011; *embarrassed Betsy's mother:* GHK, April 15, 2011.

8 - "Kimmel's tough tactics": Robert V. Cox, *Deadly Pursuit: The Pulitzer Prize–Winning Story of Terror in the Pennsylvania Mountains* (Harrisburg: Cameron House, 1977), 43, 50–51; *"awful lot of trouble":* GHK, March 14, 2012.

9 - "forcibly abducted": Cox, 116–17. Cox changes the victim's name in his book to Mary Lou Broderick, but all news accounts at the time used her real name; *into the wilds:* Paul Zdinak, "Corporal Says Hollenbaugh Faced Police Posse Calmly," Associated Press in *Gettysburg Times,* May 24, 1966; *"I never did that . . .":* Cox, 187.

10 - "largest manhunt": Zdinak article, May 25, 1966; Cox, 156. *Terry R. Anderson:* Cox, 143. While it probably goes without saying, this was not the Associated Press correspondent by that name who in the 1980s spent several years as a hostage in Beirut,

Lebanon. The FBI maintains separate walls of honor for agents killed by criminals and those who die on duty as the result of accidents. Anderson is fifteenth on the first list (www.fbi.gov/about-us/history/hallhonor/anderson), accessed March 11, 2012.
11 - "He joined the US Air Force": GHK, January 4, 2011.
12 - "A group of SDS students": GHK interview, March 14, 2012.
13 - "no idea they were being infiltrated": Jeffrey Berger, interview by the author, February 28, 2013; *undercover agent:* Pennsylvania State Police teletype bulletins, February 1, 1967, issued at 10:22 a.m. and 2:44 p.m., Shafer Papers, PSA.
14 - "black student demands": Mike Serrill, "Blacks Confront Lewis With Demands," *Daily Collegian,* May 14, 1968.
15 - "Angela Davis rally in Detroit": Angela Davis was a prominent American black radical activist beginning in the late 1960s. She was a member of the Communist Party USA and the Black Panther Party.
16 - "The state police used a complex formula": Trooper Adam Reed, coordinator, Public Information Office, Pennsylvania State Police, e-mail to the author, January 16, 2013.
17 - "had recently been promoted": Mike Simmers, conversation with the author, January 3, 2013.
18 - "phoned Keibler's mother": GHK, January 4, 2011.

Chapter 5: Miss Marple Arrives at the Library
1 - "very short": Joe Willard, interview by the author, May 5, 2011. Joe Willard is Mary Willard's nephew; *strolled purposefully into the Level 2 stacks:* GHK, April 15, 2011.
2 - "the Miss Marple of State College": Judge Charles Brown interview, January 30, 2012.
3 - "Moffat Cottage": Betty Bechtel, "Criminalistics and the Campus Brat," *Town & Gown,* May 1978, 11–12.
4 - "studied under Professor Emile Chamot": October Speakers: Mary L. Willard, October 1963, Mary L. Willard Alumni File, Division of Rare and Manuscript Collections, Cornell University; see also, "Microscopy," Encyclopedia of Industrial Chemical Analysis, Vol. 2 (New York: John Wiley & Sons, 1966), 566; *In 1899, Chamot proved:* David DeKok, *The Epidemic: A Collision of Power, Privilege, and Public Health* (Guilford, CT: Lyons Press, 2011), 45.
5 - "often sent their DUI blood tests": Simmers interview, February 22, 2011; *"highly regarded":* Memorandum, FBI Special Agent in Charge, Philadelphia, to J. Edgar Hoover, FBI Director, March 17, 1954. Obtained from the FBI under the FOIA.
6 - "he does not have qualified experts": Memorandum, FBI Special Agent in Charge, Philadelphia, to J. Edgar Hoover, FBI Director, February 20, 1961. Obtained from the FBI under the FOIA; *"simply inadequate":* Letter, Alvin B. Lewis Jr., president of the District Attorneys' Association of Pennsylvania, to Governor Raymond P. Shafer, November 9, 1967, Shafer Papers, PSA; *ambitious plan:* Letter, Governor Shafer to Lewis, January 15, 1968, Shafer Papers, PSA.
7 - "They had no training": GHK: January 4, 2011.
8 - "Those marks on her body": Warren Kornberg, "Woman Crime Lab Expert Tells

How Science Runs Down Killers," *Washington Post*, June 7, 1961; *fibers, hairs, blood:* Ann Q. Smythe, "Dr. Willard, Chemist, Is Expert on Crime Detection," *Lake Charles (La.) American Press,* January 19, 1965.

9 - "to pick up Willard": Simmers interview, April 10, 2012.

10 - "set of human remains": Joe Willard interview, May 5, 2011.

11 - "an intensive search": Triebold interview, November 3, 2011; *A soda can with a partial print:* GHK, October 10, 2011; *Nearly a hundred:* Ibid; *including books:* Charles H. Ness, interview by the author, February 11, 2012.

12 - "two glossy, illustrated books": GHK, January 4, 2011; *a specific meaning:* William B. Lockhart, chairman, *The Report of the Commission on Obscenity and Pornography* (New York: Random House, 1970), 114. This was the official report of a federal government investigating commission appointed by President Johnson; *well above the typical price:* Op. cit., *Report of the Commission on Obscenity and Pornography*, 115; *too expensive to casually abandon:* GHK, April 15, 2011.

13 - "sex pulps": Op. cit., *Report of the Commission on Obscenity and Pornography*, 112–13.

14 - "shining the light": Schleiden interview, March 31, 2011; *semen stains on the books:* Simmers interview, February 22, 2011; *"orgies on the floor":* Tyger interview, September 23, 2008; *the area "was covered":* Op. cit., Schleiden; *"You cannot imagine:"* Simmers interview, October 3, 2008.

15 - "wasted no time doffing her skirt": Trooper Jan Hoffmaster interview, October 16, 2008.

16 - "She was the expert": Judge Charles C. Brown interview, January 30, 2012.

17 - "a "very strange" explanation": GHK interview, October 10, 2011.

Chapter 6: Bringing Her Home

1 - "pick up the Aardsmas": Ron Cotts, interview by the author, October 31, 2008.

2 - "she couldn't play": JoAnn Pelon Wassenaar, e-mail to the author, April 4, 2011. *"absolutely silent":* Cotts interview, October 31, 2008; *Black Moshannon Airport:* After 1972, commercial flights switched to University Park Airport just north of State College; *including Sharon Brandt:* Brandt e-mail, February 12, 2013; *mentioned the perverts:* Letter, Ruth Cotts to Pattee Library staff, December 6, 1969.

3 - "could watch on national television": "Penn State Closes Season on TV Today," Lancaster (PA) *Intelligencer Journal* (IJ), November 29, 1969; *It was another triumph:* Steve Summers, "Penn State Defeats N.C. State, 33 to 8," *Lancaster Sunday News,* November 30, 1969. Paterno was joined by a new assistant coach on the sidelines that fall, Jerry Sandusky.

4 - "working as a waitress": Phyllis "Peggy Wich" Vandenberg (Wich), interview by the author, September 24, 2008; Coed Is Murdered in College Library, November 30, 1969, *New York Daily News.*

5 - "shaken by the same story": George Arwady, e-mail to the author, September 7, 2008; *broke down when the waiter came:* Op. cit., Cirilli.

6 - "other barracks in Troop G": Trooper Carl Cseko, Pennsylvania State Police, retired, interview by the author, March 7, 2011; *Boucke Building:* Triebold interview, November

3, 2011; *the same place Betsy Aardsma's family:* GHK interview, October 10, 2011.
7 - "dogged by morale problems": Simmers interviews, October 3, 2008, and February 22, 2011.
8 - "he was peeved": Shelar interview, March 7, 2011.
9 - "They searched in trash cans": GHK, October 10, 2011; *arranged for video cameras:* Triebold interview, November 3, 2011; *borrowed from Channel 3:* GHK, July 23, 2012; *spotted the cardboard box:* Albert Dunning, interview by the author, October 30, 2011.
10 - "attended a major-case school and conference": GHK interview, June 8, 2012.
11 - "After dropping off his wife": GHK interview, January 4, 2011; *had to run the Aardsma investigation from the inside:* Simmers interview, January 3, 2013; *"And Kimmel knew that":* Simmers interview, January 2, 2013.
12 - "went back to Atherton Hall . . .": GHK interview, January 4, 2011.
13 - "drove to the Holiday Inn": GHK, April 15, 2011; *"down and desperate":* Mike Mutch, interview by the author, February 17, 2012; *"Betsy had no enemies":* Ted Anthony, "A Vexing Mystery," *Daily Collegian,* Penn State, November 28, 1989; "*to avoid Michigan":* GHK, January 4, 2011.
14 - "The so-called Coed Murders": There are a number of accounts of the Coed Murders, also known as the Michigan Murders. The best-known is *The Michigan Murders,* by Edward Keyes, published by Readers Digest Press in 1976. The book's value as a reference source is significantly harmed, however, by the author's nearly inexplicable decision to give pseudonyms to all of the victims, a number of witnesses, and even to Collins, leaving the hapless reader to guess to whom he is referring. Wikipedia provides a concise and seemingly accurate account of the murders, as does author Katherine Ramsland in "John Norman Collins: The Coed Killer," published on TruTV.com. And of course, there are the many original news stories about the case which do not use pseudonyms.
15 - "would go to Michigan": Press release, December 12, 1969, Department of Public Information, Penn State University, Betsy Aardsma file, Box 174, in ULAD; *Sergeant Robert Milliron:* Milliron and Trooper Ronald C. Tyger are identified in Michigan State Police documents obtained by the author under the Michigan FOIA.
16 - "flew back to Michigan": "2 Suspects Sought in Coed's Death," *Holland Evening Sentinel,* December 2, 1969. *Notier-VerLee-Langeland: Holland Evening Sentinel,* December 1, 1969.
17 - "We know you share": Letter, A. Ruth Cotts to Pattee Library Staff, December 6, 1969, ULAD, Box 174, Betsy Aardsma file.
18 - "fell to pieces": Wegner interview, March 30, 2011.
19 - "was hurt by the reaction": Confidential source, June 26, 2011.
20 - "had preached similar sermons": "Aardsma Funeral Tentatively Set for Wednesday: Coed's Body Arrives Here for Rites," *Holland Evening Sentinel,* December 1, 1969.
21 - "counted only eleven roses": David L. Wright interview, November 10, 2008; *served as one of the pallbearers:* Tom Bolhuis, interview by the author, September 10, 2012.
22 - "uncertain about what to say": David L. Wright interview, November 10, 2008. Most of the facts in this paragraph are from that interview.
23 - "not Christian for us to grieve": Wegner e-mail, March 30, 2011; *"not very personal":* Olga Lozowchuk Kraska, interview by the author, September 21, 2011.

24 - "It made me so angry": Linda DenBesten Jones, interview by the author, October 11, 2008.
25 - "a loving and compassionate man": Barbara Timmer, e-mail to the author, May 1, 2012.
26 - "very, very nice family": Wright interview, November 10, 2008; *"she kept that up":* Ibid; *which he did not talk about to his own children:* Op. cit., Cirilli.

Part II: Searching for the Killer
Epigraph
1 - "It was a damn shame": Lieutenant Richwire interview, September 2008.

Chapter 7: The Running Man in the Core
1 - "As a light snow fell": "Thousands of Hunters Seek Deer," *Centre Daily Times,* December 1, 1969; *journalists were far outnumbered:* "No Prime Suspects, Police Say," *Centre Daily Times,* December 1, 1969.
2 - Lieutenant Kimmel's comments at the December 1 news conference come from a news release issued by the Penn State Department of Public Information; **"lack of material evidence":** "Two Young Men Sought in Coed Murder Case," *Associated Press* in *Reading Eagle,* Reading, Pennsylvania, December 2, 1969; *"crime without clues":* "Few Clues in Murder at Library," *Centre Daily Times,* December 2, 1969.
3 - "Nothing was found on the books": GHK, July 23, 2012.
4 - "He was concerned about her safety": Charles Madigan, "No Definite Clue in College Coed Murder," *Altoona Mirror*, December 1, 1969; *Erdely was provided with security:* James Sievers interview, October 25, 2011. Sievers was Erdely's husband. She died in 2002.
5 - "dismissed any significance": "Few Clues," *Centre Daily Times,* December 2, 1969.
6 - "The victim of the attack": "Alleged Assault on 18-Year-Old Coed is Probed," *Clarion News,* December 5, 1969; *a strange man:* "Clarion Coed Attacked, Cut in Dormitory," Associated Press in Lancaster *New Era,* Lancaster, PA, December 5, 1969; *went to another room for help:* "Report on Alleged Assault of Student," *Clarion News,* December 12, 1969.
7 - "polygraph examination": "Report on Alleged Assault of Student," *Clarion News,* December 12, 1969; *made up the account of the attack:* "Coed Says Cuts Self-Inflicted," *Clarion News,* December 19, 1969.
8 - "During the three weeks": GHK, June 8, 2012; *compile and write:* GHK, October 10, 2011; *a clerk-typist, a woman from Troop G headquarters:* GHK, January 4, 2011; *converting it to three-by-five index cards:* Ibid.
9 - "They were traffic cops": Tyger interview, September 23, 2008.
10 - "trying to interview a professor": GHK, January 4, 2011, and March 14, 2012.
11 - "'Well, that's the difference between you and me'": GHK, January 4, 2011.
12 - "Briefings are the most important thing": GHK, January 4, 2011; *didn't come home:* Viola Kimmel, interview by the author, November 7, 2011.
13 - "Ed Davis announced arrests": "Three Hippies Suspects in Murder Case," UPI in *Altoona Mirror*, Altoona, PA, December 2, 1969.

14 - "short and wiry": Paul Watkins with Guillermo Soledad, *My Life With Charles Manson* (New York: Bantam Books, 1979), 17; *Davis said four or five other suspects:* Op. cit., "Three Hippies," UPI.
15 - "Susan Atkins and two other girls": Shelly Scott, Tecopa Hot Springs, CA, interview by the author, October 1, 2012*; live-and-let-live lifestyle:* Vincent Bugliosi, *Helter Skelter: The True Story of the Manson Murders* (New York: W. W. Norton, 1974), 175.

Chapter 8: Hypnosis
1 - "who had checked out books": "Library Patrons Quizzed in Killing," UPI in *Philadelphia Daily News,* December 1, 1969; *in a hurry:* News release, Penn State Department of Public Information, December 2, 1969; *"We'll be lucky to ever find out who did this":* Betty Arnold, interview by the author, January 21, 2013.
2 - "also yielded nothing": GHK, January 4, 2011; *took Kimmel aside:* Dunning interview, October 30, 2011; *"The sons of bitches have come back!":* Ness interview, February 11, 2012; *"It wasn't him":* GHK, July 23, 2012.
3 - "singled out for suspicion": Dante Scalzi, interview by the author, October 27, 2011.
4 - "nine days after the murder": "Man Sought in Connection with Murder," UPI in Harrisburg *Evening News*, December 8, 1969.
5 - "Uafinda was the youngest": I am indebted to Dr. Mario Azevedo, a close friend of Joao Uafinda's from Mozambique, for much of my information about Uafinda's early life. Azevedo left his homeland around the same time as Uafinda and, like him, landed at the University of Rochester; *he arrived with an interpreter:* Intake form, May 13, 1954, Uafinda File, University of Rochester Library.
6 - "Keibler interviewed Uafinda": GHK, January 4, 2011; *a police officer meant danger:* GHK, April 15, 2011.
7 - "was a steelworker": "Obituary of Edward G. Erdelyi," *Beaver County Times,* Beaver, PA, July 31, 1994; *changed the family name:* Severs interview, October 25, 2011.
8 - "an honor student": *Beaver County Times,* October 28, 1963. Marilee Erdely's academic history is found in her official Penn State University transcript, which mentions the previous colleges she attended.
9 - "The strange thing about Erdely": GHK interview, January 4, 2011; *aimlessly rooting through Betsy's purse . . . :* GHK interview, March 14, 2012.
10 - "Kimmel told reporters": "Description Analyzed by Police," *Centre Daily Times,* State College, PA, December 9, 1969.
11 - "Mr. Potato Head": Simmers interview, February 22, 2011; *series of transparencies:* Cseko interview, March 7, 2011; *dated from the 1930s:* GHK, June 8, 2012; *borrow a newer version:* Ibid.
12 - "blended information received during the initial interrogations": GHK, June 8, 2012; *the witnesses couldn't agree:* Ibid; *Their release to the media was an accident:* Ibid.
13 - "It was Lieutenant Kimmel's idea": GHK, April 15, 2011; *"Hypnosis has been used":* Vernon J. Gerberth, *Practical Homicide Investigation: Tactics, Procedures, and Forensic Techniques* (New York: Elsevier, 1983), 390.
14 - "downsides to hypnosis": Gerberth, 391–92, 393.

15 - *"Harding v. Maryland":* Abstract, "Hypnotically Enhanced Testimony: Its Role and Admissibility in the Legal Process," *Law and Psychology Review,* Vol. 13 (Spring 1989), 131–46, abstract at www.ncjrs.gov/App/publications/abstract.aspx?ID=127881; *so the risk was less:* GHK, January 4, 2011.
16 - "graduated from the University of Pennsylvania": "Dr. Phillip T. Domin, Dentist, School Director," Obituary, *Standard-Speaker*, Hazleton, PA, April 15, 1994; *an injured man in the field:* Jennifer Learn, "Volunteers Recall Peer Who Helped Them Forget," *Times-Leader,* Wilkes-Barre, PA, February 26, 1995.
17 - "wired for sound": Triebold interview, November 3, 2011; *put the Mozambique student into a trance:* Ibid; *far more than he had told Keibler:* GHK, April 15, 2011.
18 - "Erdely's first hypnosis session": Simmers interview, February 22, 2011.
19 - "She was able to recall": GHK, March 14, 2012; *The second rape victim:* GHK, January 4, 2011.

Chapter 9: Frustration on the Road
1 - "a dedicated doctor's wife": "Slain PSU Coed Was Pondering Career Choice," Associated Press in *Lancaster New Era*, Lancaster, PA, December 1, 1969; *love of sketching:* Tom Boughter, "Selection of PSU Made by Dead Girl," *Pennsylvania Mirror*, State College, December 1, 1969.
2 - "overly dramatic behavior": Linda DenBesten Jones interview, October 11, 2008; *"a certain intrigue . . .":* Letter, Betsy Aardsma to Peggy Wich, September 1967. Courtesy of Peggy Wich Vandenberg.
3 - "ex-boyfriend's whereabouts": Memo of telephone call, Detective Sergeant George Smith, December 1, 1969, FOIA CR 150-09. This document and others were released by the Michigan State Police under the state's FOIA. Names of people that were of interest to the Pennsylvania State Police were redacted from the copies provided to me.
4 - "now officially attributed": Laura Wilkerson, "The Strange Case of Jane Mixer," Salon.com, January 26, 2012 (http://open.salon.com/blog/laura_wilkerson/2012/01/26/the_strange_case_of_jane_mixer_michigan_1969), accessed June 7, 2012.
5 - "they also interviewed David L. Wright's friends": Joanne Lekas, interview by the author, November 29, 2011.
6 - "got us up in the morning": Tyger interview, September 23, 2008.
7 - "clean as a whistle": Tyger interview, September 23, 2008.
8 - "one thing they did not do was attend Betsy's funeral": Ronald C. Tyger, e-mail to author, June 7, 2012.
9 - "Now as far as Betsy": Tyger interview, September 23, 2008.
10 - "Shovlin was not through with him": David L. Wright interview, November 10, 2008; *a "hippie" involved in drugs:* Ian Osborn, e-mail to the author, February 26, 2013. Osborn lived in the cottage in Hershey with Wright and the others.
11 - "asked to see Sergeant Keibler": David L. Wright interview, November 10, 2008.
12 - "not connected with the slaying": Charly Lee, "Rumors Dispelled in Library Death," *The Nittany Cub*, Penn State Behrend Campus, Erie, PA, January 23, 1970.
13 - "an ice pick or a surgical instrument": Charly Lee, January 23, 1970; *Smith*

interviewed Yunker: Report by Detective Sergeant George Smith, December 10, 1969, released by Michigan State Police in FOIA request CR 150-09. Most names, except for Betsy Aardsma and David L. Wright, were redacted from the report, but some of them could be discerned because of other information in the author's possession.
14 - "at the University of Michigan": "Academic Record of Robert Grant Durgy," released by the University of Michigan following a Michigan FOIA request from the author. The transcript also lists his place of birth and notes the serious academic problems he had during his freshman year.
15 - "Bob was a lot of fun": Martha Durgy, interview by the author, November 12, 2008; *a rising star:* Durgy's academic prizes are noted in his University of Michigan transcript; *finish his dissertation:* Ibid.
16 - "it was clinical depression": Ibid; *even buying a new car:* "2 Persons Are Killed in Traffic," *Ann Arbor News,* December 21, 1969.
17 - "never heard her name": Martha Durgy interview, November 12, 2008.
18 - "Martha Durgy is said to remember": Sascha Skucek, "The Durgy Myth," *State College* magazine, April 2004.
19 - "He saw a psychiatrist": Martha Durgy interview, November 12, 2008; *veered off the highway:* "2 Persons Are Killed in Traffic," *Ann Arbor News,* December 21, 1969; *believes her husband committed suicide:* Martha Durgy interview, November 8, 2008.
20 - "talked to a trooper over the phone": JSB e-mail, November 30, 2012.
21 - "Look for the guy in the work pants in the library": Wich interview, July 21, 2011.
22 - "She would not have gotten involved": Wich interview, September 24, 2008.

Chapter 10: Dragnet
1 - "just a little bit of background": Cseko interview, March 7, 2011.
2 - "interviewed at least two thousand students": GHK, January 4, 2011. Other troopers, such as Lee Fisher and Carl Cseko, placed the total at a more generic "thousands."
3 - "They did not like the state police": Simmers interview, February 22, 2011; *"Some of us were probably looked at as pigs":* GLK, January 4, 2011; *art students:* Ibid.
4 - "viewed the police as puppets for the government": Earl James, *Catching Serial Killers: Learning from Past Serial Murder Investigations* (Lansing: International Forensic Services, Inc., 1991), 31.
5 - "gave information if they had it": Trooper Lee Fisher, Pennsylvania State Police, retired. Interview by the author, October 15, 2008.
6 - "opened the class with consoling words": Nicholas Joukovsky, interview by the author, January 13, 2012; *if he was having an affair with Betsy:* David R. Johnson, interview by the author.
7 - "loud, arrogant behavior": Op. cit., Joukovsky interview.
8 - "seemed "incurious": Op. cit., Joukovsky interview.
9 - "pressed their student informants on campus": GHK, January 4, 2011.
10 - All of the information about the drug dealer Landis comes from my interview with Sergeant Keibler of April 15, 2011.
11 - "across the quad in front of Old Main": Simmers interview, October 3, 2008; *he was in Philadelphia at the time:* Simmers interview, February 22, 2011.

12 - "had been drug agents": John Swinton, interview by the author, October 7, 2008. Swinton was a graduate student in English at Penn State at the time of the murder; *carried out by a professional hit man:* Charly Lee, "Rumors Dispelled in Library Death," *The Nittany Cub,* Penn State University Behrend Campus, Erie, PA, January 23, 1970; *"wasn't into drugs":* Margles interview, November 11, 2008.
13 - "you can't tell who's crazy and who isn't": GHK interview, June 8, 2012; *in any major case:* GHK interview, March 14, 2012.
14 - "vicious lesbian": GHK interviews, January 4, 2011, April 15, 2011, October 10, 2011, and June 8, 2012. He brought it up frequently.
15 - "when it was still illegal under state law": GHK, January 4, 2011. Pennsylvania was still under the 1939 criminal code in 1969, which retained the anti-sodomy laws first drawn up by the Quakers. In 1970, the state adopted a new criminal code that, among other things, legalized sodomy; *One of the biggest theories:* Simmers interview, October 3, 2008; *"a hellhole":* Tyger interview, September 23, 2008; *odd positioning of five chairs:* Mutch interview, September 23, 2008, and telephone call, September 20, 2008.
16 - "It's covered in the report": Trooper Kent Bernier, interview by the author, September 30, 2008; *wrong time of day:* Roger Smith, Pennsylvania State Police, retired, interview by the author, October 9, 2008.
17 - "wanting to commit a human sacrifice": GHK, March 14, 2012.
18 - "Don't you dare tell him!": GHK, January 4, 2011, and March 14, 2012.
19 - "had to report impending crimes": GHK, March 14, 2012.
20 - "sudden interest in religion": GHK, March 14, 2012.
21 - baseball bat: GHK, March 14, 2012.
22 - "a direct, public appeal to Penn State faculty": GHK, March 14, 2012; *"criminal chromosome factor":* Fisher interview, October 15, 2008.
23 - "a nude model": GHK, January 4, 2011; *psychological problems with art students:* GHK, April 15, 2011.
24 - "lived . . . in the former Waddle School": GHK, October 10, 2011; *cofounded the Caffe Lena:* "Lena Spencer; Gave Stage to Folk Singers," *Los Angeles Times* obituary, October 25, 1989; *"Listen to him, dammit,":* Anthony Scaduto, *Dylan: An Intimate Biography* (New York: Signet, 1973), 103; *split from Lena:* Field Horne, "Founded on a Dream," *Saratoga Living,* Spring 2010; *junk cars:* GHK, October 10, 2011.
25 - "solved the Aardsma murder": GHK, October 10, 2011; *naked couple having sex:* Ibid.
26 - "'Just disregard him'": GHK, Op. cit.
27 - "There was no overtime": Cseko interview, March 7, 2011; *"No one was sharing information":* Simmers interview, February 22, 2011
28 - "Dan Brode had an ego": Simmers interview, October 3, 2008; *"He didn't have anything to hide":* GHK, April 15, 2011; *He was an eternal optimist:* Triebold interview, November 3, 2011; *this sounded like Brode:* GHK, March 14, 2012.

Chapter 11: Trouble in Old Main
1 - "wondering if it was safe": "A Dangerous Place," editorial, *Daily Collegian,* December 2, 1969; *drafted their boyfriends:* Ness interview, February 11, 2012.

2 - "horrifying but surreal": Barbara Stine Herrington, interview by the author, November 1, 2011.
3 - "most students felt safe before the murder": Rebecca Craven Greenhow, e-mail to the author, October 24, 2011.
4 - "go in together in groups": Joukovsky interview, January 13, 2012.
5 - "first in the campus directory": Marchand interview, September 6, 2011; *target all women:* Stoltz interview, June 18, 2012. While someone with the Aardsma name would have led the telephone directory in many cities in the United States, it was not the first name in the directory in Betsy's hometown of Holland, Michigan. That distinction went to the various Aalderink families.
6 - "we didn't know about grief": Linda Marsa quoted in Op. cit, Cirilli; *relive their own emotions:* Noelene Martin, interview by the author, January 26, 2012.
7 - "calculate the cost": Memo, Re: Security Guards for Winter and Spring Terms, Charles H. Ness, assistant director for public services, to W. Carl Jackson, director of libraries, December 1, 1969, ULAD.
8 - "the coed's murder": Memo, J. W. Wilson to Ralph E. Zilly, December 2, 1969, PSU Archives. Wilson was an assistant to Zilly, the vice president for business.
9 - "Penn State approved funds": Letter, Charles H. Ness, assistant director for public services, The University Library, Penn State University, to Ben C. Bowman, Director of Libraries, University of Rochester Library, Rochester, New York, October 6, 1970, ULAD; *actually objected:* Op. cit, Ness letter.
10 - "There was no question about cooperation": Lieutenant William Kimmel, Pennsylvania State Police, retired, interview by the author, October 8, 2008.
11 - "no official pressure": GHK, April 15, 2011; *sexual overtones:* Ibid; *praised Pelton's help:* GHK, January 4, 2011; *that Pelton knew about but he, Kiebler, did not:* GHK, October 10, 2011; *good working relationship with President Walker:* Ibid.
12 - "cost the state police $250,000": GHK interview, April 15, 2011; *The university provided:* Simmers interview, February 22, 2011; *"huge, nice-sized office":* Shelar interview, March 7, 2011; *further up the food chain:* Schleiden interview, March 31, 2011.
13 - "George had his hands tied": Simmers interview, February 22, 2011.
14 - "damage the image of the university": Mike Simmers talked extensively about Penn State's attitude toward the Aardsma case in our interview of February 22, 2011, but raised some of the same points during an earlier conversation on October 3, 2008.
15 - "called the situation "political": Tyger interview, September 23, 2008; *mishandling of the first ninty minutes:* Trooper Kent Bernier, interview by the author, September 30, 2008.
16 - In an e-mail to the author on February 21, 2012, Jackie R. Esposito, university archivist and head of records management programs at Penn State, said this: "The Aardsma murder records do not exist at Penn State. What, if anything, happened to them in 1969 is not documented within the Archives. . . . As University Archivist, I preserve the records I have in my custody. I cannot, however, produce what I do not have."
17 - "She was never involved": Simmers interview, October 3, 2008.

18 - "completely ignored": Phil Galewitz, "At PSU, 3 Coed Killings within 47 Years Remain Unsolved," *The Patriot*, Harrisburg, PA, March 5, 1988; *"victim is sort of pushed aside":* Ted Anthony, "A Vexing Mystery: 20 Years Later, Pattee Stabbing Still Perplexes the State Police," *Daily Collegian,* Penn State University, November 28, 1989.
19 - "claim the body": Charles L. Lewis, interview by the author, September 11, 2008; *"So nobody would know her particularly":* Raymond O. Murphy, interview by the author, September 12, 2008.

Chapter 12: Here Sits Death
1 - "A-1 suspect": "A-1 Suspects Still Elude Police Probe," *Centre Daily Times,* December 11, 1969; *an occupying army:* Kimmel interview, January 6, 1970; *Kimmel was frustrated:* Interview with Lieutenant William Kimmel by the Penn State University Department of Public Information, January 6, 1970; *sent to all twenty-six thousand students:* "Important Notice," December 19, 1969, ULAD, Betsy Aardsma folder, PSU Archives.
2 - "Aardsma's yours": GHK, October 10, 2011; *"to justify releases":* News release, Penn State Department of Public Information, December 23, 1969; *"We're stalemated right now":* Kimmel interview, January 6, 1970.
3 - "had first talked to Larry Paul Maurer": GHK, July 23, 2012.
4 - "tall and blond": *The Bruin*, Yearbook of Mahanoy Joint High School, 1964 edition; *carried a small hunting knife:* GHK, July 23, 2012; *a very quiet young man:* Joukovsky, interview, January 13, 2012.
5 - "tar baby": Larry Paul Maurer, phone call to the author, August 6, 2012.
6 - "To cut cheese": GHK interview, July 23, 2012.
7 - "so damn excited": GHK interview, April 15, 2011; *ordered that Maurer be polygraphed:* GHK interview, April 15, 2011; *drove to the Maurer farm:* Shelar interview, March 7, 2011; *not accompanied by anyone:* Shelar interview, March 7, 2011.
8 - "We actually accused him of the murder": E-mail from Thomas Shelar, July 28, 2012.
9 - "We always figured he beat the operator": E-mail from Thomas Shelar, August 8, 2012; *chin was down to the ground:* Simmers interview, January 2, 2013.
10 - "Well, they know who did it": Robert W. Sams, interview by the author, January 23, 2013.

Chapter 13: Sleep Mode
1 - "decisively lost": "Boyle Scores Easy UMW Victory," UPI dispatch in *The Evening News*, Harrisburg, PA, December 10, 1969. The official returns showed Boyle with 80,577 votes to 46,073 for Yablonski, who was on the UMWA executive board. The election was overturned by the federal government on grounds of fraud about a year later; *"a pretty, blond sociopath":* Arthur H. Lewis, *Murder by Contract: The People vs. "Tough Tony" Boyle* (New York: Macmillan, 1975), 3–5.
2 - "'Well, there goes the pressure'": Shelar interview, March 7, 2011.
3 - "They killed Aardsma, they killed Yablonski": Trooper John Holland, supplemental report, Major Case File, Yablonski Murders, January 13, 1970. Colonel Frank McKetta Papers, PSA, Harrisburg, PA. McKetta was the state police commissioner at the time.

4 - "Take all those books out of the library": GHK, October 10, 2011, and June 8, 2012.
5 - "picking the phone up and contacting me": GHK, June 8, 2012.
6 - "daily briefings on the case trailed off": Albert Dunning interview, October 30, 2011; *"fewer and fewer updates":* Brown interview, January 30, 2012; *out to Michigan:* Denise Bowman, "Police Visit Ann Arbor," *Daily Collegian,* Penn State University, University Park, PA, February 25, 1970.
7 - "Lieutenant Kimmel's idea": GHK interview, January 4, 2011; *a reward of $25,000:* "University Offers Large Reward in Murder Case," *Centre Daily Times,* March 9, 1970.
8 - "occupied the Shields Building": "50 Occupy Lobby of Building," *Centre Daily Times,* April 15, 1970; *Penn State Ogontz:* Kurilla, September 22, 1970; *latest list of demands:* "29 Held Following Campus Disorders," *Centre Daily Times,* April 16, 1970; *vandalism of wall murals:* "29 Held," *Centre Daily Times,* April 16, 1970.
9 - "put the Aardsma investigation on hold": GHK, August 13, 2012; *remove their helmets:* Ibid; *it was Major Robert A. Rice:* Mike Simmers, interview by the author, September 28, 2012.
10 - "An unidentified physician": "29 Held," *Centre Daily Times,* April 16, 1970; *taken to Beaver Stadium:* GHK interview, August 13, 2012.
11 - "they had to be careful": Jeffrey Berger interview, February 28, 2013.
12 - "bathed in blood": Joan A. Kurilla, "In Speech at University, 'Leading Yippie' Predicts New Age of Resistance," *Centre Daily Times,* April 20, 1970.
13 - "Walker was unyielding": "Students Break Windows, Start Fires on Campus," *Centre Daily Times,* April 21, 1970; *"We're going over to the president's house":* Jeffrey Berger interview, February 28, 2013; *used an uprooted stop sign:* GHK, August 9, 2012.
14 - "He could have been killed": GHK, August 9, 2012.
15 - "small fires were touched off": "Students Break Windows, Start Fires on Campus," *Centre Daily Times,* April 21, 1970; *Molotov cocktail:* John A. Brutzman and Joan A. Kurilla, "Walker Indicates Strong Disciplinary Action Likely," *Centre Daily Times,* April 22, 1970; *He was shattered by the loss:* GHK, August 13, 2012; *The last fire was reported:* Op. cit., "Students Break Windows."
16 - "contingent of 280 more state police": Brutzman and Kurilla, *Centre Daily Times,* April 22, 1970; *suspension of classes;* "Status Report on Cambodia Aftermath," May 7, 1970, R.G. 22, PennsylvaniaDepartment of Education, PSA, Harrisburg, PA; *He sued on First Amendment grounds: Keddie v. Pennsylvania State University, et al.,* 412 F. Supp. 1264 (M.D. Pa., 1976) (http://pa.findacase.com/research/wfrmDocViewer.aspx/xq/fac.19760228_0000005.MPA.htm/qx), accessed 9/4/2012.
17 - "sent it to Dick and Esther Aardsma": Linda Marsa interview, October 8, 2008.
18 - "nothing that was fruitful": Triebold interview, November 3, 2011; *"a damn shame":* Richwine interview, September 2008.
19 - "He had three theories": Ken Silverman, "Aardsma Case Still Mystery," *Daily Collegian,* Penn State, January 15, 1971; *"And in all probability, he was the killer";* GHK interview, June 8, 2012.
20 - "singularly blameless": Op. cit Silverman.

Part III: The Good Girl and the World Outside
Epigraph
1 - Three Hollanders a heresy: Traditional saying quoted by Larry Ten Harmsel in his thin but influential book, *Dutch in Michigan* (East Lansing: Michigan State University Press, 2002), 10. Ten Harmsel, who teaches at Western Michigan University, writes about Dutch-American history without ignoring inconvenient truths.

Chapter 14: Betsy Who Dreamed
1 - "Betsy Aardsma led the group": "Camp Fire Girls News Round-up," *Holland Evening Sentinel,* March 14, 1956. The Blue Birds were the youngest division of the Camp Fire Girls, founded as the sister organization of the Boy Scouts of America in 1910, two years before Juliette Gordon Low organized the rival Girl Scouts of America. The Blue Birds, whose members were between seven and nine years old, took their name from a 1908 play by Belgian author Maurice Maeterlinck about a young sister and brother who travel around the world, seeking the Bluebird of Happiness, only to discover he was in their home the whole time.
2 - "to make friends": Camp Fire Girls, Inc., *The Blue Bird Wish Comes True* (New York: Camp Fire Girls, Inc., 1960), 10.
3 - "seemingly happy marriages": Victor D. Brooks, *Boomers: The Cold-War Generation Grows Up* (Chicago: Ivan R. Dee, 2009), 37; *moved the family:* The Aardsma family's moves around Holland were discerned from their listings in the Holland City Directory, an annual publication that also mentioned where people worked.
4 - "had graduated from Hope before her": Esther Van Alsburg Aardsma obituary, *News from Hope College,* Hope College, Holland, Michigan, volume 44, number 2, October 2012.
5 - "including two great-great-uncles of Betsy Aardsma's": Mark Van Allsburg, *The Van Aalsburg Family in America* (Grand Rapids: Self-Published). This family genealogy tells the history of the emigration from the Netherlands of the Van Aalsburg family, whether spelled with one "a" or two, or one "l" or two. It is all the same family.
6 - "Also changing Holland after the war": "Holland Industry in Transition," *Holland Sentinel,* January 1978, Vertical file, "Holland-Industry-General Electric," Herrick District Library, Holland, Michigan.
7 - "bursting into tears": Sandy Vande Water, interview with the author, September 23, 2008; *"very brilliant":* Margo Hakken, interview with the author, October 5, 2008.
8 - "E. E. Fell Junior High School": Among the children who started there with Betsy that year was a boy, Pat Duncan, who would grow up to be the Hollywood screenwriter Patrick Sheane Duncan. He drew on his memories of E. E. Fell teachers and some from Hamilton High School, where he finished his secondary schooling, when he wrote the screenplay for the 1995 film, *Mr. Holland's Opus,* about a dedicated small-town music teacher.
9 - "Ted and Toshi Sasamoto": Janice Sasamoto Brandt (JSB), interview by the author, September 21, 2012.
10 - "That's how it started": JSB, interview by the author, September 25, 2012.
11 - "crashing the senior high dances": JSB, September 21, 2008.
12 - "shot to death two innocent young girls": "Dead Eye," *Front Page Detective,*

August 1961; *spotted by a local police chief:* Angeline Grysen, *The Sheriff* (Lansing: W. Curtis Company), 68–72. Grysen was the widow of longtime Ottawa County sheriff Bud Grysen.

13 - "we were pretty tight": JSB interview, September 21, 2008; *"we were pretty cute":* Wich interview, September 24, 2008.

14 - "highlight of Tulip Time since 1935": Randall P. Vande Water, *Tulip Time Treasures,* self-published for the seventy-fifth anniversary of the Tulip Festival in 2004.

15 - "a special place": A chronology of the Dutch royal family visits to Holland, Michigan, is found in the online collection register for H88-0082.1. Royal Family of the Netherlands. Papers, 1933–2004, Hope College Digital Commons (http://digitalcommons.hope.edu), accessed October 7, 2012.

16 - "no prude": JSB, November 27, 2012; *"many male friends":* Vicki Sparks Miller, interview by the author, September 24, 2008; *closest Betsy came to a serious boyfriend:* JSB, September 25, 2012.

17 - "parents who guarded them pretty closely": Kliphuis interview, March 22, 2012; *Horizon formal dance:* Betsy was active in Horizon, the senior level of the Camp Fire Girls, in high school.

18 - "second or third cousins": Tom Bolhuis, interview by the author, September 10, 2012.

19 - "They didn't dislike her": JSB interview, September 25, 2012.

20 - "I don't think they valued that": JSB interview, November 27, 2012.

21 - "She was authentic": Wich interview, July 21, 2011; *"high point of her life":* Wich interview, September 24, 2008; *"I would always volunteer to drive":* JSB interview, September 21, 2008.

22 - "smart, kind, and beautiful": Jo Ann Pelon Wassenaar, e-mail to the author, April 4, 2011; *"was just so easy":* Wich interview, September 24, 2008; *"never had any enemies":* Margo Hakken Zeedyk, interview by the author, October 5, 2008; *"just that kind of friendship":* JSB interview, September 25, 2012.

23 - "the kind of girl you wanted to marry": Jeff Lubbers, interview by the author, October 6, 2012.

24 - "a voracious reader": Wich interview, July 21, 2011; *finished the course with a straight A:* Deborah Noe Schakel, e-mail to the author, September 26, 2012. John Noe moved to E. E. Fell Junior High as principal for the 1963–64 academic year, and was there for the next seventeen years.

25 - "sources of great pain to her": Wireback article, 1972.

26 - "only about 7 percent": American Medical Association, Women Physicians Congress, *Women in Medicine: An AMA Timeline* (www.ama-assn.org/resources/doc/wpc/wimtimeline.pdf), accessed October 8, 2012; *medical illustrator:* JSB interview, September 21, 2008.

27 - "slanted toward the top kids in school": 1 Dirk Bloemendaal Sr., interview by the author, September 2008; *named the fourth of his five children after her:* Linda DenBesten Jones interview, October 11, 2008; *"Just water my plants, too":* JSB interview, November 27, 2012.

28 - "then we did the circulatory system": Bloemendaal interview, September 2008; *done at Betsy's home:* JSB interview, September 21, 2008; *"We were perfect lab partners":* JSB interview, November 27, 2012.

29 - "She was a nursing trainee, or Pinkie": "35 High School Students in Training at Hospital," *Holland Evening Sentinel,* October 29, 1964.
30 - "her favorite teacher": Sparks interview, September 24, 2008, and Wich interview, September 24, 2008; *Van Lare's intense love of poetry:* Judi Jahns Aycock, interview by the author, September 23, 2008.
31 - "American School in Yokohama": "High School Operetta Set," *Pacific Stars and Stripes*, January 19, 1950.
32 - "near-perfect grade point average": Academic transcript, Betsy R. Aardsma, Holland Public School record group, Holland Museum Archives, Holland, Michigan. The transcript also included her SAT scores and class rank; *she was one of several:* "Many Are Awarded Scholarships," *Holland Evening Sentinel,* April 30, 1965.
33 - "She was going to Hope College": Op. Cit., *Sentinel* article, April 30, 1965; *applied to Michigan, had been accepted:* DenBesten interview, October 11, 2008; *about rooming together:* JSB interview, September 21, 2008; *to please her parents:* Op. cit., DenBesten interview; *took out loans:* JSB interview, September 21, 2008, and DenBesten interview.

Chapter 15: Way Station to the World
1 - "She just never annoyed anyone": Linda DenBesten Jones interview, October 11, 2008; *"just not her thing":* Ibid.
2 - "recalled the pranks": Margo Hakken Zeedyk, interview with the author, October 5, 2008.
3 - "smart and pretty": George Arwady, e-mail to the author, September 7, 2008; *ran into her once or twice:* Bolhuis interview, September 10, 2012; *wasn't exclusive:* Op. cit., Linda DenBesten Jones, October 11, 2008.
4 - had to be back in their dorms: Linda DenBesten Jones, e-mail to author, October 19, 2012; *had to attend 8:00 a.m. chapel services:* Reverend William Hillegonds, Hope College chaplain, 1965–78, oral history, July 10, 1978. Interviewed by Conrad Strauch Jr. for the Living Heritage Oral History Project, Hope College Archives Council, Holland, Michigan; *That was an improvement:* The author's mother, Olga Kilian DeKok, told the story of how, in the mid-1940s, she could make it from her family home near the Hope campus to Dimnent Chapel in time for the morning service if she ran out the door when the chapel's bells began tolling; *"everything became immediately clear":* Op. cit., Linda DenBesten Jones e-mail; *provide the name of a relative:* "Why Do Hope Students Leave?," Hope College *Anchor*, February 24, 1967.
5 - "organic chemistry professor": Marlin D. Harmony, "History of the KU Chemistry Department, 1950–2000: A Personal Account," 2006, University of Kansas Chemistry Department, accessed at www.chem.ku.edu/docs/historyofthedepartment.pdf on October 11, 2012; *belonged to a liberal Congregationalist church:* James C. Kennedy and Caroline J. Simon, *Can Hope Endure? A Historical Case Study in Christian Higher Education* (Grand Rapids: William B. Eerdmans Publishing Company, 2005), 129; *raised as a Quaker:* Hillegonds oral history, 17; *deeply committed to the cause of civil rights:* Jack Arbolino, "Calvin A. Vander Werf: The Choice of His Peers," Fall 1980, *College Board Review*; *recruited blacks from the South:* Douglas C. Neckers, letter to *KU Giving* magazine, Spring 2010.

6 - "piety is no substitute for excellence": Kennedy and Simon, 130; *"somewhat sleepy and backward":* J. Cotter Tharin, Hope College geology professor, oral history, July 14, 1987, interviewed by Brian Williams for the Living Heritage Oral History Project, Hope College Archives Council, Holland, Michigan; *who could provide more of the financial support:* Kennedy and Simon, 138; *non-Protestant faculty:* Kennedy and Simon, 131–35; *strong reputation in the natural sciences:* Kennedy and Simon, 129.
7 - "But the changes students remembered most": Vander Werf's changes to student life and the reaction to his bringing Dick Gregory to campus are described in Kennedy and Simon, 139–42. The author attended the Gregory speech.
8 - "scared . . . Uncle Tom types": Hillegonds oral history, 25–26; *not work in their father's insurance agency:* Hillegonds oral history, 22.
9 - "He didn't work with people": Alvin Vander Bush, oral history, July 6, 1977, interviewed by Nancy A. Swinyard for the Living Heritage Oral History Program, Hope College Archives Council, Holland, Michigan; *ultimately was deposed:* Kennedy and Simon, 144–45.
10 - "by the end of her freshman year": Linda DenBesten Jones interview, October 11, 2008; *The idea of being a physician:* JSB, September 21, 2008.
11 - "I think that's pretty feminist": Linda DenBesten Jones interview, October 11, 2008.
12 - Richard M. Nixon was still in the political wilderness in 1965, but after he was elected president in 1968, Vander Bush could barely contain his disdain—and sometimes didn't. On one memorable occasion in the fall of 1971, before Watergate but well after the Cambodian invasion, Vander Bush got onto the subject of Nixon, worked up a head of steam, and then blasted out, "I can't stand that man." He was balanced ideologically on the Hope College political science faculty by Jack Holmes, a dedicated Republican who later became the Ottawa County Republican chairman.
13 - "we enjoyed him": Leslie Nienhuis Herbig interview, September 29, 2008; *"She wasn't a political nut":* Linda DenBesten Jones interview, October 11, 2008.
14 - "teach art to low-income black children": Dennis Wegner, e-mail to the author, February 13, 2012; *traveled . . . to the Mescalero Apache Reservation:* Tom Boughter, "Selection of PSU Made By Dead Girl," December 1, 1969, *Pennsylvania Mirror,* State College, PA; *poverty on the reservation:* Reverend Frank Love, interview by the author, October 28, 2011; *work in the church's Vacation Bible School:* Reverend Herman Van Galen, interview by the author, October 31, 2011; *made a presentation to her church:* "Trinity Reformed Church" news roundup, *Holland Evening Sentinel,* October 21, 1966.
15 - "the former Nibbelink-Notier Funeral Home": Randall P. Vande Water, interview by the author, October 6, 2008. The funeral home moved to 16th Street and became the Notier-VerLee-Langeland Funeral Chapel, which handled Betsy Aardsma's funeral arrangements in 1969; *Edgar Allan Poe Club:* Verne C. Kupelian talked at length about his teen clubs in Holland and Saugatuck, and about Betsy Aardsma and her friends, in an interview with the author on October 6, 2008.
16 - "driving as long as an hour": JSB, September 21, 2008; *Noah's Ark:* Kupelian interview, October 6, 2008; *"Her personality was super":* Op. cit., Kupelian.

17 - "She joined the cast of": Winnie the Pooh: "Freshmen Win Nykerk Cup," *Holland Evening Sentinel,* November 7, 1966. Betsy Aardsma is mentioned in the story.
18 - "thoughtless, inconsiderate, and immature": "Voorhees Co-eds Demonstrate: Fire Conditions Unsafe," Hope College *Anchor*, December 2, 1966.
19 - "moved to Douglas": "Last Will and Testament of Richard C. Aardsma," October 19, 1967, Allegan County Probate Court, Allegan, Michigan.
20 - "Wooden Shoe Factory bumper stickers": Andrea Yunker Marchand, interview with the author, September 6, 2011; *at the H. J. Heinz pickle factory:* JSB, September 21, 2008.
21 - "Green season": The description of work inside the H. J. Heinz pickle factory in Holland comes from the author's own experience as a fourteen-year-old temporary employee. Factory work was normally barred to children that age under federal and state law, but there was an exception for certain types of work during high production periods in food processing.
22 - "dead fish, all belly-up": US Water Pollution Control Administration, *The Alewife Explosion: The 1967 Die-Off in Lake Michigan*, published in near-record time on July 25, 1967. No one ever quite figured out what made the alewives die in such vast numbers. Some believed it was a natural phenomenon related to spawning stress, while others wondered if pesticide runoff was to blame. What scientists did know was that alewives were an ocean fish that had escaped from the Atlantic into the Great Lakes via canals dug by man in the nineteenth and early twentieth centuries. For a long time, they weren't a problem, kept in check by lake trout who found them tasty eating. But when the Welland Canal around Niagara Falls was improved in 1919, parasitic sea lampreys also found their way to Lake Michigan. Beginning in the 1930s, they devastated the lake trout. The alewife population exploded, reaching its peak in 1965. There had been die-offs before 1967, but nowhere near as bad. Michigan environmental officials devised a plan to kill off the sea lampreys by spraying larvacide in their spawning waters, then to reintroduce predators, notably the Coho salmon from the Pacific, into the Great Lakes to eat the alewives. Thankfully, it worked, although it took a few years.
23 - "Company B from Holland": "Holland Guards Patrol in Thick of Riot Area," *Holland Evening Sentinel,* July 25, 1967.

Chapter 16: A Desirable Young Woman
1 - "even though the ties are mentioned": "John D. Van Alsburg Dies Unexpectedly," *Holland Evening Sentinel,* October 29, 1953. Peter Van Allsburg, Chris Van Allsburg's grandfather, is listed as a surviving brother; *Some families just drift apart:* Chris Van Allsburg, letter to the author, June 20, 2012. Some members of the family used one "l" in the family name and others used two.
2 - "The Doors played": Alan Glenn, "The Doors Disaster at Michigan," *Michigan Today*, November 2010; *Buffy Sainte-Marie:* Philip Stine, online comment to Doors story. The article can be read online at http://michigantoday.umich.edu/2010/11/story.php?id=7894#.UJ1G545_1IA. Accessed November 9, 2012.
3 - "organized the first teach-in": Report of the President's Commission on Campus Unrest, 30; *the lover of Gilda Radner:* David Saltman, *Gilda: An Intimate Portrait* (Chicago: Contemporary Books, 1982), 58.

4 - "fell by the wayside": Margo Hakken Zeedyk interview, October 5, 2008; *"a more sensible type":* Letter, Betsy Aardsma to Peggy Wich, September 1967. Courtesy of Peggy Wich Vandenberg.
5 - "Oh, we got along great": Andrea Yunker Marchand interview, September 6, 2011.
6 - "I never considered her a saint": Andrea Yunker Marchand quoted in Kevin Cirilli, "Betsy Ruth Aardsma: 40 Years Later," *Daily Collegian,* Penn State University, State College, PA, November 20, 2009.
7 - " had been cut out of the company": Dr. Elbert Magoon, interview with the author, December 2, 2012. The circumstances of Johanna Meijer Magoon and her husband, Don Magoon, leaving the Meijer company are sharply disputed within the family. Dr. Elbert Magoon says his parents were forced out by Fred Meijer, his uncle, and got approximately ten cents on the dollar for their 40 percent equity interest. An almost opposite story is told in the 2009 book, *Fred Meijer: Stories of His Life*, by Bill Smith and Larry Ten Harmsel. The book, which was an authorized biography, contends that the Magoons wanted out of the business in the late 1950s and asked for suitable dividend payments. Fred Meijer refused, saying he needed the money for expansion. The Magoons, the book says, agreed to accept $1.25 million paid out over several years. By the time the payments were complete, the Meijer company was worth more than $100 million. The two families did not speak for years, reconciling only when Fred and Johanna were in their mid-eighties. Fred Meijer outlived his sister and her husband, dying in 2011. No Magoons were mentioned in the *Grand Rapids Press* obituary, but Dr. Magoon says he did attend his uncle's funeral.
8 - "She never tried to recruit Betsy": JSB, e-mail to author, December 1, 2012; *Jan now had a steady boyfriend:* JSB, November 27, 2012; *does not recall ever meeting Andie:* Ibid.
9 - "death of a high school friend": Leslie Nienhuis Herbig interview, September 29, 2008; *while giving first aid:* Photo caption, *Holland Evening Sentinel,* August 29, 1968. Another young man from Holland, Lieutenant David Buursma, was killed in Vietnam the previous week. He was a Holland Christian graduate, and his funeral would be a day after Freestone's.
10 - "called Betsy to break the news": JSB, November 27, 2012; *had her first drink with the bartender:* Ibid.
11 - "MCCARTHY FOR PRESIDENT buttons": Andrea Yunker Marchand interview, September 6, 2011; *various meetings of a political nature:* Terrie Newman interview, August 28, 2011.
12 - "Their apartment was on the second floor": Olga Lozowchuk Kraska, interview with the author, September 21, 2011; *lived on the same floor in Oxford Houses:* Terrie Newman interview, September 28, 2011; *who had answered an ad:* Ibid.
13 - "She did what she wanted to do": Terrie Andrews Newman interview, September 28, 2011.
14 - "assigned a human cadaver": Olga Lozowchuk Kraska, e-mail to the author, November 19, 2012; *Her opinion of Betsy dovetailed:* Olga Lozowchuk Kraska, e-mail to the author, September 21, 2011; *could whip up dinner:* Andrea Yunker Marchand interview, September 6, 2011; *was the conciliator:* Terrie Andrews Newman interview, August 28, 2011.
15 - "expectations that he would become a physician": James Schoolmaster, interview with the author, September 7, 2011.

16 - "got rid of" their dates": Schoolmaster interview, September 7, 2011.
17 - "pushing him together with Betsy": David L. Wright interview, November 10, 2008; *first date was for ice cream:* Wich interview, September 24, 2008; *They went to parties at his fraternity:* Kevin Cirilli, "Betsy Aardsma: 40 Years Later," November 20, 2009, *Daily Collegian,* Penn State; *on the eve of his twenty-first birthday:* Op. cit., Cirilli; *an entire pitcher of beer:* Andrea Yunker Marchand interview, September 6, 2011.
18 - "She was Democratic, I'm sure": David L. Wright interview, November 10, 2008; *"world's best grade-grubber":* James Schoolmaster interview, September 7, 2011; *"a hippie person":* Op. cit., Schoolmaster.
19 - "seemed to be like oil and water": Terrie Andrews Newman interview, August 28, 2011; *"just using Betsy":* Olga Lozowchuk Kraska, e-mail to the author, September 21, 2011; *"head over heels":* Andrea Yunker Marchand interview, September 6, 2011.
20 - "remembers passing Vonnegut" Chris Van Allsburg, letter to the author, June 20, 2012.
21 - "bedding any number of younger women": Charles J. Shields, *And So It Goes: Kurt Vonnegut, a Life* (New York: Henry Holt, 2011), 6, 241–42.
22 - "but finally wrote his name": Olga Lozowchuk Kraska, e-mail to the author, October 13, 2011; *talked about Vonnegut:* Linda Marsa, e-mail to author, May 17, 2012.
23 - "don't particularly like to talk to people": Daniel Okrent, "The Short, Sad Stay of Kurt Vonnegut, Jr.," *Michigan Daily,* January 25, 1969. Okrent, then a reporter for the student newspaper, later became the first public editor of the *New York Times* and author of *Last Call,* a history of Prohibition in the United States; *spent the night together:* Shields, 243.

Chapter 17: In the Shadow of a Killer

1 - "Her parents in Willis": United Press International dispatch in *Record-Eagle,* Traverse City, Michigan, July 20, 1967; *spotted her naked corpse:* UPI dispatch in *Holland Evening Sentinel,* Holland, MI, August 8, 1967; *had been chopped off:* UPI dispatch in Traverse City *Record-Eagle,* August 10, 1967.
2 - "She was another EMU coed": "Coed's Body Found in Wooded Area," UPI in *Holland Evening Sentinel,* July 6, 1968; *a blue miniskirt:* Earl James, *Catching Serial Killers: Learning from Past Serial Murder Investigations* (Lansing, MI: International Forensic Services, 1991), 20.
3 - "posted a note on the ride board": James, 33; *implicated Gary Leiterman:* Laura Wilkerson, "The Strange Case of Jane Mixer; Michigan, 1969," *Open Salon,* January 26, 2012 (http://open.salon.com/blog/laura_wilkerson/2012/01/26/the_strange_case_of_jane_mixer_michigan_1969), accessed December 4, 2012.
4 - "parents had recently moved": James, 41; *stick jammed into her vagina:* James, 42; *one of the worst things he had seen:* "Girl Found Murdered Near North Campus," *Michigan Daily,* March 26, 1969; *"somebody mentally deranged around here":* "Another Young Girl Murdered; Sex Killer on the Loose in Ann Arbor," Associated Press story in *Herald-Press,* St. Joseph, MI, March 26, 1969; *pale yellow dress:* "Funeral Services Set for Maralynn Shelton," UPI in *Holland Evening Sentinel,* March 28, 1969.
5 - "She lifted weights": James, 54; *announced that she was bored:* "Slayings Terrorize 2 University Towns," *News-Palladium,* Benton Harbor, MI, April 17, 1969.

6 - "strangled her with a piece of wire": James, 53; *must have had an accomplice:* Ibid; *Her body was found:* James, 52; *locked in rigor mortis:* Ibid.
7 - "fretted over a visit": Olga Lozowchuk Kraska, e-mail to author, September 21, 2011; *pleasant surprise:* Terrie Andrews Newman interview, August 28, 2011; *Complications also had arisen:* David L. Wright interview, November 10, 2008; *"she told me that her father had a drinking problem":* Ibid; *Betsy didn't want to attend the ceremony:* JSB interview, November 27, 2012.
8 - "as early as her freshman year": Linda DenBesten Jones interview, October 11, 2008; *people in them who were struggling to survive:* Terrie Andrews Newman interview, August 28, 2011.
9 - "sharing an apartment": Joann Manz Lekas, interview with the author, November 29, 2011.
10 - "Her beloved uncle . . . urged her to get out of Ann Arbor": Sascha Skucek, "Who Killed Betsy Aardsma?" *State College* magazine, December 1999.
11 - "She hoped he would wait for her": Op. cit., Kevin Cirilli; *"I don't know what will happen":* David L. Wright interview, November 10, 2008.
12 - "long walk on the beach": Jeff Lubbers interview, October 6, 2012; *to take her place in the bridal party:* JSB, e-mail to the author, December 11, 2012.
13 - "sex-and-bloodlust frenzy": James, 59; *needed to complete a photography project:* James, 62; *and were acquaintances:* Schoolmaster interview, September 7, 2011; *leaving a private dance party at the Depot House:* "Victim Seen Leaving Party Early Sunday," *Michigan Daily*, June 12, 1969.
14 - " ask her to follow him to Pennsylvania": JSB, November 27, 2012; *believes he finally did:* JSB, e-mail to the author, December 11, 2012; *didn't want her to leave:* Op. cit., Kevin Cirilli; *She applied soon after:* Nicholas Joukovsky, e-mail to the author, December 11, 2012; *her family was relieved:* Dennis Wegner, interview with the author, October 29, 2008; *And then, of course, there was love:* JSB, November 27, 2012.
15 - "Zodiac reveled in the public terror he created": Robert Graysmith, *Zodiac Unmasked* (New York: Berkley Books, 2007), 12.
16 - "two foolish things": UPI in *Holland Evening Sentinel,* August 15, 1969; *her face beaten beyond recognition:* Judy Sarasohn, "Police Press Search for Clues in Slaying," *Michigan Daily*, July 29, 1969; *appeared to have been rolled down:* James, 85; *large patches of her skin:* UPI in *Holland Evening Sentinel,* August 14, 1969; *marched in protest:* "Diag Vigil, March Set for Noon to Protest Harvey Search Work," *Michigan Daily,* July 29, 1969.
17 - "English major": James, 109; *found the Cliff Notes:* James, 128.
18 - "urged him to consider joining the state police": James, 105; *often hung out with cops:* James, 105–6.
19 - "murdered Beineman in Leik's basement": James, 98.
20 - "hosting some Japanese exchange students": JSB, November 27, 2012; *marrying David and having children:* JSB, September 21, 2012.
21 - They went out for drinks at Coral Gables: Wich interview, July 21, 2011; *"And that was the last I saw her":* Wich interview, September 24, 2008.

Chapter 18: Making the Best of Things

1 - **"working as a volunteer":** Wich interview, September 24, 2008; *"Let's get ready and go":* Op. cit., Kevin Cirilli.

2 - **"one of 35":** Letter, December 12, 1969, President Eric A. Walker of Penn State University to Michael Baker Jr.,of Rochester, PA, answering a question from Baker regarding how many students in the new medical school at Hershey were from in and out of state. The letter was in the Eric A. Walker Papers in the Penn State Archives in State College.

3 - **"creepy murders":** David R. Johnson, interview by the author, August 30, 2012.

4 - **"a polite smoker":** Sharon Brandt, e-mail to the author, February 26, 2013.

5 - **"unintentionally comical speech":** David Nestor, "Walker's Convocation Speech Scene for SDS, BSU Protest," *Daily Collegian,* September 24, 1969.

6 - **"They tell us not to question":** "Frosh Hear Thompson," *Daily Collegian,* September 24, 1969.

7 - **"You're a goddamn racist":** Thomas D. Witt interview, March 20, 2011; *confidential memo:* Dispatch of October 28, 1969, from Pennsylvania State Police, Rockview, Governor Raymond Shafer Papers, PSA, Harrisburg, PA; *went off without incident:* Dispatch of November 1, 1969, Pennsylvania State Police, Rockview, Shafer Papers; *Some students cheered:* David Brent, "Ignorant Armies Clash," *Daily Collegian* letter, November 5, 1969; *allowing them to be harassed:* News release of the Black Students Association, November 5, 1969, Student Activism Collection, Penn State Archives, University Park; *decried the attempt:* Lon Barash, "Close-minded Censors," *Daily Collegian,* November 5, 1969.

8 - **the state official most responsible:** David DeKok; *Fire Underground: The Ongoing Tragedy of the Centralia Mine Fire* (Guilford, CT: Globe Pequot Press, 2009), 39; *refused to apologize:* "Charmbury Says No Apology," *Daily Collegian,* November 1, 1969; *"we must not respect or even tolerate":* Jim Wiggins, "Trustee Notes Danger of Communist Pollution," *Daily Collegian,* October 29, 1969.

9 - **"her mother had been a model":** Linda Marsa, e-mail to the author, January 11, 2013; *Buffalo was a fairly radical campus:* Ibid; *"kind of an up-and-coming department":* Linda Marsa interview, October 10, 2008.

10 - **"a level of broad-minded sophistication":** Linda Marsa interview, October 10, 2008; *"She always seemed like a young Katharine Hepburn:* Op. cit.; *grilled sticky buns,* Linda Marsa, e-mail of January 10, 2013.

11 - **"required an awful lot of library work":** John Swinton, interview by the author, October 7, 2008.

12 - **"might be a useful Uncle Tom":** Letter, Representative Donald O. Bair (R-Pittsburgh) to Professor Charles T. Davis, February 3, 1969, Charles T. Davis Papers, Yale University. Bair wrote, "My congratulations to you for your stand on the student power situation. I am very pleased to see members of your race take this attitude. I am also pleased that others of your race are gaining the respect of the white community, as well as that of their own people, by organizing and operating their own businesses and industry. I realize that only a small percentage of the black people are stirring up trouble. It is a shame that a small minority can cause unrest and create disrespect for the whole black community."

13 - "favorite black writer was James Baldwin": "Slain PSU Coed Was Pondering Career Choice," Associated Press in *Lancaster New Era*, Lancaster, PA, December 1, 1969; *"This slight, dark man":* Fern Marja Eckman, *The Furious Passage of James Baldwin* (New York: M. Evans & Co., 1966), 12.
14 - "I don't think she said very much": Ian Osborn, e-mail to the author February 26, 2013; *Hershey Medical Student Wives Club:* David DeKok, "A Mystery for Almost 40 Years," *Patriot-News,* Harrisburg, PA, December 7, 2008.
15 - "two and a half men were admitted for every woman": Marianne Moughemer, "Women's Lib Continues Equality Fight," *Daily Collegian,* Penn State, April 11, 1970; *Things had been worse in 1958:* Stephanie Foti, "Sex Ratio Not Proportionate," *Daily Collegian,* May 27, 1971; *threat of litigation:* Ibid.
16 - "they met in a women's restroom": Pamella Farley, interview by the author, March 11, 2013.
17 - "the kids and the keys to the Country Squire": Linda Marsa interview, October 8, 2008. A Country Squire was a Ford station wagon that was a symbol of American family life in the 1960s.

Chapter 19: Dangerous Attraction
1 - "to become a draftman": Caption under Maurer's yearbook photo, *The Bruin,* Mahanoy Joint High School, 1964; *his high school nickname was "Aardvark":* Ibid; *how Maurer gazed at Betsy:* Simmers interview, February 22, 2011; *Marilee Erdely:* Ibid.
2 - "as highly intelligent": CLH, August 23, 2010; *his IQ was in the top 5 percent:* Judge Anthony R. Appel, "Memorandum Opinion on Degree of Contempt," February 27, 1976, *Commonwealth v. Richard Charles Haefner,* Common Pleas Court of Lancaster County (CPCLC), 7; *appear to be looking down his nose:* Daniel B. Stephens, interview with the author, June 21, 2012. Stephens, then a Penn State geology student, worked as a field assistant for Rick in Death Valley during the fall and winter of 1968; *khaki work pants:* Ibid.
3 - "Rick's home on campus": The room numbers for Larry Paul Maurer and Richard C. Haefner were obtained from the Penn State University student and faculty directories for the years 1966–69. They are on an open shelf in the reading room of the Penn State Archives at the University Park campus in State College; *conscientious, decent, and helpful:* Roger Cuffey, interview by the author, July 23, 2012.
4 - "Rick had wanted a weapon": CLH, e-mail to the author, February 17, 2013, 8:16 p.m.; *watched him sharpen the blade:* CLH, e-mail to the author, February 17, 2013, 5:06 p.m.; *to avoid nicking himself:* CLH, e-mail to the author, February 18, 2013.
5 - "no good ability to sniff out peril": Luke Kliphuis interview, March 22, 2012.
6 - "Betsy and I wrote frequently": Olga Lozowchuk Kraska interview, September 21, 2011.
7 - "they went for ice cream": Sascha Skucek, "Case Closed?," *State College* magazine, October 2010, 38; *Trooper Leigh Barrows . . . talked to Charles Hosler:* Hosler interview, November 8, 2011.
8 - "considered Rick to be "a creep": Confidential source, interview by the author, June

26, 2011; *premonitions of her own early death:* Dennis Wegner e-mail to author, March 30, 2011; *"Time has already run out on me":* Bob Quarteroni, "Ten Years Later, Woman's Death Is Still a Mystery," *Centre Daily Times,* State College, PA, November 28, 1979; *"weird feeling":* Dennis Wegner interview, October 29, 2008; *dismissed the premonitions:* Wegner e-mail, March 30, 2011.

9 - "she told David that she wanted to move": David L. Wright interview, November 10, 2008; *how "ridiculous" it was:* Op. cit., Kevin Cirilli.

10 - "Nixon put out word": "Nixon and the 1969 Vietnam Moratorium" (www.thenation.com/blog/nixon-and-1969-vietnam-moratorium), accessed February 11, 2013; *Betsy led a one-hour discussion:* "November 14 Moratorium Workshops," Student Activism Collection, Penn State Archives.

11 - "looking at engagement rings": Op. cit., Cirilli; *Everyone assumed:* David L. Wright interview, November 10, 2008.

12 - "just a real nice time": Op. cit., Wright; *no hint of any quarrel:* Dr. Steven Margles interview, November 11, 2008; *Betsy phoned her family:* "Aardsma Funeral Tentatively Set for Wednesday," *Holland Evening Sentinel,* December 1, 1969; *it was her choice to go back:* Op. cit., Cirilli; *David drove Betsy to the bus station:* Op. cit., Wright.

Chapter 20: Murder

1 - "wrote a letter to David": Op. cit., Wright; *put on a red, sleeveless dress:* Betsy Aardsma autopsy report, November 28, 1969.

2 - "Most students . . . had gone home": Joukovsky interview, January 13, 2012; *She needed to transcribe:* Ibid; *it made the English 501 students crazy:* John Swinton, interview by the author, October 7, 2008.

3 - "promising to meet for dinner at seven o'clock": Ibid; *sat down with a couple of other English 501 students:* Nicholas Joukovsky, e-mail to author, February 13, 2013.

4 - "one of the source books": It was *The Life and Works of John Arbuthnot, M.D., Fellow of the Royal College of Physicians,* written by George A. Aitken and published in 1892 by Oxford Clarendon Press; *He did not know Betsy well:* Joukovsky interview, January 13, 2012; *"It was very important":* Ibid; *offered to retrieve it and bring it to him:* Ibid.

5 - "quite a few students in the library": Pattee Library attendance figures for November 28, 1969, are found in the Statistics subgroup of the University Libraries Administrative Documents record group in the Penn State Archives; *left her coat and scarf:* Op. cit., Quarteroni; *Dean Brungart . . . saw her between two rows of books:* Mike Lenio, "Murder Conjures Memories of Pattee Stabbing in 1969," *Daily Collegian,* March 11, 1987; *his shift ended at 4:30 p.m.:* This is based on a list of Pattee Library Circulation Department employees compiled after the murder and available in the Penn State Archives. Those who left at 4:30 p.m., including Brungart, are noted.

6 - "greeted Betsy as they passed": David R. Johnson interview, August 30, 2012; *complimented her on the red dress:* Priscilla Letterman Meserole, interview by the author, November 10, 2008; *No one was following her:* GHK interview, October 10, 2011.

7 - "Two young men": Op. cit., Lenio, *Daily Collegian,* March 11, 1987; *later identified by Brungart as Larry Paul Maurer:* Trooper Mike Simmers, interview by the author, February

19, 2013. Brungart did not know Maurer on November 28, 1969, but remembered his face when the student returned to the Level 2 stacks at Pattee Library about two weeks later.
8 - "fairly disgusting" porn: Deposition of Willis Dize, chief of police, Chincoteague, Virginia, December 9, 1995, *Dr. Richard Haefner v. City of Chincoteague, et al.*, US District Court, Eastern District of Virginia.
9 - "never have allowed anyone to upend his career": CLH, August 23, 2010.
10 - "get him kicked out of Penn State on moral grounds": Roger Cuffey, interview by the author, July 23, 2012. Cuffey was speaking in general terms, not specifically about Rick Haefner.
11 - "slammed the blade horizontally into her chest": Mike Simmers interview, February 19, 2013.

Chapter 21: The Night Visitor
1 - "spent her days in private study": Obituary of Myrtle K. Wright, *Centre Daily Times,* January 4, 1990.
2 - "came face-to-face with Rick Haefner": Sascha Skucek, "Murder in the Core," *State College* magazine, January 1, 2009; *a "pretty good" geologist:* Lauren A. Wright, interview by the author, August 30, 2010.
3 - "seen running from the front of Pattee Library": News release, Penn State Department of Public Information, December 2, 1969.
4 - "Many of them desire to see blood": J. Paul de River, MD, *Crime and the Sexual Psychopath* (Springfield, IL: Charles C. Thomas, 1958), 48. De River was the founder and director of the Sex Offenses Bureau of the City of Los Angeles, California.
5 - "was not a frequent visitor": Lauren Wright interview, August 30, 2010; *being killed in Pattee Library:* Sascha Skucek, "Murder in the Core," January 1, 2009; *stayed about an hour:* Lauren Wright interview, August 30, 2010.
6 - "would have helped him bury her body": Christopher L. Haefner (CLH), interview by the author, September 15, 2010.
7 - "summoned for a routine interview": Op. cit., Skucek.
8 - "Schleiden has little or no memory": Ken Schleiden, interview by the author, February 13, 2013. The question then arises how Skucek can report authoritatively in his magazine articles what is contained in Schleiden's report. The answer could be that he, alone among writers, was given access to the report or told what it contained. In his interview with the author in 2008, Skucek mentioned in passing that the police had given him access to some of their documents on the Aardsma case; *Other retired troopers say:* Mike Simmers, interview by the author, January 3, 2013.

Part IV: Flight from Justice
Chapter 22: Bad Seed
1 - "a good citizen in every respect": Joseph Haefner obituary, IJ, Lancaster, PA, January 12, 1916; *perfecting his knowledge of the beer business:* Charles O. Lynch and John W. W. Loose, "A History of Brewing in Lancaster County, Legal and Otherwise," *Journal of the Lancaster County Historical Society*, 1966, Vol. 79, 31–33.

2 - "married "Miss Margaret Fisher": Op. cit., Lynch and Loose; *referred to Harry as "my stepson":* Joseph Haefner will, Lancaster County Archives; *The couple . . . seven more children:* Ibid.
3 - "beset by financial woes": Haefner obituary, January 12, 1916; *to open up 500,000 acres:* "Half a Million Acres of Rice Lands to Be Developed by Irrigation," *Planter and Sugar Manufacturer*, June 27, 1903; *"a large loser financially":* Op. cit., Haefner obituary.
4 - "His will made equal provision": Joseph Haefner's lengthy will is on file at the Archives of Lancaster County, 150 N. Queen Street, Lancaster, PA.
5 - "When Prohibition finally ended": Lynch, 20, 33–34.
6 - "secretary in the bursar's office": Richard Gehman, *A Murder in Paradise* (New York: Rinehart, 1954), 7–11; *bludgeoned and strangled her:* Gehman, 158; *how long it took a body to decompose:* Gehman, 95–96; *to buy the paper:* Gehman, 52–53.
7 - "son of an overprotective, smothering mother": Gehman, 63; *who also hated women:* Gehman, 95; *what he thought he was supposed to do:* Gehman, 71; *"He was devilishly clever":* Gehman, 241.
8 - "one of the better undergraduate geology programs": Lane Shultz, interview by the author, August 7, 2011; *as a volunteer guide:* Temporary teaching certificate application of Richard Charles Haefner, Pennsylvania Department of Education, June 12, 1963; *khaki pants:* Op. cit., Shultz.
9 - "born that way": Alan Zarembo, "Many Researchers Taking a Different View of Pedophilia," *Los Angeles Times*, January 14, 2013; *began carrying a homemade knife:* CLH, August 23, 2010.
10 - "first became known to police": Memo to the File, Lancaster Police Department, November 1, 1962. Obtained from Lancaster Police Department under the Pennsylvania Open Records Act. Franklin & Marshall has in its archives a confidential file on Haefner from this period that it will not release, a file that may well contain information about this and other incidents, possibly including some at the North Museum.
11 - "showing up at the front door": Michael D. Witmer, e-mail to the author, August 28, 2011; *fondled his genitals:* Ibid.
12 - "stole an important part of his childhood": Dave S., interview by the author, February 19, 2013; *seemed nonthreatening:* Ibid; *tell his parents . . . what had happened:* Witmer e-mail, August 28, 2011.
13 - "called Haefner in for a meeting": Re: Richard Charles Haefner Interview, Date 8/30/65, memo by Philip Bomberger III, director of the Lancaster Recreation Commission. This was one of a number of documents obtained by the author from the Lancaster Recreation Commission via a Pennsylvania Right To Know request (LRC-RTK). These documents provided much of the information used by the author in describing the incident in August 1965 in which Haefner molested the two boys; *sick beyond help:* Witmer e-mail, August 28, 2011*: relieved from his assistant scoutmaster position:* Ibid; *banned from Boy Scout work for life:* Op. cit., Bomberger memo, LRC-RTK. Haefner's crimes occurred a few years too early to have been included in the so-called Perversion Files, a collection of case files from all over the country released by the Boy Scouts of America in 2012 in

response to litigation settlements involving former Scouts who had been sexually abused by Scout leaders. The earliest of these documents dated from the mid- to late 1960s, and the latest from early in the twenty-first century.
14 - "second-highest rating for his leadership": "Recreation Leader's Rating Scale for Richard Haefner," Lancaster Recreation Commission, 1965.
15 - "Haefner evidently molested them both": Op. cit., Bomberger memo, LRC-RTK.
16 - "appeared very nervous and shaken": Op. cit., Bomberger memo, LRC-RTK.
17 - "a member of Sacred Heart Church": "Dr. Robert Kurey, Founder of LGH Mental Health Unit," obituary in *Lancaster New Era*, Lancaster, PA, December 16, 1993.
18 - "Rick did see Dr. Kurey": Letter, Robert J. Kurey, MD, to Albert F. Reese, Lancaster Recreation Commission, September 15, 1965, LRC-RTK.
19 - "in its attitudes toward pedophiles": Philip Jenkins, *Moral Panic: Changing Concepts of the Child Molester in America* (New Haven: Yale University Press, 1998), 2; *unlikely to cause significant harm:* Jenkins, p. 2.
20 - "obtained help from Arlen Specter": Cuffey interview, July 23, 2012.

Chapter 23: Death Valley
1 - "Wright joined the faculty": Marli B. Miller and Lauren A. Wright, *Geology of Death Valley National Park, Second Edition* (Dubuque, IA: Kendall Hunt Publishing, revised printing, 2007), v.
2 - "suggested to Haefner": Cuffey interview, July 23, 2012; *send the thesis advisor to verify the fieldwork:* Charles Hosler, interview by the author, November 8, 2011.
3 - "Rick did reasonably well in his graduate studies": Official transcript of Richard Charles Haefner, Office of the Registrar, Penn State University.
4 - "had received the 2-S student deferment": Selective Service Classification Record, Richard Charles Haefner, obtained by author via FOIA request; *were usually allowed to keep them:* Lawrence M. Baskir and William A. Strauss, *Chance and Circumstance: The Draft, The War, and the Vietnam Generation* (New York: Vintage Books, 1978), 23.
5 - "wasn't sure Rick really liked girls": Dan Stephens, interview by the author, June 21, 2012; *"a geek kind of position":* Cuffey interview, July 23, 2012.
6 - "between late September and the middle of May": Ken Lengner, interview by the author, June 3, 2011; *had signed up as Haefner's field assistant:* Joe Head, interview by the author, May 18, 2012.
7 - "Rick had his picture taken": Joe Head, e-mail to the author, April 14, 2013.
8 - "dug their own caves and lived in them": Hal Silliman, "Shoshone: Reviving Oasis in Death Valley," *Mountain Democrat*, Placerville, CA, October 15, 1999; *Fairbanks and later his descendants owned nearly everything in the town:* Ken Lengner and George Ross, "Town of Shoshone: A Family-Owned Enterprise," contained in *Remembering the Early Shoshone and Tecopa Area* (Shoshone: Deep Enough Press, second edition, 2009), 8; *Wright knew her well:* Head interview, May 18, 2012.
9 - "in the field with Rick": Joe Head interview, May 18, 2012; *about ten miles northwest*

of Shoshone: Richard C. Haefner, *Emplacement and Cooling History of a Rhyolite Lava Flow and Related Tuff at Deadman Pass, Near Death Valley, California: A Thesis in Geology*, The Pennsylvania State University, The Graduate School, Department of Geology and Geophysics, December 1969.

10 - "They seemed like they were really good friends as brothers": Joe Head interview, May 18, 2012.

11 - "was at the dinner": Joe Head was uncertain whether the dinner was over the Thanksgiving holiday or closer to Christmas. Smith College, however, did not dismiss for Christmas vacation until December 22, 1967, nearly two weeks after Head, Professor Wright, and Rick Haefner left to drive back to Pennsylvania.

12 - "knocked on Susan's door": Sascha Skucek, "Case Closed?," *State College* magazine, October 2010; *seemed to be paying close attention:* Dan Stephens, interview by the author, June 21, 2012; *dinner at the Sorrells house:* Ibid.

13 - "load up the Ford Bronco": Dan Stephens interview, June 21, 2012; *"Shoshone volcanics":* Richard C. Haefner, *Igneous History of a Rhyolite Lava-Flow Series Near Death Valley: A Thesis in Geology* (Penn State University, 1972), 2; *listened to Wolfman Jack's raspy voice:* Op. cit., Stephens.

14 - "That's a little odd for a geologist": Stephens interview, June 21, 2012; *no more important "than eating an ice-cream cone":* Vincent Bugliosi with Curt Gentry, *Helter Skelter: The True Story of the Manson Murders* (New York: W. W. Norton, 1974), 301.

Chapter 24: Left Behind

1 - "was happy in Heaven": Dennis Wegner, "Coping with Unexpected Death," unpublished manuscript provided courtesy of Wegner.

2 - "A gentle man who liked to read history": Confidential source, June 26, 2011; *And a terrible driver:* JSB, November 27, 2012; *was admitted to Holland Hospital:* Photo caption, *Holland Evening Sentinel,* February 20, 1971.

3 - "descended into deep depression": Confidential source, June 26, 2011; *kept to themselves:* JoAnn Pelon Wassenaar e-mail, April 4, 2011; *"They were quiet people":* Bernice Kolenbrander, interview by the author, October 22, 2008; *Neither parent phoned for updates:* GHK interview, June 8, 2012; *any call to the Aardsmas:* GHK interview, January 4, 2011.

4 - "grieved for "two or three months": David L. Wright interview, November 10, 2008; *first with a nursing student:* Ian Osborn, interview by the author, November 28, 2013; *She eventually became his wife:* Op. cit., Wright; *"very different from Betsy":* Joanne Lekas, interview by the author, November 29, 2011; *"now I'm totally free and I can look around":* Op. cit., Wright.

5 - "I didn't think it appropriate": Ian Osborn, e-mail to the author, February 28, 2013.

6 - "He eventually found a degree of peace": Wegner essay, 3–4.

7 - "asking him to strike down the death penalty": Marvin Cook, "Kin of Murdered Woman Implore Courts to Spare Lives of All Killers," *Capitol Times*, Madison, WI, January 13, 1972; *full support of Carole:* Dennis Wegner, e-mail to the author, May 1, 2013; *"concurred with the spirit" of the letter:* "Kin of Slain Coed Appeal for Mercy," *Evening Sentinel*, Holland, MI, January 14, 1972.

8 - "Wegner's letter to Burger": "Relative of Stab Victim Opposes Death Penalty," *Wisconsin State Journal,* Madison, WI, January 14, 1972.
9 - "down to six investigators": Barbi Stine, "Little Progress Made in Aardsma Query," *Daily Collegian,* Penn State, May 22, 1970; *an ideal number:* GHK interview, April 15, 2011; *back to Rockview:* GHK interview, January 4, 2011; *he and his investigators had talked to:* Ken Silverman, "Aardsma Case Still Mystery," *Daily Collegian,* Penn State, January 15, 1971.
10 - "always came back to the one-hour delay": GHK interview, Op. cit., Silverman.
11 - "more than twenty persons in the Core area": Op. cit, Silverman; *blamed "student apathy":* Taft Wireback, "Murder in the Stacks," *Focus Fall: Penn State's Fountain of Truth,* 1972.
12 - "Maurer dropped out of Penn State": Memorandum to Acting Director, FBI, from Special Agent in Charge, Philadelphia, April 4, 1973.
13 - "a prime suspect": Op. cit., FBI memo of April 4, 1973; *"still talking to me":* GHK interview, July 23, 2012.

Chapter 25: Hiding in Plain Sight
1 - "blot out the horror": Katherine Q. Seelye and Ian Lovett, "After Attack, Suspects Returned to Routines, Raising No Suspicions," April 26, 2013, *New York Times.*
2 - "often brought young boys with him": Charles Hosler, interview with the author, September 9, 2010.
3 - "We were very suspicious": Hosler interview, September 9, 2010; *not much else changed:* Charles Hosler, interview by the author, November 18, 2011; *a boy named Mark:* CLH, e-mail to the author, November 12, 2010, 5:10 p.m.
4 - "things that would be tolerated here": Hosler interview, November 8, 2011.
5 - "considered him a good friend": Hosler interview, November 8, 2011; *some could not reconcile:* Cuffey interview, July 23, 2012.
6 - "was arrested by police in Patton Township": Officer John R. Dodson, "Affidavit of Probable Cause for Arrest," August 27, 1981. Obtained from Patton Township via a Pennsylvania Open Records Act request. The details of the incident and arrest come from this document.
7 - "asked Lasaga to take a polygraph exam": Op. cit., Dodson Affidavit, August 27, 1981; *"Couldn't we get this thing cleared up?":* Ibid; *an incident earlier that month:* "Child Sexually Assaulted in Park," *Centre Daily Times,* August 7, 1981; *the accuracy of the test was later questioned:* Janice D'Arcy, "Yale Professor Accused Earlier," *Hartford Courant,* May 19, 2000.
8 - "much admired and loved": Hosler interview, November 8, 2011; *worshipped his talented junior colleague:* Carol Vonada, interview by the author, May 6, 2013; *paid the parents $500 to back off:* Ibid; *"I got Tony off this time":* Cuffey interview, July 23, 2012.
9 - "150,000 child pornography images": "Former Yale Professor Gets 20 Years for Molesting Boy He Mentored," *New York Times,* February 16, 2002.
10 - "When you penalize Tony for his indiscretions": Janice D'Arcy, "Ex-Professor Sentenced to 20 Years," *Hartford Courant,* February 16, 2002; *"comments so disconnected with reality":* Ibid.
11 - "his years behind bars": Late in his sentence, Lasaga was transferred to the

medium-security prison at Allenwood, Pennsylvania, seventy miles from State College, and then to FCI Petersburg in Hopewell, Virginia, a low security prison. He is scheduled for release from federal custody in February 2015, two years earlier than originally thought. His Connecticut state sentence, after credits are applied, currently runs to 2017.
12 - "related stories about a number of other professors": Charles Hosler interview, November 8, 2011.

Chapter 26: Downfall
1 - "he didn't really like teaching": CLH, August 23, 2010; *It was more like a little factory:* CLH, September 15, 2010; *sold them to the Smithsonian Natural History Museum:* CLH, August 23, 2010; *could not verify the business relationship:* Letter, Annette Fancher-Bishop, assistant general counsel, Smithsonian Institution, to the author, September 14, 2010.
2 - "Rick employed neighborhood boys": CLH, May 13, 2013; *in and out of the building "like a fly":* Harry Bambrick, interview by the author, October 21, 2010; *he would load up a trailer:* CLH, September 15, 2010.
3 - "began to pocket the ones he fancied": CLH interview, August 23, 2010; *Rick invited Chris into the rock shop:* Ibid.
4 - "Rick's world fascinated him": CLH interview, September 15, 2010; *Andy Taylor country bumpkin:* CLH interview, August 23, 2010.
5 - "an old silver mine near Pequea": CLH, August 23, 2010; *opened in the Colonial era:* Ibid; *lowered himself down the hundred-foot shaft by rope:* CLH, e-mail to the author, August 20, 2010, 10:39 p.m.
6 - "Rick and his teenage helpers": Willie Bise, interview by the author, December 6, 2010; *to collect purple lepidolite:* CLH, August 23, 2010.
7 - "Rick found two blue minerals": CLH, e-mail to the author August 24, 2010, 10:36 a.m.; *He took Chris along:* CLH, August 23, 2010.
8 - "You never had to spend a dime": CLH, August 23, 2010.
9 - "It was horrible": CLH, September 15, 2010.
10 - "too interesting to leave": CLH, August 23, 2010; *scared only that he would try to molest him again:* CLH, September 15, 2010.
11 - "hired two more boys": Complaint, *Richard C. Haefner v. The County of Lancaster, Pa., et al.*, 82-1018, March 5, 1982, US District Court for the Eastern District of Pennsylvania, 6; *would claim he fired Burkey:* Ibid; *accused him of molesting: Commonwealth of Pennsylvania vs. Richard Charles Haefner,* Criminal Complaint, August 15, 1975; *Bismoline Medicated Powder:* M. Richard Peters, interview by the author, October 19, 2010. Peters was one of the jurors in the Haefner trial; *during one of Rick's out-of-town collecting and camping trips:* Op. cit., Criminal Complaint, August 15, 1975.
12 - "then told . . . what Rick had done to him": Judge Anthony R. Appel, "Memorandum Opinion on Degree of Contempt," February 27, 1976, *Commonwealth of Pennsylvania v. Richard Charles Haefner,* CPCLC, 2: *Jimmy urged Kevin to tell their mother:* M. Richard Peters interview, October 19, 2010.
13 - "wanted to question him away from his mother": Transcription of interview,

January 5, 1981, FBI. Haefner filed a detailed complaint with the FBI against the Lancaster police early in 1981. All of the details of his arrest, interrogation, and arraignment on August 15, 1975, come from that document, which the author obtained from the FBI under the FOIA.
14 - "clear this up was to take a polygraph test": *Haefner vs. Lancaster County, et al.*, March 5, 1982; *supposedly told him he passed:* Ibid.
15 - "hired James F. Heinly . . . to represent their son": Richard Charles Haefner Waiver of Arraignment Form, CPCLC, August 15, 1975; *Richard Haefner, PhD:*. Op. cit., Waiver of Arraignment Form, August 15, 1975; *put up their house:* Richard Charles Haefner Certification of Bail and Discharge Form, CPCLC, August 15, 1975.
16 - "The story in the morning *Intelligencer Journal*": "Man Faces 3 Morals Charges," IJ, August 16, 1975.

Chapter 27: Kill Me the Way You Killed Her
1 - "Ere was agitated": CLH, e-mail to the author, May 15, 2013, 8:57 a.m.; *obscene telephone calls:* FBI interview transcript, January 5, 1981; *she took both editions:* Op. cit, CLH e-mail; *stormed outside:* CLH, August 23, 2010.
2 - "was absent from this drama": CLH, August 23, 2010; *knew nothing of his dark side:* CLH, e-mail to author, October 3, 2010, 11:15 a.m.; *conducted fire insurance inspections:* Statement on Bail Form for Richard Charles Haefner, February 18, 1976; *overheard and observed by Chris:* Ibid.
3 - "unaware that his cousin had been arrested": CLH e-mail, May 14, 2013, 8:57 a.m.; *as he often did on weekends:* CLH, e-mail to author, May 15, 2013, 9:40 a.m.; *"You might as well have killed me the way you killed her":* CLH, August 23, 2010; *"very, very clear" to him:* Ibid.
4 - "Rick did not deny his mother's accusation": Ibid; *Rick laid into Ere:* Ibid.
5 - "My world with her": CLH, September 15, 2010; *worried about keeping his job:* Ibid.
6 - "sought to pull Chris back into his camp": CLH, August 23, 2010.
7 - "began talking about what Ere had said": CLH, September 15, 2010; *mother believed he was going to get in trouble:* Ibid; *Someone was with him at Pattee Library that day:* CLH, August 23, 2010.
8 - "She wasn't a big deal, Rick said": CLH, September 15, 2010; *"saying that she was really not important":* Ibid.
9 - "already teasing him": CLH e-mail, May 14, 2013, 8:57 a.m.
10 - "soliloquies on the unimportance of individual life": CLH, September 15, 2010.
11 - "merely to hasten the inevitable end of Betsy's life": CLH, August 23, 2010.

Chapter 28: Miscarriage of Justice
1 - "set out . . . to gather incriminating evidence": CLH e-mail to the author, September 21, 2010, 9:25 p.m.
2 - "record any incriminating statements": Bise interview, December 6, 2010; *"I think there was something in there":* Ibid.
3 - "He never tried anything with me": Op. cit., Bise interview, December 6, 2010.

4 - "Haefner pursued other measures against the two boys": Op. cit., FBI interview transcript, January 5, 1981.
5 - "There was a scuffle and George was arrested": "Conviction Is Upheld by Judge," IJ, February 5, 1976.
6 - "loaned his brother $10,000": Transcript of FBI interview with George Haefner, November 18, 1996, obtained by author from FBI under FOIA. The interview was conducted during the FBI investigation of a major gem theft from a show Rick was running.
7 - "later conceded that this posed a problem": Op. cit, Judge Appel memorandum opinion, February 27, 1976; *Burkey died in 2011:* Kevin S. Burkey obituary, Lancaster Online, March 7, 2011 (http://lancasteronline.com/obituaries/local/539867_Kevin-S—Burkey.html), accessed July 1, 2013.
8 - "wrote out her last will and testament": "Last Will and Testament of Ere J. Haefner," January 25, 1976, Lancaster County Archives, Lancaster, PA.
9 - "answered "yes" to both questions": M. Richard Peters interview, October 19, 2010; *all of them white:* Ibid.
10 - "embarrassed at having to repeat the details": M. Richard Peters interview, October 19, 2010; *"He would not do that":* Ibid.
11 - "claiming to be having chest pains": Ibid.
12 - "consulting a stack of note cards": Op. cit., Judge Appel Memorandum Opinion; *a bad street kid:* M. Richard Peters interview, October 19, 2010; *how Kevin had made fun of his name:* Op. cit., M. Richard Peters interview; *"this is a great man":* Ibid.
13 - "a peaceful, honest, and law-abiding citizen": "Geologist, 32, Denies Morals Charge by Boy," IJ, February 3, 1976; *Rick had been a day camp counselor:* Ibid.
14 - "mentioned that he had secretly recorded these conversations": Op. cit., "Geologist, 32, Denies Morals Charge by Boy; *"erase the testimony of Steve Groff":* Ibid.
15 - "My religion does not condone": Mike Leary, "An Odd Case—Sprague on Defense," *Philadelphia Inquirer,* May 23, 1976.
16 - "approached by a queer": Op. cit., "Geologist, 32, Denies Morals Charge"; *"He never smiled":* Ibid.
17 - "was not likable": M. Richard Peters interview, October 19, 1975; *At one point, Haefner said, "I digress":* Ibid.
18 - "had discussed many times": Op. cit., Judge Appel Memorandum Opinion; *Judge Appel had warned them not to mention it in any way:* Ibid; *Kenneff was open to the idea:* Ibid.
19 - "I remember everything stopped": M. Richard Peters interview, October 19, 2010; *"a proven malicious boy":* "Trial of Haefner Ends in Hung Jury," IJ, February 4, 1976.
20 - "You believe one side, or you believe the other": Leary, "An Odd Case"; *"what made me realize he was guilty":* M. Richard Peters interview; *"this guy was not budging":* Ibid.
21 - "hopelessly deadlocked": Op. cit., "Trial of Haefner Ends in Hung Jury."
22 - "Rick told the intake officer": James R. Haines, "Lancaster County Prison Personal History Report on Richard Charles Haefner," February 5, 1976. Obtained from Lancaster County Prison under the Pennsylvania Open Records Act; *Rick again refused:* FBI interview transcript, January 5, 1981; *he was ordered to strip naked:* Ibid; *surrender his clothing:* "Lancaster County Prison Property Receipt for Prisoner Richard Haefner," February 5, 1976.

23 - "placed in medical quarantine": "Medical and Quarantine Report on Richard Charles Haefner," Lancaster County Prison, February 8, 1976; *scabies and a body lice outbreak:* Lancaster County Prison Board Minutes, February 9, 1976; *trying to forestall a flu epidemic:* Lancaster County Prison Board Minutes, March 8, 1976; *marched to "the hole":* FBI interview transcript, January 5, 1981.
24 - "I was in total darkness": Haefner quote in David Runkel, "Pitch Dark Cell Brought Despair," March 18, 1980, *Evening Bulletin*, Philadelphia; *"They had a Chinese dinner planned and all":* Ibid; *he now provided the names:* Op. cit., Runkel.
25 - "one of his former Boy Scouts": Michael D. Witmer interview, August 28, 2011.
26 - "received seven of them": Visitors List, Richard C. Haefner, Lancaster County Prison, undated; *have to provide a retainer of $2,500:* FBI interview transcript, January 5, 1981; *Justice Robert N. C. Nix Jr.:* Opinion of Chief Justice Benjamin R. Jones in case of *Commonwealth v. Richard Charles Haefner,* January 28, 1977.

Chapter 29: The Philadelphia Lawyer
1 - "a courtroom master": Arlen Specter with Charles Robbins, *Passion for Truth: From Finding JFK's Single Bullet to Questioning Anita Hill to Impeaching Clinton* (New York: William Morrow, 2000), 159.
2 - "to have its interests vigorously defended": "Switch-Hitter," *Time,* May 17, 1976, 53–54; *"accused of sodomizing two boys":* Ibid.
3 - "fighting for his life": Judge's opinion in *Haefner v. Sprague,* 1988; *he was dubious:* David Runkel, "Sex Case Shook His Faith in the Law," *Evening Bulletin*, March 18, 1979, Philadelphia, PA; *"This man was fighting the establishment":* Ibid.
4 - "approached him about becoming their next curator": Rick Haefner's lawsuit against Natural History Museum of Los Angeles County (Museum Suit), March 18, 1983, 5; *a giant in his field:* "Theodore Downs; Page Museum Founder," obituary in *Los Angeles Times*, March 22, 1997; *phoned Haefner to offer him the job:* Op. cit., Museum Suit. The museum confirmed the job offer to Haefner in its official answer to the lawsuit on April 28, 1983.
5 - "gave Rick several projects to complete": Op. cit., Museum Suit.
6 - "hosted an annual dinner at the show": Gary R. Hansen, "Marion Butler Stuart (1921–2000)," *Rocks and Minerals*, Vol. 76 (November/December 2001), 421; *her philanthropy was also paying for the new gem and mineral hall:* Ibid; *neither showed up at the dinner nor called:* Op. cit, Museum Suit, 7.
7 - "Stuart learned of his arrest": Op. cit., Museum Suit, 7–8.
8 - "a lifelong dream": Joe Head interview, May 18, 2012; *Price would conceive of new exhibits:* Roger Cuffey interview, July 23, 2012.
9 - "Officially, he had no idea": Op. cit., Museum Suit, 7.
10 - "marveled at a beautiful fireplace": CLH, September 15, 2010; *Crump and Randy K. talking:* Ibid; *suppression of evidence hearing:* Opinion by Judge Francis A. Berry, *Terry Hess v. County of Lancaster, et al.*, September 5, 1986, Commonwealth Court of Pennsylvania, 514 A.2d 681; *could not have seen the mirror reflections:* "Haefner Defense Tries to Quash Perjury Charge," IJ, June 5, 1976; *to represent Hess:* Op. cit., Sprague Complaint, March 5, 1987.

11 - "Sprague filed motions": "Sprague Joins Haefner Defense," IJ, May 19, 1976.
12 - "Sprague set out to show": "Petition to Quash Informations and for Rule to Show Cause," May 7, 1976, *Commonwealth of Pennsylvania v. Richard C. Haefner,* CPCLC; *Richard Peters scoffed at the idea:* M. Richard Parker interview, October 19, 2010.
13 - "packed with local lawyers": "New Trial for Haefner Postponed," IJ, May 20, 1976; *Prosecutor Kenneff argued:* Ibid.
14 - "manifest necessity": Richard A. Sprague, et al., "Petitioners Brief in Support of Petition to Quash Informations on Double Jeopardy Grounds," June 2, 1976, *Commonwealth of Pennsylvania v. Richard Charles Haefner*, CPCLC.
15 - "over the objections of the prosecution": John A. Kenneff, "Commonwealth's Brief in Opposition to Defendant's Claim of Double Jeopardy," June 1976, *Commonwealth of Pennsylvania v. Richard Charles Haefner*, CPCLC.
16 - "had been prudent and not premature": "Order of Judge Wilson Bucher," June 25, 1976, *Commonwealth of Pennsylvania v. Richard Charles Haefner,* CPCLC; *ruled that retrying Haefner would be double jeopardy:* Opinion of Pennsylvania Superior Court, March 9, 1979, *Commonwealth of Pennsylvania v. Richard C. Haefner*, 399 A2d 707.
17 - "they called the whole contempt affair "preposterous": "Opinion of Chief Justice Benjamin R. Jones, Pennsylvania Supreme Court," January 28, 1977, *Commonwealth of Pennsylvania v. Richard Charles Haefner.*
18 - "they all find out about things": Cuffey interview, July 23, 2012.
19 - "an individual of unblemished reputation": "Petition to Expunge Criminal Record of Richard Charles Haefner," August 9, 1979, *In re: Expungement Petition of Richard Charles Haefner*, CPCLC.
20 - "did not attend the hearing": Opinion of Judge Paul A. Mueller Jr., March 28, 1980, In re: Expungement Petition of Richard Charles Haefner, CPCLC; *until Haefner disproved the prosecution's prima facie case:* Ibid.
21 - "complaining that nothing had been done": Letter, Richard C. Haefner to the Hon. Paul A. Mueller Jr., October 8, 1980. Obtained from the Lancaster County District Attorney's Office under the Pennsylvania Open Records Act.
22 - "thick file of documents": Report by Notary Public Sharry Langley, March 22, 1982, and "Declaration of Robert J. Freiler," March 24, 1982. Both obtained from the Lancaster County District Attorney's Office under the Pennsylvania Open Records Act; *Haefner submitted a new petition:* "Petition for Appropriate Expungement Order," June 7, 1989. Obtained from the Lancaster County District Attorney's Office under the Pennsylvania Open Records Act.

Chapter 30: Penn State Drops the Ball
1 - "was not doing enough to help him get a museum job": Charles Hosler interview, September 9, 2010; *"was commonly in the company of younger boys":* Lauren Wright, interview by the author, August 30, 2010; *to confront Lauren Wright:* Op. cit, Hosler interview, September 9, 2010.
2 - "an open-door policy": E. Willard Miller, *The College of Earth and Mineral Sciences at Penn State* (University Park: The Pennsylvania State University Press, 1992), 62; *"was*

really fearful of him": Charles Hosler interview, November 8, 2011; *"He would never speak ill of anybody":* Charles Hosler interview, September 9, 2010.
3 - "how Haefner had appeared unexpectedly": Charles Hosler interview, November 8, 2011; *Wright described "in detail" the weapon Rick typically carried:* Ibid; *sharpened screw-driver:* Charles Hosler interview, September 9, 2010; *"a whole lot of things came together":* Ibid; *Wright would claim:* Lauren A. Wright interview, August 30, 2010; *"Had he done that":* Charles Hosler interview, November 8, 2011.
4 - "McQuaide . . . filled that role": Vicki Cheng, "Penn State Counsel McQuaide Dies at 60," *Centre Daily Times,* February 21, 1997.
5 - "an integral part of the institution": Op. cit., McQuaide Obituary, February 21, 1997; *"a great legal mind":* Ibid; *no important meetings:* Charles Hosler interview, November 8, 2011; *"concerned with doing the right thing":* McQuaide Obituary, February 21, 1997.
6 - "I didn't feel he took me terribly seriously": Charles Hosler interview, November 8, 2011; *"And that was the end of it":* Ibid.
7 - "speaking to him about Rick Haefner": GHK interview, November 21, 2011; *"We are no closer":* "Pennsylvanians Here & There," *Associated Press* in the *Washington* (PA) *Observer-Reporter*, November 3, 1976.
8 - "speculated that McQuaide": Roger Cuffey interview, July 23, 2012.
9 - "would provide the foundation for a detective story": Letter, Frank W. Merritt to Charles Ness, November 9, 1976, ULAD.
10 - "regarding the Aardsma incident": Letter, Charles H. Ness to Frank W. Merritt, November 16, 1976, ULAD.
11 - "We killed the cunt in the library": GHK interview, October 10, 2010; *Keibler found it interesting:* Ibid.
12 - "too large for any kind of practical investigation": Ibid.
13 - "conducted a remarkable survey": Nancy Bertram, "Variant Tellings About the Murder in Pattee's Stacks," Paper for C. Lit 108, 1979. Penn State University Folklore Archives, Accession # 1979-22 (1).

Part V: Monster
Chapter 31: Revenge
1 - "You didn't want to cross him": CLH, August 23, 2010; *"persistent and unrelenting":* Ernest Schreiber, interview by the author, June 3, 2013. Schreiber was the longtime editor of the Lancaster *New Era.*
2 - "boasted of his courtroom prowess": CLH, e-mail to the author, June 3, 2013.
3 - "went on for eighteen years": Neil Albert, e-mail to the author, March 29, 2011, 2:09 p.m.; *"I am sure the costs were over six figures":* Neil Albert, e-mail to the author, March 30, 2011, 2:24 p.m.
4 - "would be considered for other positions": Museum Suit, 7; *summary letter of rejection:* Ibid.
5 - "showed up at the home": CLH, September 15, 2010. There is some dispute over whether this happened in Los Angeles or at a ski chalet in Colorado, but the lawsuit complaint indicates it was in California; *would never be hired because of his arrest:* Op. cit., Museum Suit, 9.

6 - "his old F&M classmate, Harold Banks Jr.": Op. cit., Museum Suit, 12; *a character witness for Haefner:* "Geologist, 32, Denies Morals Charge by Boy," IJ, Lancaster, February 3, 1976; *urged that he not be hired:* Op. cit., Museum Suit, 10–11.
7 - "One of his stronger arguments": "Memorandum of Decision and Order," *Dr. Richard Haefner v. County of Los Angeles, et al.*, July 14, 1984, US District Court for the Central District of California, 10.
8 - "might yield a strong civil lawsuit for damages": *Haefner v. Sprague,* Court of Common Pleas, Philadelphia, PA, April Term, 1984 #2914.
9 - "no doubt he was a skilled litigator": Summary of Complaint by Richard Haefner, FBI, December 8, 1980. Obtained from the FBI via FOIA #1148254-000.
10 - "zeroed in on the statute of limitations": Opinion, US District Judge E. Mac Troutman, *Richard Haefner v. The County of Lancaster, Pa., et al.*, August 11, 1981, USDCEDP, 81-0922.
11 - "Judge Troutman did not agree": *Haefner v. Lancaster County,* March 5, 1982, 20.

Chapter 32: Paranoid and Agitated
1 - "Rick went to the offices of": Memo on Richard Haefner Civil Rights Complaint, December 10, 1980, FBI, obtained under FOIA.
2 - "My career has been in limbo": David Runkel, "Pitch Dark Cell Brought Despair," March 18, 1979, *Evening Bulletin*, Philadelphia, PA; *leaving them "destitute":* Op. cit., Runkel; *"we assume the integrity":* Ibid; *"He unlocked the truth":* Ibid.
3 - "the harassment continued": Haefner recounts the alleged harassment incidents of June 11 and October 4, 1979, and of March 5, 1980, in his complaint in *Haefner v. Lancaster County, et al*, USDCEDP, Civil Action 82-1018.
4 - "obtain video evidence": CLH, September 15, 2010.
5 - "US Senator Barry Goldwater": Memo to Director, FBI, from Special Agent in Charge, Washington Field Office, re: Richard Haefner-Victim, Civil Rights, December 10, 1980; *the entire police department in Lancaster:* Notes from interview of Richard Haefner, FBI, Washington Field Office, December 8, 1980. Both documents were obtained by the author from the FBI via FOIA #1158254-000.
6 - "did not finish taking the complaint": Letter, Richard Haefner to FBI, Harrisburg, PA, February 6 1981; *far from being finished:* Letter, Dr. Richard Haefner to Supervisory Senior Resident Agent, FBI, Harrisburg, PA, March 3, 1981. Both documents were in FBI FOIA 1158254-000.
7 - "both counterproductive and unnecessary": Memo to Director, FBI, from Special Agent in Charge, Philadelphia, March 10, 1981; *"no further investigation":* Memo, Director, FBI, to Special Agent in Charge, Philadelphia, March 27, 1981. Both documents were in FBI FOIA 1158254-000.
8 - "arrange for publication of a news story": US District Judge E. Mac Troutman, Memorandum, *Richard Haefner v. City of Lancaster,* Civ. A. No. 83-604, USDCEDP, June 22, 1983.
9 - "The subsequent police report": "Offense Report #A98257-2406, Lancaster Bureau of Police," February 6, 1981. Obtained from the Lancaster police through a

Pennsylvania Open Records Act request. Most of the details about Haefner's arrest come from this report.
10 - "more than forty-two billable hours": Civil Action Complaint, *Sprague, Higgins & Creamer v. Dr. Richard Haefner*, Case # 870301281, Court of Common Pleas, Philadelphia County, March 5, 1987.
11 - "He was persistent and unrelenting": Ernest Schreiber, interview by the author, June 3, 2013.

Chapter 33: Suing His Own Lawyer
1 - "for a total of $95,097.67": The varying amounts that Rick Haefner owed to Richard A. Sprague and his law firm for legal fees were spelled out in a lawsuit that the firm, under its then name, filed in 1987, *Sprague, Higgins & Creamer v. Dr. Richard Haefner*, Civil case #870301281, Court of Common Pleas, Philadelphia County. Kenneth Richmond, who represented Haefner in his lawsuit against Sprague, believed that Sprague's undiscounted fees would have been two to three times that amount.
2 - "filed a pro se lawsuit": The full title of the lawsuit became *Richard Haefner v. Richard A. Sprague, Edward H. Rubenstone, Sprague and Rubenstone, a Partnership, Jack L. Gruenstein, Michael Minkin & Julia T. Barsel.* It was usually abbreviated as *Haefner v. Sprague, et al.*
3 - "succumbing to a heart attack": "Heart Attack Causes Motorist's Death," IJ, December 30, 1983.
4 - "appeared in Hill's chambers": Judge Louis A. Hill, Opinion, December 21, 1988, *Haefner v. Sprague*, 23; *maintain a thin veneer of civility:* Judge Gene E. K. Pratter has an online pamphlet, "General Trial and Pretrial Procedures," which contains a chapter on "Professionalism and Civility" that could have been written in response to Rick Haefner's behavior. She pointedly notes that her rules also apply to *pro se* litigants, not just to members of the Bar. *See* www.paed.uscourts.gov/documents/procedures/prapol2.pdf, accessed June 7, 2013.
5 - "Haefner harassed Pratter": Op. cit., Hill Opinion, 27–28; *"a manipulative individual":* Ibid, 29–30.
6 - "some of Rick's more menacing behavior": Op. cit., Hill Opinion, 40–41; *"explosive, unpredictable, and impulsive":* Ibid.
7 - "subpoena the personnel file": Notes of Susan Abele, January 28, 1988. Obtained from the Lancaster Recreation Commission under the Pennsylvania Open Records Act; *"no influence on this case":* Ibid.
8 - "a hearing on his request be held": Letter, Dr. Richard Haefner to City of Lancaster and Lancaster Recreation Commission, dated April 23, 1988, hand-delivered April 25, 1988, LRC-RTK; *He appeared at the office:* Notes of Susan Abele, April 28, 1988, LRC-RTK; *Rick demanded a response:* Ibid.
9 - "offered another lawyer a $10,000 retainer": Op. cit., Hill Opinion, 26; *"material misrepresentations":* Ibid.
10 - "I have to have an attorney": Kenneth Richmond, interview by the author, June 10, 2013. All of the information about Richmond's role in *Haefner v. Sprague* comes from this interview.

11 - "in huge, illicit drug transactions": Op. cit., Richmond interview; *one emerald could equal:* Kenneth W. Richmond, interview by the author, June 15, 2013.
12 - "You could see his eyes light up": Op. cit., Richmond interview.
13 - "a deputy sheriff would remove him": Op. cit., Hill Opinion, 34.
14 - "sent a coldly worded letter": Letter, Dr. Richard Haefner to Lancaster Recreation Commission, October 19, 1989, LRC-RTK, Lancaster Recreation Commission; *LeFever stood firm:* Letter, Donald E. LeFever to Susan E. Abele, November 2, 1989, LRC-RTK.
15 - "issue a writ of mandamus": Action in Mandamus, *Richard Haefner v. City of Lancaster, Pa., School District of Lancaster, Pa., Lancaster Recreation Commission,* May 11, 1990, LRC-RTK; *if he had done anything wrong:* Bomberger, 4.

Chapter 34: Thinking about Ted Bundy
1 - "whether Bundy might have killed Betsy Aardsma": GHK, January 4, 2011.
2 - "supposedly was a student at Penn State University": Ann Rule, *The Stranger Beside Me* (New York: W. W. Norton, 1980), 27; *Ann Rule had erred:* GHK interview, October 10, 2011.
3 - impossible task: Rule, 375–76; *"He would say he was going one place":* Ibid.
4 - "a "Pennsylvania homicide detective": 375–76; *was less friendly*: GHK, June 12, 2012.
5 - "Bundy fit the description": GHK interview, April 15, 2011; *"He's five foot, eleven":* GHK, April 15, 2011; *"He's dressed better than a student":* GHK interview, July 23, 2012.
6 - "Bundy's pornography addiction was the key": Ibid; *she knew Bundy liked porn:* GHK, June 12, 2012; *observed a lot of porn:* GHK interview, January 4, 2011.
7 - "shipped to Troop G headquarters": GHK, April 15, 2011; *"For a month I'm after them":* Ibid.
8 - "would not let him go to Florida": GHK, June 12, 2012; *"That is a tragedy":* GHK, July 23, 2012; *could not prove his involvement:* GHK, June 8, 2012.
9 - "you have to have someone sitting on top of it": GHK, January 4, 2011; *"Well, make up your mind":* GHK, October 10, 2011.
10 - "No decision was ever made": Ibid.
11 - "on a bus trip": GHK, April 15, 2011; *pornography put the Devil in his head:* GHK, January 4, 2011.
12 - "didn't even find out about her death": Kliphuis interview, March 22, 2012.

Chapter 35: A Life Destroyed
1 - "Rick would sit in the car": CLH interview, June 10, 2013.
2 - "claimed to have "an intimate relationship": Richard C. Haefner, "Memorandum of Law in Opposition to Motion for Summary Judgment," *Dr. Richard Haefner v. County of Lancaster, Pennsylvania, et al.*, November 12, 1996, USDCEDP, Civil 94-3366; *who was nine years old:* Chincoteague (VA) Police Department, Report on the Detention of Bruce D., a Juvenile, May 28, 1992; *A single welfare mother:* Summary of intake interview, December 3, 1992, courtesy of Kenneth Richmond, attorney; *was deformed by spina bifida:* Kenneth Richmond interview, June 10, 2013; *had a Valium dependency problem:*

Transcript of custody hearing for Bruce J., CPCLC, June 2, 1992, 7; *at a nearby coffee shop:* Op. cit., Intake Summary; *"But he's a bastard, too":* Ibid.
3 - "little pussy Bruce": Affidavit of Richard Haefner, November 13, 1989, *Richard Haefner v. James Burkey, et al.,* CPCLC, 1399 of 1984; *warn her about Haefner's true nature:* Amended Complaint, *Dr. Richard Haefner, PhD, v. County of Lancaster, et al.,* USDCEDP, December 7, 1994, Civil Action 94-3366.
4 - "who had attention deficit disorder": Dr. Richard Haefner, Memorandum of Law in Opposition to Motion for Summary Judgment, November 12, 1996, *Dr. Richard Haefner v. County of Lancaster, Pennsylvania, et al.* (CV 94-3366); *was going to be arrested:* Complaint, January 17, 1992, *Dr. Richard Haefner v. Monica Steward and Lancaster-Lebanon Intermediate Unit 13,* CPCLC; *just five-foot-two:* Chincoteague (VA) Police Department Daily Log, May 28, 1992.
5 - "accused him of assaulting the staff": Op. cit., *Haefner v. Steward, et al.*, 4.
6 - "good, true, honest, and virtuous": *Haefner v. Steward, et al.*
7 - "stayed "with friends": Affidavit of Bruce J., December 10, 1996, *Richard Haefner, PhD, v. County of Lancaster, et al.,* US District Court for the Eastern District of Pennsylvania, Case # 94-3366; *"helped raise me as a father would":* Ibid.
8 - "did not report him missing until May 16": "City Man Charged with Taking Teen to Virginia," IJ, May 30, 1992; *"I wanted to help him to criticize the police":* Op. cit., Bruce J. Affidavit; *drove Bruce to Ocean City:* Transcript of Chincoteague, VA, police interview, May 28, 1992.
9 - "several times before": Jeff Hawkes, "City Geologist Cleared in Child Custody Case," IJ, July 28, 1992; *Dimm . . . phoned the Chincoteague police:* Chincoteague Police Department Daily Log, May 28, 1992.
10 - "Bruce, keep your mouth shut!": Report of Chincoteague, VA, Police Department, May 28, 1992; *did not want Bruce released to Rick's custody:* Deposition of Willis Dize, chief of police of Chincoteague, VA, December 9, 1995, *Richard Haefner, PhD, v. County of Lancaster, et al.,* USDCEDP, Case # 94-3366; *and, in fact, wanted Haefner arrested:* Judge Franklin S. Van Antwerpen, Memorandum and Order, July 25, 1997, Case #3366.
11 - "he will sue you, too": Op. cit., Dize Deposition; *found a large collection of pornography:* Ibid.
12 - "removing Bruce from his mother's custody": Order of Judge Wilson Bucher, June 2, 1992, CPCLC; *to prevent Rick from taking him:* Letter, Richard Haefner to Kenneth W. Richmond, March 11, 1993. Courtesy of Attorney Kenneth W. Richmond; *she had been "relieved":* Jeff Hawkes, "City Geologist Cleared in Child Sex Case," IJ, July 28, 1992; *went in a panic to the YWCA:* Op. cit, Van Antwerpen Memorandum and Order, July 25, 1997.
13 - "filed a petition . . . to adopt him": Plaintiff's Notice Regarding Adoption, May 29, 1997, Civil Action 94-3366.

Chapter 36: Neighborhood Menace

1 - Haefner's vandalism incident of June 30, 1994, is described at length in Judge Lawrence Stengel's opinion in the witness retaliation case, as well as in the police paperwork from Haefner's arrest.

2 - "he had another seizure": Joe Byrne, "Two Face Charges after Medics, Police Sprayed with Tear Gas," *The New Era,* Lancaster, PA, October 6, 1994; *ran home and called 911:* Officer Christopher DePatto, Offense Report, October 5, 1994, Lancaster (PA) Bureau of Police; *"Get the fuck out of my fucking house":* Ibid.
3 - "he sprayed them with Mace": Op. cit., Joe Byrne; *emptied it back at George and Rick:* Op. cit., Offense Report; *told that George might have a rifle:* Officer Michael S. Corso, Supplementary Report, October 5, 1994, Bureau of Police, Lancaster, PA; *"You're not getting anyone":* Ibid; *abruptly pushed the officer:* Ibid.
4 - "continued to behave like a wild man": Officer Timothy F. Goodson, Supplementary Report, October 5, 1994; *"I'm in jail again":* Op. cit., Corso; *"You're the Gestapo":* Op. cit., DePatto.
5 - "as a sort of homespun Dr. Geology": Jennifer Danner, "Pan for Gold in Gemboree," *The Patriot-News*, Harrisburg, PA, August 11, 1991.
6 - "did not want the guards in the building overnight": Lester F. Rittle deposition, October 16, 1997, *Cincinnati Insurance Co. v. Richard C. Haefner, et al.*, US District Court for the Middle District of Pennsylvania, CV-98-0052; *Haefner claimed that was Rittle's rule:* Richard C. Haefner deposition, October 16, 1997, *Cincinnati Insurance v. Haefner; didn't have keys:* North Cornwall Township Police official report on burglary and theft at the Lost Dutchman Gemboree, August 19, 1996; *out with Rick having dinner:* Ibid.
7 - "one collapsed upon discovering his losses": Andrew L. Price Deposition, October 16, 1997, *Cincinnati Insurance Co. v. Haefner, et al.*; *lost more than $275,000:* Letter, Gems & Jewelry Palace to FBI, Harrisburg, PA, August 28, 1996, FBI FOIA 115-5959712; *always had good security:* David DeKok, "$1.5 Million in Gems Stolen at Mineral Show," August 19, 1996, *The Patriot-News*, Harrisburg, PA. The $1.5 million loss figure came from one of the exhibitors. Police later revised it downward to $898,000.
8 - "had a criminal record in New York": FBI report, August 26, 1996. FBI FOIA request # 115-5959712.
9 - "Rick owed George about $30,000": Op. cit., FBI report, August 26, 1996; *He became agitated:* FBI report, November 18, 1996, FBI FOIA request #115-5959712.
10 - "Colombian gem gangs stalked shows like his": Incident memo, August 18, 1996, North Cornwall Police Department. FBI FOIA request #115-5959712; *deemed him "uncooperative":* FBI memo, November 8, 1996, FBI FOIA request #115-5959712; *not his fault:* FBI report, September 4, 1996, FBI FOIA request #1155959712; *tried to stop jewelers from calling the police:* Tom Bowman, "Troopers Were Kept from Gem Probe," *The Patriot-News,* Harrisburg, PA, August 20, 1996; *no more leads, and no suspects:* FBI memo, September 25, 1997, FBI FOIA request #115-5959712.
11 - "They just never got along": Keith Haefner, interview by the author, September 10, 2010.
12 - "accused him of cheating many people": Affidavit of Richard Haefner, April 1, 1999, *Cincinnati Insurance Co. v. Richard C. Haefner, et al.*
13 - "Haefner was off his meds": Transcript of trial (May 27, 1998), *State of Delaware v. Richard Haefner*, 177; *two well-known symptoms:* Dr. Peter Breggin,

"Long-Standing Concerns about SSRI Withdrawal Effects," *Psychiatric Drug Facts with Dr. Peter Breggin* (http://breggin.com/index.php?option=com_content&task=view&id=76), accessed June 19, 2013; *dosage was too high:* Op. cit., Transcript of trial (May 27, 1998), 182–83.
14 - "was an executive in the plastics industry": Peter A. Schuyler, interview by the author, June 20, 2013.
15 - "saw the cart start to roll": Delaware State Police, January 16, 1998, Haefner Supplemental Incident Report, 2; *Dudley was shaking:* Ibid; *take the dog to her own veterinarian:* Ibid.
16 - "They lifted Dudley from the cart": Op. cit., Haefner Supplemental Report, 2; *intending to write down his license plate number:* Affidavit of Catherine R. Schuyler, June 6, 2000, *Dr. Richard Haefner v. Catherine Schuyler*, Civil Action 00-393-RRM, US District Court for the District of Delaware.
17 - "drag her out of the vehicle": Haefner Supplemental Incident Report, 3; *try to slam her head:* Ibid, 5; *punch her in the face:* Ibid, 3.
18 - "received three stitches": Ibid, 3; *she would lose thirty-two pounds:* Restitution Order, *State of Delaware v. Richard C. Haefner; cost nearly $45,000:* Schuyler interview, June 20, 2013.
19 - "absolutely incredible": Op. cit. Transcript of Delaware Trial (May 27, 1998), 163.
20 - "have the doctor slowly take me off that medication": Op. cit., Transcript of Delaware trial, 180–81.
21 - "That scares me to death": Ibid; *proposed a quick, $10,000 settlement:* Schuyler interview, June 20, 2013; *was stalking their house:* Ibid; *beaten up another woman:* Ibid. Peter Schuyler could provide no details of this incident, and it does not show up in the Clark County, Nevada, criminal database. But if charges were dropped, it might well have been excluded; *suddenly realized she was vulnerable:* Op. cit., Schuyler.
22 - "Dr. Haefner should be aware": Judge Roderick R. McElvie, Memorandum Opinion, October 11, 2001, *Dr. Richard Haefner v. Catherine Schuyler*, US District Court for the District of Delaware, Case # 00-393-RRM.
23 - "so scared and intimidated by Mr. Haefner": Affidavit of Lisa A. Snyder, November 4, 1988, *Richard Haefner v. Lebanon Valley Exposition Corp., et al.*

Chapter 37: A Hole in the Desert
1 - "He had spoken about California": Bise interview, December 6, 2010; *"You can blend in here":* Pattie Cullison, interview by the author, September 30, 2010.
2 - "and how he thought Rick did it": Dan Stephens interview, June 21, 2012.
3 - "wanted to share what he had with others": Kathy Nixon, interview by the author, September 20, 2010.
4 - "Nixon remembered Dudley": Op. cit., Nixon interview; *also remembered Dudley:* Bennie Troxel, interview by the author, October 7, 2010; *brought Dudley with him once:* Fred Bachhuber, interview by the author September 30, 2010.
5 - "He was more a technician than a real geologist": Bachhuber interview, September 30, 2010.

6 - "The department chairman said no": Bachhuber interview, September 30, 2010.
7 - "Paul Watkins . . . was Tecopa's unofficial mayor": Cullison interview, September 30, 2010; *Las Vegas mobsters:* Ibid.
8 - "came to a verbal contract": Affidavit of Richard Haefner, January 7, 2000, *Richard Haefner v. Clifford W. Parmeter and Marjorie E. Parmeter*, Superior Court of California, Inyo County, Civil Action #24208. Dana Crom, the Parmeter lawyer, said oral agreements can be legal and enforceable in California real estate transactions, and that no lawyer is required for it to be so; *make a down payment of $5,000:* Purchase agreement for Parmeter property, May 9, 1997, *Haefner v. Parmeters.*
9 - "It is a sin how some people": Letter, Cliff and Marge Parmeter to Richard Haefner, November 12, 1997.
10 - "he renogotiated the deal with the Parmeters": Cross Complaint, February 11, 2000, *Clifford W. Parmeter and Marjorie E. Parmeter v. Richard Haefner*; *But Rick's promises this time:* Ibid.
11 - "called him a "con artist": Letter, Richard Haefner to Mr. and Mrs. Clifford Parmeter, December 28, 1998.
12 - "Rick could pay neither principal nor interest": Letter, Clifford W. Parmeter to Kirk K. Livermont, November 16, 1999; *he planned to evict Rick:* Thirty Day Termination Notice, Clifford W. Parmeter to Richard Haefner, November 16, 1999; *won a temporary restraining order:* Plaintiff's Motion for Temporary Restraining Order and/or For Rule to Show Cause, *Haefner v. Parmeter,* February 1, 2000; *had apparently resigned because he wasn't getting paid:* Dana Crom, interview by the author, September 30, 2010. Livermont declined to answer questions about the case when the author knocked on the door at his home in Independence, California. Some lawyers will never talk about their past clients, and he is one of them.
13 - "He began screaming at her": Ibid; *I know he scared my clients:* Op. cit., Crom interview, September 30, 2010.
14 - "I was shaking like a leaf": Op. cit., Crom; *then just explode:* Ibid.
15 - "I should have known something was going on": Troxel interview, October 7, 2010.
16 - "thought he had indigestion": Nixon interview, September 20, 2010; *the cremains aren't there:* CLH, August 23, 2010.

Chapter 38: The Road to Rick Haefner
1 - "until Bernier did so in the late 2000s": GHK, January 4, 2011.
2 - "began to read through the Betsy Aardsma case": Roger Smith, interview by the author, October 9, 2008; *she felt increasingly marginalized:* GHK, October 10, 2010. Trooper Sally Brown told Keibler, "They tell me I'm in charge of it, but . . ." She did not respond to an interview request for this book.
3 - "throughout the whole report": Op. cit., Smith interview.
4 - "could not put Maurer out of their thoughts": Tom Shelar, interview by the author, March 7, 2011.
5 - "I think they felt it was a dead horse": Shelar interview, March 7, 2011: The story of John Shambach's background investigation of Larry Paul Maurer comes entirely from an

interview of him by the author on March 14, 2011. Mike Simmers provided third-party verification of some of what Shambach told me.

6 - "Shelar did place a notation": Op. cit., Shelar interview.

7 - "had assignments and worked with a group": Ibid., Shambach interview.

8 - "particularly Mike Simmers": Simmers interview, February 22, 2011; *no plans to publish it:* Derrick Nunnally, *Philadelphia Inquirer*, July 31, 2008.

9 - the case she had heard so much about growing up: Kim Simmers Kravitsky, interview by the author, March 17, 2011.

10 - "one of the most memorable stories that my dad had always told us": Kravitsky interview, March 17, 2011.

11 - "Freedom of Information Act request": Roger Smith's FOIA requests to the National Security Agency in 2006 and the NSA denial letters were obtained by the author via his own FOIA request to NSA.

12 - "Simmers convened a meeting at his house": Simmers interview, February 22, 2011; *take the Aardsma case to a grand jury:* GHK, January 4, 2011; *met with Madeira:* Smith interview, March 17, 2011; *"you need some evidence":* Kent Bernier, e-mail to the author, June 27, 2013.

13 - "promise not to contact the Aardsma family": GHK interview, January 4, 2011; *she was told by a young professor:* Pamela West Kraske, e-mail to the author, June 24, 2013, 5:27 p.m.; *feared getting sued:* Derrick Nunnally, "At Penn State, a Slaying Still Haunts," *Philadelphia Inquirer*, July 31, 2008; *a science-fiction novel:* see, Pamela West, *20/20 Vision* (New York: Ballantine Books, 1990).

14 - "looking for anyone in Lancaster": "The Mysterious Murder of Penn State Student Betsy Aardsma," interview of Derek Sherwood by Todd Matthews, August 9, 2008, Yahoo! Voices (http://voices.yahoo.com/the-mysterious-murder-penn-state-student-betsy-1789847.html), accessed June 25, 2013.

15 - "at the M&M Mars candy plant": CLH, September 15, 2010; *Chris was surfing the Internet:* CLH, August 23, 2010; *Out of curiosity, he e-mailed Sherwood:* CLH, e-mail to the author, August 20, 2010, 3:47 p.m.; *told him about the murder:* CLH, August 23, 2010.

16 - Chris did more searching online: CLH, August 23, 2010; *everything he had suppressed for so long:* Ibid; *It fit Rick almost exactly:* CLH, September 15, 2010; *played the tape:* Ibid.

17 - "with a cold professionalism": CLH, September 15, 2010; *did not go to interview him in Lancaster:* CLH, August 23, 2010; *a ridiculous question:* Ibid.

18 - "did not "turn my nose up at him": Trooper Leigh Barrows, e-mail to the author, August 30, 2010, 11:19 a.m.; *told him to take down his Myspace page:* Trooper Leigh Barrows, e-mail to the author, August 30, 2010, 11:51 a.m.

19 - "all the evidence pointed": Hosler interview, November 8, 2011; *believed Haefner was the killer:* Mike Mutch, interview by the author, February 17, 2012.

20 - "She e-mailed the author": Wich, e-mail to the author, August 19, 2010, 9:59 a.m.; *Aardsma family was relieved:* Confidential source, e-mail to the author, August 19, 2010, 10:17 p.m.

21 - "We're not close to solving the Aardsma case": Trooper Jeff Pettucci, comments to author, August 22, 2010; *"don't need to explain myself":* Trooper Leigh Barrows, e-mail to author, August 30, 2010.
22 - "were going to make some arrests": CLH, September 15, 2010.

Epilogue
1 - "never truly recovered after her murder": Confidential source, e-mail to author, August 19, 2010.
2 - "looked very sad": JoAnn Pelon Wassenaar, e-mail to the author, April 4, 2011; *talk to him about Betsy:* Wich interview, July 21, 2011.
3 - "became a Reformed Church minister": Dennis Wegner interview, November 13, 2008.
4 - "You've gotta love that girl": Tyger interview, September 23, 2008.
5 - "He acknowledged, first, the criticism": GHK interview, June 26, 2013.
6 - "who could respond to any of this speculation": Bill Mahon, e-mail to the author, November 17, 2008.

Selected Bibliography

Additional source material not listed in the Selected Bibliography is listed within the Notes.

(1929). *The Netherlands.* Amsterdam: J. H. DeBussy.

(1961). *Trinity Reformed Church: Golden Anniversary, 1911–1961.* Holland, MI: Trinity Reformed Church.

Anthony, T. "A Vexing Mystery: 20 Years Later, Pattee Stabbing Still Perplexes the State Police," *Daily Collegian,* Penn State University, November 28, 1989.

Ayers, B. (2001). *Fugitive Days: A Memoir.* Boston: Beacon Press.

Baskir, L. M., and W. A. Strauss. (1978). *Chance and Circumstance: The Draft, the War, and the Vietnam Generation.* New York: Vintage Books.

Boyer, D. "1969 Murder Goes Unsolved," *Daily Collegian,* Penn State University, May 18, 1981.

Bratt, J. D. (1984). *Dutch Calvinism in Modern America: A History of a Conservative Subculture.* Grand Rapids, MI: William B. Eerdmans.

Brooks, V. D. (2009). *Boomers: The Cold-War Generation Grows Up.* Chicago: Ivan R. Dee.

Bugliosi, V., with Curt Gentry. (1974). *Helter Skelter: The True Story of the Manson Murders.* New York: W. W. Norton & Co.

Camilleri, J. A. (2008). "Pedophilia: Assessment and Treatment," *Sexual Deviance: Theory, Assessment, and Treatment.* D. R. Laws and William T. O'Donohue, eds. New York: The Guilford Press.

Cirilli, K. "Betsy Ruth Aardsma: 40 Years Later," *Daily Collegian,* Penn State University, November 20, 2009.

Cox, R. W. (1977). *Deadly Pursuit: The Pulitzer Prize–Winning Story of Terror in the Pennsylvania Mountains.* Harrisburg, PA: Cameron House.

Davis, C. T., and D. Walden (eds.). (1970). *On Being Black: Writings by Afro-Americans from Frederick Douglass to the Present.* Greenwich, CT: Fawcett Publications.

De River, D. J. P. (1958). *Crime and the Sexual Psychopath.* Springfield, IL: Charles C. Thomas.

Galewitz, P. "At PSU, 3 Coed Killings within 47 Years Remain Unsolved," *Patriot-News,* Harrisburg, PA, March 5, 1988.

Geberth, V. J. (1983) *Practical Homicide Investigation: Tactics, Procedures, and Forensic Techniques.* New York: Elsevier.

Gehman, R. (1954). *A Murder in Paradise.* New York: Rinehart.

Graysmith, R. (2007). *Zodiac Unmasked: The Identity of America's Most Elusive Serial Killer Revealed.* New York: Berkley Books.

Haefner, C. (2009). *The Silver Mine.* Bloomington, IN: Xlibris.

Heineman, K. J. (1993). *Campus Wars: The Peace Movement at American State Universities in the Vietnam Era.* New York: New York University Press.

Hillegonds, W. (1978). Oral History interview of Rev. William Hillegonds by Conrad Strauch Jr., Living Heritage Oral History Project. Hope College, Holland, Michigan.

James, E. W. K. (1991). *Catching Serial Killers: Learning from Past Serial Murder Investigations.* Lansing, MI: International Forensic Services, Inc.

Jenkins, P. (1998). *Moral Panic: Changing Concepts of the Child Molester in America.* New Haven: Yale University Press.

Kennedy, J. C., and Caroline J. Simon. (2005). *Can Hope Endure? A Historical Case Study in Christian Higher Education.* Grand Rapids, MI: William B. Eerdmans Publishing Co.

Keyes, E. (1976). *The Michigan Murders.* New York: Pocket Books division of Simon & Schuster.

Laws, D. R., and William T O'Donohue (eds.). (2008). *Sexual Deviance: Theory, Assessment, and Treatment.* New York: The Guilford Press.

Lee, J. M. (1965). *Centre County: The County in Which We Live.* State College, PA: Self-Published.

Lengner, K. E., and G. Ross. (2009). *Remembering the Early Shoshone and Tecopa Area,* 2nd ed. Shoshone, CA: Deep Enough Press.

Lenio, M. "Murder Conjures Memories of Pattee Stabbing in 1969," *Daily Collegian,* Penn State University, March 11, 1987.

Lewis, A. H. (1975). *Murder By Contract: The People vs. "Tough Tony" Boyle.* New York: Macmillan.

Lockhart, W. B. (1970). *The Report of the Commission on Obscenity and Pornography: A Special Report of the* New York Times. New York: Random House.

Lynch, C. O., and John Ward Wilson Loose. (1966). "A History of Brewing in Lancaster County, Legal and Otherwise," *Journal of the Lancaster County Historical Society,* 70.

Magnani, T. (1969) Autopsy report of Betsy Ruth Aardsma, Pathology No. A-69-41, November 28, 1969, Office of the Prothonotary, Centre County Courthouse, Bellefonte, PA.

Meisler, S. (2011). *When the World Calls: The Inside Story of the Peace Corps and Its First 50 Years.* Boston: Beacon Press.

Miller, E. W. (1992). *The College of Earth and Mineral Sciences at Penn State.* University Park, PA: The Pennsylvania State University Press.

Miller, M. and L. A. Wright. (2007). *Geology of Death Valley National Park,* revised 2nd ed. Dubuque, IA: Kendall Hunt.

Nuland, S. B. (1994). *How We Die: Reflections on Life's Final Chapter.* New York: Alfred A. Knopf.

Quarteroni, B. "10 Years Later: Woman's Death Still a Mystery," *Centre Daily Times,* State College, PA, November 28, 1979.

Redmond, L. M. (1989). *Surviving: When Someone You Love Was Murdered.* Clearwater, FL: Consultation and Education Services, Inc.

Reed, H. M., and D. Yoder. (1987). *Decorated Furniture of the Mahantongo Valley.* Lewisburg, PA: Center Gallery Publication, Bucknell University.
Rule, A. (1980). *The Stranger Beside Me.* New York: W. W. Norton & Co.
———. (2000). *The Stranger Beside Me: Updated Twentieth Anniversary Edition.* New York: W. W. Norton & Co.
Saltman, D. (1982). *Gilda: An Intimate Portrait.* Chicago: Contemporary Books.
Scranton, W. W. (1970). *The Report of the President's Commission on Campus Unrest.* New York: Arno Press.
Seto, M. C. (2008). *Pedophilia and Sexual Offending Against Children.* Washington, DC: American Psychological Association.
Shields, C. J. (2011). *And So It Goes: Kurt Vonnegut, A Life.* New York: Henry Holt.
Silverman, K. "Aardsma Case Still Mystery," *Daily Collegian,* Penn State, January 15, 1971.
Skucek, S. (1999). "Who Killed Betsy Aardsma?," *State College* magazine.
———. (2004). "Who Killed Betsy Aardsma?" (revised), *State College* magazine.
———. (2004). "The Last Reason," *State College* magazine.
———. (2009). "Murder in the Core," *State College* magazine.
———. (2010). "Case Closed? A Witness Comes Forward in a 40-Year-Old Murder Mystery, Pointing Fingers and Raising Investigators' Eyebrows," *State College* magazine.
Smit, P., and J. W. Smit. (1972). *The Dutch in America, 1609–1970: A Chronology and Fact Book.* Dobbs Ferry, NY: Oceana Publications, Inc.
Specter, A. (2000). *Passion for Truth: From Finding JFK's Single Bullet to Questioning Anita Hill to Impeaching Clinton.* New York: William Morrow.
Sunley, E. (1960). *The Bluebird Wish Comes True.* New York: Camp Fire Girls, Inc.
Ten Harmsel, L. (2002). *Dutch in Michigan.* East Lansing: Michigan State University Press.
Vande Water, R. P. (2001). *Heinz in Holland: A Century of History.* Grand Rapids, MI: Color House Graphics.
———. (2002). *Holland: The Tulip Town.* Chicago: Arcadia Publishing.
———. (2004). *Tulip Time Treasures.* Grand Rapids, MI: Color House Graphics.
Watkins, P., with Guillermo Soledad (1979). *My Life with Charles Manson.* New York: Bantam Books.
Watson, T., with Chaplain Ray (1978). *Will You Die for Me?* Old Tappan, NJ: Fleming H. Revell Co.
West, P. (1990). *20/20 Vision.* New York: Ballantine Books.
Wilber, D. Q. W. (2011). *Rawhide Down: The Near Assassination of Ronald Reagan.* New York: Henry Holt.
Wireback, H. T. (1972). "Murder in the Stacks," *Focus Fall: Penn State's Fountain of Truth.*

Index

About the Author

David DeKok is a writer of non-fiction about small towns and small-town people in crisis. A native of Holland, Michigan, he is a former investigative reporter for the *Patriot-News* in Harrisburg, Pennsylvania, where he won first-place reporting awards from The National Press Club, the Pennsylvania Newspaper Association, and Associated Press Managing Editors of Pennsylvania. His first book, *Unseen Danger: A Tragedy of People, Government, and the Centralia Mine Fire,* was published by the University of Pennsylvania Press in 1986 and reviewed in the *New York Times* Sunday Book Review. It was reissued by Globe Pequot Press in an updated edition in 2009 as *Fire Underground: The Ongoing Tragedy of the Centralia Mine Fire.* His other book, *The Epidemic: A Collision of Power, Privilege, and Public Health,* about a 1903 typhoid epidemic at Cornell University, was published by Lyons Press in 2011.

He has made many television and radio appearances discussing the Centralia mine fire, including on *Fresh Air, The Diane Rehm Show,* and the History Channel. In 2007, he appeared in the acclaimed documentary film, *The Town That Was,* which screened in competition at the Los Angeles and Philadelphia film festivals. His distinctive photographs of Centralia in the 1970s and 1980s have been used in many television productions. DeKok lives by the Susquehanna River in Harrisburg, Pennsylvania, with his wife, Lisa W. Brittingham, and daughters Elizabeth and Lydia. He can be reached via his website, daviddekok.com.